AF880848

GLOBAL PERSPECTIVES ON PARENTAL ACCEPTANCE AND REJECTION

Global Perspectives on Parental Acceptance and Rejection advances an understanding of the profound and lifelong effects that parental love (acceptance) and the absence of love (rejection) have on human development from childhood through to old age.

It draws from interpersonal acceptance-rejection theory (IPARTheory), an evidence-based theory of socialization and lifespan development that focuses on the pancultural effects, causes, and other correlates of interpersonal acceptance-rejection throughout the lifespan. Edited by Ronald P. Rohner and Sumbleen Ali, contributions from leading scholars show how few experiences have as wide-ranging, significant, and predictable consequences for human behavior well-being as experiences of parental acceptance and rejection. Key topics of parental acceptance-rejection include long-term effects in childhood; adult intimate relationships; early life stress; parental alienation; child maltreatment; and forgiveness and vengeance. It also discusses the clinical implications and practical applications of IPARTheory.

Providing vital information about parenting and human development worldwide, this book is essential for researchers, students, and practitioners in psychology, psychiatry, family sciences, sociology, human development, and the helping professions.

Ronald P. Rohner, PhD, is Professor Emeritus in the Department of Human Development and Family Sciences and Director at the Rohner Center for the Study of Interpersonal Acceptance and Rejection, University of Connecticut, USA.

Sumbleen Ali, PhD, is a Research Scientist at the Rohner Center, University of Connecticut, USA, and Assistant Professor in the Department of Human Ecology at the State University of New York at Oneonta, USA.

STUDIES IN PARENTING SERIES

Marc H. Bornstein, Series Editor

The chief aim of this series of volumes is to provide a forum for extended and integrated treatments of fundamental and challenging contemporary topics in parenting. Each volume treats a different perspective on parenting and is self-contained, yet the series as a whole endeavors to enhance and interrelate studies in parenting by bringing shared perspectives to bear on a variety of concerns prominent in parenting theory, research, practice, and application. Reflecting the nature and intent of this series, contributing authors are drawn from a broad spectrum of the humanities and sciences – anthropology to zoology – with representational emphasis placed on active contributing authorities to the contemporary literature in parenting.

Parenting Across Cultures from Childhood to Adolescence
Development in Nine Countries
Jennifer E. Lansford, W. Andrew Rothenberg, and Marc H. Bornstein

Parenting, Infancy, Culture
Specificity and Commonality in Argentina, Belgium, Israel, Italy, and the United States
Edited by Marc H. Bornstein

Parenting and Child Development in Low- and Middle-Income Countries
Marc H. Bornstein, W. Andrew Rothenberg, Andrea Bizzego, Robert H. Bradley, Kirby Deater-Deckard, Gianluca Esposito, Jennifer E. Lansford, Diane L. Putnick, and Susannah Zietz

Asian Parenting
Meanings, Characteristics, and Implications
Edited by Xinyin Chen

Global Perspectives on Parental Acceptance and Rejection
Lessons Learned from IPARTheory
Edited by Ronald P. Rohner and Sumbleen Ali

For a complete list of all books in this series, please visit the series page at:
https://www.routledge.com/Studies-in-Parenting-Series/book-series/SIP

GLOBAL PERSPECTIVES ON PARENTAL ACCEPTANCE AND REJECTION

Lessons Learned from IPARTheory

Edited by Ronald P. Rohner and Sumbleen Ali

Routledge
Taylor & Francis Group
NEW YORK AND LONDON

Designed cover image: woraput via Getty Images

First published 2025
by Routledge
605 Third Avenue, New York, NY 10158

and by Routledge
4 Park Square, Milton Park, Abingdon, Oxon, OX14 4RN

Routledge is an imprint of the Taylor & Francis Group, an informa business

© 2025 selection and editorial matter, Ronald P. Rohner and Sumbleen Ali; individual chapters, the contributors

The right of Ronald P. Rohner and Sumbleen Ali to be identified as the authors of the editorial material, and of the authors for their individual chapters, has been asserted in accordance with sections 77 and 78 of the Copyright, Designs and Patents Act 1988.

All rights reserved. No part of this book may be reprinted or reproduced or utilised in any form or by any electronic, mechanical, or other means, now known or hereafter invented, including photocopying and recording, or in any information storage or retrieval system, without permission in writing from the publishers.

Trademark notice: Product or corporate names may be trademarks or registered trademarks, and are used only for identification and explanation without intent to infringe.

Library of Congress Cataloging-in-Publication Data
Names: Rohner, Ronald Preston, 1935- editor
Title: Global perspectives on parental acceptance and rejection : lessons learned from ipartheory / edited by Ronald P. Rohner and Sumbleen Ali.
Description: New York, NY : Routledge, 2025. | Series: Studies in parenting series | Includes bibliographical references and index.
Identifiers: LCCN 2024050516 (print) | LCCN 2024050517 (ebook) | ISBN 9781032578415 hbk | ISBN 9781032563008 pbk | ISBN 9781003441243 ebk
Subjects: LCSH: Parent and child | Parental rejection | Parental acceptance | Parental deprivation
Classification: LCC HQ755.85 .G59 2025 (print) | LCC HQ755.85 (ebook) | DDC 306.874--dc23/eng/20250120
LC record available at https://lccn.loc.gov/2024050516
LC ebook record available at https://lccn.loc.gov/2024050517

ISBN: 978-1-032-57841-5 (hbk)
ISBN: 978-1-032-56300-8 (pbk)
ISBN: 978-1-003-44124-3 (ebk)

DOI: 10.4324/9781003441243

Typeset in Optima
by SPi Technologies India Pvt Ltd (Straive)

We dedicate this book with gratitude to those 100,000+ children and adults around the world who participated in our studies over the course of six plus decades.

We also dedicate the book to the scores of professionals and students who helped bring IPARTheory to its current level of maturity.

CONTENTS

ABOUT THE EDITORS

Ronald P. Rohner, PhD, Professor Emeritus, Department of Human Development and Family Sciences, & Director, Rohner Center for the Study of Interpersonal Acceptance & Rejection, University of Connecticut, Storrs, Connecticut, USA.

Rohner's work centers on the antecedents and consequences of interpersonal acceptance and rejection, recognized as interpersonal acceptance-rejection theory (IPARTheory). Rohner's journey into this field began during his doctoral studies at Stanford University, where he developed a lasting interest in investigating intricates of parental acceptance and rejection–now referred to as interpersonal acceptance-rejection theory (IPARTheory). This interest evolved into a lifetime commitment to exploring the causes, consequences, and other correlates of interpersonal acceptance and rejection on human development and wellbeing. His research interest is embedded in a larger intellectual commitment to the field of human development and family sciences, and international psychology—especially as these fields converge on issues of interpersonal acceptance-rejection in America and transnationally. Rohner's IPARTheory is recognized worldwide, and his research is cited frequently in textbooks and professional journals. Because of his dedication and lifelong commitment to international research he was given the American Psychological Association's (Division 52) Award for Distinguished Contributions to the International Advancement of Psychology; Division 52 Award for Outstanding Psychologist in the USA; Outstanding Psychologist in International Leadership; and, the Henry David International Mentoring Award. He also received the Lifetime Achievement Award from the Society for Cross-Cultural Research. Rohner has written 17 books and special issues, and over 600 articles, chapters, reviews, and technical reports while conducting research on interpersonal acceptance-rejection for more than six and one half decades (beginning 1959) on every continent except Antarctica. His work continues to shape the way researchers, clinicians and other practitioners perceive and approach the complexities of interpersonal relationships.

Sumbleen Ali, PhD, Research Scientist, Rohner Center, University of Connecticut, Storrs, Connecticut; Assistant Professor, Department of Human Ecology, State University of New York at Oneonta, Oneonta, New York, USA. Ali's work and academic training are centered on investigating the developmental outcomes of interpersonal relationships from a behavioral as well as a neuropsychological perspective. Guided by IPARTheory, her research with children, adolescents, and adults examines how various social contexts (e.g., families and peers) and individual characteristics (e.g., ethnic-racial, gender, and cultural orientations) influence psychological adjustment, emotion regulation, cognitive decline in older age, and brain functioning using fMRI. Her work seeks to understand the mechanisms underlying these developmental processes and aspires to foster optimal human development and improve family functioning across diverse cultural settings. Since 2009, Ali has been an active and valued member of the Rohner Center, where her contributions continue to advance IPARTheory and the field of human development and family sciences.

CONTRIBUTORS

Ebru Akün, PhD, Clinical Psychologist, Department of Psychology, Ankara University, Turkey. Akün's research focuses primarily on the relationship between perceived parental acceptance-rejection in childhood and the mental health and mental disorders in adulthood. She is also interested in perceived partner acceptance-rejection, attachment, and schema therapy in adulthood.

Sumbleen Ali, PhD, Assistant Professor, Department of Human Ecology, State University of New York at Oneonta, New York; Research Scientist, Rohner Center, University of Connecticut. Ali's work investigates the developmental outcomes of interpersonal relationships from a behavioral and neuropsychological perspective. Guided by IPARTheory, her research with children, adolescents, and adults examines how various social contexts and individual characteristics (e.g., ethnic-racial, gender, personality) influence psychological adjustment and emotion regulation.

Ryan J. Allred, PhD, Assistant Professor, Communication Studies, University of Wisconsin Oshkosh, Oshkosh, Wisconsin, USA. Allred's research focuses on interpersonal communication inhibitors, pro-social emotions in relationship development and maintenance, and the impact of cell phone usage on face-to-face communication. He also investigates how new technologies may influence communicative processes in the present-day digital era.

Mary Alvarez, PhD, Licensed Psychologist, Austin, Texas, USA. Alvarez, a forensic and a clinical psychologist, is experienced in forensic work in family law and custody evaluation. She is regularly appointed by courts to assess and assist high-conflict families. Witnessing the psychological impact on children in parental alienation and high-conflict situations, she co-developed "Resetting the Family."

William Bernet, MD, Psychiatrist; Professor Emeritus, Vanderbilt University School of Medicine, Nashville, Tennessee, USA. Bernet has extensive experience in parental alienation, child custody, and parenting time evaluations. Bernet helped edit DSM-5, and ICD-11. He is the founder and inaugural president of the International Parental Alienation Study Group.

Preston A. Britner, PhD, Professor of Human Development and Family Sciences, University of Connecticut, Storrs, Connecticut, USA. Britner's research interests include attachment-caregiving relationships, child maltreatment prevention, promotion of academic and social outcomes for youth in foster care, and family-focused, community-based prevention/diversion programs for children, youth, and families. Dr. Britner is a Fellow of the American Psychological Association, a University Teaching Fellow, and Editor Emeritus of the Journal of Prevention.

Kimberly Fuller, PhD, LISW-S, Associate Professor, School of Social Work, Cleveland State University, Cleveland, Ohio, US. Fuller owns Cleveland Sex & Intimacy Counseling services and conducts research on the relationships and supporting systems of LGBTQ+ individuals. She looks at the ways these relationships and systems connect to physical and mental health outcomes. Fuller is also a member of the THRiVE Research Collaborative, developing a LGBTQ+ centered sex education curriculum.

M. Selenga Gürmen, PhD, Assistant Professor, Department of Psychology, Ozyegin University, Istanbul, Turkey. Gurmen's research focuses on couple therapy effectiveness, co-parenting, and high-conflict couples. She provides therapy for individuals, couples, and families and offers seminars and training programs for couples and parents in crisis. Gürmen is also an AAMFT Approved Supervisor and Fundamentals of Supervision Course Instructor.

Fumiko Hoeft, MD, PhD, Dean & Chief Administrative Officer, University of Connecticut Waterbury campus. Hoeft is a neurophysiologist, as well as a systems and developmental cognitive neuroscientist with theoretical interests in the neurobiological mechanisms underlying individual differences in brain maturational processes.

Abdul Khaleque, PhD, Senior Research Scientist, Rohner Center, University of Connecticut, Storrs, Connecticut, USA. Khaleque, former president of the International Society for Interpersonal Acceptance and Rejection, and a member of the American Psychological Association and the Human Factors Society of America. He authored/coauthored 120+ research articles, 43 book chapters, and 15 books in psychology and human development.

Jennifer E. Lansford, PhD, Director, Center for Child and Family Policy, Sanford School of Public Policy, Duke University, North Carolina, USA. Lansford authored more than 300 publications on parenting and behavior problems during childhood and adolescence. She leads the Parenting Across Cultures Project, an international longitudinal study from nine countries. She also holds leadership positions in various organizations and is recognized as a Fellow by several psychological associations.

Jonas G. Miller, PhD, Assistant Professor, Department of Psychology, University of Connecticut, Storrs, Connecticut, USA. Miller is broadly interested in adversity, resilience, and social-emotional processes in children and adolescents, particularly empathy and prosocial behaviors. His research examines the coordination of environment, experience, and biology that underlies individual differences in health and well-being. Miller integrates methods from developmental psychology, neuroscience, and community and environmental health.

Ronald P. Rohner, PhD, Professor Emeritus, Department of Human Development and Family Sciences, & Director, Rohner Center for the Study of Interpersonal Acceptance & Rejection, University of Connecticut, Storrs, Connecticut, USA. Rohner has written 17 books and special issues, and over 600 articles, chapters, reviews, and technical reports. His research focuses on human development and family sciences, and international psychology –especially on issues of interpersonal acceptance-rejection. He received several awards from the American Psychological Association along with the Lifetime Achievement Award from the Society for Cross-Cultural Research.

Nour Zaki, PhD, Visiting Assistant Professor, Department of Psychology, American University in Cairo (AUC), Cairo, Egypt. Zaki's research focuses on perinatal psychology, maternal mental health, and parent-child attachment. She is certified in Attachment and Trauma-Focused Therapy and qualified to facilitate Circle of Security Parenting groups and the Bringing Baby Home program. Zaki is a member of the American Psychological Association, the Association for Prenatal, and Perinatal Psychology and Health.

SERIES FOREWORD

Parenting is fundamental to the survival and success of the human species. Everyone who has ever lived has had parents, and the vast majority of adults in the world become parents. Opinions about parenting abound, but still surprisingly too little solid scientific information or considered reflection exist about parenting. *Studies in Parenting* redresses this imbalance. The chief aim of this series of books is to provide a forum for extended and integrated treatments of fundament all and challenging contemporary topics in parenting. Each book treats a different perspective on parenting and is self-contained, yet the series as a whole endeavors to enhance and interrelate studies in parenting by bringing shared perspectives to bear on a variety of concerns prominent in parenting theory, research, practice, and application. As a consequence of its structure and scope, *Studies in Parenting* will appeal individually or as a series to professionals and parents alike. Reflecting the nature and intent of this series, contributing authors are drawn from a broad spectrum of the humanities and sciences—anthropology to zoology—with representational emphasis placed on active contributing authorities to the contemporary literature in parenting.

Parenting is a job whose primary object of attention and action is the child—human children do not and cannot grow up as solitary individuals—but parenting is also a vital status in the life course with consequences for parents themselves. In this forum, parenting is defined by all of children's principal caregivers and their many modes of caregiving. *Studies in Parenting* encompasses five central themes in parenting.

Who Parents

Biological and adoptive mothers, fathers, single parents, and divorced and remarried parents can be children's principal caregivers, but when siblings, grandparents, and nonfamilial caregivers as well as mentors mind children, their parenting is also pertinent.

Whom Parents Parent

Parents parent infants, toddlers, children in middle childhood, and adolescents as well as special populations of children including multiple births, preterm, ill, developmentally delayed or talented, and aggressive or withdrawn children.

The Scope of Parenting

Parenting's direct effects include parents' genetic endowment as well as the experiences they provide children that are instantiated in parents' cognitions and practices; parenting's indirect influences take place through parents' relationships with each other and their connections to community and culture. Parenting's direct and indirect effects on children can be both positive and negative.

The Determinants and Consequences of Parenting

Evolution and history; biology and ethology; family configuration; formal and informal support systems, community ties, and work; circumstances, tasks, and demands; social, educational, legal, medical, and governmental institutions; socioeconomic class, designed and natural ecology, and culture—as well as children themselves—each shapes parenting.

The Nature, Structure, and Meaning of Parenting

Parenting's pleasures, privileges, and profits as well as frustrations, fears, and failures are all explored in *Studies in Parenting*. Contemporary parenting studies are diversified, pluralistic, and specialized. This fragmented state needs counterforce in an arena that allows the extended in-depth exploration of cardinal topics in parenting. *Studies in Parenting* vigorously pursues that goal.

Marc H. Bornstein
Series Editor

PREFACE

Ronald P. Rohner, PhD and Sumbleen Ali, PhD

The book, *"Global Perspectives on Parental Acceptance and Rejection: Lessons Learned from IPARTheory,"* provides a summary of a large, widely dispersed, and growing body of literature on interpersonal acceptance-rejection theory (IPARTheory), and on the effects, causes, and other correlates of interpersonal acceptance and rejection (especially parental acceptance and rejection) worldwide. It represents the culmination of more than six decades of transcultural research with several hundred thousand children and adults on every continent except Antarctica. We intend the book to be an accessible resource for students and professionals to help facilitate their research and application in psychology, psychiatry, family sciences, law, social work, and other academically applied contexts. As you read the book, we invite you to think about yourself, your own life, and about the people who have been most important in your life. If IPARTheory is as globally powerful as we believe it is, no matter who you are or where you are, you will recognize yourself in many of the conclusions reached in the book.

We organized the book into three parts that deal with the nature and development of IPARTheory, its clinical implications, and its practical applications. Part I, "Interpersonal Acceptance-Rejection Theory (IPARTheory) and Complementary Theories," contains four chapters. Chapter 1 focuses on the nature and history of IPARTheory, especially the three great lessons learned in the theory, and on the measures and procedures used to arrive at those lessons. Chapter 2 provides a summary of 13 meta-analyses conducted to test the basic postulates of the theory. Chapters 3 and 4, discuss likeness and differences between IPARTheory and two other complementary theories: Bowlby and Ainsworth's attachment theory, and Floyd's affection exchange theory, respectively.

Part II, "Long-Term Effects of Parental Acceptance-Rejection in Childhood," comprises Chapters 5–9. Chapter 5 focuses on the way in which parental acceptance and rejection in childhood affect adult intimate relationships. Grounded in IPARTheory, Chapter 6 focuses on how adults' memories of parental acceptance-rejection in childhood affect their treatment of their now aging parents. Chapter 7 provides an overview of results from the Parenting Across Cultures (PAC) project, a longitudinal study of the developmental correlates of parental acceptance-rejection from childhood to adulthood in nine countries. Chapter 8 explains how interpersonal rejection sensitivity tends universally to be one of the personality dispositions resulting from perceived parental rejection in childhood.

IPARTheory research has consistently highlighted the significance of the gender of parents and offspring in the perception and consequences of parental acceptance and rejection. Because of that, Chapter 9 discusses how parents' gender interacts with offsprings' gender to contribute to different outcomes in sons versus daughters. Chapter 10 summarizes research showing that the number of medical problems (e.g., allergies, asthma, metabolic abnormality) experienced by young adults are associated with their memories of parental (maternal and paternal) acceptance or rejection in childhood.

Part III, "Clinical Implications and Practical Applications of IPARTheory," addresses the implications of IPARTheory for mental health and psychotherapy, as well as for practical applications in neuropsychology, LGBTQIA+ studies, and parental alienation. Chapter 11 describes an IPARTheory evidence-based approach to clinical practice and it suggests several therapy models and techniques for incorporating IPARTheory into clinical practice. Chapter 12 shows the lasting effects of acceptance and rejection in childhood on brain development and function among young adults. Chapter 13 documents the fact that the effects of parental acceptance-rejection in childhood has the same effects among LGBTQIA+ individuals cross-culturally as it does in the general population. Chapter 14 discusses the international controversy regarding parental alienation versus other forms of child maltreatment, and it discusses the use of IPARTheory measures to help the courts, clinicians, and other professionals distinguish parental alienation from parental denigration and other forms of malparenting.

Finally, the book includes two Appendices. Appendix A is a listing of IPARTheory-related measures developed by Rohner, underscoring the international reach and ongoing evolution of research in this field. Readers are encouraged to consult the Rohner Center for the Study of Interpersonal

Acceptance and Rejection's website (www.csiar.uconn.edu) or Rohner Research Publications (www.rohnerresearchpublications.com) for the latest translations and updates of measures. Appendix B provides a "Glossary of Significant Concepts in IPARTheory." It defines and operationalizes clearly and explicitly the meaning of major concepts used in the theory.

Even though the book strives to provide a reasonably comprehensive overview of major topics in IPARTheory research and practice, we acknowledge the vast scope of the theory, and apologize for any omissions or oversights. The growth of IPARTheory continues to accelerate.

Good Reading,
Ron & Sumbleen

PART I

Interpersonal Acceptance-Rejection Theory (IPARTheory) and Complementary Theories

1

INTERPERSONAL ACCEPTANCE-REJECTION THEORY (IPARTHEORY)

From Conception Through Maturity

Ronald P. Rohner and Sumbleen Ali

Interpersonal acceptance-rejection theory (IPARTheory) is an evidence-based theory of socialization and lifespan development that aims to predict and explain major consequences, causes, and other correlates of interpersonal acceptance and rejection worldwide (Rohner, 1986, 2004, 2021; Rohner & Lansford, 2017; Rohner & Rohner, 1980). Beginning in 1960, the theory focused on the effects of perceived *parental* acceptance-rejection in childhood and extending into adulthood. At that time, the theory was named "parental acceptance-rejection theory" (PARTheory). By 2000, the theory had broadened to include perceived acceptance-rejection in intimate adult relationships, relationships with siblings, peers, grandparents, teachers, and other significant interpersonal relationships throughout the lifespan. In 2014 (Rohner, 2014), this expansion in emphasis led to the transition of the theory's name from PARTheory to its current designation *Interpersonal acceptance-rejection theory (IPARTheory)*. Despite this change in name and emphasis, significant portions of the theory continue to feature the effects, causes, and other correlates of children's perceptions of parental acceptance-rejection as well as adults' memories of parental acceptance-rejection in childhood.[1]

IPARTheory's Three Great Lessons

As a result of six and a half decades of research with several hundred thousand children and adults on every continent except Antarctica, IPARTheory researchers have learned three fundamental lessons about the nature of human nature worldwide. These lessons are briefly described next.

DOI: 10.4324/9781003441243-2

Lesson 1: Individuals Perceive Themselves to be Accepted or Rejected in the Same Four Ways. Worldwide evidence supports IPARTheory's postulate that children and adults everywhere—regardless of differences in culture, race, language, gender, and other such defining conditions—understand themselves to be accepted (i.e., love/cared about) or rejected (i.e., unloved/not cared about) in the same four ways by people most important to them, shown in Figure 1.1. Acceptance-rejection is conceptualized as a continuum in IPARTheory. The acceptance end of the continuum is defined by physical acts such as hugging, kissing, and cuddling, as well as by verbal behaviors such as praising, complimenting, and saying nice things to or about the individual and by other symbolic behaviors expressing love, care, and concern. The rejection end of the continuum is defined by (1) emotional coldness/lack of affection (i.e., the significant other is emotionally cold and fails to express affectionate behavior); (2) hostility/aggression (e.g., insulting, yelling, hitting, rude gestures, and other negative, hurtful behaviors); (3) indifference/neglect (i.e., uninterested in supporting the emotional needs of the individual); and, (4) undifferentiated rejection (i.e., individuals believe that the significant other does not care about, appreciate, want, or love them, although there is no behavioral manifestation of any other expression of rejection).

Lesson 2: Individuals Respond in the Same Ten Ways to the Perception of Interpersonal Acceptance-Rejection. The second fundamental lesson learned from research in IPARTheory is that across cultures and other sociodemographic groups, perceived interpersonal acceptance and rejection from significant others—especially from parents in childhood and intimate partners in adulthood—tend worldwide to have a major influence on children's and adults' personality dispositions and overall psychological adjustment (Rohner, 1986, 2004, 2021; Rohner & Lansford 2017). For example, perceiving oneself to be rejected by an attachment figure predicts psychological maladjustment as defined by a cluster of ten personality dispositions known in IPARTheory as the acceptance-rejection syndrome described at greater length later (Rohner, 2004). These dispositions include (1) anxiety; (2) emotional insecurity; (3) anger, hostility, aggression, passive aggression, and problems with the management of hostility and aggression; (4) dependence or defensive independence depending on the form, intensity, and duration of the perceived rejection; (5) emotional unresponsiveness; (6) emotional instability; (7) impaired self-esteem; (8) impaired self-adequacy; (9) negative worldview; and (10) cognitive distortions.

Lesson 3: Responses to Interpersonal Acceptance-Rejection Are Hardwired in the Brain. The ubiquity of the first two fundamental lessons of IPARTheory suggests a biologically based, deep structure of the human affectional system (Rohner & Lansford, 2017). Behaviors noted in those

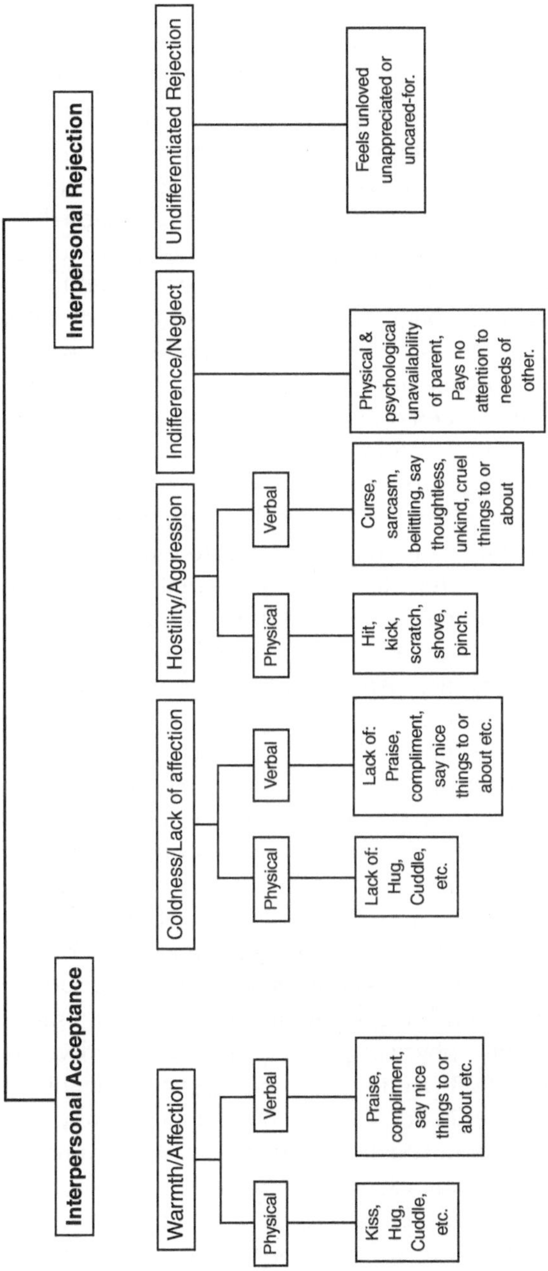

FIGURE 1.1 The Warmth Dimension of Interpersonal Relationships. © 2004, 2021, 2024, 2025 by Rohner Research Publications.

lessons occur with such near invariance across cultures, genders, races, time, and other such defining conditions that IPARTheory researchers argue they are probably embedded in a common biocultural evolution among humans everywhere. If this speculation is correct, then IPARTheorists hypothesize that specific brain mechanisms are likely to differentially characterize responses to interpersonal rejection among adults who remember having been loved/accepted by their parents in childhood versus those adults who remember having been unloved/rejected in childhood.

To test this hypothesis, Ali et al. (2024) used functional magnetic resonance imaging (fMRI) to investigate neural correlates of experimentally manipulated rejection during a computer-based ball-toss game called Cyberball. Study participants played Cyberball for 5 minutes in ten continuous alternating blocks of Inclusion and Exclusion sessions. During the Inclusion session, participants received the ball for one third of the ball throws in counterbalanced order. In the Exclusion block, study participants never received the ball. Grounded in IPARTheory, the study investigated neural activity among two groups of young adults. One group reported being loved (accepted) by both parents in childhood and self-reported being psychologically well-adjusted (AcceptedAdjusted). The other group reported having been rejected by both parents in childhood and self-reported being psychologically maladjusted (RejectedMaladjusted).

Findings revealed that during social rejection (i.e., the exclusion condition) in the ball-toss game, members of the RejectedMaladjusted group—as compared to members of the AcceptedAdjusted group—had increased activation of brain regions that critically support emotion processing and social pain. As shown in Figure 1.2, these regions include the posterior cingulate cortex (PCC) and anterior cingulate cortex (ACC), dorsolateral prefrontal cortex (dlPFC), medial prefrontal cortex (mPFC), insula, cuneus, precuneus, and amygdala. That study provided a foundation for understanding the neural mechanisms underlying emotion processing influenced by remembered parental acceptance-rejection in childhood.[2]

The pain of perceived rejection is very real (MacDonald & Jensen-Campbell, 2011). Brain imaging studies reveal that the same parts of the brain associated with physical pain are also activated when people feel rejected (Abrutyn, 2023). Additionally, peer rejection in childhood and intimate partner rejection in adolescence and adulthood also tend to be associated with activation in specific brain regions. For example, Stroud et al. (2023) found that chronic exposure to peer rejection tends to alter neural brain regions implicated in cognitive control (i.e., the dorsal striatum and the lateral prefrontal cortex). Thus, people with a history of peer rejection have to exert greater effort to maintain emotional equilibrium than do individuals with a history of peer acceptance. Moreover, different brain regions

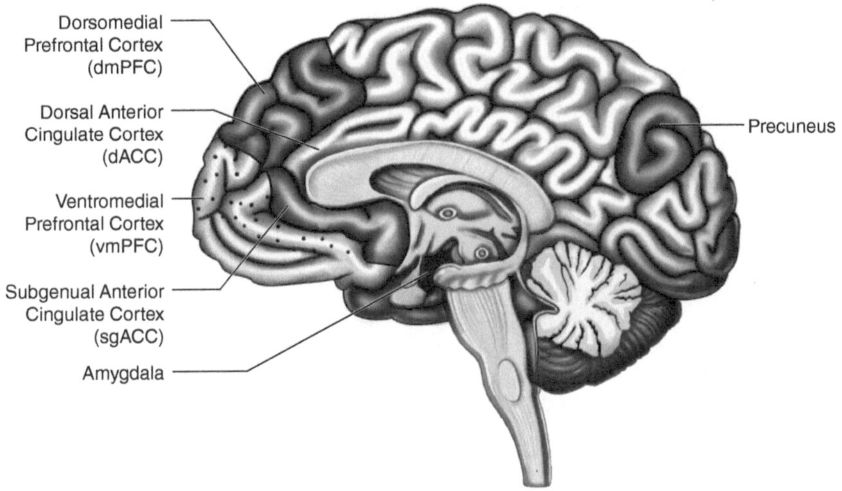

FIGURE 1.2 Regions of the Brain Associated with Interpersonal Rejection. © 2021, 2024, 2025 by Rohner Research Publications.

are activated when adults are happily in love versus those who are recently rejected by an intimate partner (DeBoer et al., 2012; Xu et al., 2011).

Research on interpersonal rejection has also found that chronic rejection disrupts early brain development in brain regions like the hippocampus, which is associated with learning, memory, emotion regulation, decision making, and level of intelligence, among other important functions (Buthmann et al., 2023). Further, parental rejection during children's early years is associated with several forms of psychiatric disorder, ultimately leading to a 45% risk for childhood onset of psychiatric disorders (Rakesh et al., 2021; Teicher & Samson, 2016). This process continues into adulthood. As a result, the nervous and immune systems associated with physical problems (e.g., allergies, asthma, metabolic abnormality, periodontal disease, and ulcers) are compromised. Ali et al. (2025; Chapter 10, this book) discuss in greater detail the association between parental rejection during childhood and medical problems in adulthood.

Perceived rejection and other forms of long-term emotional trauma are often implicated in the alteration of brain chemistry (de Haan et al., 2024; Ford & Reid, 2023). The effect of these and other neurobiological and neuropsychological changes may ultimately compromise children's and adults' central nervous systems and psychosocial development. Luby et al. (2012), however, found that the early experience of maternal love and nurturance among preschoolers is strongly predictive of larger hippocampal volume among children at school age. These results are important because, as already noted, the hippocampus is a region of the brain central to memory, emotion regulation, stress modulation, and other functions essential for healthy socio-emotional adjustment. More detail about neurobiological measures used to assess the effects of interpersonal rejection is provided toward the end of this chapter in the discussion about the eight methods or types of studies used to test IPARTheory's central postulates, assumptions, and hypotheses.

IPARTheory's Subtheories

IPARTheory is comprised of three subtheories: personality subtheory, coping subtheory, and sociocultural systems subtheory and model. Each of these is briefly discussed next.

IPARTheory's Personality Subtheory

IPARTheory's personality subtheory attempts to predict and explain major personality or psychological—especially mental health-related—consequences of perceived interpersonal acceptance and rejection. *Personality* in IPARTheory's personality subtheory is defined as an individual's more or less stable set of predispositions to respond (i.e., affective, cognitive, perceptual, and motivational dispositions) and actual modes of responding (i.e., observable behaviors) in various life situations or contexts. This definition recognizes that behavior is motivated and influenced by external (i.e., environmental) as well as internal (e.g., emotional, biological, and learning) factors and usually has regularity or orderliness across time and space.[3]

The three fundamental lessons learned about human behavior and development are embedded in personality subtheory. That is, personality subtheory argues that over the course of shared biocultural evolution, humans everywhere have developed the enduring, biologically based emotional need for positive response from the people most important to them. The need for a positive response includes a consciously or an unconsciously recognized emotional wish, desire, or yearning for comfort, support, care, concern, and nurturance. In adulthood, the need becomes more complex and differentiated, including the conscious or unconscious desire for intimacy, feeling close, and being valued by the people with whom one has an affectional bond of attachment.

According to personality subtheory, the need to feel accepted and cared about by people who are most important in one's life is a fundamental human need (Rohner, 1986, 2004, 2021). These people are called "significant others" in IPARTheory. As construed in the theory, a *significant other* is any person with whom a child or adult has a relatively long-lasting emotional tie, is uniquely important to the individual, and is interchangeable with no one else (Rohner, 2025a). In this sense, parents (in childhood) and intimate partners (in adulthood) are generally significant others. But parents and intimate partners also tend to have one additional quality not shared by most significant others. That is, children's and adults' sense of emotional security, comfort and happiness tend to depend on the quality of their relationship with their significant others. Because of that fact, these people are the kind of significant other called *attachment figures* in both IPARTheory (Rohner, 2025a) and in attachment theory (Ainsworth, 1989; Bowlby, 1982). Zaki (2025; Chapter 3, this book) provides a comprehensive review of the similarities and differences between IPARTheory and attachment theory.

IPARTheory's personality subtheory postulates that children's and adults' emotional need for positive response from significant others and attachment figures is a powerful and culturally *invariant* need. As stated previously, when children do not get this need satisfied adequately by their major caregivers—or adults do not get this need met by their intimate partners—they are predisposed to respond emotionally, behaviorally, and developmentally in the ways described in the *acceptance-rejection syndrome*. The syndrome consists of two complementary sets of factors. First, nearly 1,500 studies as of 2024 have shown that children and adults everywhere appear to organize their perceptions of interpersonal acceptance-rejection around the same four classes of behavior noted throughout this chapter. Second, as observed earlier, cross-cultural and meta-analytic evidence supports the conclusion that children and adults who experience their relationship with parents and other attachment figures as rejecting tend universally to self-report the specific form of psychological maladjustment specified in the personality subtheory. Together, these two classes of behavior comprise a *syndrome*; that is, they constitute a pattern or constellation of co-occurring behaviors, traits, and dispositions. Any single psychological disposition (e.g., anger or emotional instability) may be found in other conditions; the full configuration of dispositions composes the syndrome. Collectively, all this evidence led Rohner and Lansford (2017) to postulate a *deep structure*—that is, a biocultural co-evolutionary-foundation—to the human affectional system.

According to IPARTheory's personality subtheory and to the acceptance-rejection syndrome, individuals who feel rejected by significant others are likely to be anxious and insecure. To allay these feelings and satisfy their emotional needs, individuals who feel rejected often increase their bids for positive responses, but only up to a point. That is, they tend to become

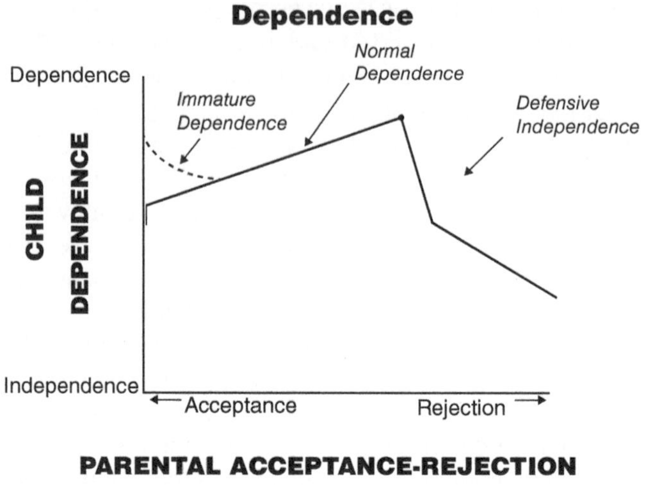

FIGURE 1.3 Dependence/Independence in Relation to Parental Acceptance-Rejection. ©2004, 2021, 2024, 2025 by Rohner Research Publications.

more dependent, as shown in Figure 1.3. Dependence is construed as a continuum in IPARTheory, with independence defining one end of the continuum and dependence the other end. Independent people have their need for positive response met well enough to feel free from frequent or intense yearning or behavioral bids for succor from significant others. On the other hand, very dependent people have a frequent and intense desire for positive response, and are likely to make many bids for such a response.

The term *dependence* in the theory refers to the internal, psychologically felt wish or yearning for *emotional* (as opposed to instrumental or task-oriented) support, care, comfort, attention, nurturance, and similar behaviors from significant others. Dependence, also refers to the actual behavioral bids children and others make for such responsiveness. For young children, these bids may include clinging to parents, whining or crying when parents unexpectedly depart, and seeking physical proximity when they return (Rohner, 2021).

Many rejected children and adults feel the need for constant reassurance and emotional support. That is particularly true of children who are immaturely dependent. According to IPARTheory, *immature dependence* comes about as a result of overly high levels of parental warmth and affection in combination with excessive protectiveness and intrusive behavioral control (i.e., moment-by-moment control over and manipulation of a child's behavior; Rohner, 1975, 2004, 2021). This parenting style is likely to produce an especially noticeable spike in the dependency curve. That is, parents who continually say, in effect, "Oh, honey, don't do that. You might hurt yourself.

Let mommy do it for you," are likely to reinforce children's dependency needs at the same time they interfere with the children's normal exploration and self-testing. These children often do not develop a complete sense of age-appropriate competence, mastery, and a realistic sense of their limits and abilities. The parent reinforces an infantilizing form of dependency. In IPARTheory, this form of parenting is sometimes called "smother love." This, in turn, may result in a fearful and emotionally needy child.

As noted earlier, children and adults who experience significant interpersonal rejection are likely to feel angry and resentful. These and other destructive emotions may become intensely painful. As a result, many rejected individuals close off emotionally to protect themselves from the hurt of further rejection. That is, they become emotionally unresponsive. In doing so, they often have problems being able or willing to express love or in knowing how to or even being capable of accepting it from others (Rohner, 2004, 2005, 2021).

Because of all this psychological hurt, some rejected people become defensively independent. Like healthy independence, *defensively independent* individuals make relatively few behavioral bids for positive response. Unlike healthy independence, however, defensively independent people continue to crave warmth and support (i.e., positive response) from the people most important to them, though they sometimes do not recognize it. Indeed, because of the overlay of anger, distrust, and other negative emotions generated by rejection, defensively independent children and adults often positively deny this need, saying in effect, "To hell with you! I don't need you. I don't need anybody!" Expressions of defensive independence such as this with their associated emotions and behaviors sometimes lead to a process of counter-rejection, where rejected individuals often reject the rejecters in return. Not surprisingly, this process sometimes escalates into a cycle of violence and other serious relationship problems (See also Ali & Rohner, 2025b; Chapter 6, this book).

In addition to dependence or defensive independence, individuals who feel rejected are predicted in IPARTheory's personality subtheory to develop feelings of impaired self-esteem and impaired self-adequacy. This comes about because—as noted in symbolic interaction theory (Cooley, 1902; Mead, 1934) —individuals tend to view themselves as they think significant others view them. Thus, as children and adults feel their attachment figures do not love them, they are likely to feel unlovable, perhaps even unworthy of being loved (Rohner, 1986, 2004, 2021).

Whereas self-esteem pertains to individuals' feelings of self-worth or value, self-adequacy pertains to their feelings of competence or mastery to perform daily tasks adequately and to satisfy their own instrumental (task-oriented) needs adequately (Rohner, 1986, 2004, 2021). Insofar as individuals feel they are not very good people they are also apt to feel they are not very good at satisfying their needs. Alternatively, insofar as people feel they are no good at satisfying their personal needs, they often come to think less well of themselves more globally.

Anger, negative self-feelings, and the other consequences of perceived rejection tend to diminish rejected persons' capacity to deal effectively with stress. Because of this, children and adults who feel rejected often have problems with emotion regulation. That is, they tend to be less emotionally stable than children and adults who feel accepted. They often become emotionally upset—perhaps tearful or angry—when confronted with stressful situations that accepted (loved) individuals can handle with greater emotional equanimity. All these acutely painful feelings associated with perceived rejection tend to induce rejected people to develop anegative worldview (Rohner, 1986, 2004, 2021). That is, according to IPARTheory, rejected persons are likely to develop a view of the world—of life, interpersonal relationships, and the very nature of human existence—as being untrustworthy, hostile, unfriendly, emotionally unsafe, threatening, or dangerous in other ways. These thoughts and feelings often extend to people's beliefs about the nature of the supernatural world (i.e., God, the gods, and other religious beliefs) (Bahaa, 2024; Najam & Batool, 2012; Rohner, 1975, 1986; Rohner et al., 2024a). This issue is discussed more fully later, in IPARTheory's sociocultural systems subtheory.

Negative worldview, negative self-esteem, negative self-adequacy, and some of the other personality dispositions described above are important elements in the social cognition or mental representations of rejected children and adults. In IPARTheory, *mental representation* (Rohner, 2025a; Appendix A, this book) refers to an individual's more-or-less organized but usually implicit conception of self, others, and the experiential world constructed from emotionally significant past and current experiences. Along with one's emotional state—which both influences and is influenced by one's conception of self and reality—mental representations shape how individuals perceive, construe, and react to new experiences, including interpersonal relationships. Mental representations also influence what and how individuals store and remember experiences (see also Baldwin, 1992; Crick & Dodge, 1994; Rohner et al., 2024a).

Once created, children's and adults' mental representations (or cognitive schemas, or implicit theories as they are sometimes called) of self, of significant others, and the world around them tend to induce people to seek or avoid certain situations and kinds of people. In effect, how individuals think about themselves and their world shapes how they live their lives. This is notably true of rejected individuals.

For example, many rejected children and adults tend to be hypersensitive to the possibility of being slighted, ignored, spurned, socially excluded, ostracized, or rejected in other ways. This is called *rejection sensitivity* (Downey & Feldman, 1996; Rohner et al., 2024b).[4] Rejection sensitive people also tend to perceive criticism or hostility where none is intended, to see deliberate rejection in unintended acts of significant others, or to devalue their sense of personal worth in the face of strong counter-information (Rohner, 2021; Rohner et al., 2024b). Moreover, rejected individuals are likely to seek, create, interpret, or perceive experiences, situations, and relationships in ways consistent with their distorted mental representations. And they often avoid or mentally reinterpret situations that are inconsistent with these representations. Additionally, rejected individuals often construct mental images of personal relationships as being unpredictable, untrustworthy, and perhaps hurtful. These negative mental representations or negative schemas are often carried forward into new relationships where rejected children and adults develop a *fear of intimacy*—finding it difficult to trust others emotionally (Ashdown et al., 2023; Phillips et al., 2013; Rohner et al., 2019).[5] Because of all this selective attention, selective perception, faulty styles of causal attribution, and distorted cognitive information-processing rejected children are generally expected in IPARTheory to self-propel along qualitatively different developmental pathways from accepted or loved children, discussed next.

Longitudinal Studies and Twin Studies of Parental Acceptance-Rejection

Longitudinal studies, including those examining monozygotic twins (Waller & colleagues, 2018) and adoptive families (Trentacosta et al., 2019), consistently demonstrate that experiences of parental acceptance-rejection directly influence children's personality development and psychological adjustment. The Parenting Across Cultures (PAC) study (see Lansford, 2025; Chapter 4 this book), for example, is a major longitudinal study of 13 cultural groups in nine countries (China, Colombia, Italy, Jordan, Kenya, Philippines, Sweden, Thailand, and the United States). Authors in the study investigate the relation between parental acceptance-rejection and cultural norms and other aspects of parenting and psychological adjustment among children and adolescents. Results of the PAC reveal that in all countries, all four forms of parental rejection (described earlier) predicted children's internalizing behavior problems (e.g., anxiety, sadness, loneliness, self-consciousness, and nervousness) and externalizing behaviors problems (e.g., lying, bullying, vandalism, disobedience, and physical violence) across ages 7 through 18 years old (Folker et al., 2023; Gorla et al., 2024; Rothenberg et al., 2022).

Moreover, other longitudinal research spanning several decades illustrates the enduring consequences of childhood adversity, including increased risk for disease, poorer overall physical health, and decline in cognitive functioning in adulthood. Studies like those conducted by Reuben et al. (2016) and Leger et al. (2021) highlight the mediating role of personality dispositions known to be associated with experiences of interpersonal rejection—particularly emotional instability—in linking perceived rejection to chronic health conditions and mortality. However, findings also suggest that parental warmth and affection can mitigate the negative impact of childhood adversity, as demonstrated by Carroll et al. (2013) and Chen et al. (2019). Carroll et al. (2013) also found that the presence of at least one loving parent essentially eliminated the impact of child abuse on the risk of later developing coronary artery problems.

Chen et al. (2019) found in their longitudinal study that adults' recollections of parental warmth and love in childhood were positively associated 10 years later with the adults' self-reports of emotional, psychological, and social well-being. Additionally, the authors found that parental warmth in childhood was negatively associated with adverse outcomes such as drug use and smoking.[6] Overall, the evidence underscores the critical importance of early experiences of acceptance or rejection in shaping both personality development and long-term health outcomes across the lifespan. The benefits of receiving warmth and affection are discussed at greater length by Ali et al. (2025; Chapter 10 of this book).

IPARTheory's Coping Subtheory

Several thousand studies spanning diverse populations, age groups, and genders, consistently conclude that about 60% to 80% of the participants worldwide support personality subtheory's expectations regarding the effects of perceived parental rejection (Ki et al., 2018). A few individuals who come from loving families, however, also display the constellation of psychological problems typically shown by rejected children. In IPARTheory, these people are called *troubled*. Many of them are adults who are or were in rejecting relationships with intimate partners or other attachment figures other than parents. This fact helps confirm IPARTheory's postulate that, for most people, perceived rejection by an attachment figure at any point in life can effectively compromise the likelihood of healthy social-emotional and physical functioning. However, it is also expected in IPARTheory that a minority of children and adults will be able to thrive emotionally despite having experienced significant rejection by parents or other attachment figures in childhood. As shown in Figure 1.4, these people are called *copers* (Rohner, 1986, 2004, 2021).

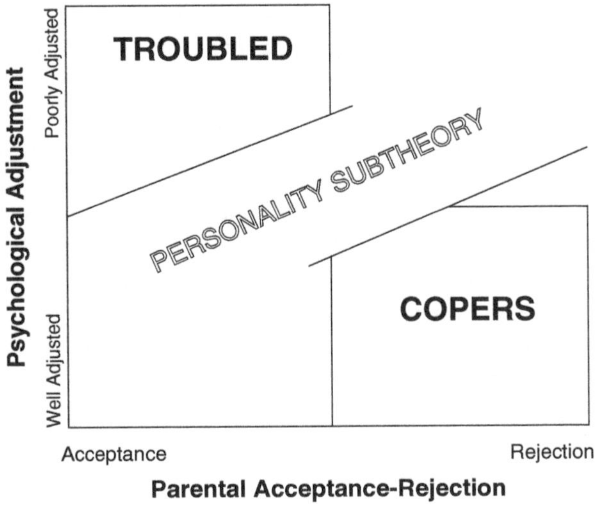

FIGURE 1.4 Copers and Troubled Individuals in Relation to IPARTheory's Personality Subtheory. © 2004, 2021, 2024, 2025 by Rohner Research Publications.

Rohner identified two forms of *copers*: (1) affective copers and (2) instrumental copers. *Affective copers* are those persons whose emotional and overall mental health is reasonably good despite having been raised in seriously rejecting families or despite being seriously rejected by other attachment figures in life (Rohner, 1986, 2004, 2021). *Instrumental copers*, on the other hand, are rejected persons whose emotional and mental health is impaired in the expected ways because of serious rejection in childhood. However, those individuals maintain high task competence and occupational performance. Instrumental copers do well in school, in their professions, occupations, and in other *task-oriented* activities. Many prominent personalities in history have been instrumental copers. Included among them are such personages as the famous trumpet player and singer, Louis "Satchmo" Armstrong; the famous British philosopher, John Stuart Mill; the 37th President of the United States, Richard Nixon; the famous American writer and poet, Edgar Allen Poe; the former First Lady of the United States, Eleanor Roosevelt; the professional baseball player, Babe Ruth (George H. Ruth, Jr); the great American writer and humorist, Mark Twain (Samuel L. Clemens); and many others (Goertzel & Goertzel, 1962; Howe, 1982). Biographies and autobiographies of these individuals reveal that even though they were successful instrumental copers, they were not affective copers. All appear to have been psychologically distressed in ways described in IPARTheory's personality subtheory.

To understand the coping process—indeed, the entire acceptance-rejection process—one must adopt a multivariate, person-in-context perspective. This perspective has three elements: self, other, and context. Specifically, the *multivariate model of behavior* employed in IPARTheory states that the individual's behavior (e.g., coping with perceived rejection) is a function of the interaction between self, other, and context. *Self*--characteristics include the individual's mental representations and other internal (biological) and external (personality) characteristics discussed earlier. *Other* characteristics include the personal and interpersonal characteristics of the rejecting other, along with the form, frequency, duration, and severity of rejection. *Context* characteristics include other significant people in the individual's life, along with social-situational characteristics of the person's environment. A specific research hypothesis from this perspective states that all other things being equal, the likelihood of children and adults being able to emotionally cope with perceived interpersonal rejection is enhanced by the presence of at least one warm, supportive attachment figure in their lives.

IPARTheory's emphasis on mental activity—including mental representations—leads IPARTheorists to expect that specific social-cognitive capabilities allow some children and adults to cope with perceived rejection more effectively than others. These capabilities include a *differentiated sense of self*, a sense of *self-determination*, and the capacity to *depersonalize* (Rohner, 1986). More specifically, coping subtheory expects that children's and adults' capacity to cope with rejection is enhanced to the degree that they have a clearly differentiated sense of self. The concept of differentiated sense of self (or self-differentiation) refers in IPARTheory to the capability of individuals to (a) understand another person's feelings, thoughts, and motivations and—crucially—(b) to clearly distinguish or differentiate those dispositions from their own feelings, thoughts, and motivations, especially in emotionally close relationships. In effect, self-differentiation involves the ability to maintain psychological individuality in the context of emotionally intense relationships.

Another attribute thought in the theory to help people cope with perceived rejection is a sense of self-determination. Self-determined individuals believe they can exert at least a modicum of control over what happens to them through their own effort or personal attributes. Other rejected individuals may feel like pawns. They feel as though things happen to them because of fate, chance, luck, or powerful others. Individuals with a sense of self-determination are believed in IPARTheory to have an internal psychological resource for minimizing some of the most damaging consequences of perceived rejection.

Similarly, individuals who can depersonalize are believed in the theory to be provided with another social-cognitive resource for dealing with perceived rejection. *Personalizing* refers to the act of "taking it personally," that is, to reflexively or automatically relating life events and interpersonal encounters to oneself—of interpreting events egocentrically in terms of oneself, usually in a negative sense. Thus, personalizers are apt to interpret inadvertent slights and minor acts of insensitivity as being deliberate acts of rejection or other hurtful intentions. This process is closely related to rejection sensitivity as discussed earlier (see also Ali & Rohner, 2025a, Chapter 8, this book). However, individuals who can depersonalize have a psychological resource for dealing more positively with inevitable ambiguities in interpersonal relationships. All three of these social cognitive capabilities are thought in IPARTheory to provide psychological shields against the most damaging effects of perceived rejection. However, these attributes also tend themselves to be affected by rejection, especially rejection occurring during the formative years of childhood. This complicates the process of assessing the independent contribution that each attribute might make in helping children and adults cope emotionally with perceived interpersonal rejection.

Rohner (1986, 2004, 2021) argued that even though the mental health status of affective copers tends to be reasonably good, it is generally not as good as that of individuals coming from loving (accepting) families or in other emotionally satisfying relationships. But it does tend to be significantly better than that of most individuals coming from rejecting families or from seriously rejecting adolescent and adult relationships. Over time, from childhood into adulthood, however, all but the most severely rejected and psychologically injured individuals are likely to have enough positive experiences outside their rejecting families of origin to help ameliorate the most damaging emotional, social, cognitive, and behavioral effects of perceived parental rejection. Thus, given the ordinary resilience characteristic of most people most of the time (Masten, 2001, 2014)—in combination with successful psychotherapy, positive work experiences, satisfying intimate relationships, and other emotionally gratifying experiences—adults who were rejected in childhood are often better adjusted emotionally and psychologically than they were as children under the direct influence of rejecting parents. This is true even though they tend not to have a sense of well-being that is as positive as adults who felt loved all along. That is, important effects of rejection are apt to linger into adulthood, placing even affective copers at somewhat greater risk for social, physical, medical, and emotional problems throughout life than those individuals who were loved continuously. This is especially true if rejection experiences in childhood seriously compromised the adult's ability to form secure, trusting relationships with an intimate partner or other adult attachment figure (Rohner, 1986, 2004, 2021). See also, Khaleque, 2025b; Chapter 5, this book.

The first empirical study to assess critical features of the affective coping process was conducted by Ki (2015; Ki et al., 2018). That study was based on 11,946 adults from 10 nations. Almost 17% of the respondents in the study reported having been seriously rejected in childhood by one or both parents. Nonetheless, 40% of the respondents fit the conceptual and operational definition of affective copers. According to Ki, significantly more women than men tended to be affective copers. At this point, it is unclear why this gender difference exists, except that women everywhere generally seek emotional support from other people more often than men (Ki et al., 2018; Tamres et al., 2002). It is worth noting that both male and female affective copers tend internationally to report significantly more maternal acceptance than paternal acceptance (Ki, 2015). However, male copers reported experiencing significantly more maternal acceptance in childhood than did women, and female copers reported experiencing more paternal acceptance in childhood than did men (for details, see Rohner, 2021). The importance of fathers' love and probable reasons for it are amplified later in this chapter as well as in Akun (2025; Chapter 9 this book).

IPARTheory's Sociocultural-Systems Subtheory and Model

Sociocultural systems subtheory is interested in predicting and explaining sociocultural and personal conditions under which parents are likely to accept or reject their children (Rohner, 1986, 2004, 2021). Is it true, for example—as the subtheory predicts—that specific psychological, familial, community, and societal factors tend to be reliably associated the world over with specific variations in parental acceptance-rejection? Second, in what way is the total fabric of society, as well as the behavior and beliefs of individuals within society, affected by the fact that most parents in that sociocultural group tend normatively to either accept or reject their children? For example, is it true—as sociocultural systems subtheory predicts—that a people's religious beliefs, artistic preferences, and other expressive beliefs and behaviors tend to be universally associated with their childhood experiences of parental love and love withdrawal (Rohner, 2021).

IPARTheory's sociocultural-systems model, shown in Figure 1.5, provides a way of thinking about the antecedents, consequences, and other correlates of interpersonal acceptance-rejection within individuals and total societies. The model has its historical roots in the early work of Kardiner (1939, 1945a, 1945b), and later in the work of Whiting and Child (1953). It also shares notable similarities with Bronfenbrenner's (1979)

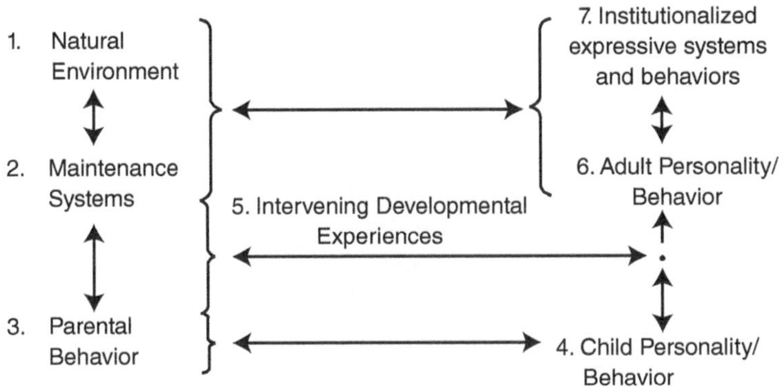

FIGURE 1.5 IPARTheory's Sociocultural-Systems Model. © 2004, 2021, 2024, 2025 by Rohner Research Publications.

ecological model and with Berry and Poortinga's (2006) eco-cultural model. It shows, for example, that the likelihood of parents (Element 3 in the model) displaying any given form of behavior (e.g., acceptance or rejection) toward their children is shaped in important ways by the *maintenance systems* (Element 2 in the model) of that society. Maintenance systems include social institutions such as society's family structure, household organization, economic organization, political organization, system of defense, and other institutions that bear directly on the survival of a culturally organized population within its natural environment (Element 1 in the model). The model also shows that parents' accepting-rejecting and other behaviors directly impact children's personality development and behavior (as postulated in the personality subtheory).

The double-headed arrows in the model show a bidirectional flow between elements, suggesting for example that parental behavior is instrumental in shaping children's personality and behavioral development. But children's personality and behavior also significantly influence the form and quality of parents' behavior toward them. Arrows in the model also reveal that—in addition to family experiences—youth have a wide variety of other influential experiences over time (Element 5 in the model) as they develop into adulthood (Element 6 in the model). Among those experiences are experiences with peers, intimate partners, and others. Additionally, they have formative experiences with institutionalized expressive systems. Institutionalized expressive systems are ubiquitous but essentially nonsurvival-oriented features of society such as a people's religious beliefs, artistic and musical traditions, their games, folklore, and the like. They are called "expressive" in IPARTheory because they are believed in the theory to express or reflect people's internal, psychological states, at least initially when the expressive systems were first created. Thus, expressive *systems* are believed in IPARTheory to be symbolic creations formed over time by multiple individuals within a society. As people change, the expressive systems and behaviors also tend to change, though sometimes haltingly—especially if the systems have been codified in writing. According to the sociocultural systems subtheory, it is important to note that even though expressive systems (such as religious traditions) are ultimately human creations, once created and incorporated into the sociocultural system, they tend to act back on individuals, shaping their further beliefs and behaviors (Rohner, 1986, 2004, 2021).

Guided by the sociocultural systems model, IPARTheory's sociocultural systems subtheory attempts to predict and explain worldwide causes and expressive correlates of parental acceptance and rejection (Rohner 1986, 2004, 2021). For example, the subtheory predicts—and substantial cross-cultural evidence confirms—that in societies where children tend to be rejected, cultural beliefs about the supernatural world (i.e., about God, gods, and the spirit world) usually portray supernaturals as being disposed toward malevolence or capable of malevolent behaviors, including hostility, treacherousness, unpredictability, capriciousness, destructiveness, or negativity in other ways (Najam & Batool, 2012; Bierman, 2005; Williams et al., 2019; Rohner, 1975,1986, 2004, 2021; Rohner et al., 2024a; Thiele, 2007). However, the supernatural world is usually thought to be more or less benevolent—warm, supportive, generous, protective, or kindly in other ways—in societies where children are typically raised with loving acceptance. These cultural differences are believed in the theory to result from aggregated individual differences in the mental representations of accepted versus rejected persons within these two types of societies.

Parental acceptance and rejection are also associated worldwide with many other expressive sociocultural correlates such as artistic traditions and artistic preferences of individuals within societies (Brown et al., 2015; Rohner & Frampton, 1982). Additionally, research suggests that the recreational and occupational choices adults make may be associated with childhood experiences of acceptance and rejection (Briana et al., 2005; Loberman & Tziner, 2011; Mantell, 1974; Rohner, 1986, 2021). Hoarding, too, tends to be associated with adults' memories of childhood rejection (Brown et al., 2015; Ma et al., 2024; Martinez-Garri, 2023). Finally, styles of humor are also associated with adults' memories of parental acceptance-rejection in childhood (Kerla, 2012). Kazarian et al. (2010), for example, found that both men and women who recalled having been loved (accepted) in childhood by both their mothers and fathers tended to use affiliative and self-enhancing styles of humor, whereas adults who recalled having been rejected in childhood tended more often to use aggressive and/or self-defeating styles of humor. *Affiliative humor* refers to humor that enhances one's relationship with others by engaging in spontaneous, witty banter to amuse others and reduce interpersonal tension. *Self-enhancing humor* uses humor to regulate emotions and cope with stress through a humorous outlook on life. *Aggressive humor*, on the other hand, involves using humor to enhance oneself at the expense of others using sarcasm, ridicule, and "put-down" humor. Finally, *self-defeating humor* involves using humor to enhance relationships at one's own expense using self-disparaging humor. All these and other expressive behaviors and beliefs appear to be byproducts of the social, emotional, and social-cognitive effects of parental acceptance and rejection.

Why do parents in most societies tend to be warm and loving, and parents in about 25% of the world's societies tend normatively to be mildly to severely rejecting (Rohner, 1975, 1986, 2021; Rohner & Rohner, 1981). What factors account for these societal differences and individual variations in parenting within societies? Questions such as these guide the second portion of IPARTheory's sociocultural systems subtheory. No single or straightforward response answers these questions, but specific factors noted below tend to be reliably associated with societal and intrasocietal variations in parental rejection. Principal among them are conditions that promote the breakdown of primary social and emotional relationships, and social support. Thus, single parents (most often mothers) in social isolation without social and emotional support—especially if the parents are young and economically deprived—appear universally to be at the greatest risk for withdrawing love and affection from their children (Rohner, 1986). However, it is useful to note that from a global perspective, poverty by itself is not necessarily associated with increased rejection. Instead, it is poverty in association with other social and emotional conditions that place children at the most significant risk. Indeed, much of humanity is now and always has been in relative poverty. But despite that, most parents worldwide raise their children with loving care (Rohner, 1975). Other risk factors such as family conflict and violence, parental substance abuse, and parental psychiatric disorder have also been shown to be significant predictors of children's and young adults' reports of parental rejection (Anderson et al., 2022; Medley & Sachs-Ericsson, 2009; Rohner, 1986, 2004, 2021).

Methods in IPARTheory Research

Six and a half decades of transcultural research in IPARTheory have been guided methodologically by conceptual models called *anthroponomy* and the *universalist approach*, respectively (Rohner, 1986; Rohner & Rohner, 1980). Anthroponomy is an approach to the human sciences characterized by a search for *universals* in human behavior, that is, by worldwide principles of behavior that can be shown empirically to generalize across our species (Homo-sapiens) under specified conditions whenever they occur. Although many propositions advanced by Western social scientists are assumed to apply to all humans, verifying such claims is complex. It involves attention to the role of culture, language, migration, history, and other factors. It also requires attention to the strengths and weaknesses of individual measurement procedures (e.g., self-report questionnaires) and general paradigms of research (e.g., the holocultural method) (Cournoyer, 2000; Cournoyer & Malcolm, 2004; Rohner, 1986).

In IPARTheory, these issues are addressed in the universalist approach, a multi-methodology and multi-procedure research strategy that searches for the convergence of results across an array of discrete measurement modalities and paradigms of research in a huge range of sociocultural and ethnic settings worldwide. More specifically, *eight* discrete methods or types of studies have been used to test IPARTheory's central postulates, assumptions, and hypotheses. These methods can be discussed in three clusters: (1) *quantitative psychological studies* (using procedures such as interviews, behavior observations, self-report questionnaires translated and adapted into the languages of the people where they are used), holocultural studies, and meta-analyses of quantitative studies; (2) *ethnographic studies* such as ethnographic case studies, and controlled comparison or concomitant variation studies; and (3) *neurobiological studies* using functional magnetic resonance imaging (fMRI) and electroencephalography (EEG). Each of these clusters is discussed below.

Quantitative Psychological Studies

The quantitative psychological studies cluster consists of three types of research. The first involves *quantitative studies* using techniques such as *interviews*, *behavior observations*, and especially *self-report questionnaires*. By 2024, Rohner had created the 35 measures relevant to IPARTheory shown in Appendix B at the end of this book (Rohner, 2025b). Some of these measures are available in up to 78 languages or dialects worldwide. All were developed to help researchers, clinicians, students, service agencies, and others conduct research and evaluation on issues of interpersonal acceptance and rejection.

Extensive information about the reliability and validity of many of these measures for use internationally and among American ethnic groups is available in the *Handbook for the Study of Parental Acceptance and Rejection* (Rohner & Khaleque, 2005) and elsewhere (e.g., Khaleque & Rohner, 2002; Rohner & Khaleque, 2003; Rohner et al., 2024b). References to approximately 6,000 quantitative psychological studies using these and related measures may be found in the Rohner Center's Bibliography (csiar.

uconn.edu/bibliography). There, interested students, researchers, and practitioners may do keyword searches to locate authors, articles, and books dealing with specific acceptance-rejection topics of special interest to them.

Holocultural studies (formerly called cross-cultural survey studies) are the second type of study in the quantitative psychological-studies category. The holocultural method is a research design for statistically testing transcultural relations between two or more theoretically defined and operationalized variables in a world sample of human societies. Several dozen holocultural studies and methodological papers (e.g., Rohner et al., 1978) have been published dealing with topics pertinent to interpersonal acceptance-rejection. Probably the single most important book dealing with this topic is Rohner's (1975), *They Love Me, They Love Me Not*. That book dealt with 101 well-described non-industrial societies worldwide. Major results of the book were later summarized and expanded in Rohner (1986), and more recently.

Meta-analyses are the third type of study in the quantitative psychological-studies category. This type of study integrates, summarizes, and synthesizes the results of a large assemblage of discrete published and unpublished psychological studies. Meta-analyses are used primarily to empirically test the basic tenets of a conceptual model or theory. As such, they are instrumental in helping confirm many of IPARTheory's central postulates about the universal effects and other correlates of interpersonal acceptance-rejection (Khaleque & Ali, 2017; Rohner, 2021). Thirteen meta-analyses involving over 150,000 children and adults from around the globe offer strong support for the central postulates of IPARTheory's basic postulates (see Khaleque, 2025a, Chapter 2, this book). Khaleque and Rohner's (2002) meta-analysis, for example, showed that 3,433 additional studies, all with nonsignificant results, would be required to disconfirm the conclusion that perceived parental acceptance-rejection in childhood is panculturally associated with *children's* psychological adjustment; 941 such studies would be required to disconfirm this conclusion among *adults*.

Ethnographic Studies

The second cluster of distinctive methods used in IPARTheory consists of two types of studies based on *ethnographic research*. The first of these is the *ethnographic case study*. These studies generally employ long-term (e.g., six months to several years) participant-observation procedures within a specific culturally organized community, along with structured and unstructured observations, interviews, and other such procedures. Such ethnographic studies produce a context-rich account of the lifeway of a people. Rohner and Chaki-Sircar's (1988) book on *Women and Children in a Bengali Village* illustrates this approach. The study involved 18 months of ethnographic and quantitative research among women and children in the village. Moreover, Rohner (1987) completed a six-month ethnographic and quantitative psychological case study of 349 9- through 16-year-old youth in St. Kitt, West Indies. He also conducted a six-month ethnographic and quantitative psychological case study of 281 9- through 18-year-old youths and their parents in a poor, biracial (African American and European American) community in southeast Georgia, USA (Rohner et al., 1996; Veneziano & Rohner, 1998). Results of all three studies support the conclusion that perceived parental acceptance-rejection is associated with the expected variations in youth's psychological adjustment.

A second method within this cluster is the *controlled comparison* or *concomitant variation study* (Naroll, 1968; Pelto & Pelto, 1978; Rohner, 1977). In these studies, investigators usually locate two or more culture-bearing populations in which one of two conditions is true: (1) Relevant variables in the sampled populations vary, but other sociocultural factors remain constant, or (2) relevant variables in the sample population remain constant while other sociocultural factors are free to vary. Rohner's (1960) comparative study of parental rejection in three Pacific societies (i.e., a Maori community of New Zealand, a traditional highland community of Bali, and the Alorese of Indonesia) illustrates this type of controlled comparison.

Neurobiological Studies

The third cluster of methods used to investigate the effects of interpersonal acceptance-rejection utilizes neurobiological measurements. Two techniques such as functional magnetic resonance imaging (fMRI) and electroencephalography (EEG) measures have helped unpack the mechanisms underlying acute rejection and acceptance experiences and the long-term neurobiological effects of experiencing interpersonal acceptance and rejection. As already noted, neurobiological studies investigating social rejection, exclusion, and acceptance have used interactive paradigms that involve social interactions. The evidence discussed earlier confirms that experimentally induced social exclusion/rejection is sufficient to induce negative affect (Wesselmann et al., 2009), increase anxiety (Oaten et al., 2008), lower mood, decrease self-esteem (Zadro et al., 2004), and create emotion dysregulation (Ali et al., 2024).

Also as noted earlier, much of what researchers know about the neural correlates of acceptance and rejection comes from *fMRI studies*. fMRI procedures rely on measuring changes in hemoglobin—the oxygen-carrying component of blood (Huettel et al., 2004). Oxygenated and deoxygenated hemoglobin respond differently in the magnetic field of an fMRI scanner. The signal generated in fMRI, commonly referred to as the Blood

Oxygenation Level Dependent (BOLD) signal, provides information about the overall level of blood oxygenation and how it varies over time as a function of neuronal activity in specific brain regions. In measuring BOLD changes, researchers infer changes in neural activity.

Using fMRI, researchers have studied the underlying circuitry of cognitive processes that form mental representations because of interpersonal acceptance-rejection. Meta-analytic reviews of fMRI studies on social exclusion/rejection identified neural circuitries engaged during social exclusion. Those circuitries include acute distress, self-relevant processing, and emotion regulation (see Cacioppo et al., 2013; Rotge et al., 2015; Vijayakumar et al., 2017). Studies examining the neural correlates of rejection reveal brain activation in multiple regions, including the amygdala (involved in emotional reactions, learning, and memory) and anterior cingulate division (involved in attention control and emotion, social reward, and pain processing). Mounting evidence suggests that positive social interactions with people—such as parents, romantic partners, or friends—lead to experiencing positive emotions (Rohner et al., 2019). Positive interactions are also linked to an increased activity in brain regions modulated by reward and relate to pleasant mood states (Minagawa-Kawai et al., 2009).

Further, fMRI research also reports that individuals who remember having experienced parental rejection in childhood—in comparison to individuals who recall having been loved/accepted by their parents—had increased activation of brain regions that critically support emotion processing and social pain. As shown earlier in Figure 1.2, these regions include the posterior cingulate cortex (PCC) and anterior cingulate cortex (ACC), dorsolateral prefrontal cortex (dlPFC), medial prefrontal cortex (mPFC), insula, cuneus, precuneus, and amygdala (Ali et al., 2024; Schulz et al., 2022).

EEG studies are another brain-based measure commonly used to study interpersonal rejection and acceptance. In these studies, researchers place sensors on the scalp to measure the electrical field potentials generated by cortical neural activity. Using EEG, Crowley et al. (2010) found similar neural activity in cortical regions previously identified in fMRI studies on social rejection, including the subgenual cortex, ventral anterior cingulate cortex, and insula, was greater when study participants were experimentally exposed to social rejection incidents.

Each of these seven types of studies contains unique strengths and weaknesses. The strengths of the psychological-study cluster, for example, include valid, reliable, and precise descriptions of phenomena. Estimates of both central tendency and variability in data generated in this methodological cluster allow sensitive and powerful statistical procedures to be employed to tease out subtle effects. However, a typical weakness of these studies is that rich contextual data is usually missing. The special strengths of the methods in the ethnographic and holocultural research cluster, on the other hand, produce ecologically valid data, culturally detailed, and sociocultural variation worldwide. A weakness of these methods, however, is that measures coded from ethnography are sometimes imprecise and, therefore, may be low in reliability. Lastly, neurobiological measurement techniques add a deeper layer to our understanding of interpersonal relationships by integrating body, brain, and interpersonal relationships. This emerging line of inquiry also offers a direct window into cognitive-emotional processes that eventually guide an individual's responses to interpersonal rejection. However, brain imaging studies are costly and usually based on a small sample size. This limits the kind of research questions that can be asked.

Benefits of Interpersonal Acceptance

It is important to emphasize that the experience of parental love (acceptance) in childhood appears to be universally associated with the development of the disposition toward forgiveness (being forgiving) and toward many other prosocial and positive developmental behaviors such as generosity, empathy, helpfulness, positive peer relations, and an overall sense of well-being and life satisfaction. The experience of parental love (acceptance) in childhood is also associated with physical health benefits in both children and adults. These benefits include lower blood pressure, lower cholesterol, lower blood glucose, and a lower incidence of serious medical problems such as cancer, cardiovascular disease, irritable bowel syndrome, and many other medical problems. Medical problems associated with perceived parental acceptance-rejection are further discussed by Ali et al. (2025; Chapter 10, this book).

Research on acceptance and affection demonstrates that affection is beneficial only if it is genuine. Deceptive affection might involve an effort to manipulate someone, pretending to care deeply about one's partner while actually using that person for their own benefit such as face-saving, conflict management/avoidance, and emotion management (Floyd & Pauley, 2010; Horan & Booth-Butterfield, 2019). When detected, deceptive affection can be emotionally damaging and erode trust between individuals (Caton & Horan, 2023). Research has found that perception of an appropriate level of love/acceptance is associated with better health and wellbeing outcomes than either excessive or insufficient love/acceptance (Hesse et al., 2023).

Clinical, Forensic, and Other Practical Applications of IPARTheory and Measures

IPARTheory and measures are used worldwide in clinical, forensic, and other applied contexts such as in mental health clinics, the courts, school systems, parent-education programs, protective services agencies, and similar settings. Here, we briefly summarize applications in two of these-contexts—in clinical settings and in the forensic context of empirically assessing parental alienation for the courts, and protective services agencies.

Clinical Applications of IPARTheory and Measures

IPARTheory researchers recognize that many of the effects of perceived rejection are also found in developmental trauma disorder (DTD; van der Kolk, 2010) and in complex posttraumatic stress disorder (Complex PTSD or simply CPTSD; Courtois, 2004). These are conditions where individuals experience repeated trauma—especially interpersonal trauma—over an extended time and developmental periods. Included among the shared effects of perceived rejection, DTD, and CPTSD are issues of hypervigilance, anxiety, often self-hatred, problems with interpersonal relationships, and suicidality, among several others. Additionally, issues of depression and substance abuse are also implicated in perceived rejection, DTD, and CPTSD.

IPARTheory concepts, measures, and/or evidence have been incorporated into the work of clinicians and others who work with clients suffering from issues such as these, but clinicians work from many different clinical perspectives. These perspectives include Cognitive Behavioral Therapy (CBT), Emotionally Focused Therapy (EFT), Eye Movement Desensitization Reprocessing Therapy (EMDR), Holistic Counseling, Interpersonal Therapy (IPT), Marriage and Family Therapy (MFT), Microcounseling, Psychodynamic Therapy, and Schema Therapy, among others. So far, the most highly developed evidence-based IPARTheory-related clinical approach was created by Rigazio-Digilio and Rohner (2008, 2015). Those authors developed and tested an interactive assessment and treatment protocol for use in relational therapy. It is based on a clinical translation of IPARTheory concepts and measures. The authors also supervised a successful study that examined how the protocol informed collaborative assessment, treatment planning, and evaluation when working with couples who had personal (e.g., emotional) problems or interpersonal difficulties associated with rejection by an intimate partner and/or parental rejection in childhood. Gurmen (2025) discusses the clinical applications of IPARTheory at a greater length in Chapter 11 of this book.

Rising and Rohner's (2021) *Recovery from Rejection: A Manual of Client Handouts for Clinical Practice* is a second major resource used by clinicians and others in the United States and internationally. The client handouts in the Manual focus on personality dispositions known to be associated worldwide with perceived rejection. The handouts are practical in nature and meant to integrate IPARTheory with clinical practice to better serve clients who are in recovery from interpersonal rejection (e.g., parental and intimate partner rejection). The Manual is available gratis as an eBook from Rohner Research Publications (rohnerresearchpublications.com). Currently it is available in English, German, Persian, Turkish, and Urdu. Additionally, it is planned for Arabic, Czech, Dutch, French, Italian, Spanish, and perhaps other languages.

Forensic Applications of IPARTheory and Measures

IPARTheory and associated measures are used in forensic psychology in the United States and internationally by helping to identify *parental alienation*. Parental alienation occurs when children ally themselves with one parent and refuse to have contact with (i.e., reject) the other parent without legitimate justification. Alienation is distinguished from *parental estrangement*, where children reject or refuse to have contact with that parent for good cause such as a history of abuse or neglect. Parental alienation generally occurs in the context of high conflict divorce or separation where one parent pits the child against the other parent. It is essential in clinical and forensic evaluation for family-law practitioners, court-appointed professionals, clinicians, and others to clearly distinguish unjustified parental alienation from justified parental estrangement, and other forms of malparenting.

To help implement this task effectively, Bernet et al. (2018, 2020) developed a technique using the Mother and Father forms of the Adult Parental Acceptance-Rejection Questionnaire (PARQ) to help distinguish parental alienation from parental estrangement and other forms of malparenting. This technique distinguished with 99% accuracy severely alienated children from non-alienated children. Because of its unusual success rate, scores of psychologists, family-law practitioners, social workers, and other professionals in many countries now use the Mother and Father PARQs in their clinical and court-related work dealing with parental alienation and other forms of malparenting. Some professionals are beginning to use the Child PAQ as well. The destructive effect of parental alienation on children and alienated parents is discussed more fully by Bernet and Alvarez (2025, Chapter 14, this book).

IPARTheory's Legacy

The empirical study of interpersonal—especially parental—acceptance-rejection has a long history going back to the 1890s (Stogdill, 1937). It was not until the 1930s, however, that a more-or-less continuous body of empirical research began to appear dealing with the effects of parental acceptance-rejection. Today, more than 6,000 studies are available on the topic (Rohner, 2021). Many individuals have contributed to this body of work, but a handful have made especially significant and sustained contributions. These individuals and groups represent different programs of research, employing distinctive concepts, measures, and research designs.

Rohner's program of research, which ultimately led to the construction of IPARTheory and associated measures in the 1970s and 1980s, grew directly out of these traditions in the United States, as well as from Rohner's own program of cross-cultural comparative research beginning in 1960 (Rohner, 1960, 1975; Rohner et al., 1978; Rohner & Rohner, 1980, 1981). This body of literature led to the development of the eight basic postulates in IPARTheory, discussed next.

IPARTheory's Eight Basic Postulates

Now, after six and a half decades of research with several hundred thousand children, adolescents, and adults in scores of countries worldwide and with members of every major American ethnic group, it seems safe to conclude that *IPARTheory's eight basic postulates* find nearly universal support. These are:

1 Over the course of shared biocultural evolution, humans everywhere have developed the enduring, biologically based emotional need to feel cared about by the people most important to them.
2 Children and adults everywhere—regardless of differences in culture, gender, race, and other defining characteristics—understand themselves to be cared about (accepted) or not cared about (rejected) in the same four ways. In IPARTheory, this is known as the warmth dimension of interpersonal relationships, including parenting.
3 Children and adults everywhere tend to respond in the same ten ways when they experience being rejected by parents in childhood and by other attachment figures throughout life. In IPARTheory, this is called the acceptance-rejection syndrome.
4 The psychological effects of parental acceptance-rejection in childhood tend to extend into adulthood and old age, though often in a less intense form than in childhood.
5 Children's perceptions of fathers' love-related (accepting-rejecting) behaviors and adults' memories of these behaviors in childhood often have as great or greater impact than children's or adults' perceptions/memories of mothers' love-related behaviors on emotional, social, behavioral, and cognitive development.
6 Some children and adults are better able than most to deal emotionally with the effects of interpersonal (especially parental) rejection. These people are known as affective copers in IPARTheory's Coping Subtheory and are distinguished from instrumental copers.

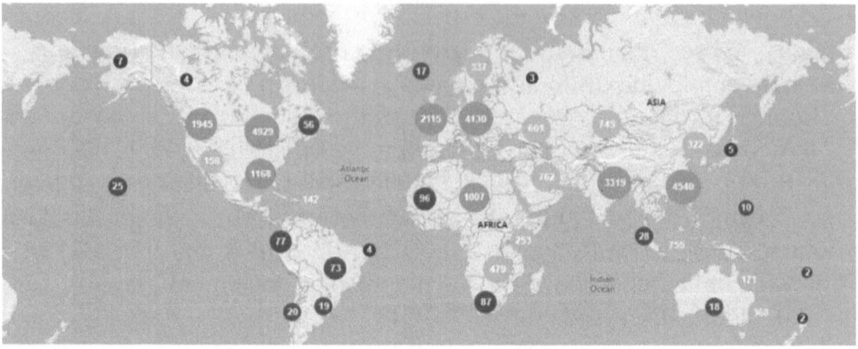

FIGURE 1.6 IPARTheory's Global Reach.

Source: Scholarworks, February, 2025

7 Specific psychological, familial, community and sociocultural factors tend to be associated worldwide with specific variations in parents' tendency to be accepting or rejecting. In IPARTheory, this pertains to the Sociocultural Systems Subtheory and Model.
8 The experience of parental acceptance-rejection in childhood tends to reliably predict expressive behaviors and beliefs of adults within a society, for example, their religious beliefs, artistic preferences, traditions, styles of humor, musical preferences, and others.

Summary: IPARTheory's Global Reach

IPARTheory is a theory of lifespan human development that investigates the consequences, causes, and other correlates of interpersonal acceptance and rejection on developmental outcomes, including cognitive, behavioral, emotional, biological, and social functioning. The theory's emphasis on the importance of positive interpersonal relationships has informed clinical practice, public policies, and welfare programs to support healthy families and promote offspring's well-being across cultures. Now the theory has a global reach, as shown graphically in Figure 1.6 by Elsevier's PlumX Metrics. That metric reveals that Rohner's 2021 article alone has been downloaded more than 33,302 times from 2,088 institutions in 171 countries (PlumX Metrics, February, 2025). That number continues to grow monthly.

Notes

1 In IPARTheory, the term parent refers to whoever the major caregiver is of the child. This can be a biological (birth) parent, adoptive parent, grandparent, other kin, or even a non-kin person.

2 Miller and Ali (2025) discuss at greater length the effects of interpersonal acceptance-rejection and neurobiological development in Chapter 12 of this book.
3 See Appendix A for the definition of all major concepts in IPARTheory.
4 IPARTheory's perspective on the fear of intimacy is amplified in Rohner et al. (2019).
5 IPARTheory's perspective on rejection sensitivity is amplified at length in Ali and Rohner (2025b; Chapter 8, this book).
6 Longitudinal studies using IPARTheory are discussed at greater length in Lansford (2025; Chapter 7, this book).

References

Abrutyn, S. (2023). Toward a sociological theory of social pain. *Journal for the Theory of Social Behaviour*, 53, 351–371. https://onlinelibrary.wiley.com/doi/pdf/10.1111/jtsb.12371

Ainsworth, M. D. S. (1989). Attachment beyond infancy. *American Psychologist, 44*, 709–716.

Akun, E. (2025). Gender differences in the effects of parental acceptance-rejection. In R. P. Rohner & S. Ali, (Eds.), *Global perspectives on parental acceptance and rejection: Lessons learned from IPARTheory* (pp. 163–190). Routledge.

Ali, S. & Rohner, R. P. (2025a). Parental rejection in childhood leads to interpersonal rejection sensitivity in adulthood. In R. P. Rohner & S. Ali, (Eds.), *Global perspectives on parental acceptance and rejection: Lessons learned from IPARTheory* (pp. 153–162). Routledge.

Ali, S., & Rohner, R. P. (2025b). As you sow, so shall you reap: Effects of adult's memories of parental acceptance-rejection in childhood on aging parents. In R. P. Rohner & S. Ali, (Eds.), *Global perspectives on parental acceptance and rejection: Lessons learned from IPARTheory* (pp. 120–135). Routledge.

Ali, S., Rohner, R. P., Britner, P. A., & Jahn, A. (2024). Longing for belonging: Feeling loved (or not) and why it matters. *Family Relations, 73(*4), 2639–2654. https://doi.org/10.1111/fare.13029

Ali, S., Rohner, R. P., Britner, P. A., Hoeft, F. (2025). Memories of parental rejection in childhood predict medical problems in adulthood. In R. P. Rohner & S. Ali, (Eds.), *Global perspectives on parental acceptance and rejection: Lessons learned from IPARTheory* (pp. 190–204). Routledge.

Anderson, A. S., Siciliano, R. E., Henry, L. M., Watson, K. H., Gruhn, M. A., Kuhn, T. M., ... Compas, B. E. (2022). Adverse childhood experiences, parenting, and socioeconomic status: Associations with internalizing and externalizing symptoms in adolescence. *Child Abuse & Neglect, 125*, 105493.

Ashdown, B. K., Brown, C. M., Faherty, A. N., & Camden, A. A. (2023). Parental rejection and fear of intimacy in the United States and Guatemala: Context and culture matter. *Current Psychology, 42*(19), 16025–16035.

Bahaa, R. (2024). *Understanding the relationship between perceived childhood experiences and relationship with God*. [Master's thesis, the American University in Cairo] AUC Knowledge Foundation. https://fount.aucegpyt.edu/etds/2324

Baldwin, M. W. (1992). Relational schemas and the processing of societal information. *Psychological Bulletin, 112*, 461–484.

Bernet, W. & Alvarez, M. (2025). From normal to lethal: The continuum of parental denigration and parental alienation. In R. P. Rohner & S. Ali, (Eds.), *Global perspectives on parental acceptance and rejection: Lessons learned from IPARTheory* (pp. 268–278). Routledge.

Bernet, W., Gregory, N., Reay, K. M., & Rohner, R. P. (2018). An objective measure of splitting in parental alienation: The Parental Acceptance–Rejection Questionnaire. *Journal of Forensic Sciences, 63*(3), 776–783.
Bernet, W., Gregory, N., Rohner, R. P., & Reay, K. M. (2020). Measuring the difference between parental alienation and parental estrangement: The PARQ-Gap. *Journal of Forensic Sciences, 65*(4), 1225–1234.
Berry, J. W., & Poortinga, Y. H. (2006). Cross-cultural theory and methodology. In J. Georgas, J. W. Berry, F. J.R. Vander Vijver, C. Kagitcibas, & Y. H. Poortinga (Eds.), *Families across cultures: A 30-Nation Psychological Study* (pp.51–71). Cambridge University Press.
Bierman, A. (2005). The effects of childhood maltreatment on adult religiosity and spirituality: Rejecting God the Father because of abusive fathers?. *Journal for the Scientific Study of Religion, 44*(3), 349–359.
Bowlby, J. (1982). *Attachment and loss, Vol. 1: Attachment*, 2nd edition. New York: Basic Books
Briana, B. K. A. C. W., Keller, K., & Whiston, S. C. (2005). The impact of parent-adolescent relationships on adult career choices. *Issues in Career Development*, 129, 145.
Bronfenbrenner, U. (1979). *The ecology of human development: Experiments by nature and by design*. Cambridge, MA: Harvard University Press.
Brown, C. M., Homa, N. L., Cook, R. E., Nadimi, F., & Cummings, N. (2015). Perceived parental acceptance-rejection and artistic preference: Replication thirty years later. *Acta de Investigacion Psicologia (Psychlogical Research Records), 5*(3), 2204–2210.
Buthmann, J. L., Miller, J. G., Uy, J. P., Coury, S. M., Jo, B., & Gotlib, I. H. (2023). Early life stress predicts trajectories of emotional problems and hippocampal volume in adolescence. *European Child & Adolescent Psychiatry*, 1–12. https://doi.org/10.1007/s00787-023-02331-4
Cacioppo, S., Frum, C., Asp, E., Weiss, R. M., Lewis, J. W., & Cacioppo, J. T. (2013). A quantitative meta-analysis of functional imaging studies of social rejection. *Scientific Reports, 3*(1), 1–3.
Carroll, J. E., Grunewald, T. L., Taylor, S. E., Janicki-Deverts, D., Matthews, K. A., & Seeman, T. E. (2013). Childhood abuse, parental warmth, and adult multisystem biological risk in the Coronary Artery Risk Development in Young Adults study. Retrieved online at http://nas.org/cji/doi/10.1073/pns.315458110
Caton, N. R., & Horan, S. M. (2023). Deceptive affection is strategically expressed under relational threat—but not towards partners with low mate value. *Journal of Social and Personal Relationships, 40*(8), 2512–2537.
Chen, Y., Kubzansky, L. D., & VanderWeele, T. J. (2019). Parental warmth and flourishing in mid-life. *Social Science & Medicine, 220*, 65–72.
Cooley, C. H. (1902). *Human nature and the social order*. New York: Scribner's.
Cournoyer, D. E. (2000). Universalist research: Examples drawing from the methods and findings of parental acceptance-rejection theory. In A. L. Comunian & U. Gielen (Eds.), *International Perspectives on Human Development* (pp.213–232). Berlin, Germany: Pabst Science Publishers.
Courtois, C. A. (2004). Complex trauma, complex reactions: Assessment and treatment. *Psychotherapy, 41*, 412–425.
Cournoyer, D. E., & Malcolm, B. P. (2004). Evaluating claims for universals: A method analysis approach. *Cross-Cultural Research, 38*, 319–342. https://doi.org/10.1177/1069397104267474
Crick, N. R., and Dodge, K. A. (1994). A review and reformulation of social information-processing mechanisms in children's social adjustment. *Psychological Bulletin, 115*, 74–101.

Crowley, M. J., Wu, J., Molfese, P. J., & Mayes, L. C. (2010). Social exclusion in middle childhood: Rejection events, slow-wave neural activity, and ostracism distress. *Social Neuroscience, 5*(5–6), 483–495.
De Boer, A., van Buel, E. M., & Ter Horst, G. J. (2012). Love is more than just a kiss: A neurobiological perspective on love and affection. *Neuroscience, 201,* 114–124.
De Haan, A., Meiser-Stedman, R., Landolt, M. A., Kuhn, I., Black, M. J., Klaus, K., ... Dalgleish, T. (2024). Efficacy and moderators of efficacy of cognitive behavioural therapies with a trauma focus in children and adolescents: an individual participant data meta-analysis of randomised trials. *The Lancet Child & Adolescent Health, 8*(1), 28–39.
Downey, G., & Feldman, S. I. (1996). Implications of rejection sensitivity for intimate relationships. *Journal of Personality and Social Psychology, 70,* 1327–1343.
Floyd, K., & Pauley, P. M. (2010). Affectionate communication is good, except when it isn't: On the dark side of expressing affection. In Cupach, W. R., & Spitzberg, B. H. (Eds.). *The dark side of close relationships II* (pp. 165–194). Routledge.
Folker, A. E., Deater-Deckard, K., Lansford, J. E., Di Giunta, L., Dodge, K. A., Gurdal, S., ... Chang, L. (2023). Intraindividual variability in parental acceptance-rejection predicts externalizing and internalizing symptoms across childhood/adolescence in nine countries. *Journal of Family Psychology, 38*(2), 333–344.
Ford, J. D., & Reid, K. (2023). Trauma Affect Regulation: Guide for Education and Therapy (TARGET) Group Therapy. *Group Approaches to Treating Traumatic Stress: A Clinical Handbook,* 105.
Goertzel, V., & Goertzel, M. G. (1962). *Cradles of eminence.* Boston: Little, Brown.
Gorla, L., Rothenberg, W. A., Lansford, J. E., Bacchini, D., Bornstein, M. H., Chang, L., ... Al-Hassan, S. M. (2024). Adolescents' relationships with parents and romantic partners in eight countries. *Journal of Adolescence, 96*(5), 940–952. Online first.
Gurmen, S. (2025). Clinical applications of interpersonal acceptance-rejection theory. In R. P. Rohner & S. Ali, (Eds.), *Global perspectives on parental acceptance and rejection: Lessons learned from IPARTheory* (pp. 207–224). Routledge.
Hesse, C., Floyd, K., & Mikkelson, A. C. (2023). Affection deprivation is more aversive than excessive affection: A test of affection exchange theory. *Personal Relationships, 30*(1), 296–313.
Horan, S. M., & Booth-Butterfield, M. (2019). Angry hugs and withheld love: An overview of deceptive affection. *The Palgrave Handbook of Deceptive Communication,* 535–550.
Howe, M. J. (1982). Biographical evidence and the development of outstanding individuals. *American Psychologist, 37*(10), 1071–1081.
Huettel, S. A., Song, A. W., & McCarthy, G. (2004). *Functional magnetic resonance imaging.* Oxford University Press.
Kardiner, A. (1939). *The Individual and his society.* New York: Columbia University Press.
Kardiner, A. (1945a). The concept of basic personality structure as an operational tool in the social sciences. In R. Linton (Ed.) *The Science of man in the world crisis* (pp. 102–122). N.Y.: Viking Fund.
Kardiner, A. (1945b). *The Psychological frontiers of society.* New York: Columbia University Press.
Kazarian, S. S., Moghnie, L., & Martin, R. A. (2010). Perceived parental warmth and rejection in childhood as predictors of humor styles and subjective happiness. *Europe's Journal of Psychology, 3,* 71–93.
Kerla, M. (2012). The Differences in Adolescent Humor Style Preferences. In *2nd International Conference on Foreign Language Teaching and Applied Linguistics."*

Intercultural Linguistic Competence and Foreign/Second Language Immersive Environments". Retrieved from http://www.academia.edu/2073460

Khaleque, A. (2025a). A systematic review of IPARTheory's constructs and measures. In R. P. Rohner & S. Ali, (Eds.), *Global perspectives on parental acceptance and rejection: Lessons learned from IPARTheory* (pp. 39–62). Routledge.

Khaleque, A. (2025b). Influence of parental acceptance-rejection on adult intimate relationships. In R. P. Rohner & S. Ali, (Eds.), *Global perspectives on parental acceptance and rejection: Lessons learned from IPARTheory* (pp. 107–119). Routledge.

Khaleque, A., & Ali, S. (2017). A systematic review of meta-analyses of research on interpersonal acceptance–rejection theory: Constructs and measures. *Journal of Family Theory & Review, 9*(4), 441–458.

Khaleque, A., & Rohner, R. P. (2002). Reliability of measures assessing the pancultural association between perceived parental acceptance-rejection and psychological adjustment: A meta-analysis of cross-cultural and intracultural studies. *Journal of Cross-Cultural Psychology, 33*, 87–99.

Ki, P. (2015). Affective coping among individuals reporting a history of rejection. [unpublished doctoral dissertation]. University of Connecticut.

Ki, P., Rohner, R. P., Britner, P. A., Halgunseth, L. C., & Rigazio-DiGilio, S. A. (2018). Coping with remembrances of parental rejection in childhood: Gender differences and associations with intimate partner relationships. *Journal of Child and Family Studies, 27*(8), 2441–2445.

Lansford, J. E. (2025). Developmental correlates of parental acceptance-rejection from childhood to adulthood in nine countries. In R. P. Rohner & S. Ali, (Eds.), *Global perspectives on parental acceptance and rejection: Lessons learned from IPARTheory* (pp. 136–152). Routledge.

Leger, K. A., Turiano, N. A., Bowling, W., Burris, J. L., & Almeida, D. M. (2021). Personality traits predict long-term physical health via affect reactivity to daily stressors. *Psychological Science, 32*(5), 755–765.

Loberman, G., & Tziner, A. (2011). The influence of the parent-offspring relationship on young people's career preferences. *Psicología del Trabajo y de las Organizaciones*, 28(2), 99–105.

Luby, J. L., Barch, D. M., Belden, A., Gaffrey, M. S., Tillman, R., Babb, C., Nishino, T., Suzuki, H., & Botteron, K. N. (2012). Maternal support in early childhood predicts larger hippocampal volumes at school age. *Proceedings of the National Academy of Sciences, 8*, 2854–2859.

Ma, H., Wu, Y., Lv, X., Yang, X., & Hu, P. (2024). Childhood environmental unpredictability and hoarding: Mediating roles of attachment and security. *Acta Psychologica, 244*, 104198.

MacDonald, G., & Jensen-Campbell, L. A. (Eds.). (2011). *Social pain: Neuropsychological and health implications of loss and exclusion*. American Psychological Association. https://doi.org/10.1037/12351-000

Mantell, D. M. (1974). *True Americanism: Green berets and war resisters: A study of commitment*. New York: Teachers College Press.

Martinez-Garri, M. (2023). Childhood Trauma: Vulnerability Factor in Geriatric Hoarding Disorder. *The American Journal of Geriatric Psychiatry, 31*(3), S.

Masten, A. S. (2001). Ordinary magic: Resilience process in development. *American Psychologist, 56*, 227–238.

Masten, A. S. (2014). Invited commentary: Resilience and positive youth development frameworks in developmental science. *Journal of Youth and Adolescence, 43*, 1018–1024.

Mead, G. H. (1934). *Mind, self, and society*. Chicago: University of Chicago Press.

Medley, A., & Sachs-Ericsson, N. (2009). Predictors of parental physical abuse: The contribution of internalizing and externalizing disorders and childhood experiences of abuse. *Journal of Affective Disorders, 113*(3), 244–254.

Miller, J. G., & Ali, S. (2025). Interpersonal acceptance-rejection and neurobiological development. In R. P. Rohner & S. Ali, (Eds.), *Global perspectives on parental acceptance and rejection: Lessons learned from IPARTheory* (pp. 225–245). Routledge.

Minagawa-Kawai, Y., Matsuoka, S., Dan, I., Naoi, N., Nakamura, K., & Kojima, S. (2009). Prefrontal activation associated with social attachment: Facial-emotion recognition in mothers and infants. *Cerebral Cortex, 19*(2), 284–292.

Najam, N., & Batool, S. (2012). Relationship between perceived parenting style, perceived parental acceptance-rejection (PAR) and perception of God among young adults. *Journal of Behavioural Sciences, 22*(1), 83–99.

Naroll, R. (1968). Some thoughts on comparative methods in cultural anthropology. In H. M. Blalock, Jr. & A. B. Blalock (Eds.), *Methodology in social research* (pp. 236–277). New York: McGraw Hill.

Oaten, M., Williams, K. D., Jones, A., & Zadro, L. (2008). The effects of ostracism on self–regulation in the socially anxious. *Journal of Social and Clinical Psychology, 27*(5), 471–504.

Pelto, P. J., & Pelto, G. H. (1978). *Anthropological research: The structure of inquiry*. New York: Cambridge University Press.

Phillips, T. M., Wilmoth, J. D., Wall, S. K., Peterson, D. J., Buckley, R., & Phillips, L. E. (2013). Recollected parental care and fear of intimacy in emerging adults. *The Family Journal: Counseling and Therapy for Couples and Families, 21*(3), 335–341.

Rakesh, D., Kelly, C., Vijayakumar, N., Zalesky, A., Allen, N. B., & Whittle, S. (2021). Unraveling the consequences of childhood maltreatment: Deviations from typical functional neurodevelopment mediate the relationship between maltreatment history and depressive symptoms. *Biological Psychiatry: Cognitive Neuroscience and Neuroimaging, 6*(3), 329–342.

Reuben, A., Moffitt, T.E., Caskpi, A., Belsky, D.W., Harrington, H., Schroeder, F. ... Danese, A. (2016). Lest we forget: Comparing retrospective and prospective assessments of adverse childhood experiences in the prediction of adult health. *Journal of Child Psychology and Psychiatry, 57*, 1103–1112.

Rigazio-DiGilio, S. A., & Rohner, R. P. (2008). Clinical adaptation of parental acceptance-rejection theory questionnaires as interactive assessment and treatment tools in relational therapy. *Acceptance: The essence of peace*, 3–23.

Rigazio-DiGilio, S. A. & Rohner, R. P. (2015). Interpersonal acceptance-rejection theory and clinical applications. In E. Kourkoutas & A. Hart (Eds.), *Innovative practices and interventions for children and adolescents with psychosocial difficulties and disorders* (pp. 476–515). Newcastle upon Tyne, UK: Cambridge Scholars Publications

Rising, D. G., & Rohner, R. P. (2021). *Recovery from Rejection: A Manual of Client Handouts for Clinical Practice*. (2nd ed. 3.0). Rohner Research Publications. www.rohnerresearchpublications.com

Rohner, R. P. (1960). *Child acceptance-rejection and modal personality in three Pacific societies*. M.A. Thesis, Stanford University.

Rohner, R. P. (1975). *They love me, they love me not: A worldwide study of the effects of parental acceptance and rejection*. New Haven, CT: HRAF Press (Available as e-book from Rohner Research Publications, Storrs, CT).

Rohner, R. P. (1977). Advantages of the comparative method of anthropology. *Behavior Science Research (now Cross-Cultural Research), 12*, 117–144.

Rohner, R. P. (1986). *The warmth dimension: Foundations of parental acceptance-rejection theory*. Beverly Hills, CA: Sage Publications, Inc. (Available as e-book from Rohner Research Publications, Storrs, CT).
Rohner, R. P. (1987). [Effects of perceived parental warmth, control, and punishment on the psychological adjustment, school conduct, and academic achievement of youth in a biracial southern community.] Unpublished data.
Rohner, R. P. (2004). The parental "acceptance-rejection syndrome:" Universal correlates of perceived rejection. *American Psychologist, 59*, 830–840.
Rohner, R. P. (2005). Glossary of Significant Concepts in Parental Acceptance-Rejection Theory. Storrs. CT: Rohner Research Publications.
Rohner, R. P. (2014). Parental acceptance-rejection theory gets a new name: Interpersonal acceptance-rejection theory (IPARTheory). *Interpersonal Acceptance, 8*(3), 6.
Rohner, R. P. (2021). Introduction to interpersonal acceptance-rejection theory (IPARTheory) and evidence. *Online Readings in Psychology and Culture, 6*(1), 1–65. Doi 10.9707/2307-0919. 1055
Rohner, R. P. (2025a). Glossary of significant concepts in parental acceptance-rejection theory. In R. P. Rohner & S. Ali, (Eds.), Appendix A, *Global perspectives on parental acceptance and rejection: Lessons learned from IPARTheory* (pp. 279–303). Routledge.
Rohner, R. P. (2025b). Self-report measures used in IPARTheory research. In R. P. Rohner & S. Ali, (Eds.), Appendix B, *Global perspectives on parental acceptance and rejection: Lessons learned from IPARTheory* (pp. 304–306). Routledge.
Rohner, R. P., Ali, S., & Lansford, J. E. (2024a). Memories of parental acceptance and rejection predict forgiveness and vengeance in the Muslim world: Introduction and overview. Forgiveness and vengeance in the Muslim world [Special Issue]. *Journal of Genetic Psychology, 185*(3), 155–161.
Rohner, R. P., Ali, S., Filus, A., Senese, V. P., Molaver, A., Ahmed, R. A., … Britner, P. A. (2024b). Reliability and validity of the interpersonal rejection sensitivity scale: A multicultural study. *Current Psychology, 43*(9), 7986–7996.
Rohner, R. P., Bourque, S. L., & Elordi, C. A. (1996). Children's perceptions of corporal punishment, caretaker acceptance, and psychological adjustment in a poor, biracial southern community. *Journal of Marriage and the Family, 58*, 842–852.
Rohner, R. P., & Chaki-Sircar, M. (1988). *Women and children in a Bengali village*. Hanover, NH: University Press of New England. (Available as e-book from Rohner Research Publications)
Rohner, R. P., Filus, A., Melendez-Rhodes, T., Kuyumcu, B., Machado, F., Roszak, J., … Roy, K. (2019). Psychological maladjustment mediates the relation between remembrances of parental rejection in childhood and adults' fear of intimacy: A multicultural study. *Cross-Cultural Research, 53*(5), 508–542. DOI: 10.1177/1069397118822992
Rohner, R. P., & Frampton, S. (1982). Perceived parental acceptance-rejection and artistic preference: An unexplained contradiction. *Journal of Cross-Cultural Psychology, 13*, 250–259.
Rohner, R. P., & Khaleque, A. (2003). Reliability and validity of the Parental Control Scale: A meta-analysis of cross-cultural and intracultural studies. *Journal of Cross-Cultural Psychology, 34*, 643–649.
Rohner, R. P., & Khaleque, A. (Eds.) (2005). *Handbook for the study of parental acceptance and rejection* (4th ed.) Storrs, CT: Rohner Research Publications.

Rohner, R. P., & Lansford, J. E. (2017). Deep structure of the human affectional system: Introduction to Interpersonal Acceptance-Rejection Theory. *Journal of Family Theory & Review, 9*, 426–440. DOI 10.1111/JFTR.12219.

Rohner, R. P., Naroll, R., Barry, III, H., Divale, W. T., Erickson, E. E., Schaefer, J. M., & Sipes, R.G. (1978). Guidelines for holocultural research. *Current Anthropology, 19*, 128–129.

Rohner, R. P., & Rohner, E. C. (1980). Worldwide tests of parental acceptance-rejection theory [Special Issue]. *Behavior Science Research, 15*(1), 1–21.

Rohner, R. P., & Rohner, E. C. (1981). Parental acceptance-rejection and parental control: Cross- cultural codes. *Ethnology, 20*, 245–260.

Rothenberg, W. A., Ali, S., Rohner, R. P., Lansford, J. E., Britner, P. A., Di Giunta, L., … Deater-Deckard, K. (2022). Effects of parental acceptance-rejection on children's internalizing and externalizing behaviors: A longitudinal, multicultural study. *Journal of Child and Family Studies, 31*(1), 29–47.

Rotge, J. Y., Lemogne, C., Hinfray, S., Huguet, P., Grynszpan, O., Tartour, E., … Fossati, P. (2015). A meta-analysis of the anterior cingulate contribution to social pain. *Social Cognitive and Affective Neuroscience, 10*(1), 19–27.

Schulz, C. C., von Klitzing, K., Deserno, L., Sheridan, M. A., Crowley, M. J., Schoett, M. J., … White, L. O. (2022). Emotional maltreatment and neglect impact neural activation upon exclusion in early and mid-adolescence: An event-related fMRI study. *Development and Psychopathology, 34*(2), 573–585.

Stogdill, R. M. (1937). Survey of experiments on children's attitudes toward parents: 1894–1936. *Journal of Genetic Psychology, 51*, 293–303.

Stroud, L. R., Morningstar, M., Vergara-Lopez, C., Bublitz, M. H., Lee, S. Y., Sanes, J. N., … Dickstein, D. P. (2023). Neural activation to peer acceptance and rejection in relation to concurrent and prospective depression risk in adolescent and pre-adolescent girls. *Biological Psychology*, 108618. https://doi.org/10.1016/j.biopsycho.2023.108618

Tamres, L. K., Janicki, D., & Helgeson, V. S. (2002). Sex differences in coping behavior: A meta-analytic review and an examination of relative coping. *Personality and Social Psychology Review, 6*, 2–30.

Teicher, M. H., & Samson, J. A. (2016). Annual research review: enduring neurobiological effects of childhood abuse and neglect. *Journal of Child Psychology and Psychiatry, 57*(3), 241–266.

Thiele, S. H. (2007). *Developing a healing God image: Young adults' reflections on paternal relational patterns as predictors of God image development during adolescence*. Unpublished Doctoral Dissertation, New Orleans Baptist Theological Seminary.

Trentacosta, C. J., Waller, R., Neiderhiser, J. M., Shaw, D. S., Natsuaki, M. N., Ganiban, J. M., … Hyde, L. W. (2019). Callous-unemotional behaviors and harsh parenting: Reciprocal associations across early childhood and moderation by inherited risk. *Journal of Abnormal Child Psychology, 47*, 811–823. Doi: 10.1007/s10802-018-0482-y

van der Kolk, B.A. (2010). Developmental trauma disorder: Towards a relational diagnosis for children with complex trauma histories. Unpublished manuscript.

Veneziano, R. A., & Rohner, R. P. (1998). Perceived paternal acceptance, paternal involvement, and youths' psychological adjustment in a rural, biracial southern community. *Journal of Marriage and the Family, 60*, 335–343.

Vijayakumar, N., Cheng, T. W., & Pfeifer, J. H. (2017). Neural correlates of social exclusion across ages: A coordinate-based meta-analysis of functional MRI studies. *NeuroImage, 153*, 359–368.

Waller, R., Hyde, L. W., Klump, K.-L., & Burt, S. A. (2018). Parenting is an environmental predictor of callous-emotional traits and aggression: A monozygotic twin difference study. *Journal of the American Academy of Child and Adolescent Psychiatry*, *57*, 955–963.

Wesselmann, E. D., Bagg, D., & Williams, K. D. (2009). "I feel your pain": The effects of observing ostracism on the ostracism detection system. *Journal of Experimental Social Psychology*, *45*(6), 1308–1311.

Whiting, J. W. M., & Child, I. L. (1953). *Child training and personality*. New Haven, CT: Yale University Press.

Williams, P. D., Hunter, W. M., Seyer, E., Sammut, S., & Breuninger, M. M. (2019). Religious/spiritual struggles and perceived parenting style in a religious college-aged sample. *Mental Health, Religion & Culture*, *22*(5), 500–516.

Xu, X., Aron, A., Brown, L., Cao, G., Feng, T., & Weng, X. (2011). Reward and motivation systems: A brain mapping study of early-stage intense romantic love in Chinese participants. *Human Brain Mapping*, *32*(2), 249–257.

Zadro, L., Williams, K. D., & Richardson, R. (2004). How low can you go? Ostracism by a computer is sufficient to lower self-reported levels of belonging, control, self-esteem, and meaningful existence. *Journal of Experimental Social Psychology*, *40*(4), 560–567.

Zaki, N. (2025). IPARTheory and attachment theo. In R. P. Rohner & S. Ali, (Eds.), *Global perspectives on parental acceptance and rejection: Lessons learned from IPARTheory* (pp. 63–92). Routledge.

2

A SYSTEMATIC REVIEW OF IPARTHEORY'S CONSTRUCTS AND MEASURES

Abdul Khaleque

Interpersonal acceptance-rejection theory (IPARTheory) is an evidence-based theory that predicts and explains effects, causes, and other correlates of interpersonal acceptance and rejection and their implications for socialization and lifespan human development worldwide (Rohner, 1986, 1998, 1999, 2004; Rohner & Lansford, 2017; Rohner et al., 2003, 2005). IPARTheory initially studied the effects of perceived *parental* acceptance-rejection in childhood. The theory was previously known as parental acceptance-rejection theory (PARTheory). But research only on parental acceptance-rejection could not provide a comprehensive explanation of lifespan development (Rohner, 2004). Gradually, PARTheory researchers began to realize that much of what the theory postulates about the effects of perceived parental acceptance-rejection is also true about the effects of perceived acceptance-rejection in virtually all attachment relationships throughout the lifespan, although the magnitude of the effects may differ (Khaleque, 2018; Rohner, 2004; Rohner & Chaki-Sircar, 2011). Thus, the theory broadened its scope beyond parental acceptance and rejection in childhood to include all forms of interpersonal acceptance and rejection throughout the individual's lifespan (Khaleque, 2007; Rohner, 2021; Rohner & Lansford, 2017).

The expansion of the theory led in 2014 to its name change from parental acceptance theory (PARTheory) to interpersonal acceptance and rejection theory (IPARTheory; Rohner, 2014b). The name change was preceded, however, by an expansion in the theory's paradigm in 1999 (Rohner, 2004; Khaleque, 2007). Initially, the theory postulated that parental rejection is

DOI: 10.4324/9781003441243-3

associated with a specific cluster of personality dispositions noted in personality subtheory. With the expansion in the postulate it says that perceived rejection by a significant other *at any point in life* is likely to be associated with the same cluster of personality dispositions found among children and adults rejected by parents in childhood.

The first empirical study to test the reformulated postulate was conducted in 2001 (Khaleque, 2001). That study explored the impact of perceived acceptance-rejection by intimate male partners on the psychological adjustment of women in the United States. Later, 14 meta-analyses provided compelling evidence about the worldwide generalizability of this postulate (Khaleque & Ali, 2017; Ali et al., 2019, 2023).

Despite the changes in name and paradigm expansion, IPARTheory heavily focuses on investigating the effects, causes, and other correlates of children's perceptions of parental acceptance-rejection on their personality, psychological adjustment, and behavioral development. The theory also explores the outcomes of adults' memories of parental acceptance-rejection in childhood on their current psychological adjustment and lifespan development (Rohner & Lansford, 2017). IPARTheory focuses on the impact of acceptance-rejection by other attachment figures, including but not limited to, peers and siblings, teachers, grandparents, intimate adult partners, and parents-in-law.

IPARTheory's Central Postulates

IPARTheory is composed of three subtheories: personality subtheory, coping subtheory, and sociocultural systems subtheory (Rohner, 1986, 2004, 2021). The overwhelming bulk of research has so far been completed on postulates 2–5 of the theory's 8 basic postulates. According to Rohner (2021) these eight postulates include the following:

1 Over the course of shared biocultural evolution, humans everywhere have developed the enduring, biologically based emotional need to feel cared about by the people most important to them.
2 Children and adults everywhere—regardless of differences in culture, gender, race, and other such defining characteristics—understand themselves to be cared-about (accepted) or not cared-about (rejected) in the same four ways. (In IPARTheory this is called the warmth dimension of interpersonal relationships, including parenting.)
3 Children and adults everywhere tend to respond in the same ten ways when they experience being rejected by parents in childhood and by other attachment figures throughout life. (In IPARTheory, this is called the acceptance-rejection syndrome.)

4 The psychological effects of parental acceptance-rejection in childhood tend to extend into adulthood and old age, though often in a less intense form than in childhood.
5 Children's perceptions of fathers' love-related (accepting) behaviors, and adults' memories of these behaviors in childhood often have as great or greater impact than children's or adults' perceptions/memories of mothers' love-related behaviors on emotional, social, behavioral, and cognitive development.
6 Some children and adults are better able than most to deal emotionally with the effects of interpersonal (especially parental) rejection. (These people are called affective copers in IPARTheory' coping subtheory and are distinguished from instrumental copers.)
7 Specific psychological, familial, community, and sociocultural factors tend to be associated worldwide with specific variations in the tendency of parents to be accepting or rejecting. (In IPARTheory this pertains to the sociocultural systems subtheory and model.)
8 The experience of parental acceptance-rejection in childhood tends to reliably predict expressive behaviors and beliefs of adults within a society (e.g., their religious beliefs, artistic preferences and traditions, styles of humor, musical preferences, and others).

Background of the Meta-Analyses

More than 6,000 studies have been completed on interpersonal acceptance-rejection from around the world (Khaleque & Ali, 2017; see also Rohner & Ali, 2025, Chapter 1, this book). Five hundred and fifty-three studies fulfilled the four specific criteria required for inclusion in the 13 meta-analyses described here. These criteria included the following: First, only those studies that used measures explicitly designed to assess perceived acceptance-rejection, psychological adjustment, and personality dispositions as conceptualized in IPARTheory's personality subtheory, were selected for these meta-analyses. Second, the data or results of every study had to be reported in sufficient detail for the computation of the effect sizes in Pearson product-moment correlations. Third, the studies had to report, or raw data had to be available for computation of total scores for the relevant self-report measures (e.g., the Parental Acceptance-Rejection Questionnaire [PARQ], Teachers' Acceptance-Rejection/Control Questionnaire [TARQ/Control], Intimate Partner Acceptance-Rejection/Control Questionnaire [IPARQ/Control], Personality Assessment Questionnaire [PAQ], and scale scores of the PARQ and the PAQ). Fourth, the samples of these studies had to be representative, and the data had to be analyzed using appropriate statistical techniques.

Studies selected for the meta-analyses were conducted over a period of 48 years (1975–2023). Fifty-one percent of the studies were published and 49% were unpublished. The studies represented an aggregated sample of 149,440 respondents selected from five continents (e.g., Africa, Asia, Europe, North America, and South America) and 32 countries: Bangladesh, Barbados, China, Colombia, Croatia, Czechoslovakia (now Czech Republic and Slovakia), Egypt, Estonia, Finland, Greece, India, Iran, Jamaica, Japan, Kuwait, Mexico, Netherlands, Nigeria, Pakistan, Peru, Poland, Portugal, Puerto Rico, Romania, South Korea, Serbia, Spain, St. Kitts, Sweden, Turkey, Ukraine, and United States. Among the 13 meta-analyses, 11 dealt with IPARTheory's personality subtheory. Two of the meta-analyses focused on the internal consistency reliability of three commonly used IPARTheory measures, the Parental Acceptance-Rejection Questionnaire (PARQ), the Personality Assessment Questionnaire (PAQ), and the behavioral control scale on of the Parental Acceptance-Rejection/Control Questionnaire (PARQ/Control). The PARQ and PAQ have been especially widely used in IPARTheory-related research globally; the behavioral control scale has been used less frequently. All 13 meta-analyses focused on IPARTheory's universalist perspective. The main goal of the studies was to assess whether children and adults everywhere—regardless of cultural, gender, ethnic, or other such differences—respond in the same way when they perceive themselves to be accepted or rejected by their parents and other attachment figures. According to IPARTheory, even though specific expressions of acceptance (e.g., warmth, affection, care, and concern) and rejection (e.g., coldness, lack of affection, indifference, neglect, aggression) may vary from culture to culture, individuals are likely to respond in the same way when they perceive themselves to be accepted or rejected by their attachment figures (Rohner, 1986, 2004, 2021).

Measures Used in the Meta-Analyses

The studies on which the meta-analyses were performed used the following measures: (a) Parental Acceptance-Rejection Questionnaire Child and Adult versions (PARQ): mother and father forms (Rohner 2004a, 2004b); (b) Parental Acceptance-Rejection/Control mother and father versions (PAR/CQ; Rohner, 2004c, d); (c) acceptance-rejection portion of the Teacher Acceptance-Rejection/Control Questionnaire (TARQ/Control; Rohner, 2005); (d) Personality Assessment Questionnaire Child and Adult (PAQ; Rohner, 2004e); and (e) Intimate Partner Acceptance-Rejection Questionnaire/Control (IPAR/CQ; Rohner, 2004f). Each of these measures is described more fully below.

PARQ

The PARQ is a self-report questionnaire that measures individuals' perception of parental acceptance-rejection. Conceptually, parental acceptance-rejection has a bipolar dimension, with acceptance at one end of the continuum and parental rejection at the other end. All versions of the PARQ consist of four subscales: (1) warmth/affection, (2) hostility/aggression, (3) indifference/neglect, and (4) undifferentiated rejection. The measure has two versions: child version and adult version. Both versions consist of 60 items. In the Child PARQ, children reflect on their mothers' or fathers' current behavior toward them; and in the Adult PARQ, adults reflect on their childhood experiences of maternal or paternal acceptance-rejection. The two versions differ only in the verb tense used: The Child PARQ uses the present tense, whereas the Adult PARQ uses the past tense. Sample items on the mother version of the Child PARQ for example are: "My mother makes me feel wanted and needed" (perceived warmth/affection), "My mother goes out of her way to hurt my feelings" (perceived hostility/aggression), "My mother ignores me as long as I do nothing to bother her" (perceived indifference/neglect), and "My mother does not really love me" (perceived undifferentiated rejection). Except for reference to "mother's" behavior or "father's" behavior, the two versions are identical. Individuals respond to items on both the versions using a 4-point Likert scale ranging from 1 = almost never true to 4 = almost always true. Scores on the four subscales are summed after reverse scoring the warmth and affection subscale to create an expression of coldness/lack of affection (i.e., rejection). Possible scores range from a low of 60 (indicating maximum perceived acceptance) to a high of 240 (indicating maximum perceived rejection).

Both versions are conceptually designed in such a way that scores ranging from 60 to about 129 indicate more acceptance than rejection, and scores from about 130 to 150 reveal the experience of increasing rejection. But scores at or above 150 to 240 indicate serious parental rejection. Extensive evidence (discussed in Rohner & Khaleque, 2005) shows robust reliability and validity of the PARQ for use in cross-cultural research globally. Khaleque and Rohner's (2002b) meta-analysis of the reliability of PARQ revealed that the size of the mean weighted coefficient alpha aggregated across all PARQ versions was .89. Moreover, mean test–retest reliability over a time period ranging from 3 weeks to 7 years (median = 15 months) as shown in the same study was .62. In addition, several cross-cultural factor analyses of the PARQ have revealed basically the same factor structure everywhere (Comunian & Gielen, 1999; Rohner & Chaki-Sircar, 1988/2011;

Rohner & Cournoyer, 1994; Rohner & Khaleque, 2005). Further, Rohner and Khaleque (2005) found the convergent validity of the Adult PARQ was .81 and that of the Child PARQ was .64.

Parental Control Scale (PCS)

The Control scale on the PARQ/Control is a 13-item self-report questionnaire assessing children's perceptions of parental behavioral control (i.e., parental permissiveness/strictness) or adults' memories of parental control in childhood. The two versions are identical except for verb tense (i.e., present tense or past tense). Items in all versions of the Control scale are scored on a 4-point Likert scale ranging from 1 = almost never true to 4 = almost always true. The total score can range from a low of 13 (i.e., minimum behavioral control; or maximum permissiveness) to a high of 52 (maximum behavioral control or restrictive behavioral control). Sample items on the mother and the father versions are: "My mother wants to control whatever I do, and "My father wants to control whatever I do". The control scale was conceptually designed in such a way that scores between 13 and 26 indicate low control (permissiveness); 27 and 39, moderate control; 40 and 45, firm control; and 46 and 52, strict or restrictive control. Low behavioral control scores indicate that parents rarely try to control children's behavior. Rather, they allow children to regulate their own behavior to the greatest possible extent. Scores in the moderate control range indicate that parents sometimes try to control children's behavior but overall, they are quite flexible in their control, or enforce compliance in some contexts but allow children considerable latitude in other contexts. Scores in the firm control range indicate that parents usually try to control children's behavior. They are demanding and directive but not unyielding. Finally, scores in the strict or restrictive control range indicate that parents almost always try to control children's behavior. Restrictive parents are strictly demanding. They want unyielding obedience and total compliance with parental directives.

TARQ/Control, Child

The acceptance-rejection portion of the TARQ/Control is a 24-item questionnaire. In the TARQ/Control children are asked to reflect on the level of warmth/affection, hostility/aggression, indifference/neglect, and undifferentiated rejection—and overall acceptance-rejection—they experience at the hands of their primary classroom teacher. The warmth or affection ubscale contains eight items; the hostility/aggression subscale and the indifference/neglect subscales contain six items; and the undifferentiated rejection subscale contains four items. Sample items on the questionnaire, include "My teacher says nice things about me" (warmth or affection), "My teacher punishes me when (s)he is angry" (hostility or aggression), "My teacher pays no attention to me" (indifference or neglect), and "My teacher seems to dislike me" (undifferentiated rejection). Responses on each item are based on a 4-point Likert scale ranging from 1 = almost never true of my teacher to 4 = almost always true of my teacher. A higher total score reveals the presence of greater perceived teacher rejection. Possible scores on the measure range from a low of 24 (indicating maximum perceived teacher acceptance) to a high of 96 (indicating maximum perceived teacher rejection). Scores at or above 60 indicate students' perception of serious teacher rejection, whereas scores between 56 and 59 indicate the perception of greater rejection than acceptance. Scores between 24 and 48 indicate the perception of substantial teacher acceptance. Coefficient alpha for the total TARQ in six studies ranged from .72 to .91, with the exception of .57 (Rohner, 2010)

PAQ

The Child PAQ and the Adult PAQ) consists of seven subscales, assessing seven of the personality dispositions most central to the IPARTheory's personality subtheory. The Child PAQ and the Adult PAQ contain 42 and 63 items respectively. Sample items on the Child PAQ, for example, are: "I think about fighting or being mean" (hostility or aggression), "I like my parents to make a fuss over me when I am hurt or sick" (dependence), "I like myself" (positive self-esteem), "I can compete successfully for the things I want" (positive self-adequacy), "It is easy for me to show my friends that I really like them" (emotional responsiveness), "I am cheerful and happy one minute and gloomy or unhappy the next" (emotional instability), and "I think the world is a good, happy place" (positive worldview). Individuals respond to items such as these on a 4-point Likert scale ranging from 1 = almost never true of me to 4 = almost always true of me. An individual's overall self-reported psychological adjustment profile is obtained by summing the seven subscale scores after reverse scoring appropriate items. Scores on the Child PAQ range from a low of 42, indicating healthy psychological adjustment to a high of 168, indicating serious psychological maladjustment. Scores on the Adult PAQ vary from a low of 63, indicating healthy psychological adjustment to a high of 252, indicating severe psychological maladjustment. The scale is designed in such a way that scores at or above the test's midpoint of 105 (child version) and 157 (adult version) indicate that individuals perceive themselves to be more psychologically maladjusted than adjusted.

The concept of psychological (mal)adjustment in the 13 meta-analyses was based on the total PAQ score for children and adults respectively. Evidence shows that both versions of the PAQ are reliable and valid for use in cross-cultural research. Khaleque and Rohner's (2002b) meta-analysis of 51 studies worldwide, for example, showed that the overall mean weighted effect size of coefficient alpha on the Child PAQ was .83. It was .86 for the Adult PAQ. Moreover, test–retest reliability across periods ranging from 1 to 18 months for the Child PAQ was .79; and the test–retest reliability across periods of 12– 18 months for the Adult PAQ was .76. The convergent and discriminant validity coefficient for the Adult PAQ subscales, ranged from .17 to .87, and for the Child PAQ subscales, these values ranged from .11 to .56 (Rohner & Khaleque, 2005). More reliability and validity evidence are documented in Rohner (1986/1999) and Rohner & Chaki-Sircar (1988/2011).

It's important to note here that IPARTheory initially postulated that the seven personality dispositions described here were among the most common psychological effects of perceived parental acceptance-rejection in childhood. Collectively, the seven dispositions are summarized under the concept of the "acceptance-rejection syndrome" (Rohner 2004). After the PAQ was developed, however, three additional personality dispositions were added to the acceptance-rejection syndrome. These were interpersonal relationship anxiety (or simply, anxiety), emotional insecurity, and cognitive distortions (Rohner, 2021). A revision of the PAQ that incorporates these three dispositions awaits future development.

IPAR/CQ

This scale consists of two discrete sections. The first section contains five items about the nature of the intimate relationship along with items that assess respondents' feelings about that relationship. The first item identifies an intimate partner by a yes response to the following question: "Are you now or have you been at any time during the past year in an emotionally deep or intimate relationship with someone you really cared about?" The other four items in that section are not relevant to the present study. The second section is the Adult PARQ/Control that represents the accepting–rejecting and behaviorally controlling behaviors of intimate partners. The PARQ/Control section contains 73 items, 60 of which represent the different expressions of perceived acceptance-rejection described earlier. It also contains 13 items relating to partners' perceived behavioral control. The acceptance-rejection portion consists of four scales: warmth/affection ("My partner says nice things about me"), hostility/aggression ("My partner hits me"), indifference/neglect ("My partner pays no attention to me"), and undifferentiated rejection ("My partner does not really love me"), control

("Lets me go any places I want without asking"). All these items are scored on a 4-point Likert scale ranging from 1 = almost never true to 4 = almost always true. Scores on the acceptance-rejection portion of the IPAR/CQ vary from a low of 60 to a high of 240. The internal consistency reliability coefficient for the behavioral control portion of the measure was .74, and for the acceptance-rejection portion it was .85 (Rohner & Khaleque, 2005).

Summary of the 13 Meta-Analyses

Eleven of the 13 meta-analyses tested IPARTheory's basic postulates, stated earlier. Table 2.1 presents detailed statistical information about those meta-analyses. Two meta-analyses examined psychometric properties of PARQ and PAQ. Table 2.2 presents detailed statistical information about those.

Meta-Analyses Testing IPARTheory's Basic Postulates

Parental Acceptance and Offspring Psychological Adjustment

Postulate 3 assumes that child and adult offspring the world over are likely to be affected in a specific way when they experience themselves to be (or to have been) accepted or rejected by their parents in childhood. This postulate was tested in the first meta-analysis (Khaleque & Rohner, 2002a). That meta-analysis specifically focused on studies dealing with children and adults to assess the postulate that perceived parental acceptance-rejection is associated with the specific form of psychological (mal)adjustment described earlier. The analysis was based on 43 studies using child and adult versions of the PARQ and PAQ. The studies represented 7,563 respondents in 15 countries and all major ethnic groups in the United States (e.g., African Americans, Asian Americans, European Americans, and Hispanic Americans). Results in Table 2.1 reveal that across all ethnocultural samples, parental acceptance-rejection has a significant association with the psychological adjustment of both children and adults. Further, the results reveal that the effect sizes of the relationships between perceived parental acceptance and psychological adjustment were significantly higher for children (r =.51) than for adults (r = .46), (z = 7.50, p = .001), as predicted in postulate 4. Moreover, perceived parental acceptance accounted for approximately 26% of variability in children's psychological adjustment and about 21% of variability in adults' psychological adjustment. The unexplained variances are likely to be accounted for by other factors, including joint, interactive, and cumulative effects of all significant persons in an individual's life—along with biological, behavioral, and genetic factors.

TABLE 2.1 Summary of Meta-Analyses Testing Theoretical Propositions in IPARTheory

Independent Variable	*Dependent Variable*	*Number of Respondents*	*Number of the Studies*	*Average Heterogeneity (probability level)*	*Weighted Mean Effect Size and Significance Level*
Parental Acceptance-Rejection and Offspring Psychological Adjustment					
Parental (maternal and paternal) acceptance-rejection	Offspring's (both male and female) psychological adjustment	7,563	43	**Adult offspring:** Heterogeneity = .00 Probability = ns **Children:** Heterogeneity = .00 Probability = ns	**Children:** $r = .51$, $p < .001$ **Adult offspring**: $r = .46$, $p < .001$
Parental (maternal vs. paternal) acceptance-rejection	Offspring's (both male vs. female and adult vs. children) psychological adjustment	19,511	66	**Adult offspring:** Heterogeneity = .00 Probability = ns **Children:** Heterogeneity = .00 Probability = ns	**Adult offspring:** $r = .45$, $p < .001$ **Children:** $r = .51$, $p < .001$ Maternal acceptance for children .49 Paternal acceptance for children .62 Maternal acceptance for adults' .45 Paternal acceptance for adults' .45, p = ns
Parental (maternal vs. paternal) acceptance-rejection	Offspring's (both male vs. female and adult vs. children) psychological adjustment	33,081	220	**Adult offspring:** Heterogeneity = .001 Probability = ns **Children:** Heterogeneity = .09 Probability = ns	**Maternal** Adult sons: $r = .44$, $p < .001$ Boys: $r = .46$, $p < .001$ Adult daughters: $r = .38$, $p < .001$ Girls: $r = .43$, $p < .001$ **Paternal** Adult sons' $r = .44$, $p < .001$ Boys: $r = .45$, $p < .001$ Adult daughters' $r = .42$, $p < .001$ Girls: $r = .42$, $p < .001$

Parental Acceptance-Rejection and Specific Aspects of Offspring Psychological Adjustment					
Parental (maternal and paternal) acceptance-rejection	Seven personality dispositions: hostility/aggression (HA), Independence (I), positive self-esteem (PSE), positive self-adequacy (PSA), emotional responsiveness (ER), emotional stability (ES), and positive worldview (PWV)	10,943	36	**Children**: Heterogeneity = .01 Probability = ns **Adult offspring**: Heterogeneity = .00 Probability = ns	**Children**: HA: M = $r = -.38, p < .001; r = -.41, p < .001$ I = M = $r = .17, p < .001; r = .17, p < .001$ PSE = M = $r = .38, p < .001; r = .41, p < .001$ PSA = M = $r = .37, p < .001; r = .37, p < .001$ ER = M = $r = .36, p < .001; r = .28, p < .001$ ES = M = $r = .30, p < .001; r = .25, p < .001$ PWV = M = $r = .37, p < .001; r = .20, p < .001$ **Adult offspring**: HA: M = $r = -.28, p < .001; r = -.23, p < .001$ I = M = $r = .11, p < .001; r = .04, p < .001$ PSE = M = $r = .36, p < .001; r = .35, p < .001$ PSA = M = $r = .34, p < .001; r = .35, p < .001$ ER = M = $r = .34, p < .001; r = .31, p < .001$ ES = M = $r = .29, p < .001; r = .29, p < .001$ PWV = M = $r = .34, p < .001; r = .38, p < .001$
Acceptance by other Attachment Figures and Psychological Adjustment					
Adult offspring's perceived parental (maternal vs. paternal) acceptance-rejection in childhood	Offspring's (men's vs. women's) psychological adjustment and perceptions of their intimate partners' acceptance-rejection	3,568	17	Heterogeneity = .00 Probability = ns	Adult sons' $r = .46$; .41, $p = .001$. Adult daughters' $r = .35$; .34, $p = .001$. Adult partner acceptance r = .42, $p <.001$ remembered paternal r = .36, $p <.001$ maternal acceptance r = .39, $p <.001$

(Continued)

TABLE 2.1 (Continued)

Independent Variable	*Dependent Variable*	*Number of Respondents*	*Number of the Studies*	*Average Heterogeneity (probability level)*	*Weighted Mean Effect Size and Significance Level*
Perceived parents' and teachers' acceptance	Youth's psychological adjustment and school conduct	2,422	9	**Psychological Adjustment** **Teachers**: Heterogeneity = .0017 Probability = ns **Parents**: Heterogeneity = .003 Probability = ns **School Conduct**: **Teachers**: Heterogeneity = .002 Probability = ns **Parents**: Heterogeneity = .004 Probability = ns	**Teacher Acceptance-Rejection**: Boys' conduct $r = .28$, $p < .001$. Girls' conduct $r = .17$, $p < .001$. Boys' psychological adjustment $r = .29$, $p < .001$ Girls' psychological adjustment $r = .34$, $p < .001$ **Paternal Acceptance-Rejection**: Boys' conduct $r = .14$, $p < .001$. Girls' conduct $r = .12$, $p < .001$. Boys' psychological adjustment $r = .38$, $p < .001$ Girls' psychological adjustment $r = .36$, $p < .001$ **Maternal Acceptance-Rejection**: Boys' conduct $r = .12$, $p < .001$. Girls' conduct $r = .13$, $p < .001$. Boys' psychological adjustment $r = .40$, $p < .001$ Girls' psychological adjustment $r = .38$, $p < .001$
Forms of Parental Acceptance-Rejection and Children's Psychological Adjustment					
Perceived parental: *Warmth/affection*	Offspring's (both male and female) psychological adjustment	12,087	30	Heterogeneity = .00 Probability = ns	Significant correlation was found with mean weighted effect size: $r = .34$, $p < .001$ children's psychological adjustment r = .33, p < .001, specific adjustment aspects r values ranged from .16 to r = .33, p <.001
Perceived parental: *Indifference/neglect*	Offspring's (both male and female) psychological maladjustment	11,755	33	Heterogeneity = .001 Probability = ns	**Maternal** ranges from r = .19 to .43, $p < .01$— .001 **Paternal** ranges from .19 to .46, $p < .01$— .001 Parental indifference/neglect and psychological adjustment ($r = .50$, $p <.001$)
Perceived parental: *Hostility/aggression*	Offspring's (both male and female) psychological maladjustment	13,406	35	Heterogeneity = .00 Probability = ns	**Maternal**: $r = .46$, $p < .001$ **Paternal**: $r = .40$, $p < .001$

Perceived parental: *Undifferentiated rejection*	Offspring's (both male vs. female and adult vs. children) psychological maladjustment	24,003	102	Adult offspring: Heterogeneity = 2.77 Probability = ns Children: Heterogeneity = 5.31 Probability = ns	**Maternal** Children = $r = .48$, $p < .001$ Adult offspring = $r = .35$, $p < .001$ **Paternal** Children = $r = .35$, $p < .001$ Adult offspring = $r = .37$, $p < .001$
Perceived parental: *Undifferentiated rejection* (maternal vs. paternal)	Offspring's psychological adjustment: hostility/aggression (HA), Independence (I), positive self-esteem (PSE), positive self-adequacy (PSA), emotional responsiveness (ER), emotional stability (ES), and positive worldview (PWV)	12,538	16	**Heterogeneity Maternal; Paternal undifferentiated Rejection** HA: Heterogeneity = 14.86; 2.89 Probability = ns; ns I: Heterogeneity = 6.22; 1.52 Probability = ns; ns PSE: Heterogeneity = 5.70; 2.06 Probability = ns; ns PSA: Heterogeneity = 9.66; 2.40 Probability = ns; ns ER: Heterogeneity = 6.71; 0.82 Probability = ns; ns ES: Heterogeneity = 3.65; 3.17 Probability = ns; ns PWV: Heterogeneity = 12.41; 5.30 Probability = ns; ns	**Maternal undifferentiated Rejection** HA: $r = .38$, $p < .001$ I: $r = .22$, $p < .001$ PSE: $r = .34$, $p < .001$ PSA: $r = .30$, $p < .001$ ER: $r = .36$, $p < .001$ ES: $r = .38$, $p < .001$ PWV: $r = .30$, $p < .001$ **Paternal Undifferentiated Rejection**: HA: $r = .34$, $p < .001$ I: $r = .12$, $p < .001$ PSE: $r = .26$, $p < .001$ PSA: $r = .30$, $p < .001$ ER: $r = .31$, $p < .001$ ES: $r = .28$, $p < .001$ PWV: $r = .23$, $p < .001$

(Adapted from Khaleque & Ali, 2017, with permission from John Wiley and Sons, 2023).
Note: ns = not significant; M = male; F = female.

TABLE 2.2 Summary of Meta-Analyses of the Psychometric Properties of the PARQ, PAQ, and Behavioral Control Scale

Measures	*Number of Respondents*	*Number of the Studies*	*Average Heterogeneity (probability level)*	*Mean Alpha Coefficients and Significance Level*
Reliability of the PARQ Reliability of the PAQ	6,898	51	PARQ: Heterogeneity = .001 Probability = ns PAQ: Heterogeneity = .002 Probability = ns	Child PARQ: .89 ($p < .001$), Adult PARQ = .95. Alpha varied for different geographic regions from .76 to .88, ($p < .001$) and for ethnic groups from .84 to .90 (p < .001). Child PAQ = .83 ($p < .001$); Adult PAQ = .86 ($p < .001$).
Reliability and validity of the behavioral control scale on the PARQ/ Control	4,203	11	Control: Heterogeneity = .00 Probability = ns	Control scale α = .73 ($p < .001$).

(Adapted from Khaleque & Ali, 2017, with permission from John Wiley and Sons, 2023).
Note: ns = not significant.

In this meta-analysis, the effect sizes of parental acceptance-rejection on the psychological adjustment of children and adults were compared separately for different American ethnic groups and for the samples from different continents (e.g., Africa, Asia, Europe, North America, South America). Results revealed no significant differences among ethno-cultural groups or geographical locations. Moreover, effect sizes of the relations between perceived parental acceptance and psychological adjustment for children and adults were approximately equivalent for the four US ethnic groups. Similarly, effect sizes for the association between perceived parental acceptance and psychological adjustment for children and adults were roughly equivalent among the samples from the five continents. Thus, the results confirm IPARTheory's third postulate about pancultural associations between perceived parental acceptance and the psychological adjustment of both children and adults.

The postulate that adults' memories of parental acceptance-rejection in childhood are likely to be associated with the same form of psychological adjustment–maladjustment as found among children—though often to a lesser extent—was also examined by Khaleque & Rohner (2012a). That meta-analysis included 66 studies involving 19,511 respondents from 22 countries on five continents. All studies in the meta-analysis used the child and adult versions of the PARQ for mothers and fathers as well as the child and adult versions of the PAQ. Results demonstrated that the effect sizes of correlations between perceived parental acceptance with offspring psychological adjustment were significant for both male and female offspring, and for both children and adults across cultures. Results also confirmed the conclusion of the first meta-analysis that there are significant relations between children's perceptions of parental acceptance and positive psychological adjustment ($r = .51$, $p < .001$).

Maternal and Paternal Acceptance and Offspring Psychological Adjustment

Two meta-analytic reviews (Ali et al., 2015b; Rohner & Khaleque, 2010) tested postulate 5 that *paternal* accepting or rejecting behaviors often have as strong or stronger effects on children's and adult offspring's psychological adjustment than do maternal accepting-rejecting behaviors. The findings showed that perceived paternal acceptance often has a greater impact ($r = .62$) on children's emotional and developmental outcomes than does perceived maternal acceptance ($r = .49$; $z = 24.29$, $p <.001$). The results of Rohner and Khaleque's (2010) meta-analysis also provided support for postulate 5.

Parental Acceptance-Rejection and Individual Personality Dispositions

Khaleque and Rohner's (2012b) meta-analysis tested postulates 3 and 4 asserting that parental acceptance–rejection is not only associated with children's and adults' overall psychological adjustment but is also transculturally associated with each of the seven personality dispositions described in the PAQ. This meta-analysis was performed on 36 studies comprising 10,943 respondents (8,573 children and 1,370 adults) from 18 countries. Results of the meta-analysis revealed that both maternal and paternal acceptance significantly correlated with all seven personality dispositions of children (r values ranged from .17 to .41, $p < .001$) across all cultures studied. Remembered maternal and paternal acceptance also correlated significantly with all seven personality dispositions of adults (r values ranged from .11 thru .36, $p < .001$; see Table 2.1). Results of this meta-analysis confirm IPARTheory's postulate that parental acceptance-rejection is related to psychological (mal)adjustment and to seven of the personality dispositions that compose the acceptance-rejection syndrome.

Acceptance-Rejection by Adult Intimate Partners and Adults' Psychological Adjustment

Rohner and Khaleque (2010) tested IPARTheory's hypothesis that the psychological adjustment of adults who perceive themselves to be accepted by their intimate partners is affected in the same way across cultures as adults who remember having been accepted by their parents in childhood. This meta-analysis was performed on 17 studies involving 3,568 adults from ten countries. Results revealed that perceived partner acceptance in adulthood ($r = .42$, $p < .001$), and remembered paternal acceptance ($r = .36$, $p < .001$) in childhood correlated significantly with the current psychological adjustment of both men and women, regardless of differences in culture, ethnicity, language, social class, gender, or other such factors. The results also showed that the more rejecting both men and women perceived their intimate partners to be, the more psychologically maladjusted they tended to be.

Parents' and Teachers' Acceptance-Rejection and Children's Psychological Adjustment and School Conduct

Ali et al. (2015a) meta-analysis examined the effects of parents' and teachers' acceptance on youth's psychological adjustment and school conduct. The meta-analysis was done on nine studies involving 2,422 school-going youth from 12 countries. The study addressed two questions: (1) To what extent are boys' and girls' perceptions of teacher acceptance related to children's psychological adjustment and school conduct? (2) To what extent are boys' and girls' perceptions of maternal and paternal acceptance related to children's psychological adjustment and school conduct? Findings showed that both maternal and paternal acceptance, and teacher acceptance all correlated significantly with the psychological adjustment and conduct of school-going children in all countries regardless of children's gender. The study also showed that children's perceptions of teacher acceptance had a significantly stronger ($z = 2.7$, $p < .001$) association with teachers' reports of boys' school conduct ($r = .28$) than with that of girls' ($r = .17$).

Effects of the Four Expressions of Parental Acceptance-Rejection on Children's Psychological Adjustment and Personality Dispositions

Four meta-analyses were performed to test IPARTheory's hypothesis that children's psychological adjustment and personality dispositions are associated with each of the following forms of parental acceptance-rejection: (a) warmth and affection, or emotional coldness and lack of affection, (b) hostility or aggression, (c) indifference or neglect; (d) and undifferentiated rejection. Khaleque's (2013) meta-analysis explored pancultural relations between perceived parental warmth and affection and children's overall psychological adjustment. That meta-analysis was performed on 30 studies involving 12,087 children from 16 countries on five continents. Results showed that perceived parental warmth and affection correlated significantly with children's positive psychological adjustment ($r = .33$, $p < .001$), and also correlated significantly with all seven personality dispositions (r values ranged from .16 to .33, $p < .001$) across cultures.

Khaleque (2015) tested relations between perceived parental indifference/neglect and children's overall psychological maladjustment and the seven personality dispositions. That meta-analysis was based on 33 studies from 15 countries on four continents. It involved 11,755 children. Results showed that both perceived maternal and paternal indifference/neglect correlated significantly ($r = .50$, $p < .001$) with overall psychological maladjustment. Perceived maternal and paternal indifference/neglect also correlated significantly with each other. The effect of maternal indifference/neglect on each of the seven personality dispositions ranged from $r = .19$ to .43, $p < .01–.001$. The effects of paternal indifference/neglect ranged from $r = .19$ to .46, $p < .01–.001$).

Khaleque (2016) tested relations between children's perceptions of parental hostility/aggression and their overall psychological maladjustment and personality dispositions. The meta-analysis was performed on 35 studies involving 13,406 children selected from 16 countries on four continents. Results revealed that both maternal and paternal hostility/aggression correlate significantly and across cultures with children's overall psychological maladjustment, as well as with all the seven negative personality dispositions on the PAQ. The results also showed that perceived maternal hostility/aggression had slightly but significantly ($z = 3.87$, $p < .001$) stronger relations with children's psychological maladjustment ($r = .46$) than did perceived paternal hostility/aggression ($r = .40$).

Ali et al. (2019) examined relations between (a) children's current perceptions of parental undifferentiated rejection and (b) adults' memories of parental undifferentiated rejection in childhood and children's and adults' overall psychological adjustment. That meta-analysis was performed on

102 studies in 17 countries on four continents. It involved 24,003 children and adults. Results demonstrated that both maternal and paternal undifferentiated rejection correlated with overall psychological maladjustment of both children and adult offspring. The results also showed that maternal undifferentiated rejection (child $r = .48$; adult $r = .39$) had a significantly stronger relationship ($z = 8.0$, $p < .001$ with children's psychological maladjustment than with perceived paternal undifferentiated rejection (child $r = .35$; adult $r = .37$). Moreover, perceived maternal undifferentiated rejection had a significantly stronger ($z = 5.50$; $p < .001$) association with children's psychological maladjustment than with adults' psychological adjustment. These meta-analyses confirm IPARTheory's postulate that each of the four forms of parental acceptance-rejection is significantly associated with children's and adults' psychological (mal)adjustment.

Finally, Ali et al. (2023) explored relations among children's perceptions of parental undifferentiated rejection and their personality dispositions. The meta-analysis was performed on 30 studies from 14 countries involving 13,045 children. Findings revealed significant relations between parental undifferentiated rejection and all seven personality dispositions, as predicted in IPARTheory. The effect sizes of correlations between perceived *paternal* undifferentiated rejection and each of the seven personality dispositions were significant (spreading from $p < .05$ to $p < .001$). The results also showed significantly stronger relations between maternal than paternal undifferentiated rejection on five personality dispositions among children, including dependence, negative self-esteem, emotional instability, emotional unresponsiveness, and negative worldview. The results further revealed that the mean weighted effect sizes between perceived *maternal* undifferentiated rejection and children's personality dispositions had significantly stronger relations than perceived paternal undifferentiated rejection in five indices (dependence, $z = 2.00$, $p < .001$; negative self-esteem, $z = 3.67$, $p < .001$; emotional unresponsiveness, $z = .88$, $p < .001$; emotional instability, $z = 5.56$, $p < .001$; and negative worldview, $z = 5.56$, $p < .001$).

Meta-Analyses Testing the Psychometric Properties of the PARQ, PAQ, and Behavioral Control Scale

As noted earlier, two meta-analyses were done to test the psychometric properties of the PARQ, PAQ, and behavioral Control scale. Khaleque and Rohner's (2002b) meta-analysis tested the reliability (alpha coefficient) of the PARQ and PAQ. This meta-analysis was based on 51 studies involving 6,898 respondents from eight countries and all major American ethnic groups. Results of the meta-analyses are presented in Table 2.2.

Results there show that the overall mean weighted effect size of alpha coefficient for the Child PARQ was .89. It was .95 for the Adult PARQ. The mean weighted effect sizes of alpha coefficients of the PARQ for different geographical regions varied from .76 to .88, and for different American ethnic groups they varied from .84 to .90. The mean weighted effect sizes of alpha coefficient for the Child PAQ was .83, and for the Adult PAQ it was .86. These results confirm the expectation that both sets of measures are reliable for use in basic and applied research in cross-cultural and multi-ethnic settings.

The second meta-analysis (Rohner & Khaleque, 2003) verified the reliability of the behavioral control scale on the PARQ/Control. That meta-analysis was performed on 11 studies involving 4,203 respondents from seven countries on four continents. Alpha coefficients and factor analyses presented in this meta-analysis confirmed that the behavioral control scale with an overall weighted mean effect size of .73, $p < .001$) is a reliable and valid measure for use in worldwide cross-cultural research.

Discussion

Findings from these meta-analyses show that both maternal and paternal acceptance are associated the world over with the psychological adjustment of children and adult offspring regardless of differences in culture, ethnicity, geographic location, race, or gender. This introduces an obvious question: Why do exogenous factors such as culture, ethnicity, or geographic location have no overriding impact on children's and adult offspring's psychological adjustment and personality dispositions. A likely answer is embedded in IPARTheory's first postulate which states that over the course of shared biocultural evolution, humans everywhere have developed the enduring, biologically based emotional need to feel cared about by the people most important to them. Evidence bearing on that postulate is provided in Rohner and Ali (2025; Chapter 1, this book) and in Miller and Ali (2025; Chapter 12, this book).

Meta-analyses summarized here reveal interesting complexities of perceived maternal versus paternal acceptance-rejection on the psychological adjustment of offspring. For instance—Rohner and Khaleque's (2010) meta-analysis concluded that paternal acceptance has a stronger effect than maternal acceptance on both boys' and girls' psychological adjustment. However, Ali et al. (2015a) found that maternal rejection—in the form of perceived maternal hostility/aggression—has a stronger effect than perceived paternal rejection on children's (both boys' and girls') psychological maladjustment. Ali et al. (2015b) also found cross-gender differences between adult sons' versus adult daughters' memories of maternal versus paternal acceptance in childhood. Specifically, adult sons' memories of maternal acceptance in childhood have significantly stronger relations with their current psychological adjustment than with that of adult daughters, whereas memories of paternal acceptance in childhood have a significantly stronger relation with adult daughters' psychological adjustment than with that of adult sons. Reasons for gender differences such as these are not clear, except for one probable reason. That is, offspring's perceptions of maternal versus paternal power and prestige often moderate the relation between perceived parental acceptance and offspring psychological adjustment (Rohner, 2014a; see also Akun, 2025; Chapter 9, this book). In male-dominant patriarchal societies, men are generally perceived to have authority over wives and children by virtue of their gender. However, in patriarchal societies, mothers are often perceived by children to have more prestige within the family than do fathers (Rohner & Carrasco, 2014; Sultana & Khaleque, 2016). Thus, offspring's differential perceptions of parental power and prestige constitute an important class of variables that often affect the relation between perceived maternal versus paternal acceptance and offspring's (male vs. female) psychological adjustment.

Beyond this cross-gender issue, results of the meta-analyses have confirmed IPARTheory's prediction that perceived parental acceptance has a stronger effect on children's psychological adjustment than on adult's psychological adjustment. For example, regardless of cultures, perceived parental acceptance accounted for about 26% of variability in children's psychological adjustment, whereas remembrances of parental acceptance in childhood accounted for about 21% of variability in adults' psychological adjustment. This small but significant difference may be due to the current (proximal) effects of parental acceptance on children and the more distal effects of remembered parental acceptance-rejection on adult offspring.

Additionally, results of the meta-analyses show that the current experience of acceptance by an intimate partner generally has a stronger effect on individuals' psychological adjustment than do memories of past experiences of acceptance by parents in childhood. In addition, findings from meta-analyses show that when partners are perceived to be warm and loving, individuals tend to be fairly well-adjusted psychologically. But as partners are perceived to be increasingly less loving, the psychological adjustment of adults tends to become increasingly more impaired, if it is not moderated by memories of parental love. For example, experiences of parental love (in childhood) appear to provide adults with a protective buffer against continued erosion of their psychological adjustment in the context of partner rejection (Khaleque, 2001; Rohner & Khaleque, 2008).

Worldwide evidence provided in these meta-analyses along with the evidence provided by several hundred other studies suggest that, in all likelihood, IPARTheory's major postulates tested in these meta-analytic reviews are panculturally generalizable, regardless of differences in culture, ethnicity, gender, geographical boundary, and other such factors. One should be cautious, however, not to overgeneralize. Because the findings have some limitations. For example, all studies included in the meta-analyses were cross-sectional and correlational, thus providing no scope for drawing causal conclusions.

Another possible limitation of these meta-analyses may involve skepticism about the reliability of respondents' subjective self-reports on questionnaires that are used in much of IPARTheory research (Rohner & Brothers, 1999). However, several empirical studies (e.g., Brewin et al., 1993; Cournoyer & Rohner, 1996) have shown that claims regarding the unreliability of self-reports on questionnaires are often exaggerated. Despite these limitations, results from the meta-analyses appear to be stable and robust because the findings are based on many studies representing a huge number of respondents globally. Thus, the results are likely to provide sufficient reason for researchers and practitioners to feel confident in using them in relevant research, policy, practice, clinical interventions, and by the courts and protective services agencies.

Finally, we should acknowledge that the association between perceived acceptance-rejection and psychological adjustment, and emotional and behavioral development of children and adults are not perfect. Approximately 74% of the variance in children's and adults' psychological and behavioral adjustment is yet to be accounted for, probably by behavioral, genetic, neurobiological, sociocultural, and other such factors (Rohner & Lansford, 2017). Nonetheless, the findings of the 13 meta-analyses discussed here confirm that IPARTheory's major postulates are generalizable across cultures worldwide, and that the major self-report measures used in IPARTheory research are reliable for cross-cultural and multiethnic research.

Clearly defined concepts and postulates, and reliable and valid research measures have encouraged and supported IPARTheory researchers across cultures since the inception of the theory in the last quarter of the 1970s. Consistently, IPARTheory research has continued to grow globally over the years since its development to the present time, making it one of the strongest evidence-based theories in the field of human development and family sciences. As IPARTheory continues to expand and grow, so too should meta-analytic studies continue to synthesize results of accumulated studies in new areas of research.

References

(Asterisks indicate already-published meta-analyses summarized in this review article).

Akun, E. (2025). Gender inconsistencies in parental acceptance-rejection and on the effects of acceptance-rejection. In R. P. Rohner & S. Ali, (Eds.), *Global perspectives on parental acceptance and rejection: Lessons learned from IPARTheory* (pp. 163–190). Routledge.

*Ali, S., Khaleque, A., & Rohner, R. P. (2015a). Influence of perceived teacher acceptance and parental acceptance on youth's psychological adjustment and school conduct: A multi-cultural meta-analysis. *Cross-Cultural Research, 47,* 204–224. https://doi.org/10.1177/1069397114552769

*Ali, S., Khaleque, A., & Rohner, R. P. (2015b). Pancultural gender differences in the relation between perceived parental acceptance and psychological adjustment of children and adult offspring: A meta-analytic review of worldwide research. *Journal of Cross-Cultural Psychology, 46,* 1059–1080. https://doi.org/10.1177/0022022115597754

*Ali, S., Khatun, M. N., Khaleque, A., & Rohner, R. P. (2019). They love me not: A meta-analysis of relations between parental undifferentiated rejection and offspring's psychological maladjustment. *Journal of Cross-Cultural Psychology, 50*(2), 185–199. 10.1177/0022022118815599

*Ali, S., Khatun, M. N., Khaleque, A., & Rohner, R. P. (2023). Perceived parental undifferentiated rejection and children's personality dispositions: A meta-analysis of multicultural studies. *Journal of Genetic Psychology, 184*(1), 9–22. 10.1080/00221325.2022.2110447

Brewin, C. R., Andrews, B., & Gotlib, I. H. (1993). Psychopathology and early experience: A reappraisal of retrospective reports. *Psychological Bulletin*, 113, 82–98.

Comunian, A. L., & Gielen, U. P. (1999). Perception of parental acceptance and rejection: An Italian study. Paper presented at the Annual Meeting of the Society for Cross-Cultural Research, Santa Fe, NM. Cournoyer, D. E., & Rohner, R. P. (1996). Reliability of retrospective reports of perceived maternal acceptance-rejection in childhood. *Psychological Reports, 78,* 147–150.

Cournoyer, D. E., & Rohner, R. P. (1996). Reliability of retrospective reports of perceived maternal acceptance-rejection in childhood. *Psychological Reports, 78*(1), 147–150. https://doi.org/10.2466/pr0.1996.78.1.147

Khaleque, A. (2001). Parental acceptance-rejection, psychological adjustment, and intimate adult relationships (Unpublished master's thesis). University of Connecticut, Storrs.

Khaleque, A. (2007). Parental acceptance-rejection theory: Beyond parent–child relationships. *Interpersonal Acceptance, 1,* 2–4.

*Khaleque, A. (2013). Perceived parental warmth and children's psychological adjustment, and personality dispositions: A meta-analysis. *Journal of Child and Family Studies, 22,* 297–306. https://doi.org/10.1007/s10826-012-9579-z

*Khaleque, A. (2015). Perceived parental neglect, and children's psychological maladjustment, and negative personality dispositions: A meta-analysis of multicultural studies. *Journal of Child and Family Studies, 24,* 1419–1428. https://doi.org/10.1007/s10826-014-9948-x

*Khaleque, A. (2016). Perceived parental hostility and aggression, and children's psychological maladjustment, and negative personality dispositions: A meta-analysis. *Journal of Child and Family Studies*. https://doi.org/10.1007/s10826-016-0637-9

Khaleque, A. (2018). Intimate Relationships Across The Lifespan: Formation. *Development, Enrichment, And Maintenance, Praeger, California*.

Khaleque, A., & Ali, S. (2017). A systematic review of meta-analyses of research on interpersonal acceptance-rejection theory: Constructs and measures. *Journal of Family Theory and Review, 9*(4), 441–458, doi: 10.1111/jftr.12228

*Khaleque, A., & Rohner, R. P. (2002a). Perceived parental acceptance-rejection and psychological adjustment: A meta-analysis of cross cultural and intracultural studies. *Journal of Marriage and Family, 64*, 54–64. https://doi.org/10.1111/j.1741-3737.2002.00054.x

*Khaleque, A., & Rohner, R. P. (2002b). Reliability of measures assessing the pancultural association between perceived parental acceptance-rejection and psychological adjustment: A meta-analysis of cross-cultural and intracultural studies. *Journal of Cross-Cultural Psychology, 33*, 87–99. https://doi.org/10.1177/0022022102033001006

*Khaleque, A., & Rohner, R. P. (2012a). Pancultural associations between perceived parental acceptance and psychological adjustment of children and adults: A meta-analytic review of worldwide research. *Journal of Cross-Cultural Psychology, 43*, 784–800. https://doi.org/10.1177/ 0022022111406120

*Khaleque, A., & Rohner, R. P. (2012b). Transnational relations between perceived parental acceptance and personality dispositions of children and adults: A meta-analytic review. *Personality and Social Psychology Review, 16*, 103–115. https://doi.org/10.1177/1088868311418986

Miller, J. G., & Ali, S. (2025). Interpersonal acceptance-rejection and neurobiological development. In R. P. Rohner & S. Ali, (Eds.), *Global perspectives on parental acceptance and rejection: Lessons learned from IPARTheory* (pp. 225–245). Routledge.

Rohner, R. P. (1986). The warmth dimension: Foundations of parental acceptance-rejection theory. Beverly Hills, CA: Sage.

Rohner, R. P. (1998). Father love and child development: History and current evidence. *Current Directions in Psychological Science, 7*, 157–161.

Rohner, R. P. (1999). Acceptance and rejection. In D. Levinson, J. Ponzetti, & P. Jorgensen (Eds.), *Encyclopedia of human emotions* (Vol. 1, pp. 6–14). Macmillan Publishers.

Rohner, R. P. (2004). The parental "acceptance-rejection syndrome": Universal correlates of perceived rejection. *American Psychologist, 59*, 830–840. https://doi.org/10.1037/0003-066X.59.8.830

Rohner, R. P. (2005). Teacher acceptance-Rejection Control Questionnaire (TARQ/CQ) test manual. In R. P. Rohner & A. Khaleque (Eds.), *Handbook for the study of parental acceptance and rejection* (4th ed., pp. 137–186). Rohner Research Publications.

Rohner, R. P. (2004a). *Parental acceptance-rejection questionnaire (PARQ) Adult Mother version*. Rohner Research Publications.

Rohner, R. P. (2004b). *Parental acceptance-rejection questionnaire (PARQ) Adult Father version*. Rohner Research Publications.

Rohner, R.P. (2004c). *Parental Acceptance-Rejection/Control Questionnaire (PARQ/Control) Child Father version*. Rohner Research Publications.

Rohner, R.P. (2004d). *Parental Acceptance-Rejection/Control Questionnaire (PARQ/Control) Child Father version*. Rohner Research Publications.

Rohner, R. P. (2004e). *Personality Assessment Questionnaire (PAQ) Child version*. Rohner Research Publications.

Rohner, R. P. (2004f). *Intimae Partner Acceptance-Rejection/Control Questionnaire (IPAR/CQ)*. Rohner Research Publications.

Rohner, R. P. (Ed.). (2010). Teacher acceptance, parental acceptance and the adjustment, achievement, and behavior of school-going youth [Special issue]. *Cross-Cultural Research, 44*, 211–309.

Rohner, R. P. (2014a). Parental power and prestige moderate the relationship between perceived parental acceptance and offspring's psychological adjustment: Introduction to the international father acceptance-rejection project. *Cross-Cultural Research, 48,* 197–213. https://doi.org/10.1177/1069397114528295

Rohner, R. P. (2014b). PARTheory gets a new name: Interpersonal acceptance-rejection theory (IPARTheory). *Interpersonal Acceptance, 8*(3), 6.

Rohner, R. P. (2021). Introduction to interpersonal acceptance-rejection theory (IPARTheory) and evidence. *Online Readings in Psychology and Culture, 6*(1), 1–65. Doi 10.9707/2307-0919.1055

Rohner, R. P., & Ali, S. (2025). IPARTheory, evidence, and methods from conception through maturity. In R. P. Rohner & S. Ali, (Eds.), *Global perspectives on parental acceptance and rejection: Lessons learned from IPARTheory* (pp. 3–38). Routledge.

Rohner, R. P., & Brothers, S. A. (1999). Perceived parental rejection, psychological maladjustment. *Emotional Abuse, 1,* 81–95.

Rohner, R. P., & Carrasco, M. A. (2014). Preface. In R. P. Rohner & M. A. Carrasco (Eds.), Parental power and prestige moderate the relationship between perceived parental acceptance and offspring's psychological adjustment [Special Issue]. *Cross-Cultural Research, 48*(3), 195–196. https://doi.org/10.1177/1069397114528292

Rohner, R. P., & Chaki-Sircar, M. (1988). *Women and children in a Bengali village.* University Press of New England.

Rohner, R. P., & Chaki-Sircar, M. (2011). *Women and children in a Bengali village.* Rohner Research Publications. (Original work published 1988)

Rohner, R. P., & Cournoyer, D. E. (1994). Universals in youth's perceptions of parental acceptance and rejection: Evidence from factor analyses within eight sociocultural groups worldwide. *Cross-Cultural Research, 28,* 371–383. https://doi.org/10.1177/106939719402800408

*Rohner, R. P., & Khaleque, A. (2003). Reliability and validity of the Parental Control Scale: A meta-analysis of cross-cultural and intracultural studies. *Journal of Cross-Cultural Psychology, 34,* 643–649. https://doi.org/10.1177/0022022103255650

Rohner, R. P. & Khaleque, A. (Eds.) (2005). *Handbook for the study of parental acceptance and rejection* (4th ed., pp. 137–186). Rohner Research Publications.

Rohner, R. P., & Khaleque, A. (2008). Relations between perceived partner and parental acceptance. In J. K. Quinn & I. G. Zambini (Eds.), *Family relations: 21st century issues and challenges.* Nova Science.

*Rohner, R. P., & Khaleque, A. (2010). Testing central postulates of parental acceptance-rejection theory (PARTheory): A meta-analysis of cross-cultural studies. *Journal of Family Theory & Review, 3,* 73–87. https://doi.org/10.1111/j.1756-2589.2010.00040.x

Rohner, R. P., Khaleque, A., & Cournoyer, D. E. (2003). Cross-national perspectives on parental Acceptance-rejection theory. *Marriage and Family Review, 35,* 85–105.

Rohner, R. P., Khaleque, A., & Cournoyer, D. E. (2005). Parental acceptance-rejection theory, methods, evidence, and implications. *Ethos, 33,* 299–334.

Rohner, R. P., & Lansford, J. E. (2017). Deep structure of the human affectional system: Introduction to interpersonal acceptance-rejection theory (IPARTheory). *Journal of Family Theory & Review, 9,* 426–440.

Sultana, S., & Khaleque, A. (2016). Differential effects of perceived maternal and paternal acceptance on male and female adult offspring's psychological adjustment. *Gender Issues, 33*(1), 42–52. https://doi.org/10.1007/s12147-015-9147-0

3

INTERPERSONAL ACCEPTANCE-REJECTION THEORY (IPARTHEORY) AND ATTACHMENT THEORY

Nour Zaki

This chapter focuses on two prominent developmental theories—attachment theory and interpersonal acceptance-rejection theory (IPARTheory). Both have greatly added to the current understanding of how interpersonal relationships impact developmental outcomes across the lifespan. Both theories emphasize the importance of the parent–child relationship as well as the quality of interpersonal relationships in general. The chapter examines the development, main postulates, and uniqueness of the theories. Then areas of convergence (i.e., similarities) and divergence (i.e., differences) between the two theories are identified. This comparison is not meant to identify one theory's superiority over the other but rather to highlight each theory's uniqueness and their areas of convergence as well as divergence.

Attachment Theory

Attachment theory is a well-established relational theory in the field of developmental psychology. It was developed by John Bowlby and Mary Ainsworth. Bowlby constructed the foundation and basic principles of the theory, whereas Ainsworth further proposed the notion of individual differences in attachment. The following section discusses Bowlby's and Ainsworth's backgrounds, and it delves into the theory's development as well as its main postulates.

DOI: 10.4324/9781003441243-4

John Bowlby's Academic Background

John Bowlby (1907–1990) was of British origin. He graduated from the University of Cambridge in 1928 with a major that is currently known as Developmental Psychology (Bretherton, 1992). When volunteer work exposed him to maladjusted children, it sparked an interest that lasted throughout his lifetime (Bretherton, 1992). He described this period saying, "when I was there, I learned *everything* that I have known; it was the most valuable six months in my life, really" (Senn 1977, quoted in van Dijken, 1997). Two boys, in particular, left a long-lasting impression on him. One was a teenage boy who lacked affect and was expelled from school after a stealing incident. The other was an 8-year-old child who anxiously followed Bowlby everywhere, to the extent that he was known as Bowlby's "shadow". It caught Bowlby's attention that both youths had a common factor in their lives: the lack of a maternal figure. From that point onward, Bowlby assumed that the mother and early family relationships are crucial for individuals' psychological adjustment. Thus, he argued, psychological deprivation may be a precursor to dysfunctional behavior in children (Coates, 2004).

These insights got him interested in studying child psychiatry, so he joined the Medical School of University College in London from 1922 to 1928 (Ainsworth, 1992). In the meantime, he also trained in psychoanalysis at the British Psychoanalytic Institute, where Melanie Klein was developing the Kleinian approach to child psychoanalysis. She introduced him to the object-relations approach, but he objected to her ideas related to internal factors causing emotional disturbances in children (e.g., libidinal forces and aggressive impulses). Instead, he was convinced that external factors, like maternal love, were overlooked. Initially, Bowlby's beliefs were not well received by the psychoanalytic community.

Bowlby's psychiatry career paused when World War II erupted in the late 1930s. It was, however, an opportunity for him to focus on research related to mother–child separation. Today, Bowlby's ideas are known to have significantly contributed to our understanding of children's ties to their mothers—particularly when the bond is disrupted through deprivation, maternal unavailability, or separation.

Personal Relevance of Attachment Theory to John Bowlby's Life

It is not uncommon for the concepts that theorists spend their lives studying to have personal relevance in their lives. This certainly applies to Bowlby's case. He was the fourth of six children. His older brother, Tony, was only thirteen months older than him. They were placed in the same classroom at school and were generally treated as twins because of the slight age difference between them. John and Tony were good friends although they had a strong sense of competition and jealousy between them (Coates, 2004).

Bowlby's father was a military surgeon. Thus, Bowlby did not spend much quality time with him (van Dijken, 1998). At the time, it was also a common parenting practice in England for mothers to spend very little time with their children. Because of that custom, Bowlby only saw his mother one hour a day during which she would read to him and his siblings (Coates, 2004). He described his mother's parenting, saying that "she held the view that it was dangerous to spoil children so her responses ... to bids of attention and affection were the opposite of what was required" (Byng-Hall, 1987 quoted in Van Dijken, 1997, p.25). According to Bowlby, what was required and needed was a more responsive mothering attitude. He disagreed with the idea that love could spoil a child, and he believed in the adverse impact of maternal separation on later psychological well-being.

Bowlby's primary caregiver for his first four years of life was his nanny, Minnie. There is nothing in the literature that explains why Minnie departed from his life. However, this separation had a great impact on Bowlby. Referring to this incident, Bowlby said "for a child to be looked after entirely by a loving nanny and then for her to leave when he is two or three, or even four or five, can be almost as tragic as the loss of a mother" (Bowlby, 1958 quoted in van Dijken, 1997, p.25). A few years later, when he was around the age of 11, Bowlby was sent to boarding school. Later he is reported to have told his wife that he would not even send a dog away from home at such a young age (Coates, 2004). In his late thirties, Bowlby experienced another significant separation when his closest friend—Evan Durbin—drowned while trying to save his two children (Coates, 2004). Bowlby's ideas extended to include concepts related to grief and mourning in interpersonal relationships after this tragic incident.

Theories that Inspired Development of Attachment Theory

The relationship between a mother and her child was conceptualized in different ways during the time Bowlby started framing his theory. Attachment theory draws on concepts from different disciplines including ethology, psychoanalysis, developmental psychology, evolutionary psychology, information processing, and control systems theory (Ainsworth, 1992; Bretherton, 1992; Tulving, 1979). For instance, Bowlby's fascination with the ethology concept of "imprinting" (Lorenz, 1935) was fruitful in understanding the early formation of emotional bonds. His contemplation of animals in their natural environment led to look into why little ducklings follow their mothers (or the first moving object they see). He took this to signal a clear indication that there is a crucial bond built on the need for proximity that forms early in life. In addition, he emphasized the importance of early relationships and their effect on subsequent social interactions, which was initially proposed in the psychoanalytic framework (Waters et al., 1991). However, Harry Harlow's (1958) experiments with rhesus monkeys were important in showing that attachment did not depend on the provision of food. Monkeys preferred to spend much more time next to a cloth mother that provided no food than a wire mother that provided nutrition. In addition, when the monkeys were scared, they immediately ran to the mother figure providing nurturance and warmth, rather than the other one who did not provide these attributes. Therefore, a clear conclusion was established from Harlow's work that *emotional* needs are most important in a relationship.

Control systems theory also influenced Bowlby's formulation of attachment theory. He considered attachment as a basic innate human need, like food, water, and shelter. Based on the evolutionary perspective, this behavioral system's primary function is to promote and maximize chances of the individual's survival. Bowlby coined the concept of the "environment of evolutionary adaptedness" through attachment behaviors (Bowlby, 1969/1982; Hinde, 2005). Building on these thoughts and more, Bowlby introduced a new conceptualization of the nature of the mother–child relationship. According to him, "the infant and young child should experience a warm, intimate, and continuous relationship with his mother (or permanent mother substitute) in which both find satisfaction and enjoyment" (Bowlby, 1951, p.13).

Origins of Attachment Theory

Starting from Bowlby's conceptualization of a group of juvenile boys in his 1949 book on *Forty-Four Juvenile Thieves* (1944), he drew an interesting connection between their common background of an adverse childhood and later criminal behavior. The idea was revolutionary at the time. A few years later, he wrote a paper entitled "The study and reduction of group tension in the family" (Bowlby, 1949). There, he proposed that children who exhibit dysfunctional behaviors are an indication of bigger issues within their family dynamics. According to him, if the child is to be helped, the parents need to be supported as well. Today, this is one of the foundational beliefs of family systems work (Byng-Hall, 2009). Later, Bowlby (1951) witnessed the importance of attachment figures in protecting their children in post-war Britain. He wrote that war bombs were less dangerous to children than separation from their attachment figures (Bowlby, 1951). Researchers at the time, however, were not convinced by his argument.

Attachment theory's origins go back to three classic papers that Bowlby presented at the British Psychoanalytic Society in London between 1958 and 1960. First, *The Nature of the Child's Tie to His Mother* (Bowlby, 1958) shed light on the difference between concepts of *dependency* and *attachment*. Bowlby proposed that a child attached to his mother is a sign of normal and healthy emotional development, as opposed to regressive behavior. Second, *Separation and Anxiety* (Bowlby, 1959) focused on rhesus monkeys who experienced maternal deprivation. And third, *Grief and Mourning in Infancy and Early Childhood* (Bowlby, 1960) further analyzed the three phases of separation response (namely, protest, despair, and denial/detachment). Later, these responses were further elaborated by Parkes (1972) into: (1) numbness, (2) yearning and protest, (3) disorganization and despair, and (4) reorganization. This more advanced conceptualization of separation responses later influenced the five stages of grief theory developed by Elizabeth Kubler-Ross (1970) in her book *On Death and Dying*.

Other important attachment theory publications include Bowlby's famous trilogy: *Attachment* (Bowlby, 1969), *Separation* (Bowlby, 1973), and *Loss* (Bowlby, 1980). This trilogy is considered classic in developmental psychology today. The three volumes laid out the main postulates of attachment theory while integrating different fields and respectfully disagreeing with other prominent authors. In total, Bowlby authored more than 150 publications. Professionals continue to draw on his work to further understand the main postulates of attachment theory and their effects on later life.

Bowlby's Initial Postulates of Attachment Theory

According to attachment theory, babies' cries often signal the need for proximity with the caregiver. The child's need for proximity and the caregiver's response together form a "goal-corrected partnership" (Bowlby, 1969). As a result of this early caregiving experience, the child forms an internal working model (IWM) of the self and others. If the caregiver is sensitive toward the child's need for proximity, the child develops an IWM of the self as valued and loved, and others as trustworthy and reliable. On the other hand, if the caregiver is unresponsive or inconsistent in providing care then the child develops an IWM of the self as incompetent and unworthy of love, and/or others as unreliable and unavailable.

Bowlby (1982) was also interested in how attachment patterns can be transmitted intergenerationally. He advocated for the provision of support to parents. For example, he wrote "if a community values its children, it must cherish its parents" (Bowlby, 1951, p.84). Bowlby believed in the universality of his theory. According to him, psychological wellbeing and attachment behavior can be understood regardless of their cultural context.

Mary Ainsworth and Her Contributions to Attachment Theory

Mary Ainsworth (1913–1999) was a Canadian-American psychologist. She graduated from the University of Toronto shortly before World War II. At the time, the anti-Freudian movement was prevalent at the University of Toronto. Later, she moved with her husband to London for his doctoral studies. There, she met Bowlby and joined his research team at the Tavistock clinic (Bretherton, 1992).

While Bowlby developed several revolutionary ideas about mother–infant attachment, it was Ainsworth who came up with the methodology to test these ideas. Through her observations in African as well as American contexts, she had a well-rounded conceptualization of individual differences in attachment relationships. She clearly highlighted the significance of *maternal sensitivity* in the mother–child relationship. She also introduced the concept of a *secure base* from which the child can explore the world while feeling safe and protected (Ainsworth, 1967).

One of Ainsworth's main contributions to attachment theory research was the introduction of *the Strange Situation Procedure* (SSP; Ainsworth & Wittig, 1969). This observation procedure was designed to explore how toddlers balance between proximity-seeking and exploration in different situations, particularly in low and high stress levels. The mother is asked to briefly step outside the observation room twice during the SSP. This allows for the examination of a brief mother–infant separation and reunion with the caregiver. Eventually, the SSP became the gold-standard of mother–infant attachment research leading to a classification system for children's attachment styles that is highly regarded today (Ainsworth et al., 1978). The SSP helps professionals understand that not all infants/toddlers respond in the same way to separation. According to Ainsworth, there are three distinct infant attachment patterns: secure attachment, ambivalent attachment, and avoidant attachment. Years later, a fourth category was introduced to the theory by Mary Main, one of Ainsworth's students. The fourth category depicted a pattern of *disorganized attachment*, which is mostly related to unresolved trauma (Main & Solomon, 1986). Later, in 1984, the Adult Attachment Interview (AAI) was developed by Mary Main and colleagues to assess adult attachment representations of their childhood.

Interpersonal Acceptance-Rejection Theory (IPARTheory)

IPARTheory was developed by Ronald P. Rohner. The following section introduces Rohner, the theory's development, and its main features. Table 3.1 provides a brief biographical comparison of the lives of Bowlby and Rohner.

TABLE 3.1 Biographical Comparison Between Bowlby & Rohner

Area of Comparison	*John Bowlby*	*Ronald P. Rohner*
Theory	Author of attachment theory	Author of IPARTheory
Nationality	British	American
Date of birth	Born in 1907 and died in 1990	Born in 1935
Studies	Child psychiatry at the Medical School of University College in London & Psychoanalysis at the British Psychoanalytic Institute	Master's and Doctor of Philosophy in Psychological Anthropology at Stanford University
Early work	Work with maladjusted/ juvenile children, sparked his lifelong interest in the significance of maternal deprivation	Senior Scientist at the Boys Town Center for the Study of Youth Development in Washington D.C., a significant step in his career
Main research interest	Mother–infant attachment, separation, and deprivation	Interpersonal (especially parental) acceptance-rejection and its worldwide implications
Primary caregiver	Nanny "Minnie", for the first four years of his life	Mother
Relationship with mother	Distant relationship	Loving and nurturing relationship
Relationship with father	Father was a military surgeon in World War II, did not spend much time with him	Father was an army officer in World War II, did not spend much time with him
Relationship with sibling	13 months older brother, relationship characterized with comparison and jealousy	Two years older sister, not a close relationship

Ronald P. Rohner's Academic Background

Rohner (1935–present) is an American born international psychologist. He received his Bachelor of Science in Psychology from the University of Oregon in 1958. He later pursued both his Master's and PhD degrees in Psychological Anthropology from Stanford University. He is currently Professor Emeritus of Human Development and Family Sciences and of

Anthropology at the University of Connecticut. He is also the current Executive Director and Former President of the International Society for Interpersonal Acceptance and Rejection (ISIPAR).

Between 1975 and 1977, Rohner was a Senior Scientist in the Boys Town Center for the Study of Youth Development in Washington D.C. In 1977—back at the University of Connecticut—he founded the Center for the Study of Parental Acceptance and Rejection which was later renamed by the University's Board of Trustees to the "Ronald and Nancy Rohner Center for the Study of Interpersonal Acceptance and Rejection". Rohner has authored or edited 27 books, monographs, and special issues of journals and 233 articles, reviews, and other publications. Additionally, Rohner is the recipient of four awards from the American Psychological Association (APA) for his distinguished contributions to the international advancement of psychology, and he is the recipient of the Lifetime Achievement Award from the Society for Cross-Cultural Research.

Personal Relevance of IPARTheory in Rohner's Life

Rohner's relationship with his mother was warm and nurturing. He recalls that "I was a kid who knew he was loved. My mom absolutely adored me, and I adored her" (N. Zaki, personal communication, July 18, 2023). On the other hand, similar to John Bowlby, he did not know his father very well since he was an army officer in World War II. He was continually sent to different bases around the United States. As a result, Rohner moved from one state or city to another every six months, which meant a frequent change of schools. This discouraged him from trying to make new friends because he knew he would be leaving them soon. However, his mother was determined to keep her family together despite the difficult circumstances. These experiences were emotionally difficult for young Rohner. He elaborates on that saying "but my mother was my anchor through it all. She was always there, always supportive, always loving" (N. Zaki, personal communication, July 18, 2023). Eventually, when he was around ten years old, Rohner got to know his father better at the end of World War II.

He had one sister, who was two years older than him. Even though he longed for her to be his good friend, their relationship did not take that direction because she was always busy with her own friends and did not have time for her little brother. Then she got married as a teenager.

Later, in 1958-59, Rohner's direct exposure to cultural differences in Morocco greatly influenced his personal life and academic career. As a college student majoring in psychology, Rohner believed that everything he learned from psychology textbooks was real and applicable to real life situations, "as if they had some kind of eternal truth for all human beings", he said (N. Zaki, personal communication, July 18, 2023). But in 1958, after graduating, he and his first wife went to Morocco for a year. They worked as the Resident Directors of a dormitory of Moroccan children, and taught in the American School of Tangier.

He had many experiences in Morocco that changed the course of his academic career. Some of those experiences led to the most important cultural lessons in his life, and helped shape the formulation and development of what was to become IPARTheory years later. For example, while in Morocco, he saw a gorgeous mosque built with spectacular Moroccan tilework in the Rif Mountains. As he was taking pictures of the building, men emerged from the mosque after morning prayer. Several boys saw him and started throwing stones at him. Soon the men started throwing bigger stones. Later, Rohner learned why the men behaved in that way. They assumed he was photographing them, in violation of their religious beliefs that photographs should not be taken of men praying in sacred places.

Another incident brought Rohner's full attention to the potential power of cultural beliefs and meanings. The Director of the school had a feast to commemorate the opening of the dormitory, which had previously been the summer palace of the former Sultan of Morocco. Elite parents in the government came for the feast. The local hostess, Mrs. Abdulwahab, spent a week preparing a special feast for the occasion. Moroccans at that time ate with their hands, especially couscous. But Rohner's mother had always discouraged him from taking food off a plate with his hands. It is important to note here that, in the Moroccan culture, eating with one's right hand is an expected practice even for left-handed people. However, Rohner—who is left-handed—did not know that. He wanted to follow Moroccan traditions as best he could, so he joined everyone in eating with his finger from a great mound of couscous heaped on a large brass tray. However, Mrs. Abdulwahab saw that he used his left hand and fled the room angrily. This was the greatest insult he could possibly have given her about her grand feast. But no one had told Rohner in advance about this custom and its importance.

Many incidents such as these had a profound influence on changing Rohner's beliefs about human behavior. He went to Morocco believing everything he had learned in psychology about how individuals think/behave was true, but he left Morocco thinking that maybe *nothing* he learned in psychology was universally true (N. Zaki, personal communication, July 18, 2023). This shifted Rohner's focus away from mainstream American psychology to psychological anthropology. He felt a great need to understand the world from people's own cultural perspective. This was more easily achieved in anthropology than in psychology at that time.

Origins of IPARTheory

The journey of IPARTheory's development started during Rohner's second semester in graduate school at Stanford University in 1960. In a class on "Culture and Personality", Rohner was told to select a research topic where the cross-cultural survey method (now called the holocultural method) could be used. This involved coding a specific set of variables in a sample of the world's well-described societies in ethnography. Looking for a suitable topic, he searched through one of his favorite undergraduate textbooks on *Abnormal Psychology and Modern Life* (Coleman, 1956). His attention was drawn to a short section on "Faulty Parent-Child Relationships". In particular, Coleman wrote about the effects of parental rejection. But Rohner's experiences in Morocco had left him feeling doubtful about the generalizability of conclusions such as those reached by psychologists regarding the effects of parental rejection. So, he thought it would be interesting to test in a cross-cultural survey some of the conclusions reached by Coleman and others. Rohner then coded a series of variables in a small holocultural sample about parental acceptance-rejection and some of the presumed effects of rejection. After doing his data analysis, he was astonished to discover that most of the reported effects of rejection appeared to be universal while others were not. He was so intrigued by these results that he did further studies on the topic in every course where he could fit it in throughout the remainder of his graduate studies.

Four years later, as a young Assistant Professor at the University of Connecticut in 1964, he began the Rejection-Acceptance Project. There, he continued exploring the construct of parental acceptance-rejection across the world's ethnographies. This work culminated in his first book on the topic, *They Love Me, They Love Me Not* (1975). Later, in a Special Issue of Behavioral Science Research (Rohner & Rohner, 1980), he introduced the concept of parental acceptance-rejection theory (PARTheory). His 1986 book on *The Warmth Dimension* amplified greatly on PARTheory. Then, during a two-year sabbatical from 1975 through 1977 at The Boys Town Center for the Study of Youth Development in Washington DC, he began to move away from holocultural research to explore intracultural variations in parental acceptance-rejection and its psychological and behavioral effects in different countries internationally. This was a major paradigm shift away from exploring anthropological descriptions of normative parenting behaviors and typical responses of children and adults in samples of societies worldwide. This paradigm shift required him to develop and validate self-report measures assessing parental acceptance-rejection and personality dispositions (known from holocultural research to be associated with parental rejection). Different versions of the "Parental Acceptance-Rejection Questionnaire"

(PARQ) and the "Personality Assessment Questionnaire" (PAQ) resulted from that endeavor (see Rohner & Ali, 2025; Chapter 1, this book).

Initially, PARTheory focused on the significance of perceived *parental* acceptance-rejection. Many studies were conducted to further develop and validate the theory across cultures internationally. However, as time passed, it came to Rohner's attention that it is not just parental acceptance-rejection that affects the individual's psychological wellbeing. He recounts a particular incident that was significant in moving PARTheory to IPARTheory. One of his former colleagues was deeply in love with a man. However, they had broken up three years earlier when he unexpectedly walked away from her. Rohner had a flash of insight as he sat behind his desk listening to his colleague talk about her experience of heartbreak. She was displaying all the personality dispositions commonly associated with experiences of perceived parental rejection. At that moment, Rohner realized that rejection by an attachment figure *at any point in life* can trigger the constellation of negative personality dispositions known to be associated with parental rejection in childhood. He realized then that children and adults everywhere probably respond in the same seven to ten ways when they perceive themselves to be accepted or rejected by their attachment figures, including parents in childhood and intimate partners in adulthood. As Rohner said, "perceived interpersonal acceptance-rejection is relevant to human beings from womb to tomb" (N. Zaki, personal communication, July 18, 2023). Because of this realization and subsequent research on it, PARTheory was renamed interpersonal acceptance-rejection theory (IPARTheory) in 2014 (Rohner, 2014) to highlight the *interpersonal* dimension of the theory.

Theories that Influenced the Development of IPARTheory

It is important to note that Rohner knew about Bowlby and attachment theory in the 1970s but attachment theory did not influence Rohner's thinking for many years. He started wondering about possible similarities and differences between the two theories in 1996. That year, Rohner co-taught a graduate seminar on attachment theory and PARTheory (as it was still called at the time). The seminar resulted in the article "Bridging Parental Acceptance-Rejection Theory and Attachment Theory in the Preschool Strange Situation" (Hughes et al., 2005).

According to Rohner, few American psychologists, especially child psychologists, held Bowlby in high regard in the 1970s. There was considerable controversy around his ideas. For example, "many professionals thought his concept of attachment was nothing more than another word for dependence" (N. Zaki, personal communication, July 18, 2023). Rohner corresponded with Bowlby a couple times between 1975 and 1977. But it was not until his last letter that he asked Bowlby about his thoughts on the relationship between dependence and attachment. Bowlby never responded. Later, Rohner learned that Bowlby was sensitive to American child psychologists who criticized him (N. Zaki, personal communication, July 18, 2023). So, even though attachment theory is consistent with IPARTheory in many ways described later, attachment theory did not shape Rohner's thinking in any significant way.

A theory that Rohner finds intriguing is Kory Floyd's Affection Exchange Theory (AET; see Allred, 2025; Chapter 4, this book). AET explores the implications and consequences of receiving affection, excessive affection, and affection deprivation. The theory considers both affection deprivation and excessive affection as aversive. However, it reports that affection deprivation has worse mental and health outcomes than excessive affection (Hesse et al., 2022). That theory drew Rohner's attention to the possible dark side of affection.

IPARTheory and Its Subtheories

IPARTheory is an evidence-based theory of socialization and lifespan developmental psychology and relationships. One of its primary aims is to explore the effects of perceived acceptance-rejection by attachment figures such as mothers, fathers, partners, peers, teachers, and other significant people in a person's life (Rohner, 2021). Acceptance and rejection are conceptualized as a continuum referred to as the "warmth dimension" that describes the quality of interpersonal relationships. The warmth dimension encompasses physical, verbal, and symbolic behaviors that characterize a relationship (Rohner, 2008). On one end of the spectrum is acceptance. It is characterized by a warm, loving, caring, considerate, and sensitive relationship. Perceived rejection, on the other hand, is characterized by coldness and lack of affection, indifference and neglect, hostility and aggression, or by the presence of undifferentiated rejection. The last category is shown when there are no clear behavioral signs of rejecting behavior, but individuals feel that significant others do not love or care about them (Rohner, 2008).

The theory posits that humans have a phylogenetically acquired need to feel cared about (i.e., accepted) by their attachment figures (Rohner, 1975, 1986; Rohner & Ali, 2025; Chapter 1, this book). When this need is not met sufficiently, individuals tend to develop a specific set of 10 dispositions in response to the perceived rejection. These are: (1) anger, hostility, aggression, and passive aggression, (2) dependence or defensive independence, (3) impaired self-esteem, (4) impaired self-adequacy, (5) emotional unresponsiveness, (6) emotional instability, (7) negative worldview, (8) anxiety, (9) insecurity, and (10) cognitive distortions (Rohner, 1986, 2004, 2021;

Rohner & Ali, 2025; Chapter 1, this book). Additionally, rejected individuals tend to develop distinct mental representations (i.e., cognitive distortions) characterized by sensitivity to rejection by others, fear of intimacy, and other cognitive distortions (Rohner, 2004).

IPARTheory is composed of three subtheories. First, *personality subtheory* explores questions related to how children and adults respond to perceived acceptance or rejection, and whether/why these responses differ. In addition, the subtheory investigates the longitudinal effects of perceptions of acceptance-rejection in childhood into adulthood (Lansford, 2025; Chapter 7, this book). The theory postulates that the effects of rejection in childhood are long-lasting and tend to influence intimate relationships in adulthood (Khaleque, 2025; Chapter 5, this book; Rohner, 2008). Second, *coping subtheory* investigates the concept of emotional resilience. More specifically, it explores factors that allow some children and adults to cope more effectively with rejection than other rejected individuals. The theory posits that emotional resilience (referred to as "affective coping") is related, among other things, to a differentiated sense of self, self-determination, and to an ability to depersonalize from external situations (Rohner, 2021). Third, *sociocultural systems subtheory and model* attempts to predict and explain worldwide causes of interpersonal acceptance and rejection. It explores why some parents behave toward their children in a caring and loving way while others appear to be cold, rejecting, insensitive, or neglectful. This is examined on an individual as well as on a societal level. The theory posits that significant differences relate to psychological, familial, community, and societal factors.

Areas of Convergence Between Attachment Theory and IPARTheory

Developmental Trajectory of Both Theories

Each theory was influenced by distinct theoretical perspectives. For instance, IPARTheory's sociocultural systems subtheory stresses the importance of a complex ecological context. This notion has theoretical roots in the early work of Kardiner (1945a, 1945b), and Whiting and Child (1953). Bronfenbrenner's (1979) ecological model was developed after Rohner's sociocultural systems model in 1975 (Rohner, 1975) and therefore had minimal influence on Rohner's thinking. Attachment theory has been influenced by several theoretical perspectives including ethology (Gould, 1986), control systems, information processing, and psychoanalysis (Bateman & Holmes, 1995). Both theories have common roots in evolutionary psychology and principles of developmental psychology.

Both IPARTheory and attachment theory are developmental in nature. Both essentially seek to explore the effects of early childhood experiences on adult development. Both also attempt to understand the influence of early interactions on developmental outcomes later in life. And both focus on the *relational* aspect of human development. Finally, both theories are fundamentally based on individuals' *perceptions* of others' behaviors and motivations.

Expanding the Concept of Attachment Relationships into Adulthood

Both theories partially align with Freud's early ideas related to the significant relationship with one's primary caregiver and its effect on future romantic relationships (Waters et al., 1991). As such, both theories started from the point of understanding the effect of the quality of the parent–child relationship on children's developmental outcomes. Later, both expanded into non-parental relationships such as siblings, peers, and intimate partners, among others.

As mentioned earlier, IPARTheory initially focused on the *parent–child* relationship, but then expanded into *interpersonal* relationships more generally. Since then, a central postulate of IPARTheory has been that important interpersonal relationships throughout life significantly affect individuals' sense of wellbeing and psychological adjustment.

Attachment theory initially focused on the mother–child dyad and its implications. Later, its focus expanded to include other important attachment figures including one's grandparents and siblings (Schaffer & Emerson, 1964). Eventually, attachment researchers stretched the theory's focus to include adult attachment relationships. For example, Hazan and Shaver (1987) applied attachment concepts (e.g., secure base, proximity seeking, separation anxiety) to romantic relationships. Hence, an "interpersonal" aspect similar to IPARTheory's has been added to attachment theory. Both theories now emphasize the importance of children's as well as adults' feelings about being loved, accepted, and cared for in their relationships with their attachment figures. Furthermore, both theories agree that other nurturing relationships (e.g., the therapist–client relationship) can lead to positive outcomes that may compensate, at least in part, for challenging experiences in childhood (Gurmen, 2025; Chapter 11, this book; Ripoll-Núñez & Carrillo, 2016). Yet, the mother–child relationship still remains one of the first things that often comes to mind when one learns about attachment theory.

Significance of the Quality of the Relationship

The *quality* of interpersonal relationships is significant in both IPARTheory and attachment theory (Ripoll-Núñez & Carrillo, 2016). Bowlby's attachment theory investigates the effect of *maternal deprivation* and the significance of *maternal sensitivity* (as developed by Ainsworth). Rohner's IPARTheory examines the implications of *perceived acceptance and rejection in relationships*.

The common underlying theme in both theories is the focus on the emotional bond as well as the quality of the relationship and how it affects individuals' developmental outcomes and future relationships.

Emphasis on Perception of the Relationship

Both theories evaluate the quality of relationships through the individual's own perceptions. IPARTheory places a high importance on the individual's perceptions of a relationship. Specifically, the research explores the notions of *perceived* acceptance and *perceived* rejection in childhood and adults' memories of parental acceptance-rejection in childhood. IPARTheory distinguishes between different expressions of rejection including coldness and lack of affection, indifference and neglect, and hostility and aggression. Furthermore, IPARTheory is unique in that it introduces the concept of "undifferentiated rejection" (i.e., individuals' perception that the attachment figure does not really care about, love, or want them, though there may be no behavioral manifestations of this behavior). IPARTheory follows Kagan's (1978) conceptualization of parental rejection, "[it] is not a specific set of actions of parents but a belief held by the child" (p.61).

Attachment theory stresses the infant's experience of responsiveness received from the caregiver. Eventually, the internal working models of self and others become based on the child's and adult's *perception* of being on the receiving end of the caregiving relationship. Some parents perceive themselves to be responsive or feel guilty for not being responsive enough. Although each of these scenarios has important implications, it is the children's own perceptions of parents' responsiveness that affect their view of themselves, others, and the world around them. Bowlby argued that "most of what goes on in the internal world is a more or less accurate reflection of what an individual has experienced in the external world.... If a child sees his mother as a very loving person, the chances are that his mother is a loving person. If he sees her as a rejecting person, she is a very rejecting person" (Bowlby et al., 1986, p.43).

The Universality of the Need to Feel Loved and Accepted

Building on the significance of fulfilling emotional needs in relationships, both theories assert that the need to feel loved and accepted is universal. According to IPARTheory, individuals have a phylogenetically acquired need to be positively regarded (i.e., cared about, comforted, nurtured) by people important to them (Rohner, 1975, 1986, 2021). This need is understood from a biocultural evolutionary perspective. Specifically, Rohner (2021) argues that "parental love is the single most important factor in a child's life". When children do not feel that this need has been fulfilled satisfactorily, they feel rejected and tend to respond in a consistent way. According to Rohner (2008), this response has been shown to be present wherever they studied this phenomenon "regardless of differences in race, gender, ethnicity, language, or other such defining conditions" (pp. 8–9). Khaleque and Ali (2017) reported on 12 meta-analyses encompassing different cultures. This multicultural meta-analysis confirmed the relation between perceived acceptance-rejection and later psychological (mal) adjustment (see Khaleque, 2025; Chapter 2, this book).

For attachment theory, on the other hand, the need for proximity is said to be innate in babies to maximize their chances of safety and survival. Like IPARTheory, the evolutionary perspective plays an important role in explaining this need. In fact, Bowlby initially defined the concept of attachment as "the universal innate propensity of humans to form protective and comforting relationships" (Crittenden, 2017, p.438). Bowlby argued that the mother-infant relationship should be experienced as warm and intimate. In addition, both the mother and the baby should ideally find satisfaction and enjoyment in the relationship (Bowlby, 1951).

Different Concepts Addressing Similar Issues in Attachment Theory and IPARTheory

Several concepts are addressed in similar ways in IPARTheory and attachment theory, even though different terms refer to them. For example: (1) internal working models in attachment theory are essentially the same thing as mental representations in IPARTheory; (2) anxious attachment style in attachment theory is related to dependence in IPARTheory; (3) avoidant attachment style in attachment theory is related to defensive independence in IPARTheory; and (4) intergenerational transmission of attachment in attachment theory is related to counter rejection in IPARTheory. These similarities in concepts are described next.

Internal Working Models (Attachment Theory) and Mental Representations (IPARTheory)

Internal working models (IWMs) and mental representations both refer to cognitive representations of self, others, and the lived world in the context of relationships. In both theories, these cognitive representations are believed to later guide one's assumptions, expectations, and core beliefs in significant interpersonal relationships (Ripoll-Núñez & Carrillo, 2016).

In attachment theory, individuals develop *internal working models* of the self, of others, and of the world. IWMs are more recently also known as "dispositional representations" (Crittenden, 2016). These IWMs depend on early experiences with primary caregivers and the sense of responsiveness and sensitivity received. For instance, Bowlby (1988) said "a child's self-model is profoundly influenced by how his mother sees and treats him; whatever she fails to recognize in him, he is likely to fail to recognize in himself" (p.132). Individuals form these IWMs in a complementary way. For instance, children whose parents are loving and attentive tend to believe they are lovable and worthy of attention (Bretherton & Munholland, 2008). Eventually these relationship-specific IWMs generalize into overall beliefs and expectations related to the self, others, and the world throughout the lifespan (Bowlby, 1988).

IPARTheory uses the term *mental representations* to refer to a similar concept. Based on the symbolic interaction theory, IPARTheory proposes that individuals' perceptions of acceptance and/or rejection affect how they cognitively view themselves. For instance, individuals who feel loved and accepted are likely to have a positive attitude toward themselves and to feel lovable. On the other hand, rejected individuals tend to develop a specific constellation of negative mental representations. These mental representations may lead rejected individuals to be predisposed toward perceiving hostility in the actions of others, even when it is not intended by the other person (Rohner, 2008). This disposition is called *rejection sensitivity* in IPARTheory. Here the rejected individual becomes hypervigilant to the slightest signs of rejection, real or imagined (Rohner, 2021, 2023). Eventually, these cognitive schemas become stable and hard to change. On the other hand, IPARTheory explains that certain social cognitive abilities tend to maximize the likelihood of coping with perceived rejection in a better way. These social cognitive abilities include having a differentiated sense of self, self-determination, and a capacity to depersonalize among other dispositions (Ki et al., 2018; Rohner, 1986).

Both theories recognize that even though these cognitive representations of the self and relationships tend to be relatively stable throughout the lifespan, some factors may lead to their revisions. These factors include developmental changes (e.g., social and cognitive development from one life stage to another) and experiencing qualitatively different relationships (e.g., a formerly loving parent becoming neglectful, or getting into an abusive relationship with an adult intimate partner) (Ripoll-Núñez & Carrillo, 2016).

Anxious Attachment Style (Attachment Theory) and Dependence (IPARTheory)

Both theories seek to conceptualize the relationship dynamic with an attachment figure characterized by clinginess and a higher-than-usual level of dependence. In attachment theory, Ainsworth proposed a classification for attachment styles to account for different relationship dynamics. One of these was *anxious attachment*. It is primarily related to the caregiver's inconsistency of responses. As a result, infants are unable to predict availability or sensitivity to their needs. The resulting dynamic becomes characterized by anxiety, heightened expression of emotions, clinginess, difficulty in being soothed, and general fear of abandonment later on.

A similar dynamic is explained in IPARTheory as *dependence* on an attachment figure. This initially takes place when the rejected individual tries unsuccessfully to elicit a positive response from a significant other to fulfill the need for feeling cared about. This behavior is called dependence in IPARTheory (Rohner, 2021). Dependence is related to an internal yearning for love, care, attention, and warmth from the attachment figure. The individual initiates different behaviors in an effort to fulfill this need. A young child may cling to the parent, whine and/or cry. In the case of an adult, an intense need for reassurance as well as jealousy may become prominent.

Avoidant Attachment Style (Attachment Theory) and Defensive Independence (IPARTheory)

Avoidant attachment is one of the main classifications of attachment patterns proposed by Ainsworth. Infants with avoidant attachment style tend to dismiss the caregiver's presence or separation, and appear to be self-sufficient. Their minimized expression of emotions is usually a response to parental unavailability. It is thought to be a coping strategy or a defense mechanism used by children to avoid further hurt and/or rejection (Bretherton, 1992). This is why this type of avoidance is referred to as *pseudo-independence* because it is different from an individual who eventually becomes independent knowing that they have a secure base to go back to when needed.

IPARTheory also distinguishes between *healthy independence* and *defensive independence* (Rohner, 1986, 2004, 2021). An individual becomes independent—in the healthy sense of the word—when their emotional need of being accepted is successfully fulfilled. On the other hand, some individuals utilize a self-protective strategy to avoid further hurt of rejection (Rohner, 2021; Zimmer-Gembeck et al., 2014). In an attempt to cope, they project an image of independence often overlaid with latent anger, emotional unresponsiveness, and other negative emotions generated by the rejection. This form of apparent independence is called defensive independence in IPARTheory. Defensively independent individuals often actively deny feeling the need for love, encouragement, and emotional support.

Intergenerational Transmission of Attachment (Attachment Theory) and Counter Rejection (IPARTheory)

Even though IPARTheory refers to the concept of intergenerational transmission of parenting practices (e.g., Rothenberg et al., 2023), the concept is more commonly associated with attachment theory. Attachment theory acknowledges that parents sometimes repeat hurtful interactions from their childhood instead of consciously changing this parent–child dynamic with their own children. For instance, a woman who experienced an insecure bond of attachment with her avoidant mother may have an avoidant attachment style with her own daughter as a coping mechanism.

IPARTheory proposes a related concept called *counter rejection*. Sometimes adults who remember having been rejected by a parent or other attachment figure end up rejecting others in turn. Counter rejection is often a way of coping with troubled relational circumstances and unfulfilled emotional needs (see Ali & Rohner, 2025; Chapter 6, this book).

Shared Mental Health Correlates of the Theories

IPARTheory and attachment theory research demonstrate a number of similar correlations with personality and lifespan dispositions. For instance, IPARTheory research has shown that perceived parental (both maternal and paternal) acceptance and rejection in childhood as well as perceived partner acceptance and rejection in adulthood tend to correlate with individuals' psychological adjustment and maladjustment everywhere (Rohner, 2008). Similarly, attachment theory research has shown positive correlations between secure attachment and emotion regulation, positive views of oneself and others, higher empathy, and a sense of belonging (e.g., Feldman, 2016). On the other hand, Bowlby wrote that "parental unavailability or unresponsiveness during early childhood may cause psychopathology later in life, manifesting itself in neurotic symptoms, personality disorders or impairment in the capacity to form lasting interpersonal relationships" (Bowlby, 1987, p.57–58). Research in IPARTheory also confirms that perceived rejection tends to affect individuals in ways similar to this, such as developmental trauma disorder and post-traumatic stress disorder (PTSD) (Courtois, 2004). These psychological disorders share their exposure to repeated stressful interpersonal relationships over an extended period of time.

Both theories predict specific neurobiological and neuropsychological outcomes. Adults with insecure attachment, for example, have been shown to have a hyper-reactive HPA axis and cortisol response to stressful situations (Quirin et al., 2008). In addition, experiences of childhood maltreatment, abuse, or neglect tend to negatively affect brain development. For instance, it results in over-pruning of the orbitofrontal cortex, which leads to a reduced capacity to effectively respond to stress (Lott, 2003). Furthermore, insecure attachment with the primary caregiver can impair the individual's dopamine reward system, thus creating a higher disposition to addictive problems and mood disorders (Gerra et al., 2009).

Perceived rejection in IPARTheory has also been shown to be related to different neurobiological and neuropsychological correlates (see Miller & Ali, 2025; Chapter 12, this book). Early exposure to maternal love and nurturance has been associated with larger hippocampal volume, which is the brain area involved in emotion regulation (Luby et al., 2012). Additionally, brain imaging (fMRI) has revealed that the brain responds similarly to both perceived rejection and actual physical pain. In both cases, brain scans show activation in the anterior cingulate cortex and the right ventral prefrontal cortex (Eisenberger, 2015). In addition, experiences of childhood maltreatment (mostly characterized by perceived rejection) are associated with a reduced amygdala volume (Souza-Queiroz et al., 2016) and a significantly reduced volume of the medial prefrontal cortex (van Harmelen et al., 2010). Both of these play a critical role in stress modulation and emotion regulation. This is partly why rejected individuals tend to struggle with emotional stability and stress management (see Miller & Ali, 2025; Chapter 12, this book for an expanded summary of the neurobiological effects of perceived acceptance-rejection).

Areas of Divergence Between IPARTheory and Attachment Theory

Conceptualization of an Attachment Figure

Even though both attachment theory and IPARTheory refer to attachment figures, they operationalize this concept differently. In attachment theory, the concept of attachment figures usually refers to parental figures. They are particularly significant in children's lives because of the sense of security (or lack of it) they provide based on parents' interaction with the child (Bowlby, 1982).

IPARTheory distinguishes between a *significant other* and an *attachment figure*. A significant other is defined in IPARTheory as someone with whom the individual has a relatively long-lasting relationship, who is emotionally important in the individual's life, and is considered to be non-interchangeable with others (Rohner, 2023). The concept of an attachment figure goes one step further. Everything related to the significant other applies to the concept of the attachment figure, with the additional requirement that one's sense of security, happiness, and wellbeing must be dependent to some extent on the quality of the relationship with this person.

Significance of the Maternal and Paternal Figures

Bowlby long emphasized the female parent (mother) when he referred to the primary caregiver. He did this so consistently that he has been criticized for supporting patriarchy and the traditional view of women as primary caregivers (Chodorow, 1978; Johnson, 1988). According to some feminist theorists, this traditional perspective leads to justified gender role stereotypes, pressuring women to leave their jobs, and placing excessive emotional demands on women (Vicedo, 2011). On the other hand, it is important to note that there is nothing in attachment theory explicitly stating that the primary caregiver *must* be the mother. This was implied to a large extent because of cultural expectations at the time of Bowlby's writings (Hazan & Shaver, 1994). Because of this emphasis in attachment theory, much is yet to be learned about father-child attachment.

IPARTheory explores the bond with mothers separately from the bond with fathers. Memories of one parent do not automatically imply similar memories with the other parent. In fact, studies often reveal that perceived paternal acceptance or rejection is a better predictor of children's psychological adjustment than perceived maternal acceptance or rejection (see Akun, 2025; Chapter 9, this book; Khaleque & Rohner, 2012; Rohner & Carrasco, 2014; Rohner & Veneziano, 2001).

Focus on Categorical Attachment Styles Versus the Warmth Dimension

Attachment theory is well known for its categorical classification of different attachment styles, whether for children or adults. A broad understanding of attachment styles refers to secure versus insecure attachment. But a closer look at these categories further divides attachment styles into several groups. For instance, the Strange Situation Procedure classifies children into secure (type B), avoidant (type A), anxious-ambivalent (type C), or disorganized (type D). Adults also have corresponding attachment categories that are classified according to the Adult Attachment Interview: autonomous-secure (giving a coherent account of their childhood), dismissing (often idealize their parents or fail to remember their childhood), preoccupied (conflicted childhood memories), or disorganized (unresolved childhood trauma) (George et al., 1984).

IPARTheory, however, does not use a categorical classification of attachment styles. Rather, acceptance and rejection are defined as being based on a *continuum* or dimension characterized by varying intensities of different behaviors and physical, verbal, and symbolic ways of showing emotions. IPARTheory also focuses on the extent to which individuals' overall well-being is affected by significant others and attachment figures (Ripoll-Núñez & Carrillo, 2016). Moreover, IPARTheory introduces new concepts that have not been commonly addressed in attachment theory's postulates such as *troubled individuals* (Rohner, 2021) and *affective copers* (Rohner, 2021). Troubled individuals are those who come from nurturing families but still display many of the personality dispositions usually associated with rejected individuals. On the other hand, affective copers are those who are able to thrive emotionally despite having been exposed to significant rejection as children.

Conceptualization of the Relationship Quality

Even though both theories are concerned with the quality of parental and interpersonal relationships, the way they operationalize that quality differs. Attachment theory focuses on the caregiver's *responsiveness* to the child, while IPARTheory emphasizes the concept of *acceptance*. Responsiveness and acceptance are not the same. As noted by Rohner, responsiveness can include different types of actions. Not all of them are positive (N. Zaki, personal communication, July 18, 2023). For example, caregivers may be intrusively responsive, controlling, or manipulative. These are obviously not ideal forms of response. Ainsworth, however, emphasized the notion of maternal *sensitivity*. Being sensitive to the child's needs usually leads to a more attuned type of responsiveness. IPARTheory's concept of acceptance includes sensitive responsiveness, or responsiveness without intrusion. According to Rohner, acceptance is essentially a matter of feeling cared about emotionally.

Universalist Versus Relativist Nature of the Theory

Both theories acknowledge a universal need to feel loved and accepted. However, one of the differences between them lies in how the universal or relativistic perspective is operationally defined. Attachment theory tends to claim universality and stability of attachment classifications. Ainsworth started by studying families in Africa, then focused on American dyads in Baltimore. However, the vast portion of attachment research focuses on Western contexts and families. This has led to several criticisms of the theory including the focus on Western middle-class families while ignoring caregiving practices considered to be common and desirable in other parts of the world (Keller, 2018).

Additionally, the theory's postulates are based on contexts characterized by high education, a low number of children, a nuclear family household, and late first parenthood (Keller, 2018). This does not represent the majority of cultures worldwide where parents may express their love and responsiveness in different ways (Keller & Chaudhary, 2017). For instance, in some sociocultural contexts, older siblings typically act as infant caregivers (Keller, 2018). Also, a concept such as *stranger anxiety*, which is believed to be a universal attachment behavior, may not exist in some cultures. For example, in Cameroon, babies rarely show stranger anxiety in response to a strange woman picking them up and moving them away from their mother because this is a common form of behavior there (Otto, 2014).

Additionally, Bowlby asserted that secure attachment is adaptive and promotes healthy wellbeing in *any* culture, just like physical well-being is independent of cultural definitions (Stevenson-Hinde, 2007). On the other hand, according to Keller (2018), a closer examination of different cultural needs and values reveals that insecure attachment can actually be adaptive in some less-than-ideal contexts. Third, the normativity assumption in attachment theory argues that secure attachment is the most prevalent attachment classification. However, several studies have revealed differences in the distribution of attachment patterns across cultures. For example, avoidant attachment may be over-represented in Germany (e.g., Grossmann et al., 1985) whereas anxious attachment may be overly represented in Japan (e.g., Miyake et al., 1985).

IPARTheory, on the other hand, takes a more relativistic stance with respect to interpersonal relationships. The theory recognizes that attachment figures express their love differently around the world. For instance, Rohner (1994) explained that when a busy, over-worked Bengali mother wants to praise her child or express her love, she can take the time to give her child a peeled and seeded orange. Words of praise are rarely used in this culture. If this mother's behavior is explored solely from an "objective" point of view, it would completely miss the cultural implications of the behavior. This partly explains why IPARTheory relies heavily on self-report measures. It allows space for individuals' own perceptions of the meaning of others' behavior.

Also, IPARTheory's sociocultural subtheory focuses on the context in which relationships happen. For example, cultural beliefs, norms, and traditions are explored with regards to their impact on different expressions of interpersonal acceptance-rejection (Rohner, 2016). IPARTheory refers to this relativistic view of behaviors as expressive behaviors (Rohner, 2016) and acknowledges their uniqueness in each society. More studies are needed to further study this concept, particularly in the context of adult relationships (Ripoll-Núñez & Carrillo, 2016).

Scope of Measures Used

For children, attachment theory's gold standard of assessment is the *Strange Situation Procedure* (SSP) which focuses on mother–infant reunion and separation. It is an observational procedure consisting of eight episodes. Coding the SSP results in identifying the child's attachment style to the caregiver. The gold standard of assessment for adults is the *Adult Attachment Interview* (AAI). It is an interview protocol exploring adults' state of mind with regards to attachment. Several *self-report measures* are also used in the literature, including the Relationship Questionnaire (RQ), and the Experience in Close Relationship scale (ECR). These questionnaires focus on attachment to one's partner instead of a parental figure.

IPARTheory's research is based to a great extent on *self-report questionnaires* developed by Rohner. Currently, the theory has 35 measures translated into 78 languages and dialects internationally (see Rohner & Ali, 2025; Chapter 1, this book). IPARTheory researchers also employ behavioral observations, interviews, and participant observation techniques in ethnographic fieldwork—along with holocultural research.

Perspective on Spoiling the Child

Attachment theory asserts that parents cannot spoil their children by being overly responsive to their needs. In fact, the theory proposes that the more the child is able to depend on their attachment figure(s), the more they can become independent when they are ready.

IPARTheory, on the other hand, acknowledges that loving yet intrusively controlling parents may lead to *immature dependence* in the child (Rohner, 2021). This is sometimes referred to as *smother love* since it interferes with the child's normal development and exploratory behavior (Hughes et al., 2005).

Clinical Applications of Attachment Theory and IPARTheory

In clinical settings, attachment theorists are concerned with understanding the sources of a dysfunctional behavioral pattern in the client (i.e., looking into the internal working models of the self and others). Ideally, therapists can be a *secure base* for clients, which enables clients to freely explore thoughts and emotions. As such, therapists are considered to be attachment figures for clients – albeit transitory. Several attachment-informed and attachment-focused therapies have developed over the years. One of the most highly developed theories is the *Dynamic Maturational Model of Attachment and Adaptation (DMM)* (Meins, 2017). IPARTheory has also developed different strategies for clinical applications of the theory's postulates. By understanding clients' background of perceived acceptance and/or rejection from attachment figures, the therapist becomes more enabled to help (see Gurmen, 2025; Chapter 11, this book for an expanded treatment of the clinical applications of IPARTheory).

Conclusion

The comparison between attachment theory and IPARTheory leads to a deeper understanding of both theories. Even though they have many similarities, they also differ in important ways that make each one of them unique. Seven areas of convergence were identified in this chapter, namely: (1) the developmental trajectory of both theories; (2) expanding the concept of attachment relationships into adulthood; (3) the significance of the *quality* of the relationship; (4) the emphasis on individuals' *perceptions* of the relationship; (5) the universality of the need to feel loved and accepted; (6) four similar concepts that are addressed in both attachment theory and IPARTheory using different terms; and, (7) the common correlates of both theories. On the other hand, eight areas of divergence were identified, namely: (1) conceptualization of an attachment figure; (2) significance of the maternal versus paternal figures; (3) focus on categorical attachment *styles* vs. the warmth *dimension*; (4) conceptualization of relationship quality; (5) universalist vs. relativist nature of the theories; (6) scope of measures used; (7) perspective on spoiling the child; and, (8) clinical applications of attachment theory and IPARTheory. This comparison helps initiate thoughtful discussions related to areas of overlap between two theories that have revolutionized our understanding of interpersonal relationships across the lifespan.

References

Ainsworth, M. D. S. (1967). *Infancy in Uganda: Infant care and the growth of love*. Baltimore, MD: The Johns Hopkins University Press.

Ainsworth, M. S. (1992). John Bowlby (1907–1990): Obituary. *American Psychologist, 47*(5), 668–668. https://doi.org/10.1037/0003-066x.47.5.668

Ainsworth, M. D. S., Blehar, M. C., Waters, E., & Wall, S. (1978). *Patterns of attachment: A psychological study of the strange situation*. Hillsdale, NJ: Erlbaum.

Ainsworth, M. D. S., & Wittig, B. A. (1969). Attachment and the exploratory behavior of one-year-olds in a strange situation. In B. M. Foss (Ed.), *Determinants of infant behavior* (Vol. 4, pp. 113–136). London: Methuen.

Akun, E. (2025). Gender differences in the effects of parental acceptance-rejection. In R. P. Rohner & S. Ali, (Eds.), *Global perspectives on parental acceptance and rejection: Lessons learned from IPARTheory* (pp. 163–190). Routledge.

Ali, S., & Rohner, R. P. (2025). As you sow, you shall reap: Effects of adults' memories of parental acceptance-rejection in childhood on aging parents. In R. P. Rohner & S. Ali, (Eds.), *Global perspectives on parental acceptance and rejection: Lessons learned from IPARTheory* (pp. 120–135). Routledge.

Allred, R. (2025). Affection, acceptance-rejection, & individual health outcomes: A heuristic juxtaposition of affection exchange theory and interpersonal acceptance-rejection theory. In R. P. Rohner & S. Ali, (Eds.), *Global perspectives on parental acceptance and rejection: Lessons learned from IPARTheory* (pp. 93–104). Routledge.

Bateman, A. W., & Holmes, J. (1995). *Introduction to psychoanalysis : Contemporary theory and practice*. Taylor & Francis Group.
Bowlby, J. (1944). Forty-four juvenile thieves: Their characters and home-life. *International Journal of Psychoanalysis, 25*, 107–128.
Bowlby, J. (1949). The study and reduction of group tensions in the family. *Human relations, 2*(2), 123–128. https://doi.org/10.1177/001872674900200203
Bowlby, J. (1951). *Maternal care and mental health. World Health Organization Monograph* (Serial no. 2). Geneva, Switzerland: World Health Organization.
Bowlby, J. (1958). The nature of the child's tie to his mother. *International Journal of Psycho-Analysis, XXXIX*, 1–23.
Bowlby, J. (1959). Separation anxiety. *International Journal of Psycho-Analysis, XLI*, 1–25.
Bowlby, J. (1960). Grief and mourning in infancy and early childhood. *The Psychoanalytic Study of the Child, VX*, 3-3. https://doi.org/10.1080/00797308.1960.11822566
Bowlby, J. (1969). *Attachment: Attachment and Loss Vol. I*. New York: Basic Books.
Bowlby, J. (1973). *Separation, Anxiety and Anger: Attachment and Loss Vol. II*. New York: Basic Books.
Bowlby, J. (1980). *Loss, Sadness and Depression: Attachment and Loss Vol. III*. New York: Basic Books.
Bowlby, J. (1982). *Attachment and loss: Vol. 1. Attachment* (2nd ed.). New York, NY: Basic Books.
Bowlby, J. (1987). Attachment. In Gregory, R.L. (ed). *The Oxford Companion to the Mind*. Oxford: Oxford University Press, pp. 57–58.
Bowlby, J. (1988). On knowing what you are not supposed to know and feeling what you are not supposed to feel. In *A Secure Base: Parent-Child Attachment and Healthy Human Development*. New York: Basic Books, pp. 99–118. https://doi.org/10.1177/070674377902400506
Bowlby, J., Figlio, K., & Young, R. M. (1986). An interview with John Bowlby on the origins and reception of his work. *Free Associations, 6*, 36–64.
Bretherton, I. (1992). The origins of attachment theory: John Bowlby and Mary Ainsworth. *Developmental Psychology, 28*(5), 759–775. https://doi.org/10.1037/0012-1649.28.5.759
Bretherton, I., & Munholland, K. A. (2008). Internal working models in attachment relationships: Elaborating a central construct in attachment theory. In J. Cassidy & P. R. Shaver (Eds.), *Handbook of attachment: Theory, research, and clinical applications* (2nd ed., pp. 102–127). New York, NY: Guilford Press.
Bronfenbrenner, U. (1979). *The ecology of human development: Experiments by nature and by design*. Cambridge, MA: Harvard University Press.
Byng-Hall, J. (2009). Foreword. In R. Dallos, & A. Vetere (Eds.), *Systemic therapy and attachment narratives: Applications in a range of clinical settings*. London, England: Routledge. https://doi.org/10.1007/978-3-030-37712-0_21
Chodorow, N. (1978). Mothering, object-relations, and the female oedipal configuration. *Feminist Studies, 4*(1), 137–158. https://doi.org/10.2307/3177630
Coates, S. W. (2004). John Bowlby and Margaret S. Mahler: Their lives and theories. *Journal of the American Psychoanalytic Association, 52*(2), 571–601. https://doi.org/10.1177/00030651040520020601
Coleman, J. C. (1956). *Abnormal Psychology and Modern Life* (2nd ed.). New York: Scott, Foresman, and Co.
Courtois, C. A. (2004). Complex trauma, complex reactions: Assessment and treatment. *Psychotherapy, 41*, 412–425. https://doi.org/10.1037/0033-3204.41.4.412

Crittenden, P. M. (2016). *Raising parents: Attachment, representation and treatment*. Routledge, Taylor & Francis Group. https://doi.org/10.4324/9781315726069
Crittenden, P. M. (2017). Gifts from Mary Ainsworth and John Bowlby. *Clinical Child Psychology and Psychiatry, 22*(3), 436–442. https://doi.org/10.1177/1359104517716214
Eisenberger, N. I. (2015). Social pain and the brain: Controversies, questions, and where to go from here. *Annual Review of Psychology, 66*(1), 601–629. https://doi.org/10.1146/annurev-psych-010213-115146
Feldman, R. (2016). The neurobiology of mammalian parenting and the biosocial context of human caregiving. *Hormones and Behavior, 77*, 3–17. https://doi.org/10.1016/j.yhbeh.2015.10.001
George, C., Kaplan, N., & Main, M. (1984). *Adult attachment interview*. Unpublished manuscript, University of California. Berkeley.
Gerra, G., Leonardi, C., Cortese, E., Zaimovic, A., Dell'Agnello, G., Manfredini, M., ... Donnini, C. (2009). Childhood neglect and parental care perception in cocaine addicts: relation with psychiatric symptoms and biological correlates. *Neuroscience & Biobehavioral Reviews, 33*(4), 601–610. https://doi.org/10.1016/j.neubiorev.2007.08.002
Gould, J. L. (1986). An introduction to ethology. P. J. B. Slater. *The Quarterly Review of Biology, 61*(4), 578–578. https://doi.org/10.1086/415243
Grossmann, K., Grossmann, K. E., Spangler, G., Suess, G., & Unzner, L. (1985). Maternal sensitivity and newbo'ns' orientation responses as related to quality of attachment in Northern Germany. In I. Bretherton & E. Waters (Eds.), Growing points of attachment theory and research, *Monographs of the Society for Research in Child Development, 50* (1-2, Serial No. 209). https://doi.org/10.2307/3333836
Gurmen, S. (2025). Clinical applications of interpersonal acceptance-rejection theory. In R.P. Rohner & S. Ali, (Eds.), *Global perspectives on parental acceptance and rejection: Lessons learned from IPARTheory* (pp. 207–224). Routledge.
Harlow, H. F. (1958). The nature of love. *American Psychologist, 13*(12), 673–685. https://doi.org/10.1037/h0047884
Hazan, C., & Shaver, P. (1987). Romantic love conceptualized as an attachment process. *Journal of Personality and Social Psychology, 52*, 511–524. https://doi.org/10.1037/0022-3514.52.3.511
Hazan, C., & Shaver, P. R. (1994). Deeper into attachment theory. *Psychological Inquiry, 5*(1), 68–79. https://doi.org/10.1207/s15327965pli0501_15
Hesse, C., Floyd, K., & Mikkelson, A. C. (2022). Affection deprivation is more aversive than excessive affection: A test of affection exchange theory. *Personal Relationships, 30*(1), 296–313. https://doi.org/10.1111/pere.12458
Hinde, R. A. (2005). Ethology and attachment theory. In K. Grossmann, K. E. Grossmann, & E. Waters (Eds.), *Attachment from infancy to adulthood: The major longitudinal studies* (pp. 1–12). New York/London: The Guilford Press.
Hughes, M. M., Blom, M., Rohner, R. P., & Britner, P. A. (2005). Bridging parental acceptance-rejection theory and attachment theory in the preschool strange situation. *Ethos, 33*(3), 378–401. https://doi.org/10.1525/eth.2005.33.3.378
Johnson, M. M. (1988). *Strong mothers, weak wives*. Berkeley: University of California Press.
Kagan, J. (1978). The parental love trap. *Psychology Today, 12*, 54–61.
Kardiner, A. (1945a). The concept of basic personality structure as an operational tool in the social sciences. In R. Linton (Ed.) *The Science of man in the world crisis* (pp. 102–122). N.Y.: Viking Fund.

Kardiner, A. (1945b). *The Psychological frontiers of society*. New York: Columbia University Press. https://doi.org/10.7312/kard94036

Keller, H. (2018). Universality claim of Attachment theory: Children's socioemotional development across cultures. *Proceedings of the National Academy of Sciences, 115*(45), 11414–11419. https://doi.org/10.1073/pnas.1720325115

Keller, H., & Chaudhary, N. (2017). Is the mother essential for attachment? *The Cultural Nature of Attachment*. https://doi.org/10.7551/mitpress/9780262036900.003.0005

Khaleque, A. (2025). Influence of parental acceptance-rejection on adult intimate relationships. In R.P. Rohner & S. Ali, (Eds.), *Global perspectives on parental acceptance and rejection: Lessons learned from IPARTheory* (pp. 39–62). Routledge.

Khaleque, A., & Ali, S. (2017). A systematic review of meta-analyses of research on interpersonal acceptance–rejection theory: Constructs and measures. *Journal of Family Theory & Review, 9*(4), 441–458. https://doi.org/10.1111/jftr.12228

Khaleque, A., & Rohner, R. P. (2012). Pancultural associations between perceived parental acceptance and psychological adjustment of children and adults: A meta-analytic review of worldwide research. *Journal of Cross-Cultural Psychology, 43*, 784–800. https://doi.org/10.1177/0022022111406120

Ki, P., Rohner, R. P., Britner, P. A., Halgunseth, L. C., & Rigazio-DiGilio, S. A. (2018). Coping with remembrances of parental rejection in childhood: Gender differences and associations with intimate partner relationships. *Journal of Child and Family Studies, 27*, 2441–2455. https://doi.org/10.1007/s10826-018-1074-8

Kubler-Ross, E. (1970). *On death and dying*. London: Tavistock. https://doi.org/10.1192/bjp.122.2.232-b

Lansford, J. E. (2025). Developmental correlates of parental acceptance-rejection from childhood to adulthood in nine countries. In R.P. Rohner & S. Ali, (Eds.), *Global perspectives on parental acceptance and rejection: Lessons learned from IPARTheory* (pp. 136–152). Routledge.

Lott, D. (2003). Brain development, attachment and impact on psychic vulnerability. *Psychiatric Times, 15*(5), 1–5.

Lorenz, K. Z. (1935). Der Kumpan in der Umwelt des Vogels [The companion in the bird's world]. *Journal fuer Ornithologie, 83*,137-213. (Abbreviated English translation published 1937 in Auk, 54, 245-273.) https://doi.org/10.1007/BF01905355

Luby, J. L., Barch, D. M., Belden, A., Gaffrey, M. S., Tillman, R., Babb, C., … Botteron, K. N. (2012). Maternal support in early childhood predicts larger hippocampal volumes at school age. *Proceedings of the National Academy of Sciences, 8*, 2854–2859. https://doi.org/10.1073/pnas.1118003109

Main, M., & Solomon, J. (1986). Discovery of an insecure-disorganized/disoriented attachment pattern. In T. B. Brazelton & M. W. Yogman (Eds.), *Affective development in infancy* (pp. 95–124). Ablex Publishing.

Meins, E. (2017, January). *The predictive power of attachment. The Psychologist, 30*(1), pp. 20–24.

Miller, J. & Ali, S. (2025). Interpersonal acceptance-rejection and neurobiological development. In R.P. Rohner & S. Ali, (Eds.), *Global perspectives on parental acceptance and rejection: Lessons learned from IPARTheory* (pp. 225–245). Routledge.

Miyake, K., Chen, S., & Campos, J. (1985). Infants' temperament, mothers' mode of interaction and attachment in Japan: An interim report. In I. Bretherton & E. Waters (Eds.), Growing points of attachment theory and research, *Monographs of the Society for Research in Child Development, 50* (1-2, Serial No. 109), 276-297. https://doi.org/10.2307/3333838

Otto, H. (2014). Don't show your emotions! Emotion regulation and attachment in the Cameroonian Nso. In *Different faces of attachment: Cultural variations on a universal human need* (pp. 215–229). Cambridge University Press. https://doi.org/10.1017/CBO9781139226684.012

Parkes, C. M. (1972). *Bereavement: Studies of grief in adult life*. New York: International Universities Press.

Quirin, M., Pruessner, J. C., & Kuhl, J. (2008). HPA system regulation and adult attachment anxiety: individual differences in reactive and awakening cortisol. *Psychoneuroendocrinology, 33*(5), 581–590. https://doi.org/10.1016/j.psyneuen.2008.01.013

Ripoll-Núñez, K., & Carrillo, S. (2016). Adult intimate relationships: Linkages between interpersonal acceptance-rejection theory and adult attachment theory. *Online Readings in Psychology and Culture*, 6(2). https://doi.org/10.9707/2307-0919.1149

Rohner, R. P. (1975). *They love me, they love me not: A worldwide study of the effects of parental acceptance and rejection*. New Haven, CT: ORAF Press. (Now available from Rohner Research Publications in Storrs, CT).

Rohner, R. P. (1986). *The warmth dimension: Foundations of parental acceptance-rejection theory*. Beverly Hills, CA: Sage Publications, Inc. (Now available from Rohner Research Publications in Storrs, CT).

Rohner, R. P. (1994). Patterns of parenting: The warmth dimension in cross-cultural perspective. In W. J. Lonner & R. S. Malpass (Eds.) *Readings in psychology and culture*. (pp.113–120). Needham Heights, MA: Allyn and Bacon.

Rohner, R. P. (2004). The parental "acceptance-rejection syndrome": Universal correlates of perceived rejection. *American Psychologist, 59*, 827–840. https://doi.org/10.1037/0003-066X.59.8.830

Rohner, R. P. (2008). Introduction: Parental acceptance-rejection theory studies of intimate adult relationships. *Cross-Cultural Research, 42*(1), 5–12. https://doi.org/10.1177/1069397107309749

Rohner, R. P. (2014). Parental acceptance-rejection theory gets a new name: Interpersonal acceptance-rejection theory (IPARTheory). *Interpersonal Acceptance, 8*(3), 6.

Rohner, R. P. (2016). Introduction to interpersonal acceptance-rejection theory (IPARTheory) and evidence. *Online Readings in Psychology and Culture*, 6(1). https://doi.org/10.9707/2307-0919.1055

Rohner, R. P. (2021). Introduction to interpersonal acceptance-rejection theory (IPARTheory) and evidence. *Online Readings in Psychology and Culture*, 6(1), 1–65. https://doi.org/10.9707/2307-0919.1055

Rohner, R. P. (2023). Glossary of significant concepts in interpersonal acceptance-rejection theory (IPARTheory). Csiar.uconn.edu.

Rohner, R. P. & Ali, S. (2025). Interpersonal acceptance-rejection theory (IPARTheory): From conception through maturity. In R.P. Rohner & S. Ali, (Eds.), *Global perspectives on parental acceptance and rejection: Lessons learned from IPARTheory* (pp. 3–38). Routledge.

Rohner, R. P. & Carrasco, M. A. (2014). Parental power and prestige moderate the effects of perceived acceptance on offsprings' psychological adjustment. *Cross Cultural Research Special Issue, 48*(3), 195–335.

Rohner, R. P. & Rohner, E. C. (1980). Worldwide tests of parental acceptance-rejection theory. *Behavior Science Research Special Issue, 15*(1), 1–88.

Rohner, R. P., & Veneziano, R. A. (2001). The importance of father love: History and contemporary evidence. *Review of General Psychology, 5*, 382–405.

Rothenberg, W. A., Lansford, J. E., Tirado, L. M. U., Yotanyamaneewong, S., Alampay, L. P., Al-Hassan, S. M., ... Bornstein, M. H. (2023). The intergenerational transmission of maladaptive parenting and its impact on child mental health: Examining cross-cultural mediating pathways and moderating protective factors. *Child Psychiatry & Human Development, 54*(3), 870–890. https://doi.org/10.1007/s10578-021-01311-6

Schaffer, H. R., & Emerson, P. E. (1964). The development of social attachments in infancy. *Monographs of the Society for Research in Child Development, 29* (Serial No. 94). https://doi.org/10.2307/1165727

Souza-Queiroz, J., Boisgontier, J., Etain, B., Poupon, C., Duclap, D., d'Albis, M.-A., Daban, C., Hamdani, N., Le Corvoisier, P., Delavest, M., Bellivier, F., Guevara, P., Leboyer, M., Henry, C., & Houenou, J. (2016). Childhood trauma and the limbic network: A multimodal MRI study in patients with bipolar disorder and controls. *Journal of Affective Disorders, 200*, 159–164. https://doi.org/10.1016/j.jad.2016.04.038

Stevenson-Hinde, J. (2007). Attachment theory and John Bowlby: Some reflections. *Attachment & Human Development, 9*(4), 337–342. https://doi.org/10.1080/14616730701711540

Tulving, E. (1979). Memory research: What kind of progress? In L. G. Nilsson (Ed.), *Perspectives on memory research: Essays in honor of Uppsala University's 500th anniversary* (pp. 19–34). Hillsdale, NJ: Erlbaum.

van Dijken, K. S. (1997). The first half of John Bowlby's life: A search for the roots of attachment theory. Doctoral dissertation, University of Leiden.

van Dijken, K. S. (1998). *John Bowlby: His early life*. London: Free Association Books.

van Harmelen, A.-L., van Tol, M.-J., van der Wee, N. J. A., Veltman, D. J., Aleman, A., Spinhoven, P., van Buchem, M. A., Zitman, F. G., Penninx, B. W. J. H., & Elzinga, B. M. (2010). Reduced medial prefrontal cortex volume in adults reporting childhood emotional maltreatment. *Biological Psychiatry, 68*(9), 832–838. https://doi.org/10.1016/j.biopsych.2010.06.011

Vicedo, M. (2011). The social nature of the mother's tie to her child: John Bowlby's theory of attachment in post-war America. *The British Journal for the History of Science, 44*(3), 401–426. https://doi.org/10.1017/s0007087411000318

Waters, E., Kondo-Ikemura, K, Posada, G., & Richters, J. (1991). Learning to Love: Mechanisms and milestones. In M. Gunnar & L. A. Sroufe (Eds.), *Self processes and development: The Minnesota Symposium on Child Psychology* (pp. 217–255). Hillsdale, NJ: Lawrence Erlbaum Associates, Inc.

Whiting, J. W. M., & Child, I. L. (1953). *Child training and personality*. New Haven, CT: Yale University Press. https://doi.org/10.2307/3537788

Zimmer-Gembeck, M. J., Trevaskis, S., Nesdale, D., & Downey, G. A. (2014). Relational victimization, loneliness and depressive symptoms: Indirect associations via self and peer reports of rejection sensitivity. *Journal of Youth and Adolescence, 43*(4), 568–582. https://doi.org/10.1007/s10964-013-9993-6

4

INTERPERSONAL ACCEPTANCE-REJECTION THEORY (IPARTHEORY) AND AFFECTION EXCHANGE THEORY

Ryan J. Allred

Affection exchange theory (AET; Floyd, 2006) and interpersonal acceptance-rejection theory (IPARTheory; Rohner, 1986, 2004, 2021) are widely used to explain why healthy relationships benefit individuals and how lack of warmth and the deprivation of affectionate communication in interpersonal relationships may cause adverse psychological and physiological outcomes. AET focuses on intimate partner relationships and attempts to explain the antecedents and effects of *affection*. IPARTheory, on the other hand, focuses on the consequences, causes, and correlates of perceived interpersonal *acceptance-rejection*, focusing on wider-array of relationships ranging from early parent-child, grandparent-child, and sibling relationships to later relationships with teachers and intimate partners among others (Rohner, 1986, 2004, 2021). Together these theories provide insight into the connection between prosocial behavior and individual/relational health.

Goals and Main Features of AET and IPARTheory

AET and IPARTheory share common goals and features. AET's primary goal is to explain the effects of *experiencing* and *expressing* affection. For example, how individuals express and interpret affectionate behaviors such as hugs, kisses, and verbal expressions of love and care. Central to AET is the idea that individuals are best served when they experience optimal levels of affection (i.e., not too much or too little; Floyd, 2006). Indeed, AET suggests that affection communication fills an innate biological need. On the other hand, IPARTheory is a theory of socialization and lifespan development

DOI: 10.4324/9781003441243-5

that attempts to explain major causes, consequences, and antecedents of perceived interpersonal acceptance and rejection. The theory suggests that the need to feel accepted in a primary relationship is a fundamental human need (Rohner, 1986, 2004, 2021).

AET focuses on communication of affection, defined as an "internal state of fondness and intense positive feeling for a living target" (Floyd, 2015, p. 310), and is founded on the evolutionary claim that all humans are driven by superordinate goals to survive and reproduce. Humans use communication to accomplish these goals, even when they are not consciously aware of procreation and survival as motivating influences (Floyd et al., 2021). AET specifically purports that humans have an inborn "need and capacity for affection" (Floyd, 2015, p. 310) such that its presence fosters individual and relational health while its absence leads to stress, depression, and reduced overall health (Floyd, 2014).

According to AET, messages of affection are communicated through *verbal affection, direct nonverbal gestures,* and *expressions of support* (Floyd, 2006). Verbal affection involves any statement that communicates liking, loving, intimacy, or appreciation. Direct nonverbal gestures are those nonverbal cues that are commonly interpreted as signs of liking, loving, intimacy, or appreciation within a given culture (e.g., holding hands, hugging, and kissing). Expressions of support include any behavior that provides tangible or emotional assistance. Expressions of support vary within any given relationship such that what constitutes support in one relationship may not be interpreted as support in another.

IPARTheory focuses on perceived acceptance-rejection on a continuum known as *the warmth dimension*, where acceptance is at one end of the dimension and rejection is on the other end. Warmth/acceptance in IPARTheory is expressed both verbally and nonverbally (e.g., signs of love, caring, affection, and emotional support). Rejection in the theory is conceptualized as the absence of warmth that can also be expressed verbally and nonverbally. IPARTheory defines four forms of rejection: emotional coldness/lack of warmth, hostility/aggression, indifference/neglect, and undifferentiated rejection (Rohner, 1986, 2004, 2021). At its core, IPARTheory suggests that individuals' experiences of acceptance and rejection by significant others—especially parents—shape their psychological, social, and physical development throughout their lives (Rohner, 1986, 2004, 2021). If an individual experiences rejection from a significant other it can lead to psychological maladjustment and negative personality dispositions such as anxiety, emotional insecurity, anger, hostility, aggression, emotional instability, impaired self-esteem, impaired self-adequacy, negative worldview, emotional instability, emotional unresponsiveness, cognitive distortion, and dependence or defensive independence depending on the form, frequency, and duration of the rejection. This cluster of personality dispositions is known as the *acceptance-rejection syndrome* in IPARTheory (Rohner, 1986, 2004, 2021; see also, Rohner & Ali, 2025, Chapter 1, this book).

Because affection is a sign of acceptance (Rohner, 1986, 2004, 2021), AET is particularly useful in exploring how individuals communicate in relationships. Indeed, Floyd (2015) conceptualizes affectionate communication as symbolic behaviors that convey messages of love, fondness, and positive regard (Floyd, 2015). AET's conceptualization of affectionate communication mirrors Rohner's (1986, 2004, 2021) explanation of the warmth dimension of acceptance and rejection as expressions of caring or lack of caring. Thus, affectionate communication promotes feelings of acceptance and reduces feelings of rejection (Denes et al., 2017).

Similarities Between AET and IPARTheory

Research suggests that affectionate communication enhances feelings of acceptance, which in turn promotes physical and mental well-being (Floyd et al., 2005; Rohner, 1986, 2004, 2021). Even though the two theories use different terminologies to explain similar concepts both aim to elucidate processes that underlie relationship formation, maintenance, and dissolution. They investigate communication patterns, emotional expressions, and relational interactions to provide insights into mechanisms shaping relationship quality and longevity. Both theories also propose that *messages/communication* of inclusion/acceptance contribute to healthy relationships while messages/communication of exclusion or scorn lead to physiological discomfort and relational distress.

Communication is thought to play a central role in both theories as a tool through which individuals convey affection/acceptance (Floyd, 2001; Rohner, 1960, 1986, 2004, 2021). IPARTheory focuses on *perceived* acceptance and rejection in that it emphasizes the subjective experience of individuals within interpersonal relationships and recognizes that individuals' perceptions of acceptance and rejection may not always align with objective reality (Rohner, 2021). What matters most is how individuals interpret and internalize the behaviors of significant others in their lives. Regardless of whether caregivers intend to convey accepting or rejecting messages, it is individuals' interpretations of these messages that influence their social, emotional, and cognitive development (Rohner, 1986, 2004, 2021). Research on AET similarly suggests that vocalic differences in message delivery determine whether a message feels affectionate regardless of how it was intended (Floyd & Ray, 2003). Thus, effective communication is vital for those seeking to enhance affection/acceptance to create and maintain individual and relational well-being.

The concept of *affection deprivation* in AET—the state of wanting greater levels of affectionate communication than is being received (Floyd, 2014; Hesse & Mikkelson, 2017)—is reflected in IPARTheory's concept of *rejection* on the acceptance-rejection continuum. Additionally, both affection deprivation and feelings of social rejection are associated with increased physical pain and poor sleep quality (Floyd, 2016; see also Miller & Ali, 2025; Chapter 12, this book).

On the other hand, both AET and IPARTheory advocate for warm and positive communication in relationships. Floyd (2015), for example, argued that successful interpersonal relationships are "initiated and maintained through the exchange of affectionate behaviors" (p. 309). Denes et al. (2017) argued that affection is an observable behavior that can be an expression of warmth as conceptualized as IPARTheory's warmth dimension. Warm/positive communication leads to better psychological adjustment which is associated with healthy interpersonal relationships (Khaleque & Ali, 2017).

Finally, both AET and IPARTheory are interested in the way in which parental communication influences offspring's development (Floyd, 2001; Rohner, 1986, 2004, 2021). As already noted, for example, evidence from research in IPARTheory has shown that individuals who perceive themselves to be rejected by significant others tend worldwide to develop the acceptance-rejection syndrome. This in turn tends to be associated with the development of *rejection sensitivity* (i.e., hypervigilance and hypersensitivity to rejection by others; Ibrahim et al., 2015; Rohner et al., 2023). Further, both IPARTheory and AET suggest that individuals who experience affection deprivation are more likely to experience depression and loneliness (Floyd & Hesse, 2017; Rohner et al., 2020). Such experiences are likely to influence patterns of affectionate communication such that those who feel rejected are less likely to communicate affectionately in future relationships.

Differences Between AET and IPARTheory

Although AET and IPARTheory have similarities, identifying differences is likely to enhance their utility and practical application. AET focuses heavily on the role of evolution and physiology and uses biological samples to measure stress. It also employs experimental and intervention-based research, qualitative research, and self-report questionnaires. IPARTheory also recognizes the evolutionary foundations of affection/acceptance. Unlike AET, however, the fundamental assumptions of IPARTheory have undergone rigorous testing and validation through eight distinct methodologies (Rohner, 2021; see also Rohner & Ali, 2025; Chapter 1, this book). These approaches can be grouped into three overarching clusters: (1) quantitative psychological studies, comprising interviews, behavior observations, self-report questionnaires translated and adapted in 78 languages internationally, holocultural studies, and meta-analyses; (2) ethnographic studies such as ethnographic case studies, and controlled comparison or concomitant variation studies; and (3) neurobiological studies using brain imaging techniques (Rohner, 2021).

IPARTheory investigates the effects of individual and cultural variations and universality in human behavior. AET is beginning to focus on matters such as these (Denes et al., 2017; Floyd, 2014; Mansson et al., 2023). IPARTheory suggests that individuals across cultures possess an innate need for feeling accepted in attachment relationships. However, the way in which individuals communicate and respond to acceptance and rejection varies somewhat from one culture to another (Denes et al., 2017; Rohner, 1986, 2021). IPARTheory's coping subtheory suggests that individual differences influence the way in which individuals respond to acceptance-rejection. For example, individuals with the ability to depersonalize, maintain a differentiated sense of self, and who are self-determined are more adept at responding less negatively in contexts of rejection (Rohner, 1986). Although AET also suggests that individuals vary in terms of their responses to less-than-optimal levels for affection (Floyd, 2018), it does not directly explain how optimal levels are developed or demonstrate why some individuals are better at responding to the lack of affectionate communication than others. Thus, IPARTheory may be helpful in explaining cultural and individual-level variations in reactions to affection and in so doing, complement AET research.

Conversely, AET is unique in its examination of *excessive affection*. AET suggests that when individuals receive more affection than they desire, adverse physiological effects are likely to occur (Hesse & Mikkelson, 2021). Although receiving excessive affection is thought to be better than affection deprivation (Hesse et al., 2023), both excessive affection and affection deprivation are likely to increase feelings of anxiety, depression, and loneliness. Understanding the effect of excessive affection may be useful as IPARTheory attempts to further explain why some individuals who grow up in supportive homes still develop maladaptive characteristics.

Additionally, IPARTheory focuses on the consequences, causes, and other correlates of interpersonal acceptance-rejection, whereas AET examines experiences and expressions of affection communication. Denes et al. (2017), for example, argued that IPARTheory may benefit from AET's focus on *giving* affection versus receiving it. Research in AET shows that the ability to give affection has health benefits over and above the benefits of *receiving* affection (Denes et al., 2017; Floyd et al., 2005). Thus, intervention-based research on the assumptions of AET may benefit IPARTheory by explaining additional ways to improve adult relationships even when childhood relationships were not optimal.

IPARTheory has a cradle-to-grave perspective. This perspective is supported by longitudinal studies demonstrating that individuals' perceptions of acceptance and rejection during childhood have long-lasting effects on their psychological functioning, well-being, as well as future relationships across the lifespan (see Lansford, 2025, Chapter 7, this book). AET is beginning to investigate the effects of affectional communication on relational quality over a period of time (Van Raalte et al., 2021).

Practical Applications of AET an IPARTheory

Practical Applications of AET

AET demonstrates the way in which healthy relationships can improve individual health, by reducing stress. Experiences of affection have consistently demonstrated the ability to reduce stress and improve mental and physical health (Hesse et al., 2020). Given its bio-evolutionary foundations, AET research often focuses on physiological markers to highlight these connections. For example, Floyd (2023) demonstrated that individuals who kiss a romantic partner seven or more times each month experience lower levels of stress than those who kiss six or fewer times each month. Stress, in turn, positively influences triglyceride levels that increase the likelihood of other physical health problems. Furthermore, even if an individual is unable to receive affectionate touch, giving verbal affection has been shown to similarly reduce physiological stress markers and improve resting heart rate, Immunoglobulin A, Immunoglobulin G, and Lymphocytes (Floyd, 2007; Floyd et al., 2018a, 2018b). IPARTheory, on the other hand, hasn't conducted intervention-based research of this sort. However, IPARTheory research has found that rejection experiences are associated with medical problems like allergies, asthma, metabolic abnormality, periodontal disease, ulcers (Rohner, 2021) and childhood obesity (Senese et al., 2020). Physical health problems associated with experiences of interpersonal acceptance-rejection are discussed in detail by Ali et al., 2025, Chapter 10 of this book.

AET has also been used to test the effects of affection on mental and physical health in ways other than physiological markers. For example, Salazar et al. (2022) indicated that affection received from grandparents increases the likelihood that grandchildren will engage in healthy activities such as physical workouts. At the same time, Mansson (2014) indicated that grandparents who give affection decreased their own feelings of loneliness and stress and improved their overall mental health. It appears that giving affection changes one's mental outlook as well as their physiology. Individuals who are able to give affection are more likely to engage with the world in positive ways. As a result, they are more likely to experience improved mental health, self-esteem, social engagement, and overall life satisfaction (Floyd, 2002).

Horan (2012) noted that affectionate communication helps individuals get through relational transgressions, particularly by reducing episodes of rumination and hurt feelings. Mansson et al. (2017) argued that affection enhances feelings of shared identity among family members. More specifically, research findings demonstrate that individuals are more likely to exhibit affection in relationships that fulfill superordinate goals. For example, Floyd and Morman (2003) found that fathers displayed more affection toward biological children than for stepchildren. Similarly, Floyd and Morr (2003) noted that adults are more likely to demonstrate affection toward biological siblings than sibling in-laws. Thus, affection influences and is influenced by both relational health and the likelihood that superordinate goals will be achieved.

Practical Applications of IPARTheory

IPARTheory's major postulates have been tested on every continent of the world except Antarctica. Results indicate that individuals experience and respond to messages of acceptance-rejection similarly across cultures. Such universal replicability implies that feelings of acceptance may fill a fundamental human need (Khaleque & Ali, 2017). Because of the worldwide near-invariance of individuals' responses to perceptions of rejection by significant others, researchers and practitioners transculturally often use evidence from IPARTheory and its associated self-report measures in applied contexts including in court systems, protective services systems, parent education programs, and clinical settings, among others.

As noted previously, many studies grounded in IPARTheory focus on acceptance-rejection in parent-child relationships. Such research is useful in improving the strength of parent-child relationships and in turn improving the health of children as they grow into adulthood. For example, Allred (2020) utilized IPARTheory to demonstrate how excessive parental phone usage can cause children to feel rejected. This subsequently increased the likelihood that the children would develop maladaptive behaviors that impaired their ability to create healthy relationships as adults (i.e., phone addiction and rejection sensitivity). These findings help parents improve communication by increasing their understanding of the way in which phone usage is perceived by their children. Other useful studies suggest that inconsistency in expressions of acceptance between parents (i.e., when one parent is significantly more or less accepting than the other) has a negative effect on adolescent adjustment (Miranda et al., 2016). Memories of those inconsistencies contribute to the development of rejection sensitivity (Ibrahim et al., 2015; Rohner et al., 2023).

Extending the Conversation

Work remains to better articulate the ways in which AET and IPARTheory influence individuals and relationships. For example, Denes et al. (2017) called for IPARTheory researchers to take a deeper look into the complexities of affectionate communication such as excessive affection and deceptive affection. Horan and Booth-Butterfield (2013) noted that individuals frequently express affection in ways that are inauthentic because of motivations for self-preservation or relationship management. Thus, despite the numerous benefits of affection, there is also a potential dark side to affection wherein individuals use affection deceitfully to manipulate or control their partners. IPARTheory may help to explain the effects of deceptive affection on perceptions of acceptance and rejection.

Thus, AET and IPARTheory will continue to extend contemporary knowledge surrounding the influence of messages/communication of inclusion/warmth and value in interpersonal relationships. When combined, these theories help explain why humans developed a need for affection, how childhood relationships and cultural influences impact patterns of affectionate communication, how messages of affection/acceptance may enhance mental and physical health as well as relationships, and ways in which individuals can heal from rejection and affection deprivation. Though each theory stands well on its own, researchers and practitioners can gain a broader perspective on messages of warmth when they include AET's distinctive literature on affection with IPARTheory's larger view on messages of acceptance-rejection. AET expands the concept of acceptance and opens additional research avenues by suggesting that not all affection is good affection. AET also benefits from IPARTheory in that the cultural nuances of acceptance-rejection may help explain additional variances in the use of affection to achieve superordinate goals. As scholars continue to use these theories in concert with one another, while also utilizing additional methodologies (i.e., neurobiological, physiological, and sociocultural), future research will provide additional insight into the way in which these prosocial messages can improve individual and relational health.

Summary

AET and IPARTheory are aimed at improving relationship quality and emotional well-being. By understanding the role of affection and interpersonal perceptions, practitioners can develop strategies for enhancing communication, resolving conflicts, and fostering intimacy in relationships. In summary, AET by Kory Floyd and IPARTheory by Ronald P. Rohner share the vision of a greater understanding of human behavior and relationships. Through their focus on affectionate communication, interpersonal dynamics, and relationship processes, they contribute to a deeper understanding of relational phenomena and inform interventions aimed at promoting healthier relationships.

References

Ali, S., Rohner, R. P., & Britner, P. A. (2025). Memories of parental rejection childhood predict medical problems in adulthood. In Rohner, R.P., & Ali. S. (Eds.). *Global perspectives on parental acceptance & rejection: Lessons learned from IPARTheory* (pp. 120–135). Routledge.

Allred, R. J., (2020). *Cell phone presence, phubbing, and rejection: Antecedents and effects of cell phone usage during face-to-face communication* (Publication No. 2569) [Doctoral dissertations, University of Connecticut]. Open Commons. https://digitalcommons.lib.uconn.edu/cgi/viewcontent.cgi?article=8918&context=dissertations

Denes, A., Bennett, M., & Winkler, K. L. (2017). Exploring the benefits of affectionate communication: Implications for interpersonal acceptance–rejection theory. *Journal of Family Theory & Review, 9*(4), 491–506.

Floyd, K. (2001). Human affection exchange: I. Reproductive probability as a predictor of men's affection with their sons. *Journal of Men's Studies, 10,* 39–50. https://doi.org/10.3149/jms.1001.39

Floyd, K. (2002). Human affection exchange: V. Attributes of the highly affectionate. *Communication Quarterly, 50*(2), 135–152.

Floyd, K. (2006). *Communicating affection: Interpersonal behavior and social context.* Cambridge University Press.

Floyd, K. (2007). Human affection exchange: XII. Affectionate communication is associated with diurnal variation in salivary free cortisol. *Western Journal of Communication, 70*(1), 47–63.

Floyd, K. (2014). Relational and health correlates of affection deprivation. *Western Journal of Communication, 78,* 383–403. 10.1080/10570314.2014.927071

Floyd, K. (2015). Affection exchange theory. In C. R. Berger & M. E. Roloff (Eds.), *The international encyclopedia of interpersonal communication* (pp. 24–31). Malden, MA: Wiley Blackwell.

Floyd, K. (2016) Affection deprivation is associated with physical pain and poor sleep quality. *Communication Studies, 67,* 4, 379–398. 10.1080/10510974.2016.1205641

Floyd, K. (2018). *Affectionate communication in close relationships.* Cambridge University Press.

Floyd, K. (2023). Lipidemic effects of kissing are mediated by stress: results from a national probability sample. *Health Communication, 38*(10), 2026–2034.

Floyd, K., & Hesse, C. (2017). Affection deprivation is conceptually and empirically distinct from loneliness. *Western Journal of Communication, 81*(4), 446–465.

Floyd, K., Hesse, C., & Generous, M. A. (2018a). Affection exchange theory: A bio-evolutionary look at affectionate communication. In D. O. Braithwaite, E. A. Suter, & K. Floyd (Eds.), *Engaging theories in family communication: Multiple perspectives* (2nd ed., pp. 17–26). Routledge. https://doi.org/10.4324/9781315204321

Floyd, K., Hesse, C., & Generous, M. A. (2021). Affection exchange theory: A bio-evolutionary look at affectionate communication. In D. O. Braithwaite, E. A. Suter, & K. Floyd (Eds.), *Engaging theories in family communication: Multiple perspectives* (3rd ed., pp. 27–38). Routledge.

Floyd, K., Hess, J. A., Miczo, L. A., Halone, K. K., Mikkelson, A. C., & Tusing, K. J. (2005). Human affection exchange: VIII. Further evidence of the benefits of expressed affection. *Communication Quarterly, 53,* 285–303. https://doi.org/10.1080 01463370500101071
Floyd, K., & Morman, M. T. (2003). Human affection exchange: II. Affectionate communication in father-son relationships. *The Journal of Social Psychology, 143*(5), 599–612.
Floyd, K., & Morr, M. C. (2003). Human affection exchange: VII. Affectionate communication in the sibling/spouse/sibling-in-law triad. *Communication Quarterly, 51*(3), 247–261.
Floyd, K., Pauley, P. M., Hesse, C., Eden, J., Veksler, A. E., & Woo, N. T. (2018b). Supportive communication is associated with markers of immunocompetence. *Southern Communication Journal, 83*(4), 229–244.
Floyd, K., & Ray, G. B. (2003). Human affection exchange: IV. Vocalic predictors of perceived affection in initial interactions. *Western Journal of Communication (includes Communication Reports), 67*(1), 56–73.
Hesse, C., Floyd, K., Rains, S. A., Mikkelson, A. C., Pauley, P. M., Woo, N. T., Custer, B. E., & Duncan, K. L. (2020). Affectionate communication and health: A meta-analysis. *Communication Monographs, 88*(2), 194–218. https://doi.org/10.1080/03637751.2020.1805480
Hesse, C., Floyd, K., & Mikkelson, A. C. (2023). Affection deprivation is more aversive than excessive affection: A test of affection exchange theory. *Personal Relationships, 30*(1), 296–313.
Hesse, C., & Mikkelson, A. C. (2017). Affection deprivation in romantic relationships. *Communication Quarterly, 65*(1), 20–38.
Hesse, C., & Mikkelson, A. (2021). Relational and health correlates of excessive affection. *Communication Quarterly, 69*(3), 320–340.
Horan, S. M. (2012). Affection exchange theory and perceptions of relational transgressions. *Western Journal of Communication, 76*(2), 109–126.
Horan, S. M., & Booth-Butterfield, M. (2013). Understanding the routine expression of deceptive affection in romantic relationships. *Communication Quarterly, 61*(2), 195–216.
Ibrahim, D. M., Rohner, R. P., Smith, R. L., & Flannery, K. M. (2015). Adults' remembrances of parental acceptance–rejection in childhood predict current rejection sensitivity in adulthood. *Family and Consumer Sciences Research Journal, 44*(1), 51–62.
Khaleque, A., & Ali, S. (2017). A systematic review of meta-analyses of research on interpersonal acceptance–rejection theory: Constructs and measures. *Journal of Family Theory & Review, 9*(4), 441–458.
Lansford, J. E. (2025). Developmental correlates of parental acceptance-rejection from childhood to adulthood in nine countries. In R. P. Rohner & S. Ali, (Eds.), *Global perspectives on parental acceptance and rejection: Lessons learned from IPARTheory* (pp. 136–152). Routledge.
Mansson, D. H. (2014). Grandparents' expressed affection for their grandchildren: examining the grandparents' own psychological health. *Communication Research Reports, 31*(4), 329–338.
Mansson, D. H., Floyd, K., & Soliz, J. (2017). Affectionate communication is associated with emotional and relational resources in the grandparent-grandchild relationship. *Journal of Intergenerational Relationships, 15*(2), 85–103.
Mansson, D. H., Marko, F., Gajdošíková Zeleiová, J., & Floyd, K. (2023). Testing the cultural scope of affection exchange theory in Slovakia. *Journal of Intercultural Communication Research,* 1–10.

Miranda, M. C., Affuso, G., Esposito, C., & Bacchini, D. (2016). Parental acceptance–rejection and adolescent maladjustment: Mothers' and fathers' combined roles. *Journal of Child and Family Studies, 25*, 1352–1362.

Miller, J., & Ali. S. (2025). Effect of early life stress on adolescent brain development. In R. P. Rohner & S. Ali, (Eds.), *Global perspectives on parental acceptance and rejection: Lessons learned from IPARTheory* (pp. 225–245). Routledge.

Rohner, R. P. (1960). *Child acceptance-rejection and modal personality in three Pacific societies*. M.A. Thesis, Stanford University.

Rohner, R. P. (1986). *The warmth dimension: Foundations of parental acceptance–rejection theory*. Beverly Hills, CA: Sage.

Rohner, R. P. (2004). The parental "acceptance–rejection syndrome": Universal correlates of perceived rejection. *American Psychologist*, 59, 830– 840. https://doi.org/10.1037/0003-066X.59.8.830

Rohner, R. P. (2021). Introduction to interpersonal acceptance-rejection theory (IPARTheory) and evidence. *Online Readings in Psychology and Culture*, 6(1), 1–65.

Rohner, R. P. & Ali, S. (2025). Interpersonal acceptance-rejection theory (IPARTheory): From conception to maturity. In Rohner, R. P., & Ali. S. (Eds.). *Global perspectives on parental acceptance & rejection: Lessons learned from IPARTheory* (pp. 3–38). Routledge.

Rohner, R. P., Ali, S., Filus, A., Senese, V. P., Molaver, A., Ahmed, R. A., … Britner, P. A. (2023). Reliability and validity of the interpersonal rejection sensitivity scale: a multicultural study. *Current Psychology*, 1–11.

Rohner, R. P., Putnick, D. L., Molaver, A. D., Ali, S., Butt, M. M., Ibrahim, D. M., … Senese, V. P. (2020). Psychological maladjustment mediates the link between remembrances of parental rejection in childhood and loneliness in adulthood: A cross-cultural comparative study. *International Journal of Psychology, 55*(4), 590–600.

Salazar, L. R., Khandelwal, P., & Castillo, Y. (2022). The effects of received grandmothers' affection on adult grandchildren's health behaviors using affection exchange theory. *BMC Public Health, 22*(1), 714.

Senese, V. P., Pezzella, M., Pasquariello, L., Ali, S., & Rohner, R. P. (2020). Effects of social exclusion and maternal rejection on Children's high-caloric food consumption. *Appetite, 145*, 104494.

Van Raalte, L. J., Floyd, K., & Mongeau, P. A. (2021). The effects of cuddling on relational quality for married couples: A longitudinal investigation. *Western Journal of Communication, 85*(1), 61–82.

PART II

Long-Term Effects of Parental Acceptance-Rejection in Childhood

5

INFLUENCE OF PARENTAL ACCEPTANCE-REJECTION ON ADULT INTIMATE RELATIONSHIPS

Abdul Khaleque

Intimacy refers to an individual's emotionally deep personal relationship with another person. Hatfield (1984) identified three components of intimacy: Cognitive component—willingness of intimate partners to disclose important information with one another; Emotional component—involves partners' deep feelings, love, care, and concern for one another; and, Physical component—consists of partners feeling comfortable and enjoyment in close physical proximity and contact. Similarly, Sherman and Thelen (1996) argued that intimacy has the following three essential elements: (1) deep feelings—very close and deeply personal relationship between partners characterized by emotional attachment, warmth, affection, and love; (2) unique importance—each partner is uniquely important to the other and interchangeable with none; (3) communication—exchange of close personal information between partners. The authors agreed that the coexistence of these elements is necessary for the existence of intimacy. The authors also thought that individuals are likely to be vulnerable or at risk of being emotionally hurt when they cannot freely exchange and share their thoughts and feelings with individuals who are highly valued to them.

Two distinctly different types of intimacy elicit different emotions and behaviors among intimate partners. They are non-romantic intimacy between parents and children, or between friends, and romantic intimacy between intimate partners (Khaleque, 2018). Intimate relationships can form, develop, and change throughout adult life from young adulthood to middle adulthood, and into late adulthood. These changes are generally related to physical, psychological, and social changes of the

DOI: 10.4324/9781003441243-7

individual. The essential elements of both romantic and non-romantic adult intimacy are based on emotional involvement and close personal relationships characterized by warmth, affection, love, care, and concern for the partner, and by responsiveness to the needs of the intimate partner (Harvey & Omarzu, 1997; Mikulincer & Shaver, 2008; Prager et al., 2013; Reis & Patrick, 1996; Rohner, 2008). In addition, the elements of intimate relationships also include trust, confidence, commitment, interdependence, mutual acceptance, self-disclose, and feeling of joy when one is with the partner and distress when separated from the partner (Berscheid et al., 2004; Collins & Miller, 1994; Hazan & Shaver, 1987; Mikulincer & Shaver, 2007).

An intimate partner can be an *attachment figure* or a *significant other* (Khaleque, 2001). A *significant other* is a person with whom one has a relatively long-lasting and important emotional bond and who is considered to be a unique, irreplaceable person, interchangeable with no one else (Rohner, 2023; Rohner & Khaleque, 2010). An *attachment figure*, on the other hand, is a significant other with whom one has a uniquely important emotional bond where the individual's sense of emotional security, comfort, and well-being are dependent to some degree on the quality of the relationship with the significant other (Ainsworth, 1989, 1991, Rohner, 2023).

Dynamics of Intimate Relationships

As the nature of intimate relationships changes from casual to close, the relationships become increasingly multi-dimensional. Several researchers (Cassidy & Shaver, 2008; Feeney, 2008; Perlman & Duck, 1987) have suggested that the following transformations take place in these relationships:

1. The frequency and length of interactions increase.
2. Individuals develop more in-depth knowledge and understanding of the personality and behavior of their partners.
3. Individuals gain more skills to identify and predict partners' opinions and behaviors.
4. Partners tend to increase their investment in their intimate partner.
5. Partners' interdependence and sense of belongingness to one another increase.
6. The magnitude of positive feelings such as liking, loving, caring, commitment, and trust toward one another increases.
7. Partners increasingly feel like staying in close proximity and avoiding separation.
8. The strength of intimacy increases as the partners perceive their relationships as unique and irreplaceable.

Dimensions of Intimate Relationships

Some authors have suggested that dimensions of intimate relationships expand to the following domains of life with the growth of intimacy (Augusburger, 1988; Chapman, 2004; Rohner & Khaleque, 2005):

1 ***Physical intimacy*** includes a variety of physical interactions between partners such as hugging, kissing, fondling, and sexual intercourse. But physical intimacy is neither limited to sexual intercourse nor does it end with it.
2 ***Emotional intimacy*** refers to a positive attachment relationship expressed with feelings and behaviors characterized by warmth, affection, love, care, concern, and support for one another. Emotional intimacy is also reflected by the spontaneity, comfort, and ease with which each partner can respond emotionally to the other partner. Emotional intimacy is a psychological phenomenon that can be achieved when the level of trust and confidence between the two partners fosters the mutual sharing of one another's deepest selves in a way that the partners can share their dreams, goals, and aspirations without the fear of losing emotional intimacy. Emotional intimacy is different from sexual intimacy because sexual intimacy can take place with or without emotional intimacy, and emotional intimacy can occur with or without sexual intimacy. Partners may experience difficult moments, with uncertainty and the risk of losing the intimate relationship. But this risk can be overcome with patience, free and sincere communication of feelings reflecting how much each partner cares for the other (Reis, 2013).

Conflict and Crisis Management in Intimate Relationships

Conflict and crisis management in intimacy depends on partners' attitudes and ability to compromise and sort out differences fairly and amicably and to reach mutually agreeable and satisfactory solutions. The most important factor that can enhance conflict and crisis management in intimacy is to recognize and accept the fact that there are no perfect and completely problem-free intimate relationships. Like any other relationship, an enduring and stable intimate relationship is more difficult to maintain than to form. Continuous monitoring, understanding, and mutual respect for partners are required to make the relationship workable and enjoyable (Khaleque, 2018).

Interpersonal Acceptance-Rejection Theory and Adult Intimate Relationships

Interpersonal acceptance-rejection theory (IPARTheory) is an evidence-based theory of socialization and lifespan human development. The theory aims to predict and explain major consequences, causes, and other correlates of interpersonal acceptance and rejection worldwide—across ethnicities, genders, cultures, and geographical boundaries. A detailed description of concepts and measures used to assess the theory's assumptions and-practical implications can be found in Rohner and Ali (2025; Chapter 1, this book).

Historically, IPARTheory focused mainly on parental acceptance and rejection. But research limited solely to parental acceptance-rejection could not provide comprehensive answers to questions about the effects of all forms of interpersonal relationships on individuals' psychosocial development throughout the lifespan. Thus, IPARTheory gradually expanded beyond its initial focus on *parental* acceptance-rejection to all aspects of *interpersonal* acceptance and rejection, including intimate partner relationships. Eventually, that led to the change of the theory's name from *parental* acceptance-rejection theory (PARTheory) to *interpersonal* acceptance-rejection theory (IPARTheory). This change of name was associated with a major reconceptualization of the theory, which now postulates that perceived rejection by an attachment figure at any point in life tends to be associated with the same cluster of personality dispositions found among rejected children (Rohner, 2014, 2021).

Although parents are generally major attachment figures for children, intimate partners are likely to be the major attachment figures for adults. A great deal of international IPARTheory research (Rohner & Khaleque, 2010) shows that parental acceptance-rejection as well as partner acceptance-rejection are associated with a specific constellation of ten personality dispositions including anxiety, emotional insecurity, hostility/aggression, dependency, impaired self-esteem, impaired self-adequacy, emotional unresponsiveness, emotional instability, negative worldview, and cognitive distortions. Together these dispositions constitute a measure of psychological maladjustment called the acceptance-rejection syndrome in IPARTheory (Rohner, 2004).

The first study to test IPARTheory's expanded postulate was conducted in 2001 (Khaleque, 2001). That study tested the impact of perceived acceptance-rejection by intimate male partners on the psychological adjustment of adult female partners. It also explored the effects of remembered childhood experiences of maternal and paternal acceptance on the relation between current partner acceptance and women's adjustment. Analyses revealed that women's adjustment was impaired to the degree that they experienced their intimate partners to be rejecting. Additionally, results showed that both partners' acceptance and paternal acceptance had a significantly greater impact on women's psychological adjustment than maternal acceptance (Khaleque & Rohner, 2004; Rohner & Khaleque, 2008). This path-breaking study sparked a great deal of international interest in IPARTheory.

Influence of Parental Acceptance-Rejection in Childhood on Adult Intimate Relationships

As already observed, the experience of parental rejection in childhood tends to be associated with emotional unresponsiveness, impaired self-esteem, and negative worldview, where rejected persons tend to perceive interpersonal relationships as being psychologically and emotionally unsafe, untrustworthy, and negative in other ways (Rohner & Lansford, 2017). Such individuals are also likely to develop a fear of intimacy (Rohner et al., 2019; Thelen et al. 2000).

Several IPARTheory studies have shown that childhood experiences of parental acceptance-rejection significantly mediate intimate relationships and adults' psychological adjustment (e.g., Aracı-İyiaydın et al. 2023; Khaleque et al., 2008; Parmar et al., 2008; Chyung & Lee, 2008; Varan et al., 2008). For example, in a sample of 354 married adults in Bangladesh, Khaleque et al. (2013) showed that the more accepting both men and women perceived their spouses to be, the better their psychological adjustment tended to be. Additionally, the more accepting both men and women remembered their parents to have been during childhood, the better was their current psychological adjustment. Multiple regression analyses revealed that *paternal* acceptance mediated the relation between perceived spouse acceptance and the psychological adjustment of both men and women, and the remembered maternal acceptance mediated the relation between men's (but not women's) perception of spouse acceptance and psychological adjustment. Several other IPARTheory studies support conclusions such as these (e.g., Khaleque, 2012, 2018; Ripoll-Nunez & Alvarez, 2008; Rohner et al., 2008; Rohner & Melendez, 2008). Rohner and Khaleque's (2010) meta-analysis of 17 cross-cultural studies involving 3,568 adults in 10 nations showed that perceived partner acceptance in adulthood and remembered paternal and maternal acceptance in childhood tended to correlate strongly with the current psychological adjustment of both men and women across all studies. The meta-analysis also showed that the perception of rejection by an intimate partner in adulthood and remembered parental rejection in childhood are associated with the same form of psychological maladjustment found among children who experienced rejection by their parents.

Effects of Paternal Versus Maternal Acceptance-Rejection in Childhood on Intimate Relationships of Adult Sons and Daughters

A substantial body of research that includes two meta-analyses shows that paternal acceptance-rejection in childhood often has as strong or even stronger effects on adult offsprings' psychological and social development than does maternal acceptance-rejection (Ali et al., 2015; Khaleque &

Rohner, 2013). In addition, parental rejection—especially paternal rejection in the forms of neglect and love withdrawal—has consistent effects on psychological maladjustment and behavioral malfunctioning of both children and adult offspring worldwide (Khaleque, 2021; Sultana & Khaleque, 2016). Results of another study (Khaleque et al., 2013) show that remembered paternal acceptance during childhood and partner acceptance during adulthood have significant independent effects on the psychological adjustment of both adult men and women. But, remember, maternal acceptance has an independent effect on the psychological adjustment of men but not on women. These findings are consistent with the findings of a growing body of cross-cultural research showing that perceived paternal acceptance often has great and sometimes greater impact on child and adult development than does perceived maternal acceptance (Parmar & Rohner, 2005, Parmar et al., 2008; Rohner 1998; Schwartz & Rubel-Lifschitz, 2009; Veneziano, 2008; see Akun, 2025; Chapter 9, this book).

To build a cumulative body of generalizable cross-cultural knowledge about parental acceptance-rejection and intimate adult relationships, Rohner (2008) analyzed 14 studies across cultures. The findings revealed that perceived partner acceptance and remembered parental (both maternal and paternal) acceptance in childhood correlated significantly with men's and women's psychological adjustment in all cultures considered. The findings further revealed that women, intimate partners, and fathers, but not mothers, often make independent contributions to psychological adjustment. However, predictors for men's psychological adjustment were much more variable. Based on these findings, Rohner observed:

> Unlike for women, no simple conclusion can be drawn about cross-cultural trends for men. More work must be done within individual nations cross-culturally to try to understand why intimate partners—or one parent versus the other—sometimes tend to drop out as unique predictors of men's and women's psychological adjustment.
>
> *(Rohner, 2008, p. 10)*

Several IPARTheory researchers, however, have offered explanations for the greater impact of paternal acceptance-rejection than maternal acceptance-rejection on offspring's psychological adjustment/maladjustment. One such explanation pertains to offspring's perceptions of paternal versus maternal power and prestige within the family. Specifically, Carrasco and Rohner (2012) reported that if offspring perceive their fathers as being more powerful in the family than their mothers, the offspring tend to be more influenced by their fathers' behaviors than by their mothers' behaviors.

However, if offspring perceive their mothers to be more powerful in the family than their fathers, then they tend to be more influenced by their mothers' behaviors. A study by Khaleque et al. (2010) showed that Bangladeshi adults who remembered their fathers as having higher power and prestige than their mothers reported better psychological adjustment than respondents who reported their fathers to have lower power and prestige than their mothers. After analyzing the results of 13 studies in 11 nations, Rohner & Carrasco (2014) later concluded that offspring's perceptions of parental power and prestige tend to moderate the relationship between perceived parental acceptance-rejection and their psychological adjustment. Depending on the perceived difference between paternal versus maternal power and prestige the authors concluded:

> Fathers' acceptance sometimes has a greater impact on the psychological adjustment of youth than do offspring's perceptions of their mothers' acceptance. Sometimes, however, offspring's perceptions of their mothers' acceptance have a greater impact on adjustment than do offspring's perceptions of their fathers' acceptance.
>
> *(Rohner & Carrasco, 2014, p. 1)*

Fear of Intimacy (FOI)

Fear of intimacy (FOI) in IPARTheory refers to conditions where individuals are fearful or anxious about forming a personal or intimate relationship with another person, especially a person who is emotionally important to them (Rohner, 2023). In other words, fear of intimacy is a subdued capacity of individuals to freely exchange or communicate deep personal thoughts and emotional feelings with an intimate partner because of anxiety (Descutner & Thelen, 1991).

These conclusions are supported by Emmons and Colby (1995) who found that individuals with a fear of intimacy had difficulty sharing personal information, and intimate feelings such as feelings of distress.

Evidence from a substantial body of IPARTheory research reveals that adults' memories of childhood rejection tend worldwide to be a major factor associated with the development of the fear of intimacy. For example, studies conducted in Bangladesh (Uddin et al., 2016), Croatia (Glavak-Tkalic et al., 2016), Greece (Giovazolias & Giotsa, 2016), Iran (Mousavi et al., 2023), Pakistan (Butt et al., 2016; Khaleque, et al., 2018), Turkey (Aracı-İyiaydın et al., 2023), and the USA (Ibrahim et al., 2015; Lindsey & Khan, 2016) confirm that experiences of parental rejection in childhood have a significant relationship with the development of the fear of intimacy in adulthood. However, a more nuanced multicultural study of 3,483 young adults in 13 nations by Rohner et al. (2019) concluded that, as expected, adults' memories of maternal and paternal rejection in childhood independently predicted fear of intimacy among both men and women in all countries. However, memories of maternal rejection were significantly stronger predictors of fear of intimacy than were memories of paternal rejection across both genders. Additionally, results confirmed the prediction that psychological maladjustment partially mediated the relation between memories of maternal and paternal rejection and adults' fear of intimacy in all 13 countries and both genders.

Psychological maladjustment tends to be a significant concomitant of the fear of intimacy. Descutner and Thelen (1991) and Hook (2003), for example, reported individuals who are high in FOI have a greater probability of being psychologically maladjusted, anxious, depressed, and having lower self-esteem than individuals who are low in FOI. In addition, Lloyd et al. (2011) concluded that adults who had two caring parents in childhood reported much lower levels of fear of intimacy than adults who had only one caring parent or no caring parent in childhood. In addition, researchers have also found that fear of intimacy and intimacy deficits are associated with many other undesirable outcomes in adulthood, including marital dissatisfaction, rape, and child molestation (Besharat et al., 2014; Bumby & Hansen, 1997).

Conclusion

To sum up, the studies reported in this chapter indicate that the childhood experience of parental acceptance-rejection is likely to have a lifelong effect on adult intimate relationships and psychological adjustment. Paternal acceptance, however, tends to have a stronger effect than maternal acceptance, depending on children's perceptions of higher paternal than maternal power and prestige in the family. Compared to other forms of interpersonal relationships, adult intimate relationships are more difficult to maintain than to form. Enduring and stable intimate relationships require continuous patience, tolerance, understanding, and mutual respect for partners to make the relationship stable and enjoyable. Individuals' fear of intimacy in adulthood tends to originate from perceived rejection by parents during childhood. Last, there needs to be more research on cultural influences on intimate relationships, especially adult intimate relationships, and psychological adjustment. Researchers should focus more on this critical area of human behavioral development and psychological adjustment.

References

Ainsworth, M. (1989). Attachment beyond infancy. *American Psychologist, 44*, 709–716.

Ainsworth, M. (1991). Attachment and other affectional bonds across the life cycle. In C. M. Parkes, J. Stevenson-Hinde, & P. Marris (Eds.), *Attachment across the life cycle* (pp. 33–51). New York: Routledge.

Akun, E. (2025). Gender inconsistencies in parental acceptance-rejection and on the effects of acceptance-rejection. In R. P. Rohner and S. Ali (Eds.), *Global perspectives on parental acceptance and rejection: Lessons learned from IPARTheory* (pp. 163–190). Routledge.

Ali, S., Khaleque, A., & Rohner, R. P. (2015). Pancultural gender differences in the relation between perceived parental acceptance and psychological adjustment of children and adult offspring: A meta-analytic review of worldwide research. *Journal of Cross-Cultural Psychology, 46*, 1059–1080.

Aracı-İyiaydın, A., Toplu-Demirtaş, E., Akçabozan-Kayabol, N. B., & Rohner, R. P. (2023). All you fear is love: The roles of rejection by intimate others. *Personal Relationships, 30*(2), 451–470.

Augusburger, D. (1988). *Sustaining Love*. Scottsdale, AZ: Regal Publishing.

Berscheid, E., Snyder, M., & Omoto, A. M. (2004). Measuring closeness: The relationship closeness inventory revisited. In D. J. Mashek & A. Aron (Eds.), *Handbook of closeness and intimacy* (pp. 81–101), Mahwah, NJ: Erlbaum.

Besharat MA, Naghshineh N, Ganji P, & Tavalaeyan T (2014) The moderating role of attachment styles on the relationship of alexithymia and fear of intimacy with marital satisfaction. *International Journal of Psychological Studies, 6*(3), 106–117.

Bumby, K. M., & Hansen, D.J. (1997). Intimacy deficits, fear of intimacy, and loneliness, among sexual offenders. *Criminal Justice and Behavior, 24*(3), 315–331.

Butt, M. M., Malik, F., & Faran M. (2016). Remembered parental acceptance rejection and fear of intimacy in married and unmarried men and women in Pakistan. In *Abstracts, 6th International Congress on Interpersonal Acceptance and Rejection, Psychology Faculty UNED, Madrid, Spain.*

Carrasco, M. A., & Rohner, R. P. (2012). Parental acceptance and children's psychological adjustment in the context of power and prestige. *Journal of Child and Family Studies, 22*(8), 1130–1137. https://doi.org/10.1007/s10826-012-9675-0

Cassidy, J., & Shaver, P. R. (Eds.) (2008). *Handbook of attachment: Theory, research and clinical applications*. New York: Guilford Publications.

Chapman, G. (2004). *Five love languages men's edition: The secret to love that lasts*. Bel Air, CA: Northfield Press.

Chyung, Y. J., & Lee, J. (2008). Intimate partner acceptance, remembered parental acceptance in childhood, and psychological adjustment among Korean college students in ongoing intimate relationships. In R. P. Rohner & T. Melendez (Eds.) Parental acceptance-rejection theory studies of intimate adult relationships. *Cross-Cultural Research, 42*(1), 77–86.

Collins, N. L., & Miller, L. C. (1994). Self-disclosure and liking: A meta-analytic review. *Psychological Bulletin, 116*, 457–475.

Descutner, C. J., & Thelen, M.H. (1991). Development and validation of a fear of intimacy scale. *Psychological Assessment, 3*, 218–225.

Emmons, R. A., & Colby, P. M. (1995). Emotional conflict and well-being: Relation to perceived availability, daily utilization, and observer reports of social support. *Journal of Personality and Social Psychology, 68*(5), 947–959.

Feeney, J. (2008). Adult romantic attachment: Developments in the study of couple relationships In J. Cassidy & P. Shaver (Eds.), *Handbook of attachment: Theory, research and clinical applications* (2nd ed., pp. 456–481). New York: The Guilford Press.

Giovazolias T. A., Giotsa, A. (2016) The mediating effect of psychological adjustment and anxiety in the relationship between parental acceptance-rejection and fear of intimacy in Greek young adults. *Abstracts, 6th International Congress on Interpersonal Acceptance and Rejection*, Psychology Faculty UNED, Madrid, Spain.

Glavak-Tkalic, R, Vulic-Prtoric, A., & Zoroja, A. (2016) Parental acceptance-rejection in childhood and fear of intimacy in adulthood among Croatian young adults: Moderating effects of anxiety and psychological adjustment. *Abstracts, 6th International Congress on Interpersonal Acceptance and Rejection*, Psychology Faculty UNED, Madrid, Spain.

Harvey, J. H., & Omarzu, J. (1997). Minding the close relationship. *Personality and Social Psychology Review, 1*(3), 224–240. https://doi.org/10.1207/s15327957pspr0103_3

Hatfield E (1984) The dangers of intimacy. In: V. Derlaga (Ed.), *Communication, intimacy, and close relationships* (pp. 207–220). New York: Academic Press, New York.

Hazan, C., & Shaver, P. (1987). Romantic love conceptualized as an attachment process. *Journal of Personality and Social Psychology, 52*, 511–524.

Hook M. K., Gerstein, L. H., Detterich, L., & Gridley, B. (2003) How close are we? Measuring intimacy and examining gender differences. *The Journal of Counseling & Development 81*(4), 462–472.

Ibrahim, D. M., Rohner, R. P., Smith, R. L., & Flannery, K. M. (2015). Adults' remembrances of parental acceptance– rejection in childhood predict current rejection sensitivity in adulthood. *Family and Consumer Sciences Research Journal, 44*(1), 51–62. DOI: 10.1111/fcsr.12119

Khaleque, A. (2001). *Parental acceptance-rejection, psychological adjustment, and intimate adult relationships*. Unpublished Master's thesis, University of Connecticut.

Khaleque, A. (2012). Adult Intimate Relationships and Psychological Adjustment. *Psychological Studies, 57*(1), 95–100

Khaleque, A. (2018). *Intimate relationships across the lifespan: Formation, development, enrichment, and maintenance*. Santa Barbara, California, and Denver, Colorado: ABC-CLIO/Praeger, USA.

Khaleque, A. (2021). Fathers' neglect of children. In T. D. Shackelford (Ed.), *The Sage handbook of domestic violence* (pp. 514–532). Thousand Oaks, California: Sage Publications.

Khaleque, A., Husain, S., Gul, S., & Zahra, S. (2018). Relations between remembered childhood parental acceptance-rejection, current fear of intimacy, and psychological adjustment among Pakistani adults. *Psychology and Behavioral Science International Journal, 10*(2), doi: 10.19080/PBSIJ.2018.10.555784

Khaleque, A. & Rohner, R. P. (2004). *Relations between partner and parental acceptance, behavioral control, and psychological adjustment among heterosexual adult women. Proceedings of the Society for Cross-Cultural Research Conference*, San Jose, California.

Khaleque, A., & Rohner, R. P. (2013). Effects of multiple acceptance and rejection on adult's psychological adjustment: A multi-cultural study. *Social Indicators Research, 113*, 393–399. doi: 10.1007/s11205

Khaleque, A., Rohner, R. P., & Laukkala, H. (2008) Intimate partner acceptance, parental acceptance, behavioral control, and psychological adjustment among Finnish adults in ongoing attachment relationships. *Cross-Cultural Research, 42*, 35–45.

Khaleque, A., Rohner, R.P., & Shirin, A. (2010, June 3–July, 28). *Impact of fathers' power, prestige, and love in Bangladreshi families. Third International Congress on Interpersonal Acceptance and Rejection*, Padua, Italy.

Khaleque, A., Shirin, A., & Uddin, M. K. (2013). Attachment relationships and psychological adjustment of married adults. *Social Indicators Research, 110*, 237–244.

Lindsey, C. R. & Khan, S. (2016). *Relationship among remembered parental acceptance, psychological adjustment, anxiety, and the fear of intimacy among African American college students. Abstracts, 6th International Congress on Interpersonal Acceptance and Rejection Psychology Faculty UNED*, Madrid, Spain.

Lloyd, J., Moore, K., Rohner, R. P. (2011) Analysis of the Adult Parental Power-Prestige Questionnaire (3PQ and Its Association with the Two-Item Measure of Parental Power and Prestige. Unpublished Manuscript, University of Chester, UK.

Mikulincer, M., & Shaver, P. R. (2007). *Attachment in adulthood*. NewYork: The Guilford Press.

Mikulincer, M., & Shaver, P. R. (2008). Adult attachment and affect regulation. In J. Cassidy & P. Shaver (Eds.), *Handbook of Attachment: Theory, research and clinical applications* (2nd ed., pp. 503–531). New York: The Guilford Press.

Mousavi, P. S. S., Khoshroo, S., Memarian, M., Ghanbari, S., & Rohner, R. P. (2023). Memories of parental rejection and fear of intimacy: The role of psychological maladjustment, interpersonal anxiety, and rejection by an intimate partner. *Current Psychology, 42*(36), 31801–31809.

Parmar, P. & Rohner, R. P. (2005). Relations among perceived intimate partner acceptance, and remembered parental acceptance, and psychological adjustment among young adults in India. *Ethos, 33*(3), 402–413.

Parmar, P., Ibrahim, M., & Rohner, R. P. (2008). Relations among perceived spouse acceptance, and remembered parental acceptance in childhood, and psychological adjustment among married adults in Kuwait. *Cross-Cultural Research, 42*(1), 67–76.

Perlman, D., & Duck, S. (1987). *Intimate relationships: Development, dynamics, and deterioration*. Newbury Park, California: Sage Publications, Inc.

Prager, K. J., Shirvani, F. K., Garcia, J. J., & Coles, M. (2013). Intimacy and positive psychology. In M. Hojjat & D. Cramer (Eds.), *Positive psychology of love* (pp. 16–29). New York: Oxford University Press.

Reis, H. T. (2013). Relationship well-being: The central role of perceived partner responsiveness. In C. Hazan & M. I. Campa (Eds.), *Human bonding: The science of affectional ties* (pp. 283–307). New York: Guilford Press.

Reis, H. T., & Patrick, B. C. (1996). Attachment and intimacy: Component process. In E. T. Higgins & A. Kruglanski (Eds.), *Social psychology: Handbook of basic principles* (pp. 523–563). New York: Guilford.

Ripoll-Nunez, K., & Alvarez, C. (2008). Perceived intimate partner acceptance, remembered parental acceptance, and psychological adjustment among Colombian and Puerto Rican youths and adults. *Cross-Cultural Research, 42*, 23–34.

Rohner, R. P. (1998). Father love and child development: History and current evidence. *Current Directions in Psychological Science, 7*, 157–161.

Rohner, R. P. (2004). The parental "acceptance-rejection syndrome": Universal correlates of perceived rejection. *American Psychologist, 59*, 827–840.

Rohner, R. P. (2008). Parental acceptance-rejection theory studies of intimate adult relationships. In R. P. Rohner & T. Melendez (Eds.), Parental acceptance-rejection theory studies of intimate adult relationships. [Special Issue]. *Cross-Cultural Research, 42*, 5–12.

Rohner, R. P. (2014). PARTheory gets a new name: Interpersonal Acceptance Rejection Theory (IPARTheroy). *Interpersonal Acceptance, 8*(3), 6.

Rohner, R. P. (2021). Introduction to interpersonal acceptance-rejection theory (IPARTheory) and evidence. *Online Readings in Psychology and Culture, 6*(1), 1–65. doi:10.9707/2307-0919.1055

Rohner, R. P. (2023). Glossary of significant concepts in parental acceptance-rejection theory. Retrieved on August 11, 2023 from https://csiar.uconn.edu/glossary/

Rohner, R. P., & Ali, S. (2025). Interpersonal acceptance-rejection theory (IPARTheory): From conception through maturity. In R. P. Rohner and S. Ali (Eds.), *Global perspectives on parental acceptance and rejection: Lessons learned from IPARTheory* (pp. 3–38). Routledge.

Rohner, R. P., & Carrasco, M. A. (Eds.) (2014). Preface. In R. P. Rohner & M. A. Carrasco (Eds.) Parental power and prestige moderate the effects of perceived acceptance on offspring's psychological adjustment (Special Issue). *Cross-Cultural Research, 48*(3), 195–196.

Rohner, R. P., Filus, A. Melendez-Rhodes, T., Kuyumcu, B., Machado, F., Roszak, J., Camden, A., Hossain, H. A., & Roy, K. (2019). Psychological maladjustment mediates the relation between remembrances of parental rejection in childhood and adults' fear of intimacy: A multicultural study. *Cross-Cultural Research, 53*, 508–542. DOI:10.1177/1069397118822992

Rohner, R. P., & Khaleque, A. (2005). *Handbook for the study of parental acceptance and rejection*. Storrs, CT, USA: Rohner Research.

Rohner, R. P., & Khaleque, A. (2008). Relations between perceived partner and parental acceptance. In J. K. Quinn & I. G. Zambini (Eds.), *Family relations: 21st century issues and challenges*. New York: Nova Science Publishers, Inc. Adjustment of Bangladeshi Adolescents. *Cross-Cultural Research, 44*, 239–252.

Rohner, R. P., & Khaleque, A. (2010). *Parental acceptance-rejection: Theory, methods, and cross-cultural evidence* (Available in compact disc for worldwide distribution). Rohner Research Publications.

Rohner, R. P., & Lansford, J. E. (2017). Deep structure of the human affectional system: Introduction to interpersonal acceptance-rejection theory. *Journal of Family Theory & Review, 9*, 426–440. DOI 10.1111/JFTR.12219

Rohner, R. P. & Melendez, T. (2008). Parental acceptance-rejection theory studies of intimate adult relationships. *Cross-Cultural Research, 42*(1), 77–86.

Rohner, R. P., Melendez, T., & Kraimer-Rickaby, L. (2008). Intimate partner acceptance, parental acceptance, and psychological adjustment among American adults in ongoing attachment relationships. *Cross-Cultural Research, 42*(1), 13–22.

Schwartz, S. H., & Rubel-Lifschitz, T. (2009). Cross-national variation in the size of sex differences in values: effects of gender equality. *Journal of Personality and Social Psychology 97(1)*, 171–185, doi: 10.1037/a0015546

Sherman, M. D., & Thelen, M. H. (1996). Fear of Intimacy Scale: Validation and extension with adolescents. *Journal of Social and Personal Relationships, 13*, 507–521.

Sultana, S., & Khaleque, A. (2016). Differential effects of perceived maternal and paternal acceptance on male and female adult offspring's psychological adjustment. *Gender Issues*, 33(1), 42–52. doi: 10.1007/s12147-015-9147-0

Thelen, M. H., Vander-Wal, J. S., & Muir T. A., & Harmon, R. (2000). Fear of intimacy among dating couples. *Behavior Modification, 24*(2), 223–240. 16.

Uddin, M. K., Khaleque, A., Akhtar, R., Hossain, M.A., & Roy, K. (2016, June 7–10). *Parental rejection in childhood predicts fear of intimacy in adults of Bangladesh.* A presentation at the 6th International Congress on Interpersonal Acceptance and Rejection, Madrid, Spain.

Varan, A., Rohner, R. P., & Eryuksel, G. (2008). Intimate partner acceptance, parental acceptance in childhood, and psychological adjustment among Turkish adults in ongoing attachment relationships. *Cross-Cultural Research, 42*, 46–56.

Veneziano, R. (2008, July 3–6). *The relative importance of fathers versus mothers for offspring's behavior: Theory and implications for future research*. Paper presented at the Second International Congress on Interpersonal Acceptance and Rejection, University of Crete, Rethymno, Greece.

6

AS YOU SOW, SO SHALL YOU REAP

Memories of Parental Acceptance-Rejection in Childhood Predict Adult Caregivers' Treatment of Aging Parents

Sumbleen Ali and Ronald P. Rohner

One in four children in the United States in 1900 had lost a parent before the age of 15 (Fingerman & Birditt, 2011). Today, however, offspring often share six or more decades of life with their aging parents. In fact, in industrialized nations, the majority of adults between 50 and 59 years of age have at least one aging parent (Hagestad & Uhlenberg, 2007). Thus, parents and offspring spend many more years together as adults than they did as parents raising young children. As a result, the relationship between adult offspring and their parents is distinct from other types of social ties due to their long-shared history and evolving relationships from the offspring's infancy into adulthood.

Offspring's early years are marked by dependency on parents, but as parents live longer, they often become increasingly reliant on their adult children for caregiving responsibilities (Fingerman & Birditt, 2011). In 2020, for example, the American Association of Retired Persons (AARP) and the National Alliance for Caregiving (NAC, 2020) estimated that 53 million adults (21.3% of Americans) served as caregivers for someone, with the majority providing care for an aging parent. By the year 2030, approximately 73 million individuals in the US will have reached the age of 65 or older (US Census, Bureau, 2020). A considerable portion of this demographic will necessitate regular aid from caregivers to maintain their quality of life, independence, and overall physical and social welfare (RAISE, 2021). It is anticipated that over two-thirds of the population in the US will encounter the need for assistance with various tasks at some stage in their lives (RAISE, 2021).

DOI: 10.4324/9781003441243-8

Therefore, because of the lack of formal support programs in the US, many adult offspring assume time-consuming, physically challenging, and emotionally draining caregiving responsibilities (Fingerman et al., 2007). Most eldercare now involves an adult offspring as primary caregiver for a parent (Wolff & Kasper, 2006). This pattern is a shift from several decades ago when the most common care provider was an aging person's spouse (Wolff & Kasper, 2006). Now offspring often serve this role because parents are less likely to be partnered in old age (Swartz, 2009).

The literature pertaining to caregiving is large, but little attention has been paid to why some adult offspring happily assume this responsibility for their parents whereas others are reluctant to do it—and consider caring for an aging parent to be a burdensome responsibility. Families have rich histories and emotional ties that may include unfinished business or tensions resulting from experiences that happened decades earlier (Kong et al., 2021). Such experiences can influence outcomes and relationships in later life. Thus, caregivers' childhood relationships with parents can influence their caregiving behaviors toward their now aging parents.

Birmingham's (1982/1985) cross-cultural survey (holocultural study) of parenting and adults' attitudes and treatment of the aged in 101 societies cross-culturally provides useful insight into worldwide relations between culturally defined (normative) styles of parenting—especially parental acceptance-rejection—and cultural attitudes toward aging and death. She found, for example, a pancultural tendency for parental affection, emotional support, love, and overall acceptance in childhood to be significantly associated with respect for the elderly. She also found that as parental neglect and hostility (i.e., rejection) increased, respect for the elderly tended to decrease. Moreover, insofar as parents lovingly accept their children, the advice of the older adults cross-culturally tends to be sought and accepted, whereas in societies where children are generally rejected, the advice of the older adult population tends to be ignored, mocked, or discounted.

Finally, Birmingham (1982/1985) found that death is recognized as a normal and natural part of life in most societies of the world, but in some societies, it is attributed to the working of evil forces. Most importantly, in some cultures where parental rejection is the norm, death is even preferable to a dependent old age: It is better to die than to be dependent on people around you in your older age, especially on your own children. Relatedly, she reported that in societies where parents normatively accept their children with loving care, old age and death are accepted as ordinary and expectable parts of life. Thus, cross-cultural evidence supports a slightly revised dictum: "As you sow rejection onto your children, so shall you reap rejection by your children in your own older age."

This cross-cultural evidence supports major postulates in interpersonal acceptance-rejection theory (IPARTheory). IPARTheory is an evidence-based theory of socialization and lifespan development that attempts to predict and explain major consequences, causes, and other correlates of interpersonal—especially parental—acceptance and rejection worldwide (Rohner, 1986, 2021). As construed in IPARTheory, interpersonal acceptance may be expressed physically, verbally, or symbolically by acts such as emotional support and caring, nurturance, or simply love. Interpersonal rejection—in contrast—is manifested in physical, verbal, and symbolically hurtful behaviors (Rohner, 1986, 2005, 2021). More specifically, IPARTheory recognizes four forms of interpersonal rejection: (1) coldness and lack of affection (i.e., the significant other is emotionally cold and fails to express either warmth or affection); (2) hostility and aggression (e.g., insulting, yelling, hitting, rude behaviors; (3) indifference and neglect (i.e., being physically or psychologically unavailable or not interested in supporting the emotional needs of the individual); and (4) undifferentiated rejection (i.e., the perception that the significant other does not really care about, appreciate, want, or love the individual, although there may be no behavioral manifestation of any of the prior three forms of rejection).

IPARTheory proposes that across cultures and other sociodemographic groups, interpersonal acceptance and rejection consistently predict the psychological and behavioral adjustment or maladjustment of children and adults (Rohner, 1986, 2004, 2021; Rohner & Ali, 2025; Chapter 1 this book). Acceptance or rejection from a significant other is postulated in the theory to have a major influence on adults' personality and psychological adjustment, as well as on future interpersonal relationships (Khaleque & Ali, 2017; Rohner & Lansford, 2017). Perceiving oneself as having been rejected has been found to be a predictor of psychological maladjustment with a cluster of ten personality dispositions including becoming anxious, insecure, being angry, and having problems with the management of hostility and aggression, becoming emotionally unresponsive, developing an impaired sense of self-esteem and self-adequacy, becoming emotionally unstable, and developing a negative worldview, including the development of other cognitive distortions (Rohner, 2021).

Research has found that adult offspring's recollections of relationship quality with parents during childhood are positively related to the adults' current level of affection toward parents, fulfillment of normative obligations toward parents (filial duties), and spending time with parents (Long & Martin, 2000; Parrot & Bengtson, 1999). Further, Fingerman (2001) conducted an in-depth study of relationships between mothers and daughters. He referred to the temporal changes in tensions and conflicts which were common among the participants as "developmental schisms." Such studies provide evidence that positive relationship quality between parents and offspring early in life places offspring on trajectories associated with positive relationships and overall wellbeing later in life.

A relatively small number of family caregiving studies have addressed the link between early parent–child relationship quality and offspring's caregiving of parents in old age. Li and Seltzer (2003), for example, found that adult daughter caregivers' perceptions of relationships with their parents were related to the adult daughters' stress. And, Daire (2002), found that adults who reported receiving limited emotional care from parents during the first 16 years of life experienced more distress in their role as primary caregiver to their parents than did adults who received substantial emotional care. Little more is known, however, about the way in which early parent–child relationships affects adult offspring who provide care to parents in old age. Understanding this is critical because care for parents with functional limitations is increasing as populations age and as advances in medicine promote longevity. The present study helps fill that gap in knowledge by testing the hypothesis within the US that adults who remember experiencing parental warmth, emotional support, and love (i.e., acceptance) from their parents in childhood are more likely to provide loving care for their aging parents than are adults who felt rejected by their parents in childhood.

Method

Participants

Sixty-three female caregivers participated in the study (age range 39–69 years; $M = 56$; $SD = 5.79$). Participants self-identified as: African American ($n = 21$), European American ($n = 20$), and Puerto Rican ($n = 22$). Only three of the caregivers lived with their parent, but all provided care for the parent who was 65 years of age or older. Six percent ($n = 4$) of the women provided care for their fathers whereas 94% ($n = 59$) provided care for their mothers. The parents ranged in age from 66 to 95 ($M = 78$, $SD = 6.3$). Sixty-seven percent ($n = 42$) of the caregivers were married. Thirty-two percent ($n = 20$) had a high school diploma, 44% ($n = 28$) completed at least two years of post-secondary education, and 24% ($n = 15$) reported having a four-year college degree or a professional diploma. Thirty-seven percent ($n = 23$) of the caregivers said they were fully employed whereas 63% ($n = 40$) reported they were retired.

Caregivers were recruited through posting flyers, using personal contacts, visiting senior centers, and support groups in the northeastern US. Inclusion criteria included: (a) the caregiver must be 18 years of age or older, (b) provide assistance with at least one instrumental activity of daily living (IADL; e.g., using a telephone and taking medications) and/or one activity of daily living (ADL; e.g., getting dressed or eating meals), (c) have contact with the parent at least five times a week, (d) reside with or in close proximity to the parent, and (e) face no financial hardship related to caregiving expenses. The parent (a) must be 65 years or older, and (b) not be seriously impaired cognitively, as assessed via the Telephone Interview for Cognitive Status (Brandt et al., 1988).

Procedure

Participation in this study was on a voluntary basis. Data were collected in two phases. Phase one determined eligibility for participation via a telephone interview with the caregiver. In addition, during telephone screening we gathered demographic information described below. A bilingual (English and Spanish) research assistant facilitated the study for caregivers who spoke Spanish.

In the second phase, a trained bilingual (English and Spanish) research assistant visited either the caregiver's home or parents' home and administered six self-report measures to the caregiver. These included the Adult version of the Parental Acceptance-Rejection Questionnaire (Adult PARQ; Rohner, 2005), Zarit Burden Interview, Positive Aspects of Caregiving (PAC) scale (Schulz et al., 1997), Satisfaction with Social Activities scale (SSA; Schulz, 2001), and Financial Difficulty (Schulz, 2001). Additionally, a 40-minute open-ended interview was conducted with the caregiver. Interview topics included (a) history of the quality of the relationship between the caregiver and her aging parent, (b) personal, religious, and cultural beliefs about illness and caregiving, and (c) stresses and satisfactions related to the caregiving process.

Measures

Personal Information Form (PIF) and Consent Form

The PIF was included in the initial screening interview. It elicits information about caregivers' age, ethnicity, marital status, number of siblings, education level, monthly income, whether they co-reside with the aging parent, duration of caregiving, any health conditions that make it difficult to provide care, other siblings or social worker (if any) who provide care to the parent, and information about instrumental activities (IADLs) or daily living activities (ADLs) they do for the parent.

Parental Acceptance-Rejection Questionnaire (PARQ)

The standard (60-item) version of the Adult PARQ (Rohner, 2005) was administered. The PARQ asks respondents to reflect on their memories of their mothers' or fathers' behavior toward them when the respondent was a child growing up at home. The Mother and Father versions of the PARQ are identical except that one asks about mothers' behavior and the other asks about fathers' behavior. If the caregiver took care of her mother only, then she completed the Mother version of the PARQ. If she took care of her father only, then she completed the Father version of the measure. Both measures consist of four summed scales: (a) a 15-item "hostility/aggression" scale (e.g., "My mother [father] nagged or scolded me when I was bad"), (b) a 10-item "undifferentiated rejection" scale (e.g., "My mother [father] did not really love me"), (c) a 15-item "indifference/neglect" scale (e.g., "My mother [father] paid no attention to me"), and (d) an 20-item "warmth/affection" scale (e.g., "My mother [father] said nice things about me). The latter scale is reverse scored to indicate coldness/lack of affection. Responses are made on a four-point Likert scale: 1 (*Almost never true)*, 2 (*Rarely true)*, 3 (*Sometimes true)*, or 4 (*Almost always true)*.

Scores on the standard PARQ range from a low of 60 (maximum perceived acceptance) to a high of 240 (maximum perceived rejection). Scores between 60 and 120 reveal respondents' perception of substantial parental love (parental acceptance). Scores between 121 and 139 reveal the feelings of increasing but not serious love withdrawal (parental rejection). Scores between 140 and 149 reveal the experience of significant levels of rejection, but not more overall rejection than acceptance. Scores at or above 150 reveal the experience of more parental rejection than acceptance. Cronbach's alpha in this study was .96.

Zarit Burden Interview

Burden was measured using the 12-item version of the Zarit Burden Interview. A sample item includes "Do you feel stressed between caring for your care recipient and trying to meet other responsibilities?" Responses were measured on a Likert scale ranging from 0 (*never*) through 4 (*nearly always*). Higher scores indicate the perception of greater burden. Cronbach's alpha in this study was.83.

Positive Aspects of Caregiving Scale

Participants completed the 11-item Positive Aspects of Caregiving scale (PAC; Schulz et al., 1997). The scale measures positive feelings and experiences derived from the caregiving role. The PAC addresses the caregiver's perception of benefits associated with the caregiving experience. Responses are on a 5-point Likert scale from 1 (*disagree a lot*) to 5 (*agree a lot*). Item scores are summed to create a total composite score. The higher the score, the more positive the caregiver's appraisal of the caregiving experience. Sample items include "Feel appreciated in what you do for the care recipient parent," "Providing care to the parent gives more meaning to my life," and "Caregiving has strengthened relationships with my parent." Cronbach's alpha in this study was .97.

Satisfaction with Social Activities Scale

Caregivers' level of social activities with their aging parent was assessed using the 6-item Satisfaction with Social Activities Scale (SSA; Schulz, 2001). Sample items include: How much you enjoyed: "spending quiet time alone with your parent," and "taking part in hobbies over the past month." Another item asked "How many times did you visit your parent over the past month." Response options include 0 (*not at all*), 1 (*a little*), and 2 (*a lot*). A higher score indicate greater satisfaction doing social activities with the parent. Cronbach's alpha in this study was .96.

Financial Difficulty Scale

Financial difficulty was assessed by asking about household income and by using a single item from Schulz (2001) Financial Difficulty Scale. Participants were asked how easy or hard it is to make ends meet such as paying for the basics such as food, housing, medical care, and heating. Responses are: 1 (*not difficult at all*), 2 (*not very difficult*), 3 (*somewhat difficult*), and 4 (*very difficult*). Coefficient alpha in this study was .70.

Qualitative Data

Qualitative data were collected in an open-ended interview format. Many items covered topics that also were measured using the self-report measures and served as follow-ups to allow caregivers the opportunity to discuss topics in their own words instead of being restricted to a set of response options. For example, offspring were asked; "Describe your relationship with your mother [father] when you were a child growing up at home (approximately ages 7 to 12 years)." Follow-up questions included, "Were you close? What are some of the good or bad things you remember from that time?" "Do you feel your relationship has changed since you started caregiving? How and why?" "Overall, from childhood until just before you started providing care for your mother [father], how would you describe changes in your relationship?" To capture a more complete picture of the current relationship, participants were asked "Do you feel your relationship has changed since you started caregiving? How and why?"

To gain a better understanding of caregivers' values and beliefs about caregiving, a series of open-ended questions was also asked. For example, "In general, when an older person needs care, who should provide that care and what would you expect them to do?" Follow-up questions included, "Are these beliefs common in your family?" "Are these beliefs common among your people or a broader group (culture) you consider yourself a part of?" Finally, the caregiver was asked to: "Describe any feelings of burden/stress that you experience related to giving care."

Data Analysis Plan

Quantitative Data

Following data entry using the Statistical Package for Social Science (IBM Corp. Released, 2020), the self-report data was analyzed in four steps. First, descriptive statistics were calculated for all variables. Second, distributions were assessed for normality and the possible undue influence of outliers. All distributions were found to be relatively normal, and none were being pulled too strongly by outliers. The missingness in data was handled using expectation-maximization (EM; Dong & Peng, 2013). Third, Pearson's product-moment correlations were computed to test associations among the major variables. Fourth, a path model was tested using multiple regression analysis (See Figure 6.1 discussed later).

Qualitative Data

Qualitative data were analyzed after tape-recorded interviews were transcribed. The text was then entered into the mixed-methods data analysis system, "Dedoose". Dedoose is a data analysis program that has the capacity to link qualitative data to respondents' quantitative data (e.g., self-reports). For qualitative data analysis we focused mainly on the expression of parental love/warmth and rejection themes. Step one was to conduct an inductive analysis of the qualitative data through coding. We followed a grounded theory approach that is, we did not impose any preconceived categories in the data, but rather let all of the themes emerge from thecaregivers' narratives (Charmaz, 2006; Corbin & Strauss, 2008; Strauss & Corbin, 1998).

This approach was well suited to the current study because our data are exploratory in nature. During the first phase of analysis each caregiver's narrative was read and coded at a granular level by three coders. The coders identified whether they thought the narrative fell into the "accepted" category or "rejected" category occurring in the narratives. Each coder evaluated a random selection of 10% of the total responses, reread them, developed open codes, and then discussed these codes with the research team. Then, as a group the team refined, renamed, or consolidated codes, and each read another 10% of the total responses and repeated the inter-rater coding process. After 30% of the responses had been coded through this process, we further developed the larger categories and themes and stopped when we achieved an interrater reliability of $\kappa = .90$ using Bowen's (2008) Kappa statistic.

Results

Descriptive and Correlational Analyses

Results displayed in Table 6.1 show that on average, caregivers recalled having been accepted in childhood by their now aging parent. Additionally, caregivers did not often feel burdened by their caregiver responsibilities. Moreover, they reported mostly positive experiences and feelings about the caregiving process, and they were mostly satisfied with the level of social activities with their aging parent. Finally, caregivers generally had little difficulty paying expenses associated with caregiving. Results in Table 6.1 also show, however, that insofar as the women experienced parental rejection in childhood, they also tended to view caregiving as a burden. Moreover, memories of childhood rejection were negatively correlated with positive aspects of caregiving and with satisfaction in sharing social activities with the aging parent. Memories of parental rejection were

TABLE 6.1 Descriptives, Intercorrelations, and Cronbach Alphas Among Study Variables

	Parental Rejection	*Caregiving Burden*	*Positive Aspects of Caregiving*	*Satisfaction with Social Activities*	*Financial Difficulty*
Caregiving Burden	.67**				
Positive Aspect of Caregiving	−.58**	−.38**			
Satisfaction with Social Activities	−.72**	−.56**	.34*		
Financial Difficulty	−.30 ns	−.21 ns	.20 ns	.06 ns	
Total Sample M(SD)	113(13.3)	22(3.6)	37(3.2)	10(4.9)	1.03(1)
Possible Range	60–240	0–48	11–55	0–12	1–4
Cronbach Alpha α	.96	.83	.97	.96	.70

Note: ns = not significant; $*p < .05$; $**p < .01$; α = Cronbach's Alpha.

unrelated to financial difficulties in caring for the aging parent. It is also worth noting that a sense of caregiving burden was negatively correlated with positive aspects of caregiving and satisfaction with engaging in social activities with the aging parent. That is, the more caregivers viewed caregiving as a burden, the fewer positive aspects of caregiving they reported and the less satisfaction they found in taking part in social activities with their aging parent. One of the items in the Satisfaction of the Social Activities scale ask caregivers how many times they visited their parents during the past month (never, a little, or a lot). That item correlated significantly ($r = .38$, $p < .01$) with the memories of childhood rejection. That is, the more rejected the caregiver remembered being as a child, the less often she visited her aging parent.

Regression Analysis

As noted above, memories of parental acceptance-rejection in childhood were associated with caregiving burden, positive aspects of caregiving, and satisfaction with social activities with the aging parent. But caregiving burden, positive aspects of caregiving, and satisfaction with social activities were also significantly correlated with each other. To estimate the *unique* (independent) association between remembered parental acceptance-rejection and each of the other variables, we computed a multiple regression analysis using SPSS (IBM SPSS Statistics Version 27). Parental acceptance-rejection was the predictor. Figure 6.1 graphically shows that women's memories of parental *rejection* in childhood uniquely predicted caregiving burden after controlling for the effect of the other two dependent variables ($b = .89$, $p < .05$). Memories of parental *acceptance* in childhood, on the other hand, uniquely predicted experiences of positive aspects of caregiving ($b = .67$, $p < .05$) and satisfaction with the social activities with the aging parent ($b = .48$, $p < .01$).

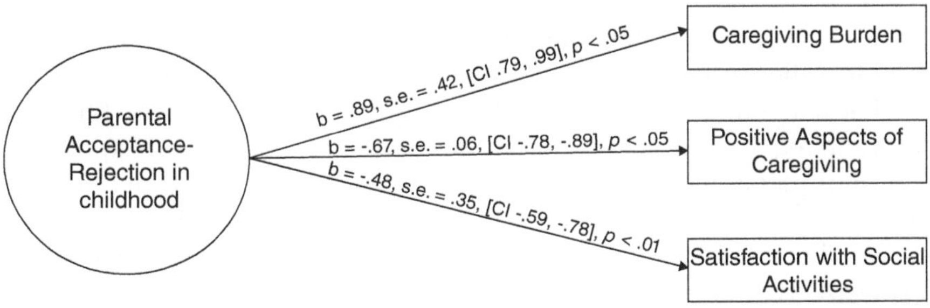

FIGURE 6.1 Regression Analysis.

Note: b = beta values; CI = Confidence Intervals.

Qualitative Results

As shown below, narrative responses from the open-ended interview with caregivers support conclusions reached in the quantitative portion of this research:

European American Mother, PARQ Score 60 = Accepted

"My mother and I are only 19 years apart in age. She and I have been super close my whole life. She was so good to me. She did everything that a mother should be doing. Now that I have to take care of her. It's like a role-reversal, you know. So, you feel more like you're the mother, you know. I'm always saying "Ma you need to drink more; you need more fluids. If you drank more maybe you wouldn't get so many UTI's," "Did you take your medicine today?", or "Do you need any refills?", or that kind of thing you know like giving instructions and taking care of her [mother] like a kid. So, it's changed. Family takes care of old people. My mother took care of her mother. So, I do the same now that my mother is old."

European American Mother, PARQ Score 70 = Accepted

"My mother loved me when I was a kid. She would always go the extra mile to support me. We both had good friendship in our relationship. We're even closer now. Now I try to be with my Ma as much as I can. She's has also mellowed in her old age. I'd say our roles have reversed. She is now the child and I'm the parent. So that's totally different. So, our relationship has changed. I try to enjoy every moment with her because I don't know when she will leave us and go to heaven. Nobody in my family takes care of old people. They go to places like senior housing or nursing home. I do it out of love. She is my mother."

African American Mother, PARQ Score 85 = Accepted

"I had a good relationship with my mother. She was a fighter parent who supported her children in every way she possibly could. So, we loved her for that unconditional support and love. But she was also strict. She had rules and regulations that I had to follow. If I would not do as I am told, then she would scold me. Now that she is old, she is softer. She is not as strict and as grumpy as she was once. I take care of my mother because it's expected that you would when family members age; it's almost like a get-back type. Family steps in and do what they can until you can't, cannot do anymore. Whatever is necessary."

Puerto Rican Mother, PARQ Score 155 = Rejected

"My relationship with my mother when I was a little girl was not the best relationship. She was harsh parent. I didn't really like my mother. We were anything but close. If there is anything positive that I recall about her it was only good food she made. My relationship with my mother in my childhood wasn't nice. Now my mother is old, and she has started depending on me. Initially, when I started taking care of her it was still a cold relationship. The relationship changed slightly when I had my first daughter. She [mother] showed love and affection toward my child. The love that she never had for me. Since then, our relationship became interesting. As a kid I didn't like her much, but now I think to myself she can't be all bad because she loves my daughter. We share experiences of motherhood. I think you have to step up to the plate; you have to do what you have to do whatever's involved. Family and relatives in my family take care of older people. I expect that my daughter will take care of me when I will be old. So, I love her as I know that she is the one who will love me back when I need the most."

African American Mother, PARQ Score 170 = Seriously Rejected

"She was who she was. She was very firm. Very, very, firm. You weren't getting away with anything, um-hmm. We [siblings] used to get spankings. She would spank all of us at one time. She'd make us stand in a queue and spank. She'd say: "And this is because you did it, and…this is so you, you, and you won't do it again." Hmm. We were not close. Na…I didn't like being spanked. So, I was waiting for the day I could leave home. Yeah, Relationship has changed. She can't spank me no more. Right! She started getting mellower as she aged. It took me a while to realize that because my whole life I knew her as hard person. She never liked my food. Now that she is old, she complains no more. She knows that if she would I ain't making no more food for her. I do my job. That is all. Blood relatives have to take care of old people in my family. If they have kids they will do it, or anyone who is related does it."

Puerto Rican Father, PARQ Score 190 = Very Seriously Rejected

"Well, when I was little my father used to drink a lot, and I was always receiving a lot of spankings and beatings. My mother used to hide me [from my father]. I was always the one that would pay for everybody's "broken dish." Things changed since I turned 12 years old. Because I stood up for myself when my father would batter me, to whoever would hit me. I told him [father], "One day you are going to get old, and the one who is going to take care of you is going to be me!" And since that day my father never hit me again. It is not that he became a loving father, but I was not battered no more. So, now that I have to take care of my father, he is become better. No more cursing and abusing and bickering about me. I have to do things for my father because Puerto Rican people believe in "Familismo". You got no choice. So, I do what I can. I don't go out of my means and bounds to provide for him. I do what I am expected of."

European American Mother, PARQ Score 230 = Profoundly Rejected

"I was never close to my mom. She and I were so different. She never cooked for us. We had to fetch for ourselves. So, I started fixing meals for me when I was about 6 years. I don't remember if she ever made food for us. Our relationship hasn't changed because there is no reason why it would change. So, I don't know [how] much love I have for my mother, but I'm obligated, and I feel a deep obligation. She's my mom but as far as deeply caring, loving, I don't feel that way. This is a definite obligation thing that I'm doing. And I feel bad that I feel that way but that's the way that it is. We've just never been close, so this is difficult. In my family children are expected to take care of older parents. So, I do it not because I want to but because I have to. So, you know, there is sometimes you don't have a choice, but ideally if we could care for our own elderly that would be the way to go, I think."

Discussion

This study provides insight into the influence of early parent–child relationships on adults' feelings about taking care of their aging parents. Results of the work show that adults who experienced parental rejection during childhood report fewer positive feelings or experiences in the process of caregiving for their now-aging parents than do adults who felt loved and accepted in childhood. Additionally, adults who were rejected in childhood tend to be more dissatisfied with doing social activities with their aging parents than do accepted adults, and rejected adults tend to perceive caregiving as more burdensome than do adults who felt loved in childhood. These results are consistent with IPARTheory's expectations about the long-term effects of parental acceptance and rejection (see Rohner, 2021; Rohner & Ali, 2025; Chapter 1 in this book).

The results are also consistent with cross-cultural survey data regarding relations between culturally defined (normative) styles of parenting and cultural attitudes toward aging and death. Specifically, the older adults tend to be respected in societies where children are raised by their parents with emotional support, love, and overall acceptance. Moreover, insofar as parents lovingly accept their children, the advice of the aged cross-culturally tends to be sought and accepted. However, in societies where children are rejected the advice of the older adults tends to be ignored, mocked, or discounted. Respect for the elderly tends to decrease significantly in societies where parents typically reject their children. In fact, in some societies where parental rejection is the norm, death is preferable to a dependent old age. There, people often believe it is better to be dead than have to depend on their own children or others in old age. In societies where parental acceptance is the norm, however, old age and death are accepted as ordinary and expectable parts of life. Thus, intracultural evidence and cross-cultural evidence support the ancient proverb, "As you sow, so shall you reap."

Limitations and Implications

Conclusions reported here are limited by the fact that neither the cross-sectional American evidence nor the cross-cultural comparative evidence allows causal inferences to be drawn. Longitudinal data would be required for that. Additionally, the sample of Americans emphasized here is too small to allow strong, generalizing conclusions—especially about possible ethnic differences in attitudes toward caring for aging parents. Nonetheless, despite these limitations work reported year has the distinctive strength of providing converging evidence from self-report data in a sample of individuals intraculturally along with evidence from normative (cultural) data in a large sample of societies cross-culturally.

Although research in this area is growing, there are still far more unanswered than answered questions in need of research. As emphasized in IPARTheory, effects of childhood rejection continue into adulthood through ongoing cognitive engagement and meaning-making about past hurts and long-held beliefs and mental representations about self and others (see Rohner & Ali, 2025; Chapter 1 in this book). Culturally congruent family-centered therapeutic interventions based on evidence in IPARTheory can be designed to support interactions between adult caregivers and their aging parents.

Data availability statement

The data that support the findings of this article are available on request from Sumbleen Ali (sumbleen.ali@uconn.edu) or Ronald P. Rohner (rohner@uconn.edu)

References

Birmingham, M. T. (1982). *Treatment accorded the elderly and the young: A holocultural study* (Doctoral dissertation). Rohner Center for the Study of Interpersonal Acceptance and Rejection. University of Connecticut, Storrs. CT. Results published in Rohner, R.P., (1986). The Warmth Dimension Foundations of Parental Acceptance-Rejection Theory.

Bowen, G. A. (2008). Naturalistic inquiry and the saturation concept: a research note. *Qualitative research, 8*(1), 137–152.

Brandt, J., Spencer, M., & Folstein, M. (1988). The telephone interview for cognitive status. *Neuropsychiatry, Neuropsychology and Behavioral Neurology, 1*(2), 111–117.

Charmaz, K. (2006). *Constructing grounded theory: A practical guide through qualitative analysis*. Russell Sage Foundation.

Corbin, J., & Strauss, A. (2008). *Basics of qualitative research: Techniques and procedures for developing grounded theory*. Sage Publications.

Daire, A. P. (2002) The influence of parental bonding on emotional distress in caregiving sons for a parent with dementia. *The Gerontologist, 42*, 766–771.

Dong, Y., & Peng, C. Y. J. (2013). Principled missing data methods for researchers. *SpringerPlus, 2*, 1–17.

Fingerman, K. L. (Ed.). (2001). *Aging mothers and their adult daughters: A study in mixed emotions*. Springer Publishing Company.

Fingerman, K. L., & Birditt, K. S. (2011). Relationships between adults and their aging parents. In *Handbook of the psychology of aging* (pp. 219–232). Academic Press.

Fingerman, K. L., Hay, E. L., Dush, C. M. K., Cichy, K. E., & Hosterman, S. J. (2007). Parents' and offspring's perceptions of change and continuity when parents experience the transition to old age. *Advances in life course research, 12*, 275–306.

Hagestad, G. O., & Uhlenberg, P. (2007). The impact of demographic changes on relations between age groups and generations: A comparative perspective. In K. W. Schaie & P. Uhlenberg (Eds.). *Social structures: Demographic changes and the well-being of older persons* (pp. 239–261). New York: Springer Publishing Co.

IBM Corp. Released 2020. IBM SPSS Statistics for Windows, Version 27.0. Armonk, NY: IBM Corp.

Khaleque, A., & Ali, S. (2017). A systematic review of meta-analyses of research on interpersonal acceptance-rejection theory: Constructs and measures. *Journal of Family Theory & Review, 9*(4), 441–458.

Kong, J., Kunze, A., Goldberg, J., & Schroepfer, T. (2021). Caregiving for parents who harmed you: A conceptual review. *Clinical Gerontologist, 44*(5), 507–519.

Li, L. W., & Seltzer, M. M. (2003). Parent care, intergenerational relationship quality, and mental health of adult daughters. *Research on aging, 25*(5), 484–504.

Long, M. V., & Martin, P. (2000). Personality, relationship closeness, and loneliness of oldest old adults and their children. *The Journals of Gerontology Series B: Psychological Sciences and Social Sciences, 55*(5), P311–P319.

National Alliance for Caregiving (NAC) and AARP. (2020). Caregiving in the US: A focused look at family caregivers of adults age 50+ a *National Survey*. Retrieved on January 25, 2023, from https://www.caregiving.org/research/caregiving-in-the-us/caregiving-in-the-us-2020/

Parrot, T., & Bengtson, V. (1999). The effects of earlier intergenerational affection, normative expectations, and family conflict on contemporary exchanges of help and support. *Research on Aging, 21*, 73–105.

RAISE Family Caregiving Advisory Council (2021). *Recognize, Assist, Include, Support, & Engage (RAISE) Family Caregivers Act. (2021). Initial Report to Congress*. Administration for Community Living. Retrieved on January 25, 2023, from https://acl.gov/sites/default/files/RAISE-InitialReportToCongress2021_Final.pdf

Rohner, R. P. (1986). *The warmth dimension: Foundations of parental acceptance-rejection theory*. Sage Publications.

Rohner, R. P. (2005). Parental acceptance-rejection questionnaire (PARQ): Test manual. In R. P. Rohner & A. Khaleque (Eds.), *Handbook for the study of parental acceptance and rejection* (4th ed., pp. 43–106). Storrs: Rohner Research Publications.

Rohner, R. P. (2004). The parental "acceptance-rejection syndrome": Universal correlates of perceived rejection. *American Psychologist, 59*(8), 830.

Rohner, R. P. (2021). Introduction to Interpersonal Acceptance-Rejection Theory (IPARTheory) and Evidence. *Online Readings in Psychology and Culture*, 6(1), 1–65. https://doi.org/10.9707/2307-0919.1055

Rohner, R. P. & Ali, S. (2025). Interpersonal acceptance-rejection theory (IPARTheory): From conception through maturity. In Rohner, R. P., & Ali. S. (Eds.). *Global perspectives on parental acceptance and rejection: Lessons learned from IPARTheory* (pp. 3–38). Routledge.

Rohner, R. P., & Lansford, J. E. (2017). Deep structure of the human affectional system: Introduction to interpersonal acceptance-rejection theory. *Journal of Family Theory & Review, 9*(4), 426–440.

Schulz, J. H. (2001). *The economics of aging*. ABC-CLIO.

Schulz, R., Newsom, J., Mittlemark, M., Burton, L., Hirsch, C., & Jackson, S. (1997). Health effects of caregiving: The Caregiver Health Effects Study: An ancillary study of the cardiovascular health study. *Annals of Behavioral Medicine, 19*, 110–116.

Strauss, A., & Corbin, J. (1998). *Basics of qualitative research: Techniques and procedures for developing grounded theory* (2nd ed.). Sage Publications, Inc.

Swartz, T. T. (2009). Intergenerational family relations in adulthood: Patterns, variations, and implications in the contemporary United States. *Annual Review of Sociology*, 191–212.

U.S. Census Bureau, Population Division (2020). *Projected Age Groups and Sex Composition of the Population: Main Projections Series for the United States, 2017–2060*. Retrieved on January 25, 2023, from https://www.census.gov/data/tables/2017/demo/popproj/2017-summary-tables.html

Wolff, J. L., & Kasper, J. D. (2006). Caregivers of frail elders: Updating a national profile. *The Gerontologist, 46*(3), 344–356.

7

DEVELOPMENTAL CORRELATES OF PARENTAL ACCEPTANCE-REJECTION FROM CHILDHOOD TO ADULTHOOD IN NINE COUNTRIES

Jennifer E. Lansford

Interpersonal Acceptance-Rejection Theory (IPARTheory) argues that interpersonal acceptance and rejection predict individuals' psychological and behavioral adjustment from childhood through adulthood (Rohner & Lansford, 2017; see Rohner & Ali, 2025; Chapter 1, this book). The theory's central tenets have been supported in thirteen meta-analyses, concluding that interpersonal acceptance-rejection is cross-culturally important for well-being across age groups (Khaleque & Ali, 2017). This chapter provides an overview of the Parenting Across Cultures (PAC) project, a longitudinal study of children, mothers, and fathers in nine countries that addresses many questions related to parental acceptance-rejection. The chapter briefly describes the methodology of the PAC project. The chapter next describes findings from the project regarding trajectories of parental acceptance-rejection over time, predictors and developmental outcomes associated with parental acceptance-rejection, and parental acceptance-rejection as a mediator of links among prior risk and protective factors and child adjustment. The chapter then describes the limitations of the project, future directions, and implications for practice and policy.

Parenting Across Cultures Project

Participants

Children and their parents (both mothers and fathers) were recruited from public and private schools that serve socioeconomically diverse families in 13 groups in nine countries: China (Jinan and Shanghai), Colombia

DOI: 10.4324/9781003441243-9

(Medellín), Italy (Rome and Naples), Jordan (Zarqa), Kenya (Kisumu), the Philippines (Manila), Sweden (Trollhättan/Vänersborg), Thailand (Chiang Mai), the United States (African American, European American, and Latino families in Durham, NC). At the time of recruitment, children ranged from 7 to 10 years of age (N = 1,298, M = 8.29 years, SD = .66, 51% girls). Mothers (N = 1,275, M_{age} = 36.93 years, SD_{age} = 6.27) and fathers (N = 1,032, M_{age} = 39.96 years, SD_{age} = 6.52) also provided data. Most participating parents were married (82%) and biological parents (97%) of their children; some nonresidential/non-biological parents also provided data. Participants have been followed annually since 2008, with data collection ongoing. Attrition has remained low throughout the project. Attriters do not differ from continuous participants on parents' age at the time of the child's birth, parents' education, or the child's gender.

Procedure

Self-report measures described below were administered in Mandarin Chinese (China), Spanish (Colombia and the United States), Italian (Italy), Arabic (Jordan), Dholuo (Kenya), Filipino (the Philippines), English (the Philippines and the United States), Swedish (Sweden), and Thai (Thailand) following forward- and back-translation and methodological validation to ensure the conceptual equivalence of the instruments (Erkut, 2010). Previous research with the Parenting Across Cultures sample has addressed measurement invariance (Huang et al., 2012; Rothenberg et al., 2020a). Interviews lasting 1.5–2 hours were conducted at each age after parent consent and child assent were obtained in participant-chosen locations. At first assessment for parents and until age 10 for children, interviews were conducted orally. Subsequently, participants chose to complete written or oral measures.

Measurement of Parental Acceptance-Rejection

When children were, on average, between 8 and 14 years of age, children, mothers, and fathers completed the short version of the Child Parental Acceptance-Rejection/Control Questionnaire (PARQ/Control, Rohner, 2005). This is a measure with excellent reliability, convergent and discriminant validity, and measurement invariance that has been used in scores of cultures worldwide and has been used successfully with families in all nine participating countries by our own and other research teams (Lansford, Rothenberg et al., 2018a; Rohner, 2005). Children provided separate ratings about their mothers and fathers. Warmth was computed as the average of eight items from the warmth scale, such as "I make my child feel wanted and needed" or "My mother/father makes me feel wanted and needed." Hostility was computed as the average of six items, such as "I punish my child severely when I am angry" or "My mother/father punishes me severely when she/he is angry." Neglect was computed as the average of six items, such as "I pay no attention to my child when (s)he asks for help" or "My mother/father pays no attention to me when I ask for help." Rejection was computed as the average of four items, such as "I do not really love my child" or "My mother/father does not really love me." Frequency of behavior was rated on a modified 4-point scale (1 = *almost never* to 4 = *every day*). In some analyses, we used each subscale separately. In others, we used the total acceptance-rejection scale, computed as the sum of the items for warmth-affection (reversed), hostility, rejection, and neglect (high score equals more rejection). In others—based on Rohner and Cournoyer's (1994) analysis of the factor structure of the PARQ scale in eight cultural groups—two subscales were derived, measuring parental warmth separately from hostility/neglect/rejection.

Trajectories of Parental Acceptance-Rejection Over Time

Several sets of PAC analyses have examined trajectories of parental acceptance-rejection over time. We conducted these analyses by age rather than by waves of data collection to account for variations in children's ages within a given wave and to enable us to examine trajectories spanning ages 7–18 years. These analyses provided evidence for both cultural specificity as well as cultural universality in trajectories. In terms of universality, we found that across the nine countries in the PAC sample, parents' and children's reports of parents' warmth generally decreased over time from age 7 to 18 years, with an inflection point between 11 and 12 years of age showing pronounced decrease in warmth (Bornstein et al., 2021). Regarding specificity, there were some nuances across countries in whether the decrease in warmth happened uniformly across this age range or first increased to a certain degree before decreasing (Bornstein et al., 2021). One reason for the decrease in parental warmth across adolescence could be that parents spend less time with adolescents than with younger children, so parents may have fewer opportunities to demonstrate warmth. Parents may also find it more challenging to continue demonstrating warmth in the face of more frequent conflict, which often characterizes the transition to adolescence (Branje, 2018).

We also examined whether changes in warmth were a function of the child's age, puberty, or both. These analyses showed steeper declines in parental warmth after age 11 than before. In addition, even after controlling for effects of age, greater progression through puberty at a particular age was associated with less parental warmth at that age than was otherwise typical (Lansford et al., 2021b). The intercept, slope prior to age 11, and slope after age 11 all varied significantly, suggesting that within individual families, some parents started higher or lower than others in warmth and changed at different rates from the average trajectory. The parental warmth trajectory did not differ for boys versus girls.

Predictors of Parental Acceptance-Rejection

In addition to age and pubertal status, several PAC papers found a range of developmental predictors of parental acceptance-rejection. Some of these predictors are sociodemographic. For example, in six of the nine countries, parental education significantly predicted trajectories of warmth through adolescence, with more educated parents providing slightly more warmth (Bornstein et al., 2021). Across countries, mothers and fathers generally reported high levels of warmth and low levels of hostility, rejection, and neglect. In some countries (China, Italy, the Philippines, Sweden, and Thailand), we found that mothers reported higher warmth than fathers, whereas in Kenya, fathers reported higher warmth than mothers (Putnick et al., 2012). In Sweden, mothers reported less hostility, rejection, and neglect than fathers (Putnick et al., 2012). Mothers' and fathers' reports of warmth were significantly correlated in Italy, Jordan, Kenya, the Philippines, and the United States (ranging from .18 to .38; Putnick et al., 2012). Mothers' and fathers' reports of hostility, rejection, and neglect were significantly correlated in China, Colombia, Italy, Jordan, Thailand, and the United States (ranging from .21 to .36; Putnick et al., 2012). Child gender did not predict parental warmth consistently across countries or ages. In some analyses, parents provided more warmth toward girls in China and Kenya and more warmth toward boys in Jordan. Also, in some analyses parents provided more warmth toward girls at some ages, and boys at other ages in Italy, whereas there were no gender differences in other countries (Bornstein et al., 2021).

Beyond sociodemographic predictors, we tested the hypothesis that parents' recollections of their own parents' acceptance-rejection when they were growing up would predict the acceptance-rejection they showed to their own children. Researchers who study intergenerational relationships refer to these individuals as Generation 1 (G1; the children's grandparents), Generation 2 (G2; the children's parents), and Generation 3 (G3; the-children). We found that G2 parents' recollections of their G1 parents' rejection predicted an increase in G2s' rejection of their G3 children,-especially in cultural contexts with higher normative levels of parental rejection (Rothenberg et al., 2023a, 2023b). In addition, this intergenerational transmission of parental rejection predicted more G3 externalizing and internalizing behavior problems in children. However, the intergenerational transmission of paternal rejection was disrupted by fathers' participation in a parenting program in cultures where parental rejection tended to be normative. Intergenerational transmission of maternal rejection was disrupted by an increase of more than five percent in a family's income, regardless of cultural context. These results suggest that interventions that provide families with income supplements or parenting skills help disrupt the intergenerational transmission of parental rejection.

Parental acceptance and rejection are also predicted by children's own positive and negative behaviors, respectively. For example, children who showed more prosocial behaviors (such as helping and sharing) at age 9 elicited more maternal warmth the following year (Pastorelli et al., 2016). In addition, from ages 8 to 13 years, children with higher levels of externalizing and internalizing behaviors in one year elicited less parental warmth the following year. These child effects were more pervasive across this developmental period than were the effects of parental warmth, predicting fewer externalizing and internalizing problems the following year, which were concentrated at earlier ages (Lansford, Godwin, et al., 2018b). Children's internalizing and externalizing behaviors predicted lower maternal and paternal warmth in ways that were mostly consistent across countries (Rothenberg et al., 2020c). We disaggregated different types of externalizing behaviors. We found that compared to children's rule-breaking behavior, children's aggression—especially before age 10—was likely to evoke a decrease in subsequent parental warmth (Rothenberg et al., 2020d).

Parental acceptance-rejection was also predicted by parents' personal characteristics and the characteristics of parents' environments. For example, parents' religiousness when children were 8 years old was associated with more parental rejection. But parental religiousness was associated with more parental efficacy and warmth when children were 9 years old. This led us to conclude that religiousness is a mixed blessing as far as parenting is concerned, with benefits as well as drawbacks (Bornstein et al., 2017). In addition, neighborhood danger predicted harsher maternal parenting, and household chaos predicted harsher maternal parenting and less maternal warmth (Deater-Deckard et al., 2019).

Methodologically, self-enhancing response biases are a risk in any research reliant on self-reports. In the study, we administered a social desirability scale (Reynolds, 1982) to control for such self-enhancing biases. We also examined whether socially desirable responses were related to parental warmth, parental hostility/neglect/rejection, or to both. We found that for both mothers and fathers and across countries, socially desirable responding was associated more strongly with self-reports of parental hostility/neglect/rejection than warmth (Bornstein et al., 2015). Only 4 of 36 associations tested differed by parent gender, and only 2 of 36 associations tested differed across countries. Thus, when interpreting parents' reports of their acceptance-rejection, it is important to remember that they may have a tendency to under-report behaviors that indicate hostility, neglect, and rejection.

Because individuals are nested within families that are nested within cultural groups, the design of the PAC project is well suited for understanding between-culture versus within-culture sources of variance. For mothers, the proportion of the between-person variance accounted for by culture was .16 for hostility, .08 for neglect, .20 for rejection, and .20 for warmth for mothers' reports (.16, .05, .12, and .14, respectively, for child reports; Deater-Deckard et al., 2018). For fathers, the proportion of between-person variance accounted for by culture was .33 for hostility, .15 for neglect, .45 for rejection, and .36 for warmth for fathers' reports (.13, .06, .13, and .12, respectively, for child reports; Deater-Deckard et al., 2018). These findings reveal much more variance within cultures than between cultures in mothers' and fathers' acceptance and rejection.

Parental acceptance and rejection are also concurrently correlated with other dimensions of parenting. For example, across the 13 cultural groups in our nine-country study, the concurrent correlation between parental warmth and behavioral control ranged from −.35 to .85 (Deater-Deckard et al., 2011). Because we had parent and child reports of warmth and control, we examined four correlations between warmth and control for each-parent–child relationship. The correlations for each cultural group were as follows: Jinan (.01 to .24, n.s.) and Shanghai, China (−.10, n.s., to .26, $p < .05$); Colombia (.07, n.s., to .60, $p < .05$); Naples (.12, n.s., to .68, $p < .05$) and Rome, Italy (.16, n.s., to .45, $p < .05$); Jordan (−.14, n.s., to .35, $p < .05$); Kenya (.44 to .85, $p < .05$); Philippines (.22, n.s., to .54, $p < .05$); Sweden (−.13, n.s., to .48, $p < .05$); Thailand (.21, n.s., to .71, $p < .05$); and Black (.28, n.s., to .46, $p < .05$), White (−.35 to −.18, n.s.), and Latino families (.23, n.s., to .62, $p < .05$) in the United States. All the significant correlations (25 of the 52 tested) were positive. Perhaps because warmth and control were not related to one another in the same way across cultures, warmth and control were also related somewhat differently to child adjustment across cultures. We found, for instance, that parental warmth protected against the onset and increase of children's internalizing and externalizing problems over time across cultures. However, there was more variability in associations of behavioral control with children's internalizing and externalizing problems (Rothenberg et al., 2020c).

Child Development Outcomes Associated with Parental Acceptance-Rejection

As was already observed, mothers' and fathers' warmth predicts a decrease in children's externalizing and internalizing problems over time (Rothenberg et al., 2020c). When we disaggregated different types of externalizing problems, we found that parental warmth predicted less subsequent child rule-breaking behavior more consistently across development than less child aggression (Rothenberg et al., 2020c). When we disaggregated different aspects of internalizing problems, we found that lower parental warmth most pervasively predicted children's withdrawn/depressed problems, followed by anxious/depressed problems. Parental warmth least pervasively predicted children's somatic problems across development (Rothenberg et al., 2020b). In addition, parental warmth when children were 9 and 10 years old predicted an increase in children's prosocial behaviors from age 10 to 12 (Pastorelli et al., 2021; Putnick et al., 2018).

For mothers and fathers across all nine countries, higher perceived parental rejection, by contrast, predicted an increase in internalizing and externalizing problems and a decrease in school achievement across three years (Putnick et al., 2015). These analyses controlled for within-wave relations, stability across waves, and parental age, education, and social desirability response bias. Likewise, for mothers and fathers across countries, parental warmth promoted and parental hostility, neglect, and rejection hindered children's flourishing, as indicated by engagement, perseverance, optimism, connectedness, and happiness (Rothenberg et al., 2021). In Sweden, child agency is an important cultural value aligned with the emphasis on children's rights as equal to those of adults (Sorbring et al., 2021). For both boys and girls, we found that parental warmth predicted subsequent child agency, but child agency did not predict subsequent parental warmth (Gurdal et al., 2016). These findings suggest that parental acceptance may be one way in which culturally valued aspects of child development are promoted.

Parental rejection is also related to developmental outcomes downstream from internalizing and externalizing problems. For example, we found a significant indirect effect of maternal rejection on youth self-efficacy in dealing with anger via youth aggression (Di Giunta et al., 2022). That is, maternal rejection predicted more youth aggressive behavior, which in turn was significantly related to lower youth self-efficacy in dealing with anger. We also found significant effects of maternal rejection on youths' beliefs about lower self-efficacy regarding the regulation of sadness. Dysregulation of sadness was related to more youth depressive symptoms (Di Giunta et al., 2022). Thus, it appears that parental acceptance-rejection affects youth well-being by shaping how youth regulate their emotions (especially anger and sadness) and their sense of self-efficacy regarding how well they can regulate these emotions. Thus, we have robust evidence that parental acceptance-rejection is related longitudinally to a range of child adjustment outcomes.

To test the relative strength of a range of predictors of child externalizing and internalizing behaviors, we used a machine learning approach in which 79 possible predictors were compared to ascertain the predictive power of each (Rothenberg et al., 2023a, 2023b). In each analysis, predictors at age 10 were ranked in terms of their importance for predicting externalizing and internalizing behaviors at ages 13 and 17. In predicting externalizing behavior among 13-year-olds, youth reports of their mothers' and fathers' hostility, their mothers' neglect, and youths' reports of their fathers' rejection emerged in the top 15 predictors. In predicting externalizing behavior among 17-year-olds, mother-reported hostility, youth-reported maternal hostility, and youth-reported paternal warmth were among the top 15 predictors. In predicting internalizing behavior among 13-year-olds, youth-reported maternal warmth and youth-reported paternal neglect were among the top 15 predictors. Finally, in predicting internalizing behavior at age 17, youth-reported maternal and paternal neglect were among the top 15 predictors. Taken together, these findings suggest that key components of parental acceptance-rejection in middle childhood predict subsequent internalizing and externalizing behaviors in adolescence.

In addition to finding evidence that parental acceptance-rejection is related longitudinally to subsequent developmental outcomes during childhood and adolescence, we have also found that parental acceptance-rejection in one generation tends to predict parental acceptance-rejection and child outcomes in the next generation (Rothenberg et al., 2021). Intergenerational transmission of parental acceptance-rejection also showed cultural specificity. Intergenerational transmission of warmth was more likely in cultures above average in parent warmth, and intergenerational transmission of hostility, neglect, and rejection was less likely in cultures below average in hostility, neglect, and rejection.

The design of the Parenting Across Cultures project—with children, mothers, and fathers nested within families, that are in turn nested within cultures—is well suited for comparing within-culture effects to between-culture effects. For example, we found that within cultures, hostility, neglect, rejection, and lack of warmth are each independently associated with internalizing and externalizing behaviors from ages 7 to 14 (Rothenberg et al., 2022). In addition, we found between-culture effects in that children's internalizing behaviors were more persistent over time in cultures in which mothers' and fathers' neglect was higher than average compared to other cultures (Rothenberg et al., 2022).

In addition to the main effects of parental acceptance-rejection on child outcomes, we also have found that parental acceptance-rejection may moderate associations between variables and child outcomes. For example, maternal warmth tends to moderate the link between corporal punishment and changes in children's anxiety and aggression in some countries (Lansford et al., 2014). Children's anxiety decreased most over time if their mothers were high in warmth and low in the use of corporal punishment. This trend was followed by children whose mothers were low in both warmth and the use of corporal punishment. Anxiety, however, increased rather than decreased over time among children whose mothers were high in both warmth and the use of corporal punishment. One explanation is that these incongruent forms of parenting were unsettling for children, making them unsure of whether their mothers would treat them harshly or warmly.

Overall, parental warmth is related to a range of adaptive child outcomes, but cultural normativeness of parental warmth can strengthen or weaken these associations. We found that children displayed more social competence within a given culture when their mothers were warmer than the cultural mean (Lansford, Rothenberg, et al., 2018a). In addition, the association between fathers' warmth and children's social competence was stronger in cultures where paternal warmth was more normative. Children also behaved more prosocially when their mothers' and fathers' warmth was higher than the within-culture mean. Likewise, the association between maternal warmth and children's prosocial behavior was more robust in cultures in which maternal warmth was more normative. Children's academic achievement was higher when fathers' warmth was higher relative to others in their culture and in cultures with paternal warmth higher than the grand mean across cultures. These associations were significant above and beyond prior adjustment and sociodemographic covariates.

Because we had child, mother, and father reports of parents' acceptance-rejection, we were able to examine whether each person's perspective carries unique predictive value for children's subsequent adjustment. For example, within the US sample, we used a multitrait-multimethod confirmatory factor analysis to isolate adolescents' distinct views of parental rejection from the portion of the adolescents' view that overlaps the parents' view (Jager et al., 2016). We found that adolescents' unique perspectives of parental rejection predicted more adolescent internalizing and externalizing problems one year later. This conclusion is consistent with IPARTheory's central postulate about the importance of individuals' perceptions of parental acceptance-rejection.

Parental Acceptance-Rejection as a Mediator of Links Between Prior Risk and Protective Factors and Child Adjustment

We also tested whether parental acceptance-rejection mediates the relation between prior risk and protective factors and subsequent child adjustment. For example, in one study, we focused on China, Colombia, Jordan, Kenya, the Philippines, and Thailand. We found that maternal harshness (reflecting hostility, neglect, rejection, and psychological control) when children were 14 years old statistically mediated the relation between household chaos and neighborhood danger when children were age 13 years and subsequent externalizing, internalizing, and school performance problems at age 15 years (Deater-Deckard et al., 2019). That is, one mechanism through which living in a dangerous neighborhood or chaotic household can affect children's adjustment is via harsh maternal parenting.

In Italy, we administered a set of items focused on maternal self-efficacy and found that maternal warmth mediated the association between maternal self-efficacy and adolescents' subsequent prosocial behaviors (Luengo Kanacri et al., 2021). In the Philippines, maternal hostility, neglect, and rejection mediated the association between parental self-efficacy and children's delinquent behavior (Daganzo et al., 2014). Thus, it appears that one way that both environmental risk factors and parental characteristics affect children's adjustment is through their effects on parental acceptance-rejection.

Even the way in which experiences within the parent–child relationship affect children's adjustment may be accounted for by whether the experiences lead children to feel accepted or rejected by their parents. In a precursor to the PAC study, for example, we found in a sample of mother-child dyads in China, India, the Philippines, and Thailand that mothers' use of corporal punishment and harsh verbal discipline predicted mothers' reports of children's anxiety and aggression (Lansford et al., 2010). Children's perceptions of maternal hostility mediated three of those four links. Children were more likely to perceive harsh verbal discipline as being hostile in cultural contexts in which harsh verbal discipline was less normative. The meaning children attach to parents' behaviors may be more important than the actual behaviors in predicting children's adjustment.

Limitations and Future Directions

The ongoing Parenting Across Cultures project has numerous strengths, including the availability of longitudinal data on parental acceptance-rejection spanning ages 7–18, and including children's, mothers', and fathers' reports of parental acceptance-rejection in nine countries. But the project also has limitations. First, the samples are not nationally representative, so care must be taken not to generalize to entire countries or beyond these nine countries to other countries. Second, data collection started in middle-childhood. It is possible that parental acceptance-rejection is predicted by and predicts different constructs in infancy and early childhood as well as later in life.

Advances in neuroscience allow future research to examine possible brain mechanisms involved in parental acceptance-rejection. For example, previous research has found that children who have been spanked show a different neural response to perceived threats than children who have not been spanked (Cuartas et al., 2021). It is possible that parental acceptance-rejection likewise alters brain structure and function (e.g., see Miller & Ali, 2025; Chapter 12, this book). Psychophysiological studies on stress responses also suggest that the hypothalamic-pituitary-adrenal axis is affected by interpersonal adversity during childhood (Huang & Starr, 2020). These mechanisms may be responsible for some of the links between parental rejection and poor child adjustment and are worthy of additional research attention. The use of ecological momentary assessments and daily diaries could make it possible in future research to understand fluctuations in parental acceptance-rejection that might occur from day to day or during the course of a given day. Measurement of these fluctuations could provide additional insights above and beyond assessments that provide a snapshot at a single point in time (Odgers et al., 2023).

Implications for Practice and Policy

In terms of practice, one implication of our findings is that in therapeutic interventions designed to improve adolescents' well-being, it is important to target adolescents' *perceptions* of their parents' behavior (Jager et al., 2016). Regardless of whether parents perceive themselves as accepting or rejecting (and regardless of whether an impartial observer would regard the parents as accepting or rejecting), if adolescents perceive themselves as being rejected by their parents, their well-being is likely to suffer. There is value in working with parents to change their behaviors in ways that will improve the quality of parent–adolescent relationships. But it is equally important to work with adolescents as needed to help cognitively reframe issues that might be leading them to perceive their parents as rejecting.

In terms of policy, the United Nation's (2023) Sustainable Development Goals (SDG) guiding the international agenda through 2030 include SDG 3, which is to "ensure healthy lives and promote well-being for all at all ages." SDG Target 3.4 is to promote well-being and mental health. Parental acceptance and other positive social relationships are among the most important predictors of well-being and mental health. In the PAC project, as described above, we have documented numerous links between mothers' and fathers' acceptance and fewer child internalizing and externalizing behaviors, more child prosocial behavior, better social competence, and better school performance (e.g., Lansford, Rothenberg et al., 2018a; Putnick et al., 2015). SDG 5 promotes "gender parity and equitable life chances." In the project, we have found that associations between parental acceptance-rejection and child well-being are generally consistent across cultural contexts and for both mothers and fathers. Both mothers' and fathers' parenting play important roles (e.g., Rothenberg et al., 2023a, 2023b). Taken together, the findings suggest the value of policies that are supportive of warm parent–child relationships and gender equity such as paid parental leave for both mothers and fathers. Longitudinal developmental research provides evidence that can be used by policymakers to implement programs and policies supportive of well-being, mental health, and gender equity (Lansford et al., 2021a).

Conclusions

Using longitudinal data from a sample of children followed through adolescence and their mothers and fathers in nine countries, we draw several conclusions about developmental correlates of parental acceptance-rejection. As children move into and through adolescence, parental warmth tends to show a downward trajectory across countries. Pubertal status, in addition to age itself, predicts this decrease. Parental acceptance-rejection is predicted by several sociodemographic factors such as parents' own experiences of parental acceptance-rejection when they were children, behaviors of their children, and personal characteristics of parents and their environments. More variance in parental acceptance-rejection is accounted for by within-culture than between-culture factors. Parental acceptance-rejection predicts a range of child behavioral and psychological development outcomes, such as internalizing and externalizing problems, academic achievement, and prosocial behavior. Associations of risk and protective factors with child adjustment are sometimes mediated by parental acceptance-rejection. Understanding the importance of mothers' and fathers' acceptance has implications for programs and policies to advance the UN's international agenda of promoting well-being and gender parity at all ages.

References

Bornstein, M. H., Putnick, D. L., Lansford, J. E., Al-Hassan, S. M., Bacchini, D., Bombi, A. S., Chang, L., Deater-Deckard, K., Di Giunta, L., Dodge, K. A., Malone, P. S., Oburu, P., Pastorelli, C., Skinner, A. T., Sorbring, E., Steinberg, L., Tapanya, S., Uribe Tirado, L. M., Zelli, A., & Alampay, L. P. (2017). "Mixed blessings": Parental religiousness, parenting, and child adjustment in global perspective. *Journal of Child Psychology and Psychiatry, 58*, 880–892.

Bornstein, M. H., Putnick, D. L., Lansford, J. E., Pastorelli, C., Skinner, A. T., Sorbring, E., Tapanya, S., Uribe Tirado, L. M., Zelli, A., Alampay, L. P., Al-Hassan, S. M., Bacchini, D., Bombi, A. S., Chang, L., Deater-Deckard, K., Di Giunta, L., Dodge, K. A., Malone, P. S., & Oburu, P. (2015). Mother and father socially desirable responding in nine countries: Two kinds of agreement and relations to parenting self-reports. *International Journal of Psychology, 50,* 174–185.

Bornstein, M. H., Rothenberg, W. A., & Lansford, J. E. (2021). Change over time in four domains of parenting in diverse international contexts: Specificity and universality, country and culture, determinants, strengths, and limitations, future directions and implications. In J. E. Lansford, W. A. Rothenberg, & M. H. Bornstein (Eds.), *Parenting across cultures from childhood to adolescence: Development in nine countries* (pp. 227–263). Routledge.

Branje, S. (2018). Development of parent–adolescent relationships: Conflict interactions as a mechanism of change. *Child Development Perspectives, 12,* 171–176.

Cuartas, J., Weissman, D. G., Sheridan, M. A., Lengua, L., & McLaughlin, K. A. (2021). Corporal punishment and elevated neural response to threat in children. *Child Development, 92*(3), 821–832.

Daganzo, M. A. A., Alampay, L. P., & Lansford, J. E. (2014). Filipino mothers' self-efficacy in managing anger and in parenting, and parental rejection as predictors of child delinquency. *Philippine Journal of Psychology, 47,* 1–26.

Deater-Deckard, K., Godwin, J., Lansford, J. E., Bacchini, D., Bombi, A. S., Bornstein, M. H., Chang, L., Di Giunta, L., Dodge, K. A., Malone, P. S., Oburu, P., Pastorelli, C., Skinner, A. T., Sorbring, E., Steinberg, L., Tapanya, S., Alampay, L. P., Uribe Tirado, L. M., Zelli, A., & Al-Hassan, S. M. (2018). Within- and between-person and group variance in behavior and beliefs in cross-cultural longitudinal data. *Journal of Adolescence, 62,* 207–217.

Deater-Deckard, K., Godwin, J., Lansford, J. E., Uribe Tirado, L. M., Yotanyamaneewong, S., Alampay, L. P., Al-Hassan, S. M., Bacchini, D., Bornstein, M. H., Chang, L., Di Giunta, L., Dodge, K. A., Oburu, P., Pastorelli, C., Skinner, A. T., Sorbring, E., Steinberg, L., & Tapanya, S. (2019). Chaos, danger, and maternal parenting in families: Links with adolescent adjustment in low- and middle-income countries. *Developmental Science, 22*(5), e12855.

Deater-Deckard, K., Lansford, J. E., Malone, P. S., Alampay, L. P., Sorbring, E., Bacchini, D., Bombi, A. S., Bornstein, M. H., Chang, L., Di Giunta, L., Dodge, K. A., Oburu, P., Pastorelli, C., Skinner, A. T., Tapanya, S., Uribe Tirado, L. M., Zelli, A., & Al-Hassan, S. M. (2011). The association between parental warmth and control in thirteen cultural groups. *Journal of Family Psychology, 25,* 790–794.

Di Giunta, L., Lunetti, C., Gliozzo, G., Rothenberg, W. A., Lansford, J. E., Eisenberg, N., Pastorelli, C., Basili, E., Fiasconaro, I., Thartori, E., Favini, A., & Virzì, A. T. (2022). Negative parenting, adolescents' emotion regulation, self-efficacy about emotion regulation, and psychological adjustment. *International Journal of Environmental Research and Public Health, 19,* 2251.

Erkut, S. (2010). Developing multiple language versions of instruments for intercultural research. *Child Development Perspectives, 4,* 19–24.

Gurdal, S., Lansford, J. E., & Sorbring, E. (2016). Parental perceptions of childreńs agency: Parental warmth, school achievement and adjustment. *Early Child Development and Care, 186,* 1203–1211.

Huang, L., Malone, P. S., Lansford, J. E., Deater-Deckard, K., Di Giunta, L., Bombi, A. S., Bornstein, M. H., Chang, L., Dodge, K. A., Oburu, P., Pastorelli, C., Skinner, A. T., Sorbring, E., Tapanya, S., Uribe Tirado, L. M., Zelli, A., Alampay, L.,

Al-Hassan, S. M., & Bacchini, D. (2012). Measurement invariance of mother reports of discipline in different cultural contexts. *Family Science, 2*, 212–219.
Huang, M., & Starr, L. R. (2020). Interpersonal childhood adversity and stress generation in adolescence: Moderation by HPA axis multilocus genetic variation. *Development and Psychopathology, 32*(3), 865–878.
Jager, J., Mahler, A., An, D., Putnick, D. L., Bornstein, M. H., Lansford, J. E., Dodge, K. A., Skinner, A. T., & Deater-Deckard, K. (2016). Early adolescents' unique perspectives of maternal and paternal rejection: Examining their across-dyad generalizability and relations with adjustment one year later. *Journal of Youth and Adolescence, 45*, 2108–2124.
Khaleque, A., & Ali, S. (2017). A systematic review of meta-analyses of research on interpersonal acceptance–rejection theory: Constructs and measures. *Journal of Family Theory & Review, 9*(4), 441–458.
Lansford, J. E., Godwin, J., Al-Hassan, S. M., Bacchini, D., Bombi, A. S., Bornstein, M. H., Chang, L., Chen, B.-B., Deater-Deckard, K., Di Giunta, L., Dodge, K. A., Malone, P. S., Oburu, P., Pastorelli, C., Skinner, A. T., Sorbring, E., Steinberg, L., Tapanya, S., Alampay, L. P., Uribe Tirado, L. M., & Zelli, A. (2018b). Longitudinal associations between parenting and youth adjustment in twelve cultural groups: Cultural normativeness of parenting as a moderator. *Developmental Psychology, 54*, 362–377.
Lansford, J. E., Malone, P. S., Dodge, K. A., Chang, L., Chaudhary, N., Tapanya, S., Oburu, P., & Deater-Deckard, K. (2010). Children's perceptions of maternal hostility as a mediator of the link between discipline and children's adjustment in four countries. *International Journal of Behavioral Development, 34*, 452–461.
Lansford, J. E., Rothenberg, W. A., Jensen, T. M., Lippold, M. A., Bacchini, D., Bornstein, M. H., Chang, L., Deater-Deckard, K., Di Giunta, L., Dodge, K. A., Malone, P. S., Oburu, P., Pastorelli, C., Skinner, A. T., Sorbring, E., Steinberg, L., Tapanya, S., Uribe Tirado, L. M., Alampay, L. P., & Al-Hassan, S. M. (2018a). Bidirectional relations between parenting and behavior problems from age 8 to 13 in nine countries. *Journal of Research on Adolescence, 28*, 571–590.
Lansford, J. E., Rothenberg, W. A., Riley, J., Uribe Tirado, L. M., Yotanyamaneewong, S., Alampay, L. P., Al-Hassan, S. M., Bacchini, D., Bornstein, M. H., Chang, L., Deater-Deckard, K., Di Giunta, L., Dodge, K. A., Gurdal, S., Liu, Q., Long, Q., Malone, P. S., Oburu, P., Pastorelli, C., Skinner, A. T., Sorbring, E., Tapanya, S., & Steinberg, L. (2021b). Longitudinal trajectories of four domains of parenting in relation to adolescent age and puberty in nine countries. *Child Development, 92*, e493–e512.
Lansford, J. E., Rothenberg, W. A., Tapanya, S., Uribe Tirado, L. M., Yotanyamaneewong, S., Alampay, L. P., Al-Hassan, S. M., Bacchini, D., Bornstein, M. H., Chang, L., Deater-Deckard, K., Di Giunta, L., Dodge, K. A., Gurdal, S., Liu, Q., Long, Q., Malone, P. S., Oburu, P., Pastorelli, C., Skinner, A. T., Sorbring, E., & Steinberg, L. (2021a). Achieving the Sustainable Development Goals: Evidence from the longitudinal Parenting Across Cultures Project. In P. Banati (Ed.), *Sustainable human development: Evidence from longitudinal studies in childhood and adolescence* (pp. 89–111). Bristol University Press.
Lansford, J. E., Sharma, C., Malone, P. S., Woodlief, D., Dodge, K. A., Oburu, P., Pastorelli, C., Skinner, A. T., Sorbring, E., Tapanya, S., Uribe Tirado, L. M., Zelli, A., Al-Hassan, S. M., Alampay, L. P., Bacchini, D., Bombi, A. S., Bornstein, M. H., Chang, L., Deater-Deckard, K., & Di Giunta, L. (2014). Corporal punishment, maternal warmth, and child adjustment: A longitudinal study in eight countries. *Journal of Clinical Child and Adolescent Psychology, 43*, 670–685.

Luengo Kanacri, B. P., Pastorelli, C., Thartori, E., Lunetti, C., Di Giunta. L., Bacchini, D., & Lansford, J. E. (2021). Longitudinal relations among maternal self-efficacy, maternal warmth, and early adolescents' prosocial behavior. *Parenting: Science and Practice, 21*, 24–46.

Miller, J. G., & Ali, S. (2025). Effect of early life stress on adolescent brain development. In R. P. Rohner & S. Ali (Eds.), *Global perspectives on parental acceptance and rejection: Lessons learned from IPARTheory* (pp. 225–245). Routledge.

Odgers, C. L., Godwin, J., Rothenberg, W. A., Lansford, J. E., Dodge, K. A., & Copeland, W. E. (2023). Daily parenting and household chaos uniquely predict children's behavior and maternal depression. Manuscript submitted for publication

Pastorelli, C., Lansford, J. E., Luengo Kanacri, B. P., Malone, P. S., Di Giunta, L., Bacchini, D., Bombi, A. S., Zelli, A., Miranda, M. C., Bornstein, M. H., Tapanya, S., Uribe Tirado, L. M., Alampay, L. P., Al-Hassan, S. M., Chang, L., Deater-Deckard, K., Dodge, K. A., Oburu, P., Skinner, A. T., & Sorbring, E. (2016). Positive parenting and children's prosocial behavior in eight countries. *Journal of Child Psychology and Psychiatry, 57*, 824–834.

Pastorelli, C., Zuffianò, A., Lansford, J. E., Thartori, E., Bornstein, M. H., Chang, L., Deater-Deckard, K., Di Giunta, L., Dodge, K. A., Gurdal, S., Liu, Q., Long, Q., Oburu, P., Skinner, A. T., Sorbring, E., Steinberg, L., Tapanya, S., Uribe Tirado, L. M., Yotanyamaneewong, S., Al-Hassan, S., Alampay, L. P., & Bacchini, D. (2021). Positive youth development: Parental warmth, values, and prosocial behavior in 11 cultural groups. *Journal of Youth Development, 16*(2–3), 379–401.

Putnick, D. L., Bornstein, M. H., Lansford, J. E., Chang, L., Deater-Deckard, K., Di Giunta, L., Dodge, K. A., Malone, P. S., Oburu, P., Pastorelli, C., Skinner, A. T., Sorbring, E., Tapanya, S., Uribe Tirado, L. M., Zelli, A., Alampay, L. P., Al-Hassan, S. M., Bacchini, D., & Bombi, A. S. (2018). Parental acceptance-rejection and child prosocial behavior: Developmental transactions across the transition to adolescence in nine countries, mothers and fathers, and girls and boys. *Developmental Psychology, 54*, 1881–1890.

Putnick, D. L., Bornstein, M. H., Lansford, J. E., Chang, L., Deater-Deckard, K., Di Giunta, L., Gurdal, S., Dodge, K. A., Malone, P. S., Oburu, P., Pastorelli, C., Skinner, A. T., Sorbring, E., Tapanya, S., Uribe Tirado, L. M., Zelli, A., Alampay, L. P., Al-Hassan, S. M., Bacchini, D., & Bombi, A. S. (2012). Agreement in mother and father acceptance-rejection, warmth, and hostility/rejection/neglect of children across nine countries. *Cross-Cultural Research, 46*, 191–223.

Putnick, D. L., Bornstein, M. H., Lansford, J. E., Malone, P. S., Pastorelli, C., Skinner, A. T., Sorbring, E., Tapanya, S., Uribe Tirado, L. M., Zelli, A., Alampay, L. P., Al-Hassan, S. M., Bacchini, D., Bombi, A. S., Chang, L., Deater-Deckard, K., Di Giunta, L., Dodge, K. A., & Oburu, P. (2015). Perceived mother and father acceptance-rejection predict four unique aspects of child adjustment across nine countries. *Journal of Child Psychology and Psychiatry, 56*, 923–932.

Reynolds, W. M. (1982). Development of reliable and valid short forms of the Marlowe-Crowne Social Desirability Scale. *Journal of Clinical Psychology, 38*, 119–125.

Rohner, R. P. (2005). Parental Acceptance-Rejection/Control Questionnaire (PARQ/Control): Test manual. In R. P. Rohner & A. Khaleque (Eds.), *Handbook for the study of parental acceptance and rejection* (4th ed., pp. 137–186). University of Connecticut.

Rohner, R. P. & Ali, S. (2025). IPARTheory, evidence, and methods from conception through maturity. In Rohner, R. P., & Ali, S. (Eds.). *Global perspectives on parental acceptance and rejection: Lessons learned from IPARTheory* (pp. 3–38). Routledge.

Rohner, R. P., & Cournoyer, D. E. (1994). Universals in youths' perceptions of parental acceptance and rejection: Evidence from factor analyses within eight sociocultural groups worldwide. *Cross-Cultural Research, 28,* 371–383.
Rohner, R. P., & Lansford, J. E. (2017). Deep structure of the human affectional system: Introduction to Interpersonal Acceptance-Rejection Theory. *Journal of Family Theory & Review, 9,* 426–440.
Rothenberg, W. A., Ali, S., Rohner, R. P., Lansford, J. E., Britner, P. A., Di Giunta, L., Dodge, K. A., Malone, P. S., Oburu, P., Pastorelli, C., Skinner, A. T., Sorbring, E., Steinberg, L., Tapanya, S., Uribe Tirado, L. M., Yotanyamaneewong, S., Alampay, L. P., Al-Hassan, S. M., Bacchini, D., Bornstein, M. H., Chang, L., & Deater-Deckard, K. (2022). Effects of parental acceptance-rejection on children's internalizing and externalizing behaviors: A longitudinal, multicultural study. *Journal of Child and Family Studies, 31,* 29–47.
Rothenberg, W. A., Bizzego, A., Esposito, G., Lansford, J. E., Al-Hassan, S. M., Bacchini, D., Bornstein, M. H., Chang, L., Deater-Deckard, K., Di Giunta, L., Dodge, K. A., Gurdal, S., Liu, Q., Long, Q., Oburu, P., Pastorelli, C., Skinner, A. T., Sorbring, E., Tapanya, S., Steinberg, L., Uribe Tirado, L. M., Yotanyamaneewong, S., & Alampay, L. P. (2023b). Predicting adolescent mental health outcomes across cultures: A machine learning approach. *Journal of Youth and Adolescence, 52,* 1595–1619.
Rothenberg, W. A., Lansford, J. E., Alampay, L. P., Al-Hassan, S. M., Bacchini, D., Bornstein, M. H., Chang, L., Deater-Deckard, K., Di Giunta, L., Dodge, K. A., Malone, P. S., Oburu, P., Pastorelli, C., Skinner, A. T., Sorbring, E., Steinberg, L., Tapanya, S., Uribe Tirado, L. M., & Yotanyamaneewong, S. (2020d). Examining effects of mother and father warmth and control on child externalizing and internalizing problems from age 8 to 13 in nine countries. *Development and Psychopathology, 32,* 1113–1137.
Rothenberg, W. A., Lansford, J. E., Al-Hassan, S. M., Bacchini, D., Bornstein, M. H., Chang, L., Deater-Deckard, K., Di Giunta, L., Dodge, K. A., Malone, P. S., Oburu, P., Pastorelli, C., Skinner, A. T., Sorbring, E., Steinberg, L., Tapanya, S., Uribe Tirado, L. M., Yotanyamaneewong, S., & Alampay, L. P. (2020a). Examining effects of parent warmth and control on internalizing behavior clusters from age 8 to 12 in 12 cultural groups in nine countries. *Journal of Child Psychology and Psychiatry, 61,* 436–446.
Rothenberg, W. A., Lansford, J. E., Bacchini, D., Bornstein, M. H., Chang, L., Deater-Deckard, K., Di Giunta, L., Dodge, K. A., Malone, P. S., Oburu, P., Pastorelli, C., Skinner, A. T., Sorbring, E., Steinberg, L., Tapanya, S., Uribe Tirado, L. M., Yotanyamaneewong, S., Alampay, L. P., & Al-Hassan, S. M. (2020c). Cross-cultural effects of parent warmth and control on aggression and rule-breaking from ages 8–13. *Aggressive Behavior, 46,* 327–340.
Rothenberg, W. A., Lansford, J. E., Bornstein, M. H., Chang, L., Deater-Deckard, K., Di Giunta, L., Dodge, K. A., Malone, P. S., Oburu, P., Pastorelli, C., Skinner, A. T., Sorbring, E., Steinberg, L., Tapanya, S., Uribe Tirado, L. M., Yotanyamaneewong, S., Alampay, L. P., Al-Hassan, S. M., & Bacchini, D. (2020b). Effects of parental warmth and behavioral control on adolescent externalizing and internalizing trajectories across cultures. *Journal of Research on Adolescence, 30,* 835–855.
Rothenberg, W. A., Lansford, J. E., Bornstein, M. H., Uribe Tirado, L. M., Yotanyamaneewong, S., Alampay, L. P., Al-Hassan, S. M., Bacchini, D., Chang, L., Deater-Deckard, K., Di Giunta, L., Dodge, K. A., Liu, Q., Long, Q., Malone, P. S., Oburu, P., Pastorelli, C., Skinner, A. T., Sorbring, E., Tapanya, S., & Steinberg, L. (2021). Cross-cultural associations of four parenting behaviors with child flourishing: Examining cultural specificity and commonality in

cultural normativeness and intergenerational transmission processes. *Child Development, 92*, e1138–e1153.

Rothenberg, W. A., Lansford, J. E., Uribe Tirado, L. M., Yotanyamaneewong, S., Alampay, L. P., Al-Hassan, S. M., Bacchini, D., Chang, L., Deater-Deckard, K., Di Giunta, L., Dodge, K. A., Gurdal, S., Liu, Q., Long, Q., Oburu, P., Pastorelli, C., Skinner, A. T., Sorbring, E., Tapanya, S., Steinberg, L., & Bornstein, M. H. (2023a). The intergenerational transmission of maladaptive parenting and its impact on child mental health: Examining cross-cultural mediating pathways and moderating protective factors. *Child Psychiatry and Human Development, 54*, 870–890.

Sorbring, E., Gurdal, S., & Rothenberg, W. A. (2021). Four domains of parenting in Sweden. In J. E. Lansford, W. A. Rothenberg, & M. H. Bornstein (Eds.), *Parenting across cultures from childhood to adolescence: Development in nine countries* (pp. 151–171). Routledge.

United Nations. (2023). Global Sustainable Development Report (GSDR) 2023. Available https://sdgs.un.org/gsdr/gsdr2023

8

PARENTAL REJECTION IN CHILDHOOD LEADS TO INTERPERSONAL REJECTION SENSITIVITY IN ADULTHOOD

Sumbleen Ali and Ronald P. Rohner

Rejection sensitivity has been conceptually and operationally defined in various ways over time. In 1973, Horney first introduced the term explaining how individuals dealing with psychological maladjustment and neuroticism have difficulty socializing with other people and have difficulty maintaining intimate relationships. She explained rejection sensitivity in the context of abuse, humiliation, and betrayal. She viewed anxiety as an underlying concept in rejection sensitivity. More specifically, she defined rejection sensitivity as a negative emotional response to "any rejection or rebuff no matter how slight, [for example], a change in an appointment, having to wait, failure to receive an immediate response" (Horney, 1937, pp. 135-136).

In 1950, Erikson re-defined rejection sensitivity as a form of mistrust of others in personal and interpersonal relationships. Later, in 1970 Mehrabian conceptualized rejection sensitivity as the tendency to be reserved or lack self-assurance in social interactions with others. Mehrabian found that individuals who were rejection sensitive tended to elicit less positive response from others than did individuals who were less rejection sensitive. Individuals interacting with rejection-sensitive persons tended to view them as being less congenial (Mehrabian, 1970, 1976).

Today the concept of rejection sensitivity is generally defined either in terms of *interpersonal* rejection sensitivity, which deals with generalized concerns about socializing with others in social situations (Boyce & Parker, 1989; Harb et al., 2002)—or *personal* rejection sensitivity, that is, the concerns that individuals may have about how they will be treated in a social situation by a specific other person (Downey & Feldman, 1996; Feldman &

DOI: 10.4324/9781003441243-10

Downey, 1994; Garthe et al., 2020). Interpersonal acceptance-rejection theory (IPARTheory; Rohner, 2021)—an evidence-based theory of socialization and lifespan development that aims to understand consequences, causes, and correlates of interpersonal acceptance and rejection—defines interpersonal rejection sensitivity (IRS) as a heightened readiness or disposition to perceive negative or hurtful intent in the behavior of others in any social situation, even when no such intent is objectively present or intended. As such, it involves hypervigilance or watchfulness for the possibility of being criticized, ridiculed, slighted, disrespected, minimized, ignored, excluded, or rejected in some other way (Rohner, 2023). IRS is also associated with the experience of hurt feelings or emotional pain, including but not limited to sadness, dejection, depression, anger, and irritation resulting from real or imagined rejection by others.

Emotional and Cognitive Processes Underlying Rejection Sensitivity

The field of psychology has made progress in identifying potential emotional and cognitive mechanisms linking early parent–child relationships to rejection sensitivity. Research supports the conclusion that rejection sensitivity tends to develop as a result of parental rejection and neglect (see for instance, Rohner et al., 2024; Kim & Cicchetti, 2010; Lansford et al., 2002; Mischel & Shoda, 1995; Rohner, 2021; Wolfe et al., 2004). Perceived interpersonal rejection consistently evokes strong emotional reactions suggesting interpersonal rejection had serious consequences (Rohner, 2021).

Beginning in the first few months of life, infants use interactions with their caregivers to help regulate affect (Emde, 1989). IPARTheory argues that these interactions can influence the form, and intensity with which emotion is experienced. Thus, infants generally notice congruencies between their affective state and their caregiver's response. When caregivers do not respond with love, warmth, and care, for example, infants' affect may become flattened, sad, or despondent. This is one indicator of the extent to which the affective state of infants is subject to interpersonal influence (Rohner, 2004, 2021). London et al. (2007) argue that children's early caregiving experiences shape moment-to-moment cognitive and affective processes that ultimately form what IPARTheory calls children's mental representations of self, others, and context (Rohner, 2023). Contemporary cognitive psychologists and interpersonal relationship researchers support the notion that children's early experiences shape expectations, values, attributes, biases, and self-regulatory behaviors that underlie how children socialize with others (Feldman & Downey, 1994; Mischel & Shoda, 1995).

Research supports the idea that human beings have a bio-psychological mechanism to inform themselves of threats to acceptance (Scott et al.,

2022). Excessive and inappropriate affect can give rise to mental representations that are characterized by rejection sensitivity to protect oneself from social threat. An individual becomes ready for immediate action to avert the danger/threat by being emotionally and cognitively self-defensive (Rohner, 2021, 2023). Mental representations are biologically mediated psychological dispositions that are typical elements in the social cognition of rejected individuals (Rohner & Ali, 2025; Chapter 1, this book). Mental representations are individuals' implicit conceptions of existence and emotional states which shape the way individuals perceive, construe, and react to social situations and interpersonal relationships, as well as how they encode memory (Rohner, 2021). When activated in a less than benign social world, such mental representations undermine the chances of maintaining supportive and satisfying interpersonal relationships.

Rejection sensitivity originates within a system of mental representations when children experience parental rejection, thereby increasing the likelihood of maladaptive social behaviors such as social avoidance (Jittayuthd & Karl, 2022). Because of parental rejection, children often close off emotionally to protect themselves from the hurt of further rejection (Zimmer-Gembeck et al., 2016; Rohner & Ali, 2025; Chapter 1, this book). That is, they are likely to become emotionally unresponsive and defensively independent (Rohner, 1986, 2021). Moreover, rejected individuals are likely to develop distorted mental images where they reinterpret experiences to align with their existing mental representations (Rohner, 2021). Due to these distorted or negative mental representations, individuals often come to regard interpersonal relationships as being untrustworthy and hurtful, making it difficult for them to trust new relationships (Rohner, 2021).

IPARTheory researchers have found that individuals tend to respond in 10 ways when they experience being rejected by parents in childhood and by other attachment figures throughout life (Rohner, 2021; Rohner & Ali, 2025, Chapter 1, this book). These responses to perceived rejection include the development of (1) anxiety; (2) insecurity; (3) anger, hostility, and aggression, or problems with the management of anger and aggression; (4) dependence or defensive independence depending on the form, frequency, duration, and intensity of the rejection experienced; (5) impaired self-esteem; (6) impaired self-adequacy; (7) emotional unresponsiveness; (8) emotional instability; (9) negative worldview; and (10) cognitivedistortions, including rejection sensitivity.

Additionally, prior research has found that rejection sensitivity tends to be a highly stable personality trait across time and context (London et al., 2007; Marston et al., 2010; Zimmer-Gembeck et al., 2016). Further, compared to individuals with low rejection sensitivity, individuals with high rejection sensitivity show heightened physiological activity (Downey et al., 2004), and are on alert for rejection-related cues. Additionally, they automatically process rejection-related content (Berenson et al., 2009), show a greater readiness for detecting social threats, and see cues of rejection as more negative than persons who are low on rejection sensitivity (Olsson et al., 2013). Moreover, they tend to engage in biased encoding and recall of rejection-related information (Mor & Inbar, 2009), and they are prone to personalize ambiguous cues of rejection (Downey & Feldman, 1996). Collectively, these findings lend support to IPARTheory's conceptualization of rejection sensitivity as an enduring personality disposition that once acquired contributes to clinically relevant cognitive distortions and maladaptive behaviors in response to situations where rejection could be possible.

Neuroscientific investigations also suggest that individuals who are high on measures of rejection sensitivity show greater activity in the anterior cingulate cortex (ACC) and anterior insula (Powers et al., 2013) in response to rejecting stimuli than do people low in rejection sensitivity (Burklund et al., 2007). Activity in these regions correlates with self-reported social distress in response to rejection (Masten et al., 2009).

Impact of Rejection Sensitivity on Mental Health and Wellbeing

Studies have examined how rejection sensitivity affects interpersonal behaviors, relationship quality, social interactions, and mental health and wellbeing (Downey & Feldman, 1996; Rohner et al., 2024; Romens & Pollak, 2012; Wilbarger et al., 2010). For instance, individuals high in rejection sensitivity may engage in self-protective behaviors such as avoiding new relationships or overreacting to minor cues of rejection (Inman & London, 2022). Rejection-sensitive individuals readily perceive other people's facial expressions as negative (Wilbarger et al., 2010). Moreover, children with a history of parental rejection tend to have difficulty regulating their emotions because they pay more attention to sad and depression-relevant cues and less to happy and positive emotion cues (Romens & Pollak, 2012). These attentional patterns of rejection sensitive children are risk factors for depression in later life, thus, making it difficult to form and maintain supportive and satisfying relationships during childhood and during adult life (Khaleque et al., 2019).

Some rejected individuals have such a heightened concern about the possibility of being rejected by others that they find it almost overwhelmingly difficult to maintain positive interpersonal relationships. Such-individuals are often hypervigilant and hypersensitive to the slightest possibility of being rejected (Rohner, 2021). As a result, rejection sensitivity is often significantly associated with depression (Pearson et al., 2011), anxiety (Thomas & Bowker, 2015), loneliness (Normansell & Wisco,

2017; Watson & Nesdale, 2012), borderline personality disorder (Bungert et al., 2015), increased risk of domestic violence (Murphy & Russell, 2016), and low self-esteem (Lin & Fan, 2022). Gao et al. (2017) found in their meta-analytic review that these mental health domains associated with rejection sensitivity remain fairly stable over time. This, in turn, can take a further toll on individuals' interpersonal relationships (Lin & Fan, 2022).

Measuring Rejection Sensitivity

Interpersonal rejection sensitivity versus personal rejection sensitivity has been measured predominantly by Boyce and Parker's (1989) Interpersonal Sensitivity Measure (IPSM; see also Harb et al., 2002). The IPSM deals with the self-presentation difficulties individuals may have when socializing with others across social situations. It involves the tendency to expect disapproval from them and to be overly worried about their approval. It also involves the tendency to be reticent or inhibited about expressing self-assurance or assertiveness in social interactions. This perspective follows from the work of Rosenfeld (1979) who studied personality dispositions involving the need for affiliation and fear of rejection from an expectancy-value perspective. That perspective assumes that the motivation for an outcome is dependent on the significance for the individual of the outcome and on the likelihood of achieving the outcome.

Personal rejection sensitivity, on the other hand, is measured most often by the Rejection Sensitivity Questionnaire (RSQ; Downey & Feldman, 1996; Feldman & Downey, 1994), and also by the Adult Rejection Sensitivity Questionnaire (A-RSQ; Berenson et al., 2009). Here rejection sensitivity is defined as the tendency in ongoing personal relationships to be concerned about whether a *specific* significant other will want to be supportive or continue participating in a desired relationship—and to expect that they will not want to do so (Berenson et al., 2009; Downey & Feldman, 1996; Feldman & Downey, 1994). Thus, an expectancy-value perspective also informs the concept of *personal* rejection sensitivity. RSQ is primarily based on how an individual might react in a *hypothetical* social interaction with others.

The literature summarized in this chapter details mechanisms underlying the link between accepting-rejecting experiences in childhood and the subsequent development of *generalized* interpersonal rejection sensitivity. It is essential to have a self-report measure that reliably assesses this construct for cross-cultural comparative research, as well as for multiethnic research within the United States. Although depression, social anxiety, and other mental health outcomes have commonly been examined in relation to *personal* rejection sensitivity (Gao et al., 2017), much less is known about how *interpersonal* rejection sensitivity is related to these issues. Because of these problems, Rohner et al., (2020) created the Interpersonal Rejection Sensitivity Scale (IRSS).

Interpersonal Rejection Sensitivity Scale (IRSS; Rohner et al., 2020)

The IRSS is an 11-item self-report questionnaire measuring an individual's sensitivity to the possibility of being rejected in interpersonal relationships. Sample items include: "If my friends are in a bad mood, I tend to wonder if it is because of me," and "I worry very little about what others may think of me" (reverse scored). Items are scored on a 4-point Likert scale ranging from (1) "not at all true of me" through (4) "very true of me." Possible scores range from a low of 11 (i.e., no self-reported rejection sensitivity) through a high of 44 (i.e., maximum possible self-reported rejection sensitivity). The measure was conceptually designed in such a way that scores at the midpoint of 28 would reveal the perception of mild interpersonal rejection sensitivity, whereas scores equal to or greater than 33 would reveal significant self-reported rejection sensitivity.

To assess the reliability and validity of the IRSS for use in the US and internationally, Rohner et al. (2020, 2024) collected data from 3,083 individuals (M_{Age} = 26; *SD* = 2.3) in eight countries. They found that rejection sensitivity is equally prevalent in collectivist societies such as Bangladesh, Egypt, Kuwait, and Pakistan as it is in individualist societies such as Bulgaria, Spain, Italy, and the USA. Chronbach's alphas for the IRSS in these eight countries spread from .84 through .95.

Conclusion

The concept of rejection sensitivity was initially formulated by Horney in 1937. But it evolved over time to include two distinct variants, (1) personal rejection sensitivity and (2) interpersonal rejection sensitivity. IPARTheory provides a comprehensive framework for understanding interpersonal rejection sensitivity as a disposition marked by hypervigilance to the possibility of negative intent in an interpersonal relationship. IPARTheory research traces the emotional and cognitive roots of interpersonal rejection sensitivity back to early parent-child relationships, highlighting its association with parental rejection and neglect. These formative experiences shape mental representations, influencing individuals' expectations, biases, and self-regulatory behaviors in social contexts. Moreover,-interpersonal rejection sensitivity is associated with various maladaptive-personality dispositions, including anxiety, aggression, and emotional instability. Neuroscientific findings corroborate these behavioral patterns, indicating heightened neural activity in response to interpersonal rejection experiences among rejection-sensitive individuals. The repercussions of interpersonal rejection sensitivity extend beyond individual personality dispositions to impact an individual's overall mental health and wellbeing. High rejection sensitivity correlates with depression, anxiety, loneliness, and a variety of other mental health issues, thus posing challenges for forming and maintaining fulfilling interpersonal relationships.

Despite significant advancements, the study of interpersonal rejection sensitivity faces several limitations. Most of the research is based on self-report measures, though research employing multimodal approaches such as neuroimaging with behavioral assessments tends to support conclusions from self-reports. Longitudinal studies could better elucidate the developmental trajectories of interpersonal rejection sensitivity and its enduring effects on individuals' social and emotional functioning. Furthermore, advancements in technology, such as ambulatory assessments, offer possible novel avenues for studying interpersonal rejection sensitivity in ecologically valid settings.

In conclusion, interpersonal rejection sensitivity is a multifaceted construct with profound implications for individuals' lives. Ongoing research, however, holds the promise of deepening an understanding and informing interventions aimed at fostering healthier interpersonal relationships and thereby enhancing individuals' psychological well-being.

References

Berenson, K. R., Gyurak, A., Ayduk, Ö., Downey, G., Garner, M. J., Mogg, K., Bradley, B. P., Pine, D. S. (2009). Rejection sensitivity and disruption of attention by social threat cues. *Journal of Research in Personality, 43*(6), 1064–1072.

Boyce, P., & Parker, G. (1989). Development of a scale to measure interpersonal sensitivity. *Australian and New Zealand Journal of Psychiatry, 23*(3), 341–351. doi:10.3109/00048678909068291

Bungert, M., Koppe, G., Niedtfeld, I., Vollstädt-Klein, S., Schmahl, C., Lis, S., & Bohus, M. (2015). Pain processing after social exclusion and its relation to rejection sensitivity in borderline personality disorder. *PloS One, 10*(8), 1–22.

Burklund, L. J., Eisenberger, N. I., & Lieberman, M. D. (2007). The face of rejection: Rejection sensitivity moderates dorsal anterior cingulate activity to disapproving facial expressions. *Social Neuroscience, 2*(3–4), 238–253.

Downey, G., & Feldman, S. I. (1996). Implications of rejection sensitivity for intimate relationships. *Journal of Personality and Social Psychology, 70*(6), 1327.

Downey, G., Mougios, V., Ayduk, O., London, B. E., & Shoda, Y. (2004). Rejection sensitivity and the defensive motivational system: Insights from the startle response to rejection cues. *Psychological Science, 15*(10), 668–673.

Emde, R. N. (1989). The infant's relationship experience: Developmental and affective aspects. In A. J. Sameroff & R. N. Emde (Eds.), *Relationship disturbances in early childhood*. (pp. 35–51). Basic Books.

Erikson, E. (1950). *Childhood and society*. W. W. Norton & Company.

Feldman, S., & Downey, G. (1994). Rejection sensitivity as a mediator of the impact of childhood exposure to family violence on adult attachment behavior. *Development and Psychopathy*, *6*(1), 231–247.

Gao, S., Assink, M., Cipriani, A., & Lin, K. (2017). Associations between rejection sensitivity and mental health outcomes: A meta-analytic review. *Clinical Psychology Review*, 57, 59–74. doi:10.1016/j.cpr.2017.08.007

Garthe, K., Dingley, C. E., & Johnson, M. J. (2020). A historical and contemporary literature review of rejection sensitivity in marginalized populations. *Journal of Health Disparities Research and Practice*, *13*(1), 1.

Harb, G. C., Heimberg, R. G., Fresco, D. M., Schneier, F. R., & Liebowitz, M. (2002). The psychometric properties of the interpersonal sensitivity measure in social anxiety disorder. *Behaviour Research and Therapy*, *40*(8), 961–980. doi:10.1016/S0005-7967(01)00125-5

Horney, K. (1937). *Neurotic personality of our time* (Vol. 10). W. W. Norton & Company.

Inman, E. M., & London, B. (2022). Self-silencing mediates the relationship between rejection sensitivity and intimate partner violence. *Journal of Interpersonal Violence*, *37*(13–14),12475–12494.

Jittayuthd, S., & Karl, A. (2022). Rejection sensitivity and vulnerable attachment: Associations with social support and PTSD symptoms in trauma survivors. *European Journal of Psychotraumatology*, *13*(1), 2027676.

Khaleque, A., Uddin, M. K., Hossain, K. N., Siddique, M. N. E. A., & Shirin, A. (2019). Perceived parental acceptance-rejection in childhood predict psychological adjustment and rejection sensitivity in adulthood. *Psychological Studies*, *64*, 447–454.

Kim, J., & Cicchetti, D. (2010). Longitudinal pathways linking child maltreatment, emotion regulation, peer relations, and psychopathology. *Journal of Child Psychology and Psychiatry*, *51*(6), 706–716.

Lansford, J. E., Dodge, K. A., Pettit, G. S., Bates, J. E., Crozier, J., & Kaplow, J. (2002). A 12-year prospective study of the long-term effects of early child physical maltreatment on psychological, behavioral, and academic problems in adolescence. *Archives of Pediatrics and Adolescent Medicine*, *156*(8), 824–830.

Lin, Y., & Fan, Z. (2022). The relationship between rejection sensitivity and social anxiety among Chinese college students: The mediating roles of loneliness and self-esteem. *Current Psychology*, 1–10.

London, B., Downey, G., Bonica, C., & Paltin, I. (2007). Social causes and consequences of rejection sensitivity. *Journal of Research on Adolescence*, *17*(3), 481–506.

Marston, E. G., Hare, A., & Allen, J. P. (2010). Rejection sensitivity in late adolescence: Social and emotional sequelae. *Journal of Research on Adolescence*, *20*(4), 959–982.

Masten, C. L., Eisenberger, N. I., Borofsky, L. A., Pfeifer, J. H., McNealy, K., Mazziotta, J. C., & Dapretto, M. (2009). Neural correlates of social exclusion during adolescence: Understanding the distress of peer rejection. *Social Cognitive and Affective Neuroscience*, *4*(2), 143–157.

Mehrabian, A. (1970). The development and validation of measures of affiliative tendency and sensitivity to rejection. *Educational and Psychological Measurement*, *30*(2), 417–428.

Mehrabian, A. (1976). Questionnaire measures of affiliative tendency and sensitivity to rejection. *Psychological Reports*, *38*(1), 199–209.

Mischel W., Shoda Y. (1995). A cognitive-affective system theory of personality: Reconceptualizing situations, dispositions, dynamics, and invariance in personality structure. *Psychological Review*, 102, 246–268.

Mor, N., & Inbar, M. (2009). Rejection sensitivity and schema-congruent information processing biases. *Journal of Research in Personality, 43*(3), 392–398.

Murphy, A. M., & Russell, G. (2016). Rejection sensitivity, jealousy, and the relationship to interpersonal aggression. *Journal of Interpersonal Violence, 91*(4), 626–641.

Normansell, K. M., & Wisco, B. E. (2017). Negative interpretation bias as a mechanism of the relationship between rejection sensitivity and depressive symptoms. *Cognition and Emotion, 31*(5), 950–962.

Olsson, A., Carmona, S., Downey, G., Bolger, N., & Ochsner, K. N. (2013). Learning biases underlying individual differences in sensitivity to social rejection. *Emotion, 13*(4), 616.

Pearson, K. A., Watkins, E. R., & Mullan, E. G. (2011). Rejection sensitivity prospectively predicts increased rumination. *Behaviour Research and Therapy, 49*(10), 597–605.

Powers, K. E., Somerville, L. H., Kelley, W. M., & Heatherton, T. F. (2013). Rejection sensitivity polarizes striatal–medial prefrontal activity when anticipating social feedback. *Journal of Cognitive Neuroscience, 25*(11), 1887–1895.

Rohner, R. P. (1986). *The warmth dimension: Foundations of parental acceptance-rejection theory*. Sage Publications, Inc. [Now available from Rohner Research Publications]

Rohner, R. P. (2004). The parental "acceptance-rejection syndrome:" Universal correlates of perceived rejection. *American Psychologist, 59*, 830–840.

Rohner, R. P. (2021). Introduction to Interpersonal Acceptance-Rejection Theory (IPARTheory) and Evidence. *Online Readings in Psychology and Culture, 6*(1), 1–65.

Rohner R. P. (2023). *Glossary of significant concepts in Interpersonal Acceptance-Rejection Theory (IPARTheory)*. Rohner Research Publications.

Rohner, R. P. & Ali. S. (2025). Interpersonal acceptance-rejection theory (IPARTheory): From conception through maturity. In R. P. Rohner & S. Ali (Eds.) *Global perspectives on parental acceptance and rejection: Lessons learned from IPARTheory* (pp. 3–38). Routledge

Rohner, R. P., Ali, S., Filus, A., Senese, V. P., Molaver, A., Ahmed, R. A., Carrasco, M. A., Ibrahim, M., Koltcheva, N., Sajid, B., Uddin, K. M., Izquierdo-Sotorrío, E., Khaled, Z. E., Nasti, C., Shahnaz, I., Zeb, R., Holgado-Tello, F. P., Massaro, R., Riaz, M., ... Britner, P. A. (2024). Reliability and validity of the interpersonal rejection sensitivity scale: A multicultural study. *Current Psychology*, 43, 7986–7996. https://doi.org/10.1007/s12144-023-04980-9

Rohner, R. P., Molaver, A., & Ali, S. (2020). *Interpersonal Rejection Sensitivity Scale (IRSS)*. Rohner Research Publications.

Romens, S. E., & Pollak, S. D. (2012). Emotion regulation predicts attention bias in maltreated children at-risk for depression. *Journal of Child Psychology and Psychiatry, 53*(2), 120–127.

Rosenfeld, L. B. (1979). Self-disclosure avoidance: Why I am afraid to tell you who I am. *Communications Monographs, 46*(1), 63–74.

Scott, W., Tyser, J., Penningroth, S. L., & Strauch, C. (2022). Assessing self-schema content: The relationship of psychological needs to early maladaptive schemas, rejection sensitivity, and personality traits. *Self and Identity, 21*(3), 317–338.

Thomas, K., & Bowker, J. (2015). Rejection sensitivity and adjustment during adolescence: Do friendship, self-silencing, and parent support matter? *Journal of Child and Family Studies*, *24*(3), 608–616.

Watson, J., & Nesdale, D. (2012). Rejection sensitivity, social withdrawal, and loneliness in young adults. *Journal of Applied Social Psychology*, *42*(8), 1984–2005.

Wilbarger, J., Gunnar, M., Schneider, M., & Pollak, S. (2010). Sensory processing in internationally adopted, post-institutionalized children. *Journal of Child Psychology and Psychiatry*, *51*(10), 1105–1114.

Wolfe, D. A., Wekerle, C., Scott, K., Straatman, A.-L., & Grasley, C. (2004). Predicting abuse in adolescent dating relationships over 1 year: The role of child maltreatment and trauma. *Journal of Abnormal Psychology*, *113*(3), 406–415.

Zimmer-Gembeck, M. J., Nesdale, D., Webb, H. J., Khatibi, M., & Downey, G. (2016). A longitudinal rejection sensitivity model of depression and aggression: Unique roles of anxiety, anger, blame, withdrawal, and retribution. *Journal of Abnormal Child Psychology*, *44*, 1291–1307.

9

GENDER INCONSISTENCIES IN PARENTAL ACCEPTANCE-REJECTION

Ebru Akün

According to the interpersonal acceptance-rejection theory (IPARTheory; Rohner, 2021), perceived parental acceptance and rejection in childhood are associated with personality and psychological consequences in childhood and adulthood across cultures (Rohner, 1986, 2021, Rohner and Ali, 2025, Chapter 1, this book). IPARTheory suggests that the gender of the child and the gender of the parent often play important roles in the relations between perceived parental acceptance-rejection and offspring's developmental outcomes. However, there is conflicting evidence in studies investigating the contribution of parent and child genders, making it difficult to draw firm conclusions. The chapter examines how the gender of parents and children uniquely impacts the consequences, causes, and other correlates of perceived parental acceptance and rejection. The chapter also emphasizes the social, emotional, relational, and psychological outcomes of perceived parental acceptance-rejection.

Gender Differences in Overall Parenting Behaviors

From an evolutionary perspective, both parents—regardless of gender—can care for and provide for a child's necessities for survival and healthy development (Parke, 2013). Research has found that fathers can be as sensitive and responsive as mothers to newborn infant cues and older children's needs for optimal development (Lewis & Lamb, 2003). However, parenting (i.e., caregiving) is generally seen as a gendered activity (Parke, 2013).

DOI: 10.4324/9781003441243-11

The term gender differences refers to variations in behaviors and characteristics that distinguish females from males within social and cultural contexts, unlike the term sex differences, which refers to biological differences between males and females (Palkovitz, 2013). Fathers and mothers often interact with their children differently. These interactional differences provide a unique opportunity to foster children's cognitive, linguistic, and emotional regulation skills (Parke, 2013).

Many studies have shown significant quantitative and qualitative differences between maternal and paternal parenting behaviors (Möller et al., 2016). Mothers usually spend more time with their children than fathers in most countries (Geary, 2021; Möller et al., 2016). Although there has been a recent increase in paternal involvement in some countries, mothers cross-culturally still tend to be viewed as primary caregivers.

Gender differences in parenting styles have biological, evolutionary, psychological, social, and cultural bases (Veneziano, 2003). Biologically, for example, hormones affect maternal and paternal caregiving behaviors. Women experience notable hormonal shifts during pregnancy, childbirth, and postpartum. Male partners often also undergo hormonal adjustments during these phases due to their proximity to their pregnant or breastfeeding partner and their interaction with the newborn after birth (Rajhans et al., 2019). Men who are attached to their partners are likely to have elevated prolactin and decreased testosterone when they become new parents. This appears to contribute to their ability to respond with greater empathy, nurturance, and sensitivity to their children. On the other hand, men who are not attached to their partners usually have higher testosterone levels and tend to be less engaged in parental caregiving (Rilling, 2013). Oxytocin increases in both parents, but its effect on parenting differs. An elevated level of oxytocin in mothers is linked to more affectionate parenting such as sensitive touch, parent gaze, and "motherese" vocalization. A high level of oxytocin in fathers is associated with more stimulatory parenting such as proprioceptive touch, tactile stimulation, and object-oriented play (Gordon et al., 2010).

Parents may exhibit different parenting behaviors based on the child's gender. For example, fathers often interact differently with their sons versus daughters, including the length and content of conversations, conflict resolution styles, playing games, and socializing strategies (Palkovitz, 2013).

Gender Inconsistencies in the Perception of Parental Acceptance-Rejection

Prior literature has heavily focused on mothers' behavior. For example, Rohner and Veneziano (2001) noted that studies on "parenting" were defined exclusively in terms of "mothering" until the mid-1920s, and research on "fathering" did not really begin until the 1960s and 1970s, except for a few clinical studies in earlier years. Rohner's research on parental acceptance-rejection, however, has emphasized the impact of perceived maternal and paternal acceptance-rejection since its origins in the 1960s (Li & Meier, 2017; Rohner, 1975).

According to IPARTheory, children's perceptions of their mothers' and fathers' physical, verbal, and symbolic behaviors expressing acceptance-rejection influence their personality, psychological adjustment, and behavioral development. These effects tend to continue into adulthood. Parental acceptance refers to warmth, affection, care, and support, whereas parental rejection refers to behaviors and emotions that are physically and psychologically hurtful. It includes the absence or withdrawal of warm and accepting behaviors. Parental rejection occurs in four forms: (1) cold and unaffectionate, (2) hostile and aggressive, (3) indifferent and neglecting, and (4) undifferentiated rejection, that is, children believe their parents do not really love them, want them, or care about them though there may be no *behavioral* manifestation of rejecting behaviors.

Findings comparing maternal versus paternal acceptance-rejection have varied over six decades of IPARTheory research. Most studies often conclude that offspring tend to perceive their mothers as warmer and more accepting than fathers (Giaouzi & Giovazolias, 2015; Klein et al., 2020; Miranda et al., 2016). Dwairy (2010), for instance, found that despite cultural differences in nine nations, fathers on average tended to be perceived as less loving and accepting than mothers. Several other studies, however, have found that sons and daughters do not perceive a significant difference between maternal versus paternal warmth and acceptance (Anonas & Alampay, 2015; Dmitrieva & Espel, 2023).

Findings have varied regarding boys' versus girls' perceptions of parental acceptance. Many studies, for example, report that girls tend to perceive significantly more maternal and paternal acceptance than do boys (İbrahim et al., 2015; Khaleque et al., 2018; Miranda et al., 2016). Other studies, however, have not found significant gender differences between boys' and girls' perceptions of parental acceptance-rejection (Anonas & Alampay, 2015; Giaouzi & Giovazolias, 2015; Papadaki & Giovazolias, 2015).

In some studies, the parent's gender interacted with the offspring's gender and showed same-gender or cross-gender effects on the perception of parental acceptance-rejection. Specifically, male offspring sometimes report more *paternal* rejection than female offspring (Giaouzi & Giovazolias, 2015), whereas female offspring report greater *maternal* rejection than male offspring (Klein et al., 2020). Some findings also reveal that female offspring remember more emotional warmth and less rejection from fathers than do male offspring (Klein et al., 2020), but male offspring perceive slightly higher maternal acceptance than did female offspring (Parmar & Rohner, 2010). It is unclear at this time why these gender-of-parent by gender-of-offspring differences appear.

Gender Inconsistencies in the Effects of Parental Acceptance-Rejection

Research on gender differences in the *effects* of perceived parental acceptance and rejection also shows mixed results. That is, some studies conclude that (a) perceived maternal and paternal acceptance equally predict specific offspring (child and adult) outcomes; (b) one parent's acceptance predicts specific outcomes better than the other parent's; (c) perceived parental acceptance moderates the effects of one parent's behavior on the other parent's behavior (buffering or exaggerating the effects); and (d) parent's gender interacts with offspring's gender and leads to different outcomes in sons versus daughters. Based on these mixed trends, the following section evaluates the effects of parental rejection on psychological maladjustment in childhood and adulthood.

Parental Acceptance-Rejection and Psychological Maladjustment in Children and Adults

IPARTheory argues that people have a biologically based emotional need for positive responses (i.e., to feel cared about) from the most important people in their lives (Rohner, 2021). When these needs are not adequately met (from parents in childhood, intimate partners during adulthood, and other significant others), children and adults worldwide—regardless of differences in gender, culture, race, or ethnicity—tend to develop a specific set of personality dispositions (Rohner, 2021). These are affective, cognitive, perceptual, and motivational dispositions, referred to as *psychological (mal)adjustment* in IPARTheory. The dispositions include (1) anger, hostility, aggression, or problems with the management of anger; (2) anxiety; (3) dependence or defensive independence; (4) impaired self-esteem; (5) impaired self-adequacy; (6) emotional unresponsiveness; (7) emotional instability; (8) insecurity; (9) negative worldview; and (10) cognitive distortions (Rohner, 1986, 2021).

Research reveals mixed findings about how parents' and offspring's gender play a role in the relation between perceived parental acceptance-rejection and psychological (mal)adjustment (see Khaleque, 2025; Chapter 2, this book). A meta-analysis by Khaleque and Rohner (2012a) drew attention to the importance of the *parent's gender*. The authors reported a significantly stronger worldwide association between *paternal* acceptance-rejection and overall psychological (mal)adjustment for children (but not adult offspring) compared to maternal acceptance-rejection. Moreover, recent studies conducted with adult offspring in Bangladesh revealed that perceived paternal rejection has a more negative impact on the current psychological maladjustment of adult offspring in comparison to maternal rejection (Khaleque et al., 2021b; Sultana & Khaleque, 2016). Another meta-analysis emphasized the importance of the *offspring's gender*. In that study, Rohner and Khaleque (2010) found that recollections of parental (maternal and paternal) acceptance contributed more to adult sons' psychological adjustment than to adult daughters'.

Several meta-analyses have examined the relation between offspring's psychological (mal)adjustment, parental acceptance/warmth, and the four forms of parental rejection (Ali et al., 2023; Khaleque, 2013, 2015, 2017). These meta-analyses showed that parents' gender did not have a differential effect on warmth/affection or on indifference/neglect (see, for example, Khaleque, 2015). However, perceived maternal hostility/aggression (Khaleque, 2017) and undifferentiated rejection (Ali et al., 2023) had a more robust relationship with offspring's psychological maladjustment than did perceived paternal hostility/aggression and undifferentiated rejection.

Various studies have also found that parents' as well as offspring's gender may play a joint role in the relation between parental acceptance-rejection and psychological (mal)adjustment. For example, a meta-analytic study by Ali et al. (2015a) emphasized the importance of the cross-gender effect on adult offspring's psychological maladjustment. More specifically, they found a significantly stronger association between adults' memories of maternal rejection in childhood and adult sons' current psychological maladjustment as compared to adult daughters. Furthermore, recollections of paternal acceptance were more closely associated with adult daughters' current psychological adjustment than with adult sons. This cross-gender effect was supported in Sultana and Khaleque's (2016) study for adult daughters. There, only paternal rejection made a significant independent contribution to the psychological maladjustment of adult daughters. However, both paternal and maternal rejection also made independent contributions to the current psychological maladjustment of adult sons. Ramírez-Uclés et al.'s (2018) study concluded that the effect of perceived parental rejection during childhood on psychological maladjustment was more robust for daughters than sons. Offspring's gender also moderated the relation between parental acceptance-rejection and some dimensions of psychological (mal)adjustment. Specifically, perceived paternal rejection (but not maternal rejection) led to increased levels of emotional instability and negative self-esteem for daughters but not sons.

Parental Acceptance-Rejection and Children's Socioemotional Development

The caregiver–infant relationship is central to emotional development (Rohner, 2021) because this primary relationship is vital in forming a child's emotion-regulation skills (Thomson et al., 2003). Many studies have found the mother–child relationship to be more prominent than the father–child relationship in helping offspring regulate their emotions. Laible and Carlo (2004), for example, found that greater perceived maternal (but not paternal) support was related to greater sympathy and self-worth in adolescent offspring. Interestingly, the same study revealed that children benefited from the support of their mothers by buffering them against an unsupportive relationship with their fathers (Laible & Carlo, 2004). A review of empirical literature by Li and Meier (2017) on the impact of maternal and paternal acceptance on children's outcomes also found that positive socioemotional development is more likely to be influenced by maternal acceptance than paternal acceptance.

Contrary to conclusions such as these, many studies argue that paternal acceptance contributes as much as maternal acceptance to positive expressions of socioemotional development such as prosocial behavior, altruism, and empathy. For example, Putnick et al. (2018) showed that maternal and paternal acceptance were related to children's prosocial behavior. Similarly, Saha et al. (2020) reported that both maternal and paternal acceptance predicted altruistic behavior in adolescence regardless of the child's gender.

Miklikowska et al.'s (2011) 3-wave longitudinal study revealed that both perceived maternal and paternal acceptance were related to empathy among offspring. More specifically, perceived maternal acceptance consistently predicted changes in empathic concern in daughters over time; however, paternal acceptance predicted changes over time in perspective-taking abilities in sons and daughters. Further, Miklikowska et al. (2011) reported that mothers offered more affection, emotional assistance, and psychological support to their children, especially daughters, than fathers. Fathers, on the other hand, taught their children values and socially appropriate behaviors, and encouraged independence—especially to their sons. In a one-year longitudinal study, Vergara-Lopez et al. (2022) found that perceived maternal acceptance was important in helping adolescent girls express and regulate negative emotions like sadness initially and at 1-year follow-up. Perceived paternal acceptance, however, did not show an association with adolescent girl's sadness initially, but was linked to decreased sadness one year later.

Research has also pointed out that marital relations between mothers and fathers can contribute to youths' socioemotional development. Han et al. (2017), for example, investigated longitudinal relationships among marital conflict, parenting behaviors, emotion regulation, and peer relationships in preschool children. Their findings indicate that parents' marital conflict when children were three years old was indirectly related to children's emotional regulation problems two years later when children turned five. Further, lower maternal warmth when children were four years old was indirectly associated with less adaptive peer relationships one year later.

Parental Acceptance-Rejection, Academic Achievement, and Children's School Conduct

Parents are critically important in offspring's school conduct and academic performance (Rohner, 2010). A study conducted in Spain by Bully et al. (2019), for example, showed that low levels of paternal (but not maternal) warmth were associated with increased school conduct problems, which in turn were associated with poorer academic performance for adolescent boys but not girls. The same study found lower levels of maternal (but not paternal) warmth were associated with adolescent girls' school conduct problems. Further, Dumka et al. (2009) found that in Mexico, fathers' warmth was associated with fewer school conduct problems, and fathers' harshness was associated with more problems in peer relationships among male than female adolescents. However, maternal harshness was associated with better grades for girls. Dumka et al. (2009) explained that the variation in these findings could be because adolescent girls in Mexico perceive mothers' harshness as a sign that their mothers care about their future.

Kara and Sümer (2022) found in Türkiye that paternal warmth was more influential than maternal warmth on boys' math self-efficacy, whereas maternal warmth was more influential than paternal warmth on girls' literature self-efficacy. In Germany, Raufelder et al. (2015) concluded that girls' school engagement tended to be negatively influenced by their mothers' behavioral control/pressure, but boys' school engagement and test anxiety were negatively influenced by both their mothers' and fathers' behavioral control/pressure. According to Uddin (2011), academic achievement among Bangladeshi children is associated with parental warmth, regardless of parents' and children's gender.

A meta-analytic study consisting of respondents from 12 countries (Ali et al., 2015b) revealed that perceived parental rejection is significantly associated with school conduct (disruptive behaviors such as defying teachers' authority, cheating, lying, stealing, and disobedience), regardless of parents' and children's gender. Khaleque et al. (2021a, 2021b) reported that maternal and paternal acceptance were both related to Portuguese female and male adolescents' motivation for learning and academic performance via psychological adjustment. Complementing these studies, a longitudinal study by Putnick et al. (2015) revealed that parental rejection predicted a decline in offspring's school performance across three years.

Parental Acceptance-Rejection and Internalizing Behavior Problems in Childhood

Internalizing behavior problems include anxiety, depression, social withdrawal, and somatic concerns (Achenbach et al., 2016). Several meta-analyses (McLeod et al., 2007a, 2007b; Pinquart, 2017a), longitudinal studies (Jager et al., 2016; Putnick et al., 2015), and cross-sectional studies (Vazsonyi et al., 2022; Weitkamp & Seiffge-Krenke, 2019) all report that both maternal and paternal rejection are associated with offspring's depression, anxiety, and other internalizing psychological problems. Meta-analytic reviews indicate that childhood depression is more strongly related to parental rejection than to parental control (McLeod et al., 2007b), while childhood anxiety tends to be more strongly associated with parental control than parental rejection (McLeod et al., 2007a).

Pinquart (2017a) reported that parental warmth is associated with fewer internalizing symptoms among daughters than sons. Several IPARTheory-related studies reported that both parents were equally influential on children's and adolescents' internalizing symptoms, regardless of the child's gender across cultures (Miranda et al., 2016; Rothenberg et al., 2022). Additionally, Rothenberg et al. (2022) highlighted that children's internalizing problems across nine countries tend to be more persistent in cultures where both maternal and paternal indifference/neglect scores are higher than average, regardless of the child's gender.

Longitudinal studies also provide evidence that the contribution of maternal and paternal warmth and rejection may have long-lasting effects on the development of internalizing problems. In a 3-wave study, Del Barrio et al. (2016), for example, showed that consistent paternal and maternal warmth over three years reduced the severity of depressive symptoms, regardless of the child's gender. More specifically, Del Barrio and colleagues found that the impact of parental warmth on the child's depressive symptoms was influenced longitudinally by the preceding levels of warmth exhibited by both the mother and father. However, the authors reported a more significant effect of maternal warmth than paternal warmth on the development of depression. These results were invariant across children's sex. Rueger et al. (2013) investigated if support from mothers, fathers, and teachers affects adolescents' depressive symptoms during their transition to middle school. At the beginning of the seventh grade, low social support from mothers, fathers, and teachers equally predicted depressive symptoms. However, after two years, a lack of support from mothers and fathers (but not teachers) predicted depressive symptoms. This issue is discussed at greater length in Gurmen (2025; Chapter 11, this book).

Maternal and paternal warmth affect offspring internalizing symptoms differently. For example, Rueger et al. (2013) reported that maternal support had a more significant impact on reducing daughters' depressive symptoms than sons'. Rothenberg et al. (2020), however, found that paternal warmth and control across cultures had a more significant effect on offspring's internalizing symptoms than maternal warmth. But Lila et al. (2007) argued that maternal acceptance directly affects children's internalizing symptoms, but paternal acceptance mediates children's internalizing symptoms via maternal acceptance.

Rohner (2021) argued that the love of only one parent is significant but not ideal for offspring's normal development. In line with that argument, Graziano et al. (2009) found that one parent's support may be able to compensate for the lack of support from the other parent for adolescents' depressive feelings. Liu et al. (2022) argued that maternal warmth, however, does not always provide a sufficient buffering effect against paternal harshness. The authors reported that despite experiencing maternal warmth, girls perceived their fathers' punitive attitude as rejecting and thus reported feeling more anxious.

Studies also reveal that differences in parental socialization with sons versus daughters are associated with internalizing symptoms in children and adolescents (Anonas & Alampay, 2015; Dmitrieva & Espel, 2023). Anonas and Alampay (2015) reported that mothers' (but not fathers) use of verbal punishment predicted both girls' and boys' internalizing symptoms. Dmitrieva and Espel (2023) found that perceived maternal warmth tended to reduce girls' depression and anxiety symptoms. However, perceived paternal warmth tended to reduce girl's depressive symptoms only. They also reported that perceived paternal hostility (but not maternal) was related to higher depression and anxiety symptoms.

Parental Acceptance-Rejection and Externalizing Behavior Problems in Childhood

Externalizing behavior problems include behavior such as lying, truancy, vandalism, bullying, drug and alcohol use, disobedience, tantrums, sudden mood change, and physical violence (Achenbach et al., 2016). Meta-analyses (Kawabata et al., 2011; Pinquart, 2017b) have shown that externalizing problems are strongly associated with parental rejection and behavioral control. Kawabata et al. (2011) indicated cross-gender differences in parenting: relational aggression was more strongly associated with paternal psychological control than maternal psychological control in girls. However, Pinquart (2017b) found no differences between maternal and paternal psychological control and the offspring's relational aggression regardless of the offspring's gender.

Studies have also supported Pinquart's (2017b) finding that mothers and fathers make equal contributions to aggression and externalizing symptoms in children (Rothenberg et al., 2022) and adolescents (Vazsonyi et al., 2022; Weitkamp & Seiffge-Krenke, 2019), regardless of the child's gender. Externalizing problems were positively related to parents who are low in warmth but high in behavioral control and hostility. Parents' warmth and support, however, were negatively related to externalizing problems. IPARTheory research has revealed that maternal and paternal rejection are significant predictors of offspring's externalizing symptoms from six months to three years later (Jager et al., 2016; Putnick et al., 2015). Unlike other studies, Carrasco et al. (2009) reported that maternal hostility in Spain was associated in secondary school children with higher aggression one to two years later than paternal hostility.

Guzel et al. (2018) reported that children with special needs such as ADHD perceived more maternal rejection (but not paternal rejection) than healthy controls. Studies reveal that maternal rejection is directly associated with children's externalizing symptoms. In contrast, the effect of perceived paternal rejection on children's symptoms was indirect via perceived maternal rejection or via children's satisfaction with overall relationships in the family (Lila et al., 2007; Jin & Roopnarine, 2023). Longitudinal studies have also drawn attention to the long-lasting effects of mother's hostility (Carrasco et al., 2009) and indifference/neglect (Rothenberg et al., 2022) on aggression and externalizing symptoms in children and adolescents (regardless of child gender). A few studies, however, have reported that paternal rejection is more strongly associated with offspring's externalizing problems than is maternal rejection. Marcone et al. (2020) reported that fathers' lack of warmth but high control were directly related to children's hyperactivity/distractibility symptoms. Rothenberg et al. (2020) reported that even though the effects of both parents were significant, the lack of paternal warmth was a stronger predictor of offspring's externalizing behavior than the lack of maternal warmth.

Studies have also reported that at times, one parent's (i.e., mothers' versus fathers') lack of warmth/rejection can have a more significant impact on children's or adults' externalizing problems than the other parent's. For example, Anonas and Alampay (2015) reported that maternal verbal punishment was related more than paternal verbal punishment to externalizing behavior problems and physical aggression in both boys and girls. Paternal verbal punishment was associated more than maternal verbal punishment with higher externalizing behavior problems in girls. Additionally, paternal control was related to lower antisocial behavior in girls, but not sons

(Kosterman et al., 2004). Maternal relational aggression was related to more relational aggression in boys but not in girls (Kawabata & Crick, 2016). Similarly, the maternal authoritarian parenting style (i.e., rejecting and restrictive controlling) made a more substantial contribution to sons' than daughters' externalizing behavior problems (Bolkan et al., 2010).

According to Papadaki and Giovazolias (2015), paternal acceptance tends to reduce the adverse effects of maternal rejection on the development of depressive symptoms, thereby preventing offspring from engaging in bullying behavior. Murray et al. (2014) showed how supportive father–child and mother–child relationships buffer adolescent aggression. The supportive father–son relationship tended to reduce the negative impact of mothers' psychological control on adolescent boys' aggressive behavior. Further, the relationship between paternal corporal punishment and child externalizing problem behaviors was strengthened by maternal hostility for boys, but not for girls. Xing and Wang (2017) found that paternal hostility also exacerbated the relationship between paternal corporal punishment and child externalizing problem behavior for girls but not boys. Similarly, a study by Verhoeven et al. (2010) showed that maternal warmth strengthened the relation between maternal spanking and externalizing symptoms for toddler boys. According to the authors, this finding could indicate that giving the child both supportive and aggressive signals may elicit internal distress and negative emotions that lead to externalizing behaviors (Verhoeven et al., 2010).

Memories of Parental Acceptance-Rejection in Childhood and Intimate Relationships in Adulthood

Children who experience acceptance from their parents also tend to perceive acceptance from their partners in adulthood. A series of studies conducted in eight countries (see Rohner, 2008) revealed that memories of maternal and paternal acceptance in childhood were significantly associated among adults with perceived partner acceptance for both men and women. Correlations ranged from .18 to .65 for women and .22 to .84 for men. The relation between recollections of father acceptance and current partner acceptance in women was significant in all countries (with correlations ranging from .18 to .51). Additionally, the independent contribution of intimate partner and father acceptance to psychological adjustment among women was often significant but not necessarily for men. However, studies in Türkiye (Eryavuz, 2006) and India (Parmar & Rohner, 2008) showed that the continuity between perceived parental acceptance in childhood and partner acceptance in adulthood was more robust for men than for women.

Further, parental rejection in childhood is also associated in adulthood with interpersonal rejection sensitivity, that is, with the perception of rejection even when it is unintended, and with the overreaction to actual or perceived rejection (Rohner, 2021). İbrahim et al. (2015) found that there was a strong association between men's and women's rejection from their same-sex parent and rejection sensitivity. Specifically, paternal rejection for men and maternal rejection for women had a substantial effect on the development of adults' rejection sensitivity.

Adults' memories of parental rejection in childhood are also associated with fear and anxiety in intimate relations. A study conducted by Rohner et al. (2019) in 13 countries, for example, indicated that adults' memories of parental rejection in childhood predicted adults' fear of intimacy, that is, being anxious about establishing an intimate relationship with a significant other. However, maternal rejection was a stronger predictor of this than paternal rejection. Additionally, the relation between recollections of maternal and paternal rejection and fear of intimacy was mediated by psychological maladjustment, regardless of the offspring's gender.

Recent studies conducted in Italy (Senese et al., 2020), the USA (Ashdown et al., 2023), and Iran (SeyedMousavi et al., 2022) support the finding that there is a cross-cultural association between memories of parental rejection in childhood and fear of intimacy in adulthood, regardless of the parent's and offspring's gender. However, a study in Türkiye (Aracı-İyiaydın et al., 2023) showed that both maternal and paternal rejection for women but only paternal rejection for men were associated with psychological adjustment problems and fear of intimacy when the adults perceived partner rejection. Studies also emphasized the direct effects of perceived paternal rejection on fear of intimacy (Khaleque et al., 2018) and dating anxiety (Epli et al., 2021). Both studies concluded that maternal rejection did not have a direct effect on fear of intimacy and dating anxiety. However, maternal rejection did have an indirect effect through psychological maladjustment and cognitive distortions. However, a study by Giovazolias and Paschalidi (2022) found that rejection sensitivity seems to enhance interpersonal anxiety, which in turn can lead to a fear of intimacy in women. However, maternal acceptance moderated these relationships. Specifically, memories of maternal acceptance buffered the negative effects of rejection sensitivity on fear of intimacy via interpersonal anxiety, only in women.

Memories of Parental Acceptance-Rejection in Childhood and Loneliness in Adulthood

Perceived parental acceptance-rejection in childhood tends to contribute to the experience of loneliness in adulthood. A study conducted by Rohner et al. (2020) in five countries (Iraq, Pakistan, Italy, the Netherlands, and the United States), for example, revealed that memories of parental rejection predicted feelings of loneliness, regardless of parents' or childs' gender. Paternal rejection, however, was a stronger predictor in those studies than maternal rejection. However, Brekalo and Keresteš (2023) concluded in their study that maternal acceptance, but not paternal acceptance, significantly predicted loneliness in adulthood. Putnick et al. (2020) found that memories of perceived parental rejection were associated with loneliness only through the mechanism of psychological maladjustment in men but memories of parental rejection had a direct effect on the development of loneliness among women.

Parental Acceptance-Rejection in Childhood and Self and Personality in Adulthood

IPARTheory suggests that one of the consequences of parental rejection in childhood is the tendency to become psychologically maladjusted in adulthood as well as in childhood (Rohner, 1975, 1986, 2021). Crawford (2003) compared the effects of perceived parental acceptance-rejection on self-view (including self-concept, self-esteem, and self-efficacy) in college-age emerging adults. Parental acceptance-rejection was the most potent predictor of self-view, regardless of the youth's gender. Studies conducted in several countries (e.g., Rasmi et al., 2012; Koutra et al., 2022) also found significant and positive relationships between parental acceptance and self-esteem, self-efficacy, self-compassion, and self-acceptance among both males and females. A few studies, however, report cross-gender effects of parental acceptance and youth's self-view. Crawford (2003), for example, reported a stronger correlation between female adolescents' self-views and their fathers' acceptance than their mothers'. Kuyumcu and Rohner (2018) also highlighted cross-gender effects in Türkiye. Paternal acceptance there predicted women's self-acceptance, whereas maternal acceptance predicted self-acceptance for men.

Research also suggests that parental rejection in childhood sometimes becomes linked to specific personality traits known as the "dark triad": Machiavellianism, psychopathy, and narcissism (Guo et al., 2021; Yendell et al., 2022). Machiavellianism (i.e., manipulation and exploitation of others) and psychopathy (i.e., absence of empathy and guilt as well as the presence of impulsivity) tend to be negatively correlated with parental acceptance. At the same time, they tend to be positively associated with parental rejection, regardless of parent and child gender. Backman et al. (2021) argued that parental rejection predicts offspring's psychopathic traits. Further, Gao et al. (2010) reported that the strongest predictor of psychopathy was low maternal care, followed by paternal overprotection. Parental rejection also tends to be a significant and consistent predictor of narcissism (i.e., self-perception of grandiosity, lack of empathy, and entitlement). Guo et al. (2021) and Yendell et al. (2022) reported that parental rejection was positively associated with adults' narcissism. Green et al. (2020) and Imamoglu and Durak Batıgün (2020) concluded that paternal rejection and overprotectiveness predicted sons' narcissistic symptoms.

Parental Acceptance-Rejection and Psychological Disorders in Adulthood

Research has demonstrated strong relations between recollections of parental acceptance-rejection in childhood and adults' psychological disorders (see also Gurmen, 2025; Chapter 11, this book). However, the results of this research are inconsistent with respect to gender differences. For example, Akün (2017) and Someya et al. (2000) found that adults who reported high social anxiety and panic disorder also reported more maternal rejection than paternal rejection. However, offspring diagnosed with borderline personality disorder (Rohner & Brothers, 1999) and obsessive-compulsive disorder (Hofer et al., 2018) were reported to have experienced more paternal rejection than maternal rejection.

In many studies, the gender of adult offspring is significant, with women often appearing to be more susceptible to the adverse effects of parental rejection than men. This vulnerability is evident in various contexts, including (1) the impact of maternal neglect on positive schizophrenia symptoms (Akün et al., 2018); (2) the impact of both maternal and paternal rejection on negative schizophrenia symptoms (Akün & Durak Batıgün, 2019); (3) the impact of parental neglect on lifetime suicide attempts (Ehnvall et al., 2008); (4) and the impact of parental rejection on daughters' anxiety and depression. However, Giaouzi and Giovazolias (2015) reported that both maternal and paternal rejection in childhood contributed more to social anxiety among men than women.

Parent's gender also appears to play a significant role in the development of adults' psychological disorders. For example, Klein et al. (2020) reported that the risk of depression was associated more with paternal rejection among both men and women than with maternal rejection. Koutra et al. (2022) noted that recollections of maternal rejection were more related than memories of paternal rejection to adults' depressive and anxiety symptoms, but recollections of paternal rejection were more associated than maternal rejection with adult offspring's anxiety symptoms. Richter et al. (1991) reported that perceived maternal rejection (but not paternal rejection) was a risk factor for offspring's depression. In contrast, others have found that paternal (but not maternal) rejection significantly predicted offspring depression in Italian, Japanese, and European American young adults (Rostad et al., 2014; Senese et al., 2022). However, Rostad et al. (2014) reported that maternal rejection of adult sons and paternal rejection of adult daughters were associated with depression symptoms.

Parental Acceptance-Rejection and Substance Abuse in Adults

Several systematic reviews have revealed an association between parental rejection in childhood and alcohol and substance abuse in adolescents and adults (Čablová et al., 2014; Ryan et al., 2010). Studies conducted on men (Koşar, 2021; Pomini et al., 2014) with substance use disorder (SUD) reported more maternal and paternal rejection in childhood than men without SUD. Additionally, a longitudinal study by Ford et al. (2023) found that young adults who reported having experienced parental acceptance in adolescence had a lower incidence of alcohol use, cannabis abuse symptoms, nicotine dependence, and other drug use symptoms. On the other hand, Lippold et al.'s (2018) longitudinal study reported that parental hostility in early adolescence was associated with an elevated risk for later tobacco and polysubstance use.

Several studies have found that paternal rejection contributes more to offspring's involvement in substance abuse than maternal rejection. For example, paternal rejection significantly predicted SUD in college students (Patock-Peckham & Morgan-Lopez, 2006) and in adults (Butt et al., 2022). Research comparing offspring in Italy (Caliendo et al., 2017) and Pakistan (Butt et al., 2022) indicated that offspring who had SUD reported more paternal rejection (but not maternal) during childhood than the control group. In the Pakistan study, additionally, paternal rejection and psychological maladjustment were found to distinguish men with SUD from men with lifelong abstinence with 97.3% accuracy (Butt et al., 2022). Shin et al. (2019) also found that offspring who experienced paternal warmth were at a low risk of involvement in alcohol-related problems. Few studies have found that maternal rejection is associated with offspring's alcohol problems, marijuana use, and age of onset of tobacco and alcohol use (Icick et al., 2013; Luk et al., 2015).

The findings about same-gender and cross-gender parenting effects were also noteworthy in the relation between SUD and parental acceptance-rejection. Studies have shown that same-sex high warmth and low-control parenting was found to be negatively associated with offspring's risk for alcohol abuse and dependence (Patock-Peckham et al., 2001; Patock-Peckham & Morgan-Lopez, 2006). Patock-Peckham et al. (2001) argued that mother–daughter and father–son relationships in childhood may be critical in alcohol dependency-related problems in young adulthood. Yang et al. (2019) also reported that maternal and paternal rejection of girls, and maternal rejection of boys significantly predict adult offspring's drug use.

Conclusion

Since the 1960s, IPARTheory research has consistently highlighted the significance of the gender of parents and offspring in the perception and consequences of parental acceptance and rejection. Research on gender differences, however, has shown mixed findings in the effects of perceived parental acceptance and rejection. Briefly summarized, some studies found that perceived maternal and paternal acceptance are equally predictive of offspring's outcomes (both child and adult) (e.g., Khaleque & Rohner, 2012b, Pinquart, 2017a). Several studies, however, emphasized the importance of the parent's gender. Specifically, some studies indicated that maternal acceptance is the sole significant predictor of specific outcomes (e.g., Del Barrio et al., 2016; Laible & Carlo, 2004). Some studies, in contrast, reported that paternal acceptance is the sole significant predictor of specific outcomes (e.g., Jager et al., 2016; Rothenberg et al., 2020). Some studies assessing parent's gender also revealed that one parent's acceptance may buffer or exaggerate the effects of the other parent's behavior (e.g., Graziano et al., 2009; Papadaki & Giovazolias, 2015). Numerous studies also demonstrated the importance of offspring' gender rather than parent's gender (e.g., Putnick et al., 2020; Ramírez-Uclés et al., 2018). In addition, some studies concluded that there is an interaction between the parent's gender and the offspring's gender, resulting in different outcomes for sons versus daughters (e.g., Kuyumcu & Rohner, 2018; Patock-Peckham et al., 2001).

Even though research on gender differences reveals mixed findings, they support the idea that both maternal acceptance and paternal acceptance contribute to children's optimal development. As mothers tend to spend more time with their children and provide daily caregiving than fathers in most countries (Geary, 2021; Lewis & Lamb, 2003), it is not surprising that maternal acceptance contributes significantly to offspring's psychological and behavioral adjustment. It is noteworthy that fathers are generally as influential as mothers in most outcomes. In fact, paternal acceptance may even be more influential in some outcomes (e.g., feelings of loneliness in adulthood, substance abuse disorder) than maternal acceptance. However, the source of the inconsistent findings associated with one parent having a greater developmental impact on the offspring's outcomes than the other is not yet well understood.

According to IPARTheory, the fact that one parent's acceptance or rejection has a greater impact on offspring's psychological outcomes than the other parent's acceptance or rejection may be explained by the perceived interpersonal power and prestige of mothers and fathers in the family. Rohner (2014, p.199) defines interpersonal power as "a person's ability to influence the opinions and behavior of others." Unlike the concepts of authority and patriarchy, IPARTheory emphasizes that interpersonal power only arises through informal interactions between family members. Prestige, on the other hand, is defined as being approved, respected, appreciated, or admired by family members (Rohner, 2014). A series of studies in 11 countries simultaneously examined the moderating roles of parental power and prestige in the relationship between parental acceptance-rejection and offspring's adjustment. In 62% of the studies (i.e., 8 of the 13 studies), maternal versus paternal power or prestige (or both power and prestige) significantly moderated the relationship between perceived parental acceptance (maternal and/or paternal) and adjustment of the offspring (Rohner, 2014). However, this moderating effect differs in terms of parent's gender across countries. Specifically, in some countries (e.g., Türkiye and Portugal), the higher power and/or prestige of one parent (mothers or fathers) in comparison to another intensifies the effects of this parent's acceptance on the offspring's adjustment (Börkan et al., 2014; Machado et al., 2014). In some countries (e.g., Greece and Korea), in contrast, the higher power and/or prestige of one parent (mothers or fathers) in comparison to the other diminishes the relationship between this parent's acceptance and the offspring's adjustment (Giotsa & Touloumakos, 2014; Lee & Chyung, 2014).

Mixed findings in gender studies on perceived parental acceptance and offspring's outcomes may also be due to cultural values and time. Parenting behaviors are often influenced by social roles and cultural values. Furthermore, children also tend to interpret their parents' behavior in the context of their cultural background (Lansford, 2022). For example, a behavior that is seen as an expression of warmth in one culture may be perceived as rejecting behavior in another culture. When parents behave in accordance with their cultural values, children are less likely to interpret this as rejecting behavior. This may weaken the relationship between maternal and/or paternal rejection and offspring outcomes (Lansford, 2022). Additionally, cultural values may change over time, resulting in changes in parental behavior and their effects on the child (Lansford et al., 2021).

Differences in samples and methodologies may also explain some of the inconsistent results among gender studies in perceived parental acceptance-rejection and offspring's behavioral and psychological outcomes. Methodologically, most studies use cross-sectional designs which are more open to the influence of confounding variables, such as the use of small, heterogeneous, and nonrepresentative samples. Multimethod longitudinal studies can provide greater insight into possible causal relations, considering the "mother and/or father effect," "offspring's gender effect," and "bidirectional effect" in the relationship (Power et al., 2013).

References

Achenbach, T. M., Ivanova, M. Y., Rescorla, L. A., Turner, L. V., & Althoff, R. R. (2016). Internalizing/externalizing problems: Review and recommendations for clinical and research applications. *Journal of the American Academy of Child & Adolescent Psychiatry, 55*(8), 647–656. https://doi.org/10.1016/j.jaac.2016.05.012

Akün, E. (2017). Relations among adults' remembrances of parental acceptance-rejection in childhood, self-reported psychological adjustment, and adult psychopathology. *Comprehensive Psychiatry, 77*, 27–37. https://doi.org/10.1016/j.comppsych.2017.05.002

Akün, E., & Durak Batıgün, A. (2019). Negative symptoms and recollections of parental rejection: The moderating roles of psychological maladjustment and gender. *Psychiatry Research, 275*, 332–337. https://doi.org/10.1016/j.psychres.2019.03.042

Akün, E., Durak Batıgun, A., Devrimci Özgüven, H., & Başkak, B. (2018). Positive symptoms and perceived parental acceptance-rejection in childhood: The moderating roles of socioeconomic status and gender. *Turkish Journal of Psychiatry*. https://doi.org/10.5080/u22681

Ali, S., Khaleque, A., & Rohner, R. P. (2015a). Pancultural gender differences in the relation between perceived parental acceptance and psychological adjustment of children and adult offspring. *Journal of Cross-Cultural Psychology, 46*(8), 1059–1080. https://doi.org/10.1177/0022022115597754

Ali, S., Khaleque, A., & Rohner, R. P. (2015b). Influence of perceived teacher acceptance and parental acceptance on youth's psychological adjustment and school conduct. *Cross-Cultural Research, 49*(2), 204–224. https://doi.org/10.1177/1069397114552769

Ali, S., Khatun, M. N., Khaleque, A., & Rohner, R. P. (2023). Perceived parental undifferentiated rejection and children's personality dispositions: A meta-analysis of multicultural studies. *The Journal of Genetic Psychology, 184*(1), 9–22. https://doi.org/10.1080/00221325.2022.2110447

Anonas, M. R., & Alampay, L. P. (2015). The moderating role of parental warmth on the relation between verbal punishment and child problem behaviors for same-sex and cross-sex parent-child groups. *Philippine Journal of Psychology, 48*(1), 115–152.

Aracı-İyiaydın, A., Toplu-Demirtaş, E., Akçabozan-Kayabol, N. B., & Rohner, R. P. (2023). All you fear is love: The roles of rejection by intimate others. *Personal Relationships, 30*(2), 451–470. https://doi.org/10.1111/pere.12473

Ashdown, B. K., Brown, C. M., Faherty, A. N., & Camden, A. A. (2023). Parental rejection and fear of intimacy in the United States and Guatemala: Context and culture matter. *Current Psychology, 42*(19), 16025–16035. https://doi.org/10.1007/s12144-020-01021-7

Backman, H., Laajasalo, T., Jokela, M., & Aronen, E. T. (2021). Parental warmth and hostility and the development of psychopathic behaviors: A longitudinal study of young offenders. *Journal of Child and Family Studies, 30*(4), 955–965. https://doi.org/10.1007/s10826-021-01921-7

Bolkan, C., Sano, Y., De Costa, J., Acock, A. C., & Day, R. D. (2010). Early adolescents' perceptions of mothers' and fathers' parenting styles and problem behavior. *Marriage & Family Review, 46*(8), 563–579. https://doi.org/10.1080/01494929.2010.543040

Börkan, B., Erkman, F., & Keskiner, P. (2014). Effects of parental power/prestige and acceptance on the psychological adjustment of Turkish youth. *Cross-Cultural Research, 48*(3), 316–325.

Brekalo, M., & Keresteš, G. (2023). Remembrances of childhood rejection and loneliness in female university students: A mediating role of rejection sensitivity. *Current Psychology, 43*(9), 8252–8260. https://doi.org/10.1007/s12144-023-05010-4

Bully, P., Jaureguizar, J., Bernaras, E., & Redondo, I. (2019). Relationship between parental socialization, emotional symptoms, and academic performance during adolescence: The influence of parents' and teenagers' gender. *International Journal of Environmental Research and Public Health, 16*(12). https://doi.org/10.3390/ijerph16122231

Butt, M. M., Watson, R. J., Rohner, R. P., & Malik, F. (2022). Memories of parental rejection in childhood and current psychological maladjustment predict substance abuse in a collectivist religious country. *Journal of Child and Family Studies, 31*(9), 2608–2617. https://doi.org/10.1007/s10826-022-02323-z

Čablová, L., Pazderková, K., & Miovský, M. (2014). Parenting styles and alcohol use among children and adolescents: A systematic review. *Drugs: Education, Prevention and Policy, 21*(1), 1–13. https://doi.org/10.3109/09687637.2013.817536

Caliendo, C., Senese, V. P., & Cantone, D. (2017). Parental rejection, addiction and current fathering: A comparative study. *Rivista di Psicologia Clinica, 1*, 59–69.

Carrasco, M. A., Holgado, F. P., Rodríguez, M. A., & del Barrio, M. V. (2009). Concurrent and across-time relations between mother/father hostility and children's aggression: A longitudinal study. *Journal of Family Violence, 24*(4), 213–220. https://doi.org/10.1007/s10896-009-9222-y

Crawford, T. R. W. (2003). *Fathers' parenting: Effects of behavioral style and availability on the child's self-concept at early adulthood.* [Unpublished doctoral dissertation]. University of Connecticut.

Del Barrio, V., Holgado-Tello, F. P., & Carrasco, M. A. (2016). Concurrent and longitudinal effects of maternal and paternal warmth on depression symptoms in children and adolescents. *Psychiatry Research, 242*, 75–81. https://doi.org/10.1016/j.psychres.2016.05.032

Dmitrieva, J., & Espel, E. V. (2023). The role of paternal and maternal warmth and hostility on daughter's psychosocial outcomes: The insidious effects of father warmth combined with high paternal hostility. *Frontiers in Psychology, 14*, 930371. https://doi.org/10.3389/fpsyg.2023.930371

Dumka, L. E., Gonzales, N. A., Bonds, D., & Millsap, R. E. (2009). Academic success of Mexican origin adolescent boys and girls: The role of mothers' and fathers' parenting and cultural orientation. *Sex Roles, 60*(7-8), 588–599. https://doi.org/10.1007/s11199-008-9518-z

Dwairy, M. (2010). Parental acceptance–rejection: A fourth cross-cultural research on parenting and psychological adjustment of children. *Journal of Child and Family Studies, 19*(1), 30–35. https://doi.org/10.1007/s10826-009-9338-y

Ehnvall, A., Parker, G., Hadzi-Pavlovic, D., & Malhi, G. (2008). Perception of rejecting and neglectful parenting in childhood relates to lifetime suicide attempts for females–but not for males. *Acta Psychiatrica Scandinavica, 117*(1), 50–56. https://doi.org/10.1111/j.1600-0447.2007.01124.x

Epli, H., Vural Batık, M., Doğru Çabuker, N., & Balcı Çelik, S. (2021). The relationship between perceived parental rejection and dating anxiety: The mediating role of interpersonal cognitive distortions. *International Journal of Progressive Education, 17*(3), 70–85. https://doi.org/10.29329/ijpe.2021.346.5

Eryavuz, A. (2006). *Çocuklukta algılanan ebeveyn kabul veya reddinin yetişkinlik dönemi yakın ilişkileri üzerindeki etkileri.* [Unpublished doctoral dissertation]. Ege University.

Ford, C. A., Pool, A. C., Kahn, N. F., Jaccard, J., & Halpern, C. T. (2023). Associations between mother-adolescent and father-adolescent relationships and young adult health. *JAMA Netw Open, 6*(3), e233944. https://doi.org/10.1001/jamanetworkopen.2023.3944

Gao, Y., Raine, A., Chan, F., Venables, P. H., & Mednick, S. A. (2010). Early maternal and paternal bonding, childhood physical abuse and adult psychopathic personality. *Psychological Medicine, 40*(6), 1007–1016. https://doi.org/10.1017/S0033291709991279

Geary, D. C. (2021). *Male, female: The evolution of human sex differences* (3rd ed.). American Psychological Association. https://doi.org/10.1037/0000181-000

Giaouzi, A., & Giovazolias, T. (2015). Remembered parental rejection and social anxiety: The mediating role of partner acceptance-rejection. *Journal of Child and Family Studies, 24*(11), 3170–3179. https://doi.org/10.1007/s10826-015-0120-z

Giotsa, A., & Touloumakos, A. K. (2014). Perceived parental acceptance and psychological adjustment: The moderating role of parental power and prestige among Greek pre-adolescents. *Cross-Cultural Research, 48*(3), 250–258.

Giovazolias, T., & Paschalidi, E. (2022). The effect of rejection sensitivity on fear of intimacy in emerging adulthood. *European Journal of Psychology Open, 81*(1), 1–12. https://doi.org/10.1024/2673-8627/a000019

Gordon, I., Zagoory-Sharon, O., Leckman, J. F., & Feldman, R. (2010). Oxytocin and the development of parenting in humans. *Biological Psychiatry, 68*(4), 377–382. https://doi.org/10.1016/j.biopsych.2010.02.005

Graziano, F., Bonino, S., & Cattelino, E. (2009). Links between maternal and paternal support, depressive feelings and social and academic self-efficacy in adolescence. *European Journal of Developmental Psychology, 6*(2), 241–257. https://doi.org/10.1080/17405620701252066

Green, A., MacLean, R., & Charles, K. (2020). Recollections of parenting styles in the development of narcissism: The role of gender. *Personality and Individual Differences, 167*. https://doi.org/10.1016/j.paid.2020.110246

Guo, J., Zhang, J., & Pang, W. (2021). Parental warmth, rejection, and creativity: The mediating roles of openness and dark personality traits. *Personality and Individual Differences, 168*. https://doi.org/10.1016/j.paid.2020.110369

Gurmen, S. (2025). Clinical Applications of interpersonal acceptance-rejection theory (IPARTheory). In R. P. Rohner & S. Ali (Eds.), *Global perspectives on parental acceptance and rejection: Lessons learned from IPARTheory* (pp. 207–224). Routledge.

Guzel, H. S., Guney, E., & Senses Dinc, G. (2018). Assessment of perceived parental acceptance-rejection and psychological adjustment levels of children diagnosed with attention-deficit hyperactivity disorder. *Dusunen Adam: The Journal of Psychiatry and Neurological Sciences, 31*(1), 50–60. https://doi.org/10.5350/dajpn2018310105

Han, Y., Rudy, D., & Proulx, C. M. (2017). Longitudinal relationships among marital conflict, maternal and paternal warmth and control, and preschoolers'

socioemotional outcomes in South Korea. *Journal of Cross-Cultural Psychology, 48*(10), 1522–1536. https://doi.org/10.1177/0022022117732300
Hofer, P. D., Wahl, K., Meyer, A. H., Miché, M., Beesdo-Baum, K., Wittchen, H.-U., & Lieb, R. (2018). The role of behavioral inhibition, perceived parental rearing, and adverse life events in adolescents and young adults with incident obsessive-compulsive disorder. *Journal of Obsessive-Compulsive and Related Disorders, 19*, 116–123. https://doi.org/10.1016/j.jocrd.2018.10.003
Ibrahim, D. M., Rohner, R. P., Smith, R. L., & Flannery, K. M. (2015). Adults' remembrances of parental acceptance–rejection in childhood predict current rejection sensitivity in adulthood. *Family and Consumer Sciences Research Journal, 44*(1), 51–62. https://doi.org/10.1111/fcsr.12119
Icick, R., Lauer, S., Romo, L., Dupuy, G., Lepine, J. P., & Vorspan, F. (2013). Dysfunctional parental styles perceived during childhood in outpatients with substance use disorders. *Psychiatry Research, 210*(2), 522–528. https://doi.org/10.1016/j.psychres.2013.06.041
Imamoglu, A., & Durak Batıgün, A. (2020). The assessment of the relationship between narcissism, perceived parental rearing styles, and defense mechanisms. *Dusunen Adam-Journal of Psychiatry and Neurological Sciences, 33*(4), 388–401.
Jager, J., Mahler, A., An, D., Putnick, D. L., Bornstein, M. H., Lansford, J. E., Dodge, K. A., Skinner, A. T., & Deater-Deckard, K. (2016). Early adolescents' unique perspectives of maternal and paternal rejection: Examining their across-dyad generalizability and relations with adjustment 1 year later. *Journal of Youth and Adolescence, 45*(10), 2108–2124. https://doi.org/10.1007/s10964-016-0509-z
Jin, B., & Roopnarine, J. L. (2023). Pathways of influence between maternal and paternal acceptance and childhood outcomes among Korean immigrant families. *Asian American Journal of Psychology*. https://doi.org/10.1037/aap0000333
Kara, D., & Sümer, N. (2022). The role of paternal parenting and co-parenting quality in children's academic self-efficacy. *Frontiers in Psychology, 13*. https://doi.org/10.3389/fpsyg.2022.772023
Kawabata, Y., Alink, L. R. A., Tseng, W.-L., van Ijzendoorn, M. H., & Crick, N. R. (2011). Maternal and paternal parenting styles associated with relational aggression in children and adolescents: A conceptual analysis and meta-analytic review. *Developmental Review, 31*(4), 240–278. https://doi.org/10.1016/j.dr.2011.08.001
Kawabata, Y., & Crick, N. R. (2016). Differential associations between maternal and paternal parenting and physical and relational aggression. *Asian Journal of Social Psychology, 19*(3), 254–263. https://doi.org/10.1111/ajsp.12139
Khaleque, A. (2013). Perceived parental warmth, and children's psychological adjustment, and personality dispositions: A meta-analysis. *Journal of Child and Family Studies, 22*(2), 297–306. https://doi.org/10.1007/s10826-012-9579-z
Khaleque, A. (2015). Perceived parental neglect, and children's psychological maladjustment, and negative personality dispositions: A meta-analysis of multicultural studies. *Journal of Child and Family Studies, 24*(5), 1419–1428. https://doi.org/10.1007/s10826-014-9948-x
Khaleque, A. (2017). Perceived parental hostility and aggression, and children's psychological maladjustment, and negative personality dispositions: A meta-analysis. *Journal of Child and Family Studies, 26*(4), 977–988. https://doi.org/10.1007/s10826-016-0637-9
Khaleque, A. (2025). A systematic review of IPARTheory's constructs and measures. In R. P. Rohner & S. Ali, (Eds.), *Global perspectives on parental acceptance and rejection: Lessons learned from IPARTheory* (pp. 39–62). Routledge.

Khaleque, A., Hussain, S., Gul, S., Zahra, S. (2018). Relations between remembered childhood parental acceptance-rejection, current fear of intimacy, and psychological adjustment among Pakistani adults. *Psychology and Behavioral Science, 10*(2), 1–8.

Khaleque, A., Reboredo, A. R., Monteiro, V., & Uddin, M. K. (2021a). Effects of parental acceptance-rejection, psychological adjustment, academic self-concept, and learning motivation on adolescents' academic achievement. *International Journal of Biomed Research, 1*(4).

Khaleque, A., & Rohner, R. P. (2012a). Pancultural associations between perceived parental acceptance and psychological adjustment of children and adults: A meta-analytic review of worldwide research. *Journal of Cross-Cultural Psychology, 43*(5), 784–800. https://doi.org/10.1177/0022022111406120

Khaleque, A., & Rohner, R. P. (2012b). Transnational relations between perceived parental acceptance and personality dispositions of children and adults: A meta-analytic review. *Personality and Social Psychology Review, 16*(2), 103–115. https://doi.org/10.1177/1088868311418986

Khaleque, A., Uddin, M., & Aktar, R. (2021b). Relations between bicultural attitudes, paternal versus maternal acceptance, and psychological adjustment of ethnic minority youth in Bangladesh. *Journal of Ethnic and Cultural Studies, 8*(3), 149–168. https://doi.org/10.29333/ejecs/694

Klein, E. M., Brähler, E., Petrowski, K., Tibubos, A. N., Burghardt, J., Wiltink, J., Michal, M., Wild, P. S., Schulz, A., & Münzel, T. (2020). Recalled parental rearing behavior in adult women and men with depressive and anxiety symptoms: Findings from a community study. *Zeitschrift für Psychosomatische Medizin und Psychotherapie, 66*(3), 243–258.

Kosterman, R., Haggerty, K. P., Spoth, R., & Redmond, C. (2004). Unique influence of mothers and fathers on their children's antisocial behavior. *Journal of Marriage and Family, 66*(3), 762–778. https://doi.org/10.1111/j.0022-2445.2004.00051.x

Koşar, E. (2021). *Investigation of substance use among late adolescents in terms of its relationship with parental acceptance rejection, self-control, anger and peer deviance*. [Unpublished master thesis]. TED University.

Koutra, K., Paschalidou, A., Roumeliotaki, T., & Triliva, S. (2022). Main and-interactive retrospective associations between parental rearing behavior and psychological adjustment in young adulthood. *Current Psychology, 42*(22), 18761–18776. https://doi.org/10.1007/s12144-022-03011-3

Kuyumcu, B., & Rohner, R. P. (2018). The relation between remembered parental acceptance in childhood and self-acceptance among young Turkish adults. *International Journal of Psychology, 53*(2), 126–132. https://doi.org/10.1002/ijop.12277

Lansford, J. E. (2022). Annual research review: Cross-cultural similarities and differences in parenting. *Journal of Child Psychology and Psychiatry, 63*(4), 466–479. https://doi.org/10.1111/jcpp.13539

Lansford, J. E., Zietz, S., Al-Hassan, S. M., Bacchini, D., Bornstein, M. H., Chang, L., … & Alampay, L. P. (2021). Culture and social change in mothers' and fathers' individualism, collectivism and parenting attitudes. *Social Sciences, 10*(12), 459. https://doi.org/10.3390/socsci10120459

Lee, J., & Chyung, Y. J. (2014). Parental power–prestige and the effects of paternal versus maternal acceptance on the psychological adjustment of Korean children. *Cross-Cultural Research, 48*(3), 259–269.

Lewis, C., & Lamb, M. E. (2003). Fathers' influences on children's development: The evidence from two-parent families. *European Journal of Psychology of Education, 18*, 211–228. https://doi.org/10.1007/BF03173485

Li, X., & Meier, J. (2017). Father love and mother love: Contributions of parental acceptance to children's psychological adjustment. *Journal of Family Theory & Review*, *9*(4), 459–490. https://doi.org/10.1111/jftr.12227

Laible, D. J., & Carlo, G. (2004). The differential relations of maternal and paternal support and control to adolescent social competence, self-worth, and sympathy. *Journal of Adolescent Research*, *19*(6), 759–782. https://doi.org/10.1177/0743558403260094

Lila, M., Garcia, F., & Gracia, E. (2007). Perceived paternal and maternal acceptance and children's outcomes in Colombia. *Social Behavior and Personality*, *35*(1), 115–124.

Lippold, M. A., Hussong, A., Fosco, G. M., & Ram, N. (2018). Lability in the parent's hostility and warmth toward their adolescent: Linkages to youth delinquency and substance use. *Developmental Psychology*, *54*(2), 348–361. https://doi.org/10.1037/dev0000415

Liu, L., Zhai, P., & Wang, M. (2022). Parental harsh discipline and migrant children's anxiety in China: The moderating role of parental warmth and gender. *Journal of Interpersonal Violence*, *37*(19-20), NP18761–NP18783. https://doi.org/10.1177/08862605211037580

Luk, J. W., Patock-Peckham, J. A., & King, K. M. (2015). Are dimensions of parenting differentially linked to substance use across Caucasian and Asian American college students? *Substance Use & Misuse*, *50*(10), 1360–1369. https://doi.org/10.3109/10826084.2015.1013134

Machado, M., Machado, F., Neves, S., & Fávero, M. (2014). How do parental acceptance–rejection, power, and prestige affect psychological adjustment? A quantitative study with a sample of Portuguese college students. *Cross-Cultural Research*, *48*(3), 295–304.

Marcone, R., Affuso, G., & Borrone, A. (2020). Parenting styles and children's internalizing-externalizing behavior: The mediating role of behavioral regulation. *Current Psychology*, *39*(1), 13–24. https://doi.org/10.1007/s12144-017-9757-7

McLeod, B. D., Wood, J. J., & Weisz, J. R. (2007a). Examining the association between parenting and childhood anxiety: A meta-analysis. *Clinical Psychology Review*, *27*(2), 155–172. https://doi.org/10.1016/j.cpr.2006.09.002

McLeod, B. D., Weisz, J. R., & Wood, J. J. (2007b). Examining the association between parenting and childhood depression: A meta-analysis. *Clinical Psychology Review*, *27*(8), 986–1003. https://doi.org/10.1016/j.cpr.2007.03.001

Miklikowska, M., Duriez, B., & Soenens, B. (2011). Family roots of empathy-related characteristics: The role of perceived maternal and paternal need support in adolescence. *Developmental Psychology*, *47*(5), 1342–1352. https://doi.org/10.1037/a0024726

Miranda, M. C., Affuso, G., Esposito, C., & Bacchini, D. (2016). Parental acceptance–rejection and adolescent maladjustment: Mothers' and fathers' combined roles. *Journal of Child and Family Studies*, *25*(4), 1352–1362. https://doi.org/10.1007/s10826-015-0305-5

Möller, E. L., Nikolić, M., Majdandžić, M., & Bögels, S. M. (2016). Associations between maternal and paternal parenting behaviors, anxiety, and its precursors in early childhood: A meta-analysis. *Clinical Psychology Review*, *45*, 17–33. https://doi.org/10.1016/j.cpr.2016.03.002

Murray, K. W., Dwyer, K. M., Rubin, K. H., Knighton-Wisor, S., & Booth-LaForce, C. (2014). Parent-child relationships, parental psychological control, and aggression: Maternal and paternal relationships. *Journal of Youth & Adolescence*, *43*(8), 1361–1373. https://doi.org/10.1007/s10964-013-0019-1

Palkovitz, R. (2013). Gendered parenting's implications for children's well-being: Theory and research in applied perspective. In W. B. Wilcox & K. K. Kline (Eds.), *Gender and Parenthood: Biological and Social Scientific Perspectives* (pp. 215–248). Columbia University Press.

Papadaki, E., & Giovazolias, T. (2015). The protective role of father acceptance in the relationship between maternal rejection and bullying: A moderated-mediation model. *Journal of Child and Family Studies, 24*(2), 330–340. https://doi.org/10.1007/s10826-013-9839-6

Parke, R. D. (2013). Gender differences and similarities in parental behavior. In W. B. Wilcox & K. K. Kline (Eds.), *Gender and Parenthood: Biological and Social Scientific Perspectives* (pp. 120–163). Columbia University Press

Parmar, P., & Rohner, R. P. (2008). Relations among spouse acceptance, remembered parental acceptance in childhood, and psychological adjustment among married adults in India. *Cross-Cultural Research, 42*(1), 57–66. https://doi.org/10.1177/1069397107309763

Parmar, P., & Rohner, R. P. (2010). Perceived teacher and parental acceptance and behavioral control, school conduct, and psychological adjustment among school-going adolescents in India. *Cross-Cultural Research, 44*(3), 253–268. https://doi.org/10.1177/1069397110367613

Patock-Peckham, J. A., Cheong, J., Balhorn, M. E., & Nagoshi, C. T. (2001). A social learning perspective: A model of parenting styles, self-regulation, perceived drinking control, and alcohol use and problems. *Alcoholism: Clinical and Experimental Research, 25*(9), 1284–1292. https://doi.org/10.1111/j.1530-0277.2001.tb02349.x

Patock-Peckham, J. A., & Morgan-Lopez, A. A. (2006). College drinking behaviors: Mediational links between parenting styles, impulse control, and alcohol-related outcomes. *Psychology of Addictive Behaviors, 20*(2), 117–125. https://doi.org/10.1037/0893-164X.20.2.117

Pinquart, M. (2017a). Associations of parenting dimensions and styles with internalizing symptoms in children and adolescents: A meta-analysis. *Marriage & Family Review, 53*(7), 613–640. https://doi.org/10.1080/01494929.2016.1247761

Pinquart, M. (2017b). Associations of parenting dimensions and styles with externalizing problems of children and adolescents: An updated meta-analysis. *Developmental Psychology, 53*(5), 873–932. https://doi.org/10.1037/dev0000295

Pomini, V., Gournellis, R., Kokkevi, A., Tomaras, V., Papadimitriou, G., & Liappas, J. (2014). Rejection attitudes, poor parental bonding, and stressful life events in heroin addicts' families. *Substance Use & Misuse, 49*(14), 1867–1877. https://doi.org/10.3109/10826084.2014.913629

Power, T. G., Sleddens, E. F., Berge, J., Connell, L., Govig, B., Hennessy, E., ... St. George, S. M. (2013). Contemporary research on parenting: conceptual, methodological, and translational issues. *Childhood Obesity, 9*(s1), S87–94.

Putnick, D. L., Bornstein, M. H., Lansford, J. E., Chang, L., Deater-Deckard, K., Di Giunta, L., Dodge, K. A., Malone, P. S., Oburu, P., Pastorelli, C., Skinner, A. T., Sorbring, E., Tapanya, S., Uribe Tirado, L. M., Zelli, A., Alampay, L. P., Al-Hassan, S. M., Bacchini, D., & Bombi, A. S. (2018). Parental acceptance-rejection and child prosocial behavior: Developmental transactions across the transition to adolescence in nine countries, mothers and fathers, and girls and boys. *Developmental Psychology, 54*(10), 1881–1890. https://doi.org/10.1037/dev0000565

Putnick, D. L., Bornstein, M. H., Lansford, J. E., Malone, P. S., Pastorelli, C., Skinner, A. T., Sorbring, E., Tapanya, S., Uribe Tirado, L. M., Zelli, A., Alampay, L. P., Al-Hassan, S. M., Bacchini, D., Bombi, A. S., Chang, L., Deater-Deckard, K., Di

Giunta, L., Dodge, K. A., & Oburu, P. (2015). Perceived mother and father acceptance-rejection predict four unique aspects of child adjustment across nine countries. *Journal of Child Psychology and Psychiatry, 56*(8), 923–932. https://doi.org/10.1111/jcpp.12366

Putnick, D. L., Uddin, M. K., Rohner, R. P., Singha, B., & Shahnaz, I. (2020). Remembrances of parental rejection are associated with loneliness as mediated by psychological maladjustment in young Bangladeshi men but not women. *International Journal of Psychology, 55*(3), 354–363. https://doi.org/10.1002/ijop.12609

Rajhans, P., Goin-Kochel, R. P., Strathearn, L., & Kim, S. (2019). It takes two! Exploring sex differences in parenting neurobiology and behaviour. *Journal of Neuroendocrinology, 31*(9), e12721. https://doi.org/10.1111/jne.12721

Ramírez-Uclés, I., González-Calderón, M. J., del Barrio-Gándara, V., & Carrasco, M. Á. (2018). Perceived parental acceptance-rejection and children's psychological adjustment: The moderating effects of sex and age. *Journal of Child and Family Studies, 27*(4), 1336–1348. https://doi.org/10.1007/s10826-017-0975-2

Rasmi, S., Chuang, S. S., & Safdar, S. (2012). The relationship between perceived parental rejection and adjustment for Arab, Canadian, and Arab Canadian Youth. *Journal of Cross-Cultural Psychology, 43*(1), 84–90. https://doi.org/10.1177/0022022111428172

Raufelder, D., Hoferichter, F., Ringeisen, T., Regner, N., & Jacke, C. (2015). The perceived role of parental support and pressure in the interplay of test anxiety and school engagement among adolescents: Evidence for gender-specific relations. *Journal of Child and Family Studies, 24*(12), 3742–3756. https://doi.org/10.1007/s10826-015-0182-y

Rilling, J. K. (2013). The neural and hormonal bases of human parental care. *Neuropsychologia, 51*(4), 731–747. https://doi.org/10.1016/j.neuropsychologia.2012.12.017

Richter, J., Eisemann, M., & Richter, G. (1991). Perceived parental rearing and state versus trait aspects of adult depression. *Psychopathology, 24*(1), 25–30.

Rohner, R. P. (1975). *They love me, they love me not: A worldwide study of the effects of parental acceptance and rejection*. New Haven, CT: HRAFLEX Press.

Rohner, R. P. (1986). *The warmth dimension: Foundations of parental acceptance-rejection theory*. Beverly Hills, CA: Sage Publications, Inc. (Available as e-book from Rohner Research Publications, Storrs, CT).

Rohner, R. P. (2008). Parental acceptance-rejection theory studies of intimate adult relationships. *Cross-Cultural Research, 42*(1), 5–12. https://doi.org/10.1177/1069397107309749

Rohner, R. P. (2010). Perceived teacher acceptance, parental acceptance, and the adjustment, achievement, and behavior of school-going youths internationally. *Cross-Cultural Research, 44*(3), 211–221.

Rohner, R. P. (2014). Parental power and prestige moderate the relationship between perceived parental acceptance and offspring's psychological adjustment: Introduction to the international father acceptance–rejection project. *Cross-Cultural Research, 48*(3), 197–213.

Rohner, R. P. (2021). Introduction to interpersonal acceptance-rejection theory (IPARTheory) and evidence. *Online Readings in Psychology and Culture, 6*(1), 1–65. https://doi.org/10.9707/2307-0919.1055

Rohner, R. P. & Ali, S. (2025). IPARTheory, evidence, and methods from conception through maturity. In Rohner, R. P., & Ali, S. (Eds.). *Global perspectives on parental acceptance and rejection: Lessons learned from IPARTheory* (pp. 3–38). Routledge.

Rohner, R. P., & Brothers, S. A. (1999). Perceived parental rejection, psychological maladjustment, and borderline personality disorder. *Journal of Emotional Abuse, 1*(4), 81–95. https://doi.org/10.1300/J135v01n04_05

Rohner, R. P., Filus, A., Melendez-Rhodes, T., Kuyumcu, B., Machado, F., Roszak, J., Hussain, S., Chyung, Y.-J., Senese, V. P., Daneshmandi, S., Ashdown, B. K., Giovazolias, T., Glavak-Tkalić, R., Chen, S., Uddin, M. K., Harris, S., Gregory, N., Fávero, M., Zahra, S., ... Roy, K. (2019). Psychological maladjustment mediates the relation between remembrances of parental rejection in childhood and adults' fear of intimacy: A multicultural study. *Cross-Cultural Research, 53*(5), 508–542. https://doi.org/10.1177/1069397118822992

Rohner, R. P., & Khaleque, A. (2010). Testing central postulates of parental acceptance-rejection theory (PARTheory): A meta-analysis of cross-cultural studies. *Journal of Family Theory & Review, 2*(1), 73–87. https://doi.org/10.1111/j.1756-2589.2010.00040.x

Rohner, R. P., Putnick, D. L., Molaver, A. D., Ali, S., Butt, M. M., Ibrahim, D. M., Aurino, C., Blom, M. J. M., Darwesh, F. H., Auricchio, S., Radha, A. H., Miranda, M. C., Adamsons, K., & Senese, V. P. (2020). Psychological maladjustment mediates the link between remembrances of parental rejection in childhood and loneliness in adulthood: A cross-cultural comparative study. *International Journal of Psychology, 55*(4), 590–600. https://doi.org/10.1002/ijop.12621

Rohner, R. P., & Veneziano, R. A. (2001). The importance of father love: History and contemporary evidence. *Review of General Psychology, 5*(4), 382–405. https://doi.org/10.1037/1089-2680.5.4.382

Rostad, W. L., Medina, A. M., & Hurtig-Crosby, P. (2014). Fathers in the dorm room: the unique influence of fathers and mothers on young adult functioning. *Fathering: A Journal of Theory, Research, and Practice, 12*(1), 3–17. https://doi.org/10.3149/fth.1201.3

Rothenberg, W. A., Ali, S., Rohner, R. P., Lansford, J. E., Britner, P. A., Giunta, L. D., Dodge, K. A., Malone, P. S., Oburu, P., Pastorelli, C., Skinner, A. T., Sorbring, E., Steinberg, L., Tapanya, S., Uribe Tirado, L. M., Yotanyamaneewong, S., Alampay, L. P., Al-Hassan, S. M., Bacchini, D., ... Deater-Deckard, K. (2022). Effects of parental acceptance-rejection on children's internalizing and externalizing behaviors: A longitudinal, multicultural study. *Journal of Child and Family Studies, 31*(1), 29–47. https://doi.org/10.1007/s10826-021-02072-5

Rothenberg, W. A., Lansford, J. E., Alampay, L. P., Al-Hassan, S. M., Bacchini, D., Bornstein, M. H., Chang, L., Deater-Deckard, K., Di Giunta, L., Dodge, K. A., Malone, P. S., Oburu, P., Pastorelli, C., Skinner, A. T., Sorbring, E., Steinberg, L., Tapanya, S., Tirado, L. M. U., & Yotanyamaneewong, S. (2020). Examining effects of mother and father warmth and control on child externalizing and internalizing problems from age 8 to 13 in nine countries. *Development and Psychopathology, 32*(3), 1113–1137. https://doi.org/10.1017/S0954579419001214

Rueger, S. Y., Chen, P., Jenkins, L. N., & Choe, H. J. (2013). Effects of perceived support from mothers, fathers, and teachers on depressive symptoms during the transition to middle school. *Journal of Youth and Adolescence, 43*(4), 655–670. https://doi.org/10.1007/s10964-013-0039-x

Ryan, S. M., Jorm, A. F., & Lubman, D. I. (2010). Parenting factors associated with reduced adolescent alcohol use: A systematic review of longitudinal studies. *Australian & New Zealand Journal of Psychiatry, 44*(9), 774–783.

Saha, A. K., Linte, M. A., & Kumar, P. (2020). Impact of parental acceptance-rejection on children's altruistic behavior. *Journal of Psychosocial Research, 15*(1), 349–359. https://doi.org/10.32381/jpr.2020.15.01.30

Senese, V. P., Miranda, M. C., Lansford, J. E., Bacchini, D., Nasti, C., & Rohner, R. P. (2020). Psychological maladjustment mediates the relation between recollections of parental rejection in childhood and adults' fear of intimacy in Italy. *Journal of Social and Personal Relationships, 37*(6), 1968–1990. https://doi.org/10.1177/0265407520912339

Senese, V. P., Shinohara, K., Venuti, P., Bornstein, M. H., Rosanio, V., Nasti, C., Neoh, M. J., Maresca, M., & Esposito, G. (2022). The interaction effect of parental rejection and oxytocin receptor gene polymorphism on depression: A cross-cultural study in non-clinical samples. *International Journal of Environmental Research and Public Health, 19*(9). https://doi.org/10.3390/ijerph19095566

SeyedMousavi, P., Khoshroo, S., Memarian, M., Ghanbari, S., & Rohner, R. P. (2022). Memories of parental rejection and fear of intimacy: the role of psychological maladjustment, interpersonal anxiety, and rejection by an intimate Partner. *Current Psychology, 42*(36), 31801–31809. https://doi.org/10.1007/s12144-022-04160-1

Shin, S. H., Wang, X., Yoon, S. H., Cage, J. L., Kobulsky, J. M., & Montemayor, B. N. (2019). Childhood maltreatment and alcohol-related problems in young adulthood: The protective role of parental warmth. *Child Abuse & Neglect, 98*, 104238. https://doi.org/10.1016/j.chiabu.2019.104238

Someya, T., Kitamura, H., Uehara, T., Sakado, K., Kaiya, H., Tang, S. W., & Takahashi, S. (2000). Panic disorder and perceived parental rearing behavior investigated by the Japanese version of the EMBU scale. *Depression and Anxiety, 11*(4), 158–162. https://doi.org/10.1002/1520-6394(2000)11:4<158::AID-DA2>3.0.CO;2-4

Sultana, S., & Khaleque, A. (2016). Differential effects of perceived maternal and paternal acceptance on male and female adult offspring's psychological adjustment. *Gender Issues, 33*(1), 42–52. https://doi.org/10.1007/s12147-015-9147-0

Thomson, R. A., Easterbrooks, M. A., & L. M. Padilla-Walker. (2003). Social and emotional development in infancy. In R. M. Lerner, M. A. Easterbrooks, & J. Mistry (Eds.), *Handbook of Psychology: Developmental Psychology* (Vol. 6, pp. 120–163). Columbia University Press

Uddin, M. K. (2011). Parental warmth and academic achievement of adolescent children. *Journal of Behavioural Sciences, 21*(1), 1–12.

Vazsonyi, A. T., Ksinan, A. J., Javakhishvili, M., Scarpate, J. M., & Kahumoku-Fessler, E. (2022). Links between parenting and internalizing and externalizing problems: Cross-cultural evidence from ten countries. *Child Psychiatry & Human Development, 53*(4), 667–683. https://doi.org/10.1007/s10578-021-01153-2

Veneziano, R. A. (2003). The importance of paternal warmth. *Cross-Cultural Research, 37*(3), 265–281. https://doi.org/10.1177/1069397103253710

Vergara-Lopez, C., Sokol, N. A., Bublitz, M. H., Gaffey, A. E., Gomez, A., Mercado, N., Silk, J. S., & Stroud, L. R. (2022). Exploring the impact of maternal and paternal acceptance on adolescent girls' emotion regulation. *Child Psychiatry & Human Development, 55*(2), 320–326. https://doi.org/10.1007/s10578-022-01405-9

Verhoeven, M., Junger, M., Van Aken, C., Deković, M., & Van Aken, M. A. G. (2010). Mothering, fathering, and externalizing behavior in toddler boys. *Journal of Marriage and Family, 72*(2), 307–317. https://doi.org/10.1111/j.1741-3737.2010.00701.x

Weitkamp, K., & Seiffge-Krenke, I. (2019). The association between parental rearing dimensions and adolescent psychopathology: A cross-cultural study. *Journal of Youth and Adolescence, 48*(3), 469–483. https://doi.org/10.1007/s10964-018-0928-0

Xing, X., & Wang, M. (2017). Gender differences in the moderating effects of parental warmth and hostility on the association between corporal punishment and child externalizing behaviors in China. *Journal of Child and Family Studies, 26*(3), 928–938. https://doi.org/10.1007/s10826-016-0610-7

Yang, Y., Li, M., & Lin, H. C. (2019). Parental rejection, resilience, and health-risk behavior in emerging adults. *American Journal of Health Behavior, 43*(5), 898–911. https://doi.org/10.5993/AJHB.43.5.3

Yendell, A., Clemens, V., Schuler, J., & Decker, O. (2022). What makes a violent mind? The interplay of parental rearing, dark triad personality traits and propensity for violence in a sample of German adolescents. *PLoS One, 17*(6), e0268992. https://doi.org/10.1371/journal.pone.0268992

10

PARENTAL REJECTION IN CHILDHOOD PREDICTS MEDICAL PROBLEMS IN ADULTHOOD

Sumbleen Ali, Ronald P. Rohner, Preston A. Britner, and Fumiko Hoeft

Both positive and negative early life experiences, whether retrospectively reported or prospectively reported, are known to have a lifelong impact on individuals' social, emotional, and physical well-being (Fisher et al., 2011; Matthews & Gallo, 2011; Solís et al., 2015; Varese et al., 2012). Family scientists have long argued that reports of adverse childhood experiences (ACEs) are associated with an increased likelihood of adverse *mental health* outcomes in adulthood (e.g., Anda et al., 2009; Norman et al., 2012; Rich-Edwards et al., 2010; Rohner, 1986, 2021). For example, emotional abuse, which involves verbal threats of violence or other verbal aggression and ridiculing from caregivers (Norman et al., 2012), is associated with adverse outcomes even after controlling for all other forms of abuse (Spertus et al., 2003). Research has also found that childhood adversity can lead to serious increases in the risk of medical problems (physical health) such as cancer, cardiovascular diseases, and irritable bowel syndrome (Anda et al., 2010).

Much of the foundational research on associations between childhood adversity and subsequent health-outcomes stems from the ACE study (Felitti et al., 1998, 2019), a collaborative research project between the U.S. Centers for Disease Control (CDC) and Kaiser Permanente (a network of health care organizations). Beginning in 1997, the ACE study collected data about childhood adversity and its relation to adult health outcomes from 17,337 participants who sought health services from Kaiser Permanente (Felitti et al., 1998). ACEs were defined as children's exposure (prior to the age of 18) to child abuse and neglect, domestic violence,

DOI: 10.4324/9781003441243-12

mental illness in the household, substance abuse in the household, imprisonment of a family member, parental divorce, and/or other forms of family dysfunction (CDC, 2013; Felitti et al., 1998). Compelling evidence now shows that ACEs are associated with vulnerability to many medical problems (Fagundes et al., 2013; Matthews et al., 2014).

To develop pediatric policies and practices for health and wellbeing across the lifespan in response to findings in the ACEs project, the American Academy of Pediatrics developed the eco-bio-developmental (EBD) framework (see Garner et al., 2012). That framework helped pediatricians and others understand complex relationships among adverse childhood experiences and early-life origins of many adult diseases (Garner et al., 2012). The EBD framework argued that the potential effects on brain development of excessive and prolonged early-life stress can threaten children's adaptive capacities and coping skills, thus creating long-term implications for negative psychological and physical-health outcomes (see Davidson et al., 2010; Pesonen & Räikkönen, 2012).

As the number of ACEs that a child experiences increases, the risk for physical health problems, mental health problems, and behavioral problems in adulthood is also likely to increase (Dong et al., 2004). For instance, as scores on measures of ACEs increase, so does the likelihood of adulthood substance abuse, suicide attempts, depression, smoking, heart and pulmonary diseases, liver disease, intimate partner violence, and sexually transmitted diseases, among other problems (CDC, 2013).

When the physiological stress response is activated frequently or when it remains activated for a prolonged period of time, excessive demands are often placed on the body's regulatory systems for maintaining allostasis—the process of maintaining physiological stability or homeostasis during periods of stress (McEwen & Seeman, 1999). Such excessive demands are likely to lead to a state of physiological dysregulation across multiple systems (Kiecolt-Glaser et al., 2020). The cost of chronic exposure to such a state of stress is termed allostatic load. (McEwen & Seeman, 1999; Seeman et al., 2010). Allostatic load has been observed across a number of physiological regulatory systems in relation to childhood adversity, including elevated cholesterol levels, poor cardiovascular health, increased inflammation, accelerated cellular aging, and metabolic syndrome (Drury et al., 2012; Kiecolt-Glaser et al., 2011; Miller et al., 2011a, 2011b). Likewise, neuroendocrine changes have been observed in adults reporting childhood stress. These changes include greater sympathetic nervous system (SNS) activity, disrupted hypothalamic-pituitary-adrenal (HPA) activity, and autonomic imbalance (Seeman et al., 2010; Miller et al., 2011a, 2011b). Additionally, researchers have found that ACEs are associated with immune dysregulation in patients with cancer and among cancer survivors (Fagundes et al., 2013).

It is important to note here that interpersonal rejection, emotional abuse, neglect, and emotional maltreatment are forms of ACEs (see Dong et al., 2004). Recent evidence suggests that rejecting and neglectful parental behaviors can influence offspring's physical health outcomes in adulthood (Repetti et al., 2011). For instance, Witek-Janusek et al.' (2013) longitudinal study of 40 women diagnosed with early-stage breast cancer who were followed for nine months after tumor resection, showed that childhood physical neglect (but not physical abuse) was associated with women's perceived stress. The study also showed that the women experienced greater fatigue, depressive symptoms, and poorer quality of life, as well as lower natural killer cell activity (NKCA).

Positive dimensions of parenting (e.g., parental warmth, affection, sensitivity, and responsiveness), on the other hand, are associated with lower levels of emotional, behavioral, physical, and psychological problems (see Chen et al., 2019; Rothenberg, 2019; Rohner, 2021; Rohner & Britner, 2002). Further, Wegman and Stetler (2009) conducted a meta-analysis of the long-term health consequences of childhood maltreatment including neglect. Their analysis included 48,000 individuals. In comparison with children who experienced no maltreatment, the authors reported that children who experienced maltreatment reported more severe medical problems, including cardiovascular, respiratory, metabolic, musculoskeletal, and autoimmune conditions. Thus, children are most likely to have healthy developmental outcomes in environments where adversity is minimal and parents are warm and caring (Bayer et al., 2006; Rohner, 1986, 2021; van IJzendoorn & Juffer, 2006). These conclusions are consistent with a large body of multicultural research drawing on interpersonal acceptance-rejection theory (IPARTheory).

Interpersonal Acceptance-Rejection Theory (IPARTheory)

IPARTheory is an evidence-based theory of socialization and lifespan development that aims to predict and explain major consequences, causes, and other correlates of perceived interpersonal, especially parental, acceptance and rejection (Rohner, 1986, 2004a, 2021). The theory was born from questions about how parental acceptance and rejection in childhood are related to children's adjustment and developmental outcomes over the lifespan and across cultures (Rohner, 1986, 2021; Rohner & Lansford, 2017). IPARTheory's personality subtheory postulates that humans everywhere have developed over the course of common biocultural evolution the enduring, biologically based emotional need for positive responses (i.e., warmth, care, emotional support) from the people most important in their lives, especially parents in childhood (Rohner, 1986, 2021; Rohner & Lansford, 2017).

The extent to which children experience positive response depends on where their parents' behavioral expressions fall along the warmth dimension of parenting (Rohner, 1986; Rohner & Lansford, 2017). As construed in IPARTheory, one end of the warmth dimension is defined by parental warmth, affection, and other expressions of acceptance—that is by behaviors that convey love, emotional care, affection, nurturance, and emotional support. The other end of the dimension is defined by parental rejection—that is, by parental coldness, lack of affection, hostility/aggression, indifference/neglect, and undifferentiated rejection (Rohner, 1986, 2021; Rohner & Lansford, 2017). Undifferentiated rejection refers to children's belief that their parents do not really care about or love them without necessarily having objective indicators that the parents are hostile or aggressive, neglecting, or lacking in affection (Rohner, 2021).

IPARTheory further postulates that because the need for warmth and affection is biologically based, children's *psychological* health is likely to worsen in direct proportion to the level of parental rejection they experience—regardless of differences in cultural context, race, language, gender, or other such defining conditions (Khaleque & Ali, 2017; Rohner, 1986, 2021; Rohner & Lansford, 2017). Thirteen meta-analyses (e.g., Khaleque & Ali, 2017; Khaleque, 2013; Pinquart, 2017) involving 149,440 respondents, along with several longitudinal studies involving 12 ethnocultural groups across nine nations worldwide (Lansford et al., 2018; Rothenberg, 2019; Rothenberg et al., 2020), support these conclusions.

However, it is unclear at this time if adults' memories of parental acceptance and rejection in childhood influence their *physical health* in adulthood. Because of that deficiency, this study examined relations between young adults' memories of maternal and paternal acceptance-rejection in childhood and their reports of medical problems in adulthood.

Method

Participants and Procedure

Initially, 1,299 students from a public research university in the northeastern US responded to an online survey that included the measures discussed below. Students from the psychological sciences research participant pool voluntarily participated in the study. Thirty-one responses were excluded because they had more than 60% missingness in their responses to the measures. Thus, 1,268 adults were included in the final study. Less than 3% of the data was missing. We used the Multiple Imputation technique to deal with that missingness.

The sample consisted of 71% women, 26% men, and 2% self-reported transgender/non-binary adults. Participants ranged in age from 18 to 48 years (*M* = 20, *SD* = 3.05). In total, 53% of them were European American (White other than Hispanic), 24% Asian American (e.g., Korean and Chinese), 10% Hispanic American (e.g., Puerto Rican and Mexican), and 7% African American. Six percent self-identified as bi-racial (e.g., African European, African Hispanic. and Asian European).

The study required participants to be 18 years of age or older and to have been raised in two-parent families. Participants from two-parent households were recruited because the objective of the study was to investigate the influence of both maternal and paternal acceptance-rejection on offspring's physical health. Participants in the study could enter a gift card raffle of $100. A total of five raffles of $100 each were drawn after the closing of the survey. The research was approved by the university's Institutional Review Board, and informed consent was obtained from participants. The data were analyzed using descriptive statistics (means and standard deviations), Pearson's correlations, and multiple regression analysis after controlling for demographic variables described next.

Measures

Demographic Characteristics and Medical Problems

Demographic information (e.g., age, gender, ethnicity, socio-economic background, and education level) was obtained using a Personal Information Form. An open-ended question asked participants to list all medical problems they currently have or had experienced in the immediate past. Using that information—in conjunction with available literature on medical problems associated with ACEs—we grouped respondents' medical problems into nine categories. These included: (1) allergies (see Israel et al., 2014), (2) asthma (see Israel et al., 2014), (3) blood pressure problems (see Lehman et al., 2009), (4) cancer (see Fagundes et al., 2013); (5) cardiovascular issues, including open-heart surgery not due to any condition present at birth, but also including the implantation of stents and pacemakers (see Carroll et al., 2013; Suglia et al., 2020); (6) periodontal disease (see Reuben et al., 2016), (7) irritable bowel syndrome (see Drossman et al., 1990), (8) metabolic abnormality (see Israel et al., 2014), and (9) ulcers (see Springer, 2009). Each of these medical problems was scored 1 = "yes, if present" and 0 = "no, not mentioned by the participant". Possible scores ranged from 0 (no medical problem) through 9 medical problems.

Parental Acceptance-Rejection Questionnaire (PARQ-Short Form; Mother and Father Versions)

Adult versions of the Parental Acceptance-Rejection Questionnaire-Short Form (PARQ-SF; Rohner, 2004b, 2004c) were administered to assess participants' memories of maternal and paternal warmth/affection (or coldness/lack of affection), hostility/aggression, indifference/neglect, and undifferentiated rejection in childhood. Adults reported these memories on 4-point Likert scale where 4 = *almost always true*, 3 = *sometime true*, 2 = *rarely true*, or 1 = *almost never true*. Eight PARQ items capture parental warmth/affection (e.g., "my mother[father] made me feel wanted and needed"). These items become a measure of parental coldness/lack of affection when they are reverse scored. Six items capture parental hostility/aggression (e.g., "my mother[father] went out of her[his] way to hurt my feelings"); six items capture parental indifference/neglect (e.g., "my mother[father] paid no attention to me"); and, four items capture undifferentiated rejection (e.g., "my mother[father] did not really love me"). The sum of the four scales provides a total acceptance-rejection score. Possible scores range from a minimum of 24 through a maximum of 96. Higher scores reveal the experience of greater rejection than lower scores. The short form of the PARQ is designed in such a way that scores between 28 and 47 conceptually reveal the experience of remembered parental acceptance whereas scores between 52 and 96 conceptually reveal memories of parental rejection (Rohner, 2005).

Three major systematic reviews and meta-analyses have established that the PARQ has excellent reliability (α = .89; Rothenberg et al., 2020), convergent and discriminant validity (Rohner & Khaleque, 2005), and factorial invariance (Khaleque & Ali, 2017; Rohner & Khaleque, 2005) in over 60 nations worldwide. Reliability, validity, and factorial invariance have also been replicated in several studies (e.g., Lansford et al., 2018; Putnick et al., 2015; Rothenberg, 2019). The alpha value for the mother version of the PARQ in this study was .70 [95% CI .57–.79]. For the father version, it was .80 [95% CI .65–.86].

Results

Scores on the mother and father versions of the PARQ ranged in this study from 24 through 95. As shown in Table 10.1, adults who experienced no medical problems reported substantial maternal acceptance (M = 33, SD = 9, 95% CI, 32.92–34.09), as well as paternal acceptance (M = 37, SD = 11, 95% CI, 36.04–38.55). Adults who experienced one medical problem reported more overall acceptance than rejection, though with minor signs

TABLE 10.1 Means, Standard Deviations, and T-Tests of Differences Between Mothers' Versus Fathers' PARQ Scores

Medical Problems (Number)	*Sample Size*	*PARQ Score*				*t(df)*
		Maternal		**Paternal**		
		M(SD)	*CI*	*M(SD)*	*CI*	
0	913	*33(9)*	32.92–34.09	*37(11)*	36.04–37.55	8.50(1824)***
1	202	*49(11)*	47.58–50.62	53*(14)*	51.47–55.38	3.19(402)***
2	128	*65(11)*	63.60–67.36	*70(12)*	67.52–71.76	3.47(254)***
3 or more	25	*77(8)*	74.15–80.65	*76(12)*	71.43–81.29	–0.35(48) *ns*

Note: PARQ scores 24 – 47 = memories of substantial parental acceptance in childhood; 48 – 57 = more acceptance than rejection, though with minor signs of rejection; 60 – 79 =serious rejection; *** $p < .001$.

ns = not significant.

of maternal rejection ($M = 49$, $SD = 11$, 95% CI, 47.58–50.62), and especially paternal rejection ($M = 53$, $SD = 14$, 95% CI, 51.47–55.38). These adults tended to report slightly elevated levels of parental coldness/lack of affection, hostility/aggression, indifference/neglect, or undifferentiated rejection. Adults who experienced two or more medical problems reported serious signs of both maternal rejection ($M = 65$, $SD = 11$, 95% CI, 63.60–67.36), and paternal rejection ($M = 70$, $SD = 12$, 95% CI, 67.52–71.76). Adults' who experienced three or more medical problems reported even more serious maternal rejection ($M = 77$, $SD = 8$, 95% CI, 74.15–80.65), and paternal rejection ($M = 76$, $SD = 12$, 95% CI, 71.43–81.29). These scores reveal significant linear relations between the number of medical problems reported by the adults and their reports of childhood maternal acceptance-rejection ($r = .77$, $p <.01$) as well as paternal acceptance-rejection ($r = .70$, $p < .01$). These linear relations are displayed graphically in Figure 10.1.

The figure shows *linear* trendlines up to three or more medical problems, at which point the trendlines tend to flatten somewhat. Table 10.1 also shows that mothers of adults with up to two serious medical problems were remembered to have been significantly more loving (accepting) than fathers. However, both mothers and fathers were reported to have been rejecting to about the same extent among adults with three or more medical problems.

Figure 10.2 displays the relation between memories of parental acceptance-rejection in childhood, and the percentage of young adults with specific medical problems. It reveals that the number of adults who report any given form of medical problem increases substantially the more rejected they remember having felt as children. The only exception to this

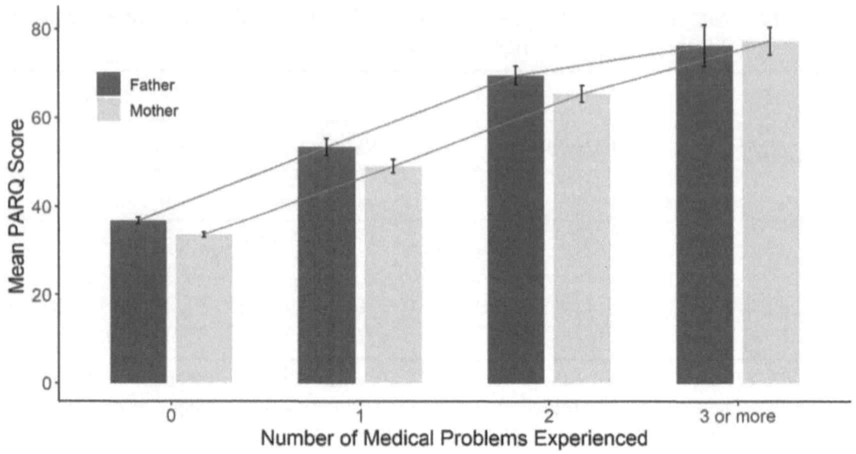

FIGURE 10.1 Relation Between Remembered Parental Acceptance-Rejection in Childhood and Number of Medical Problems Experienced.

Note: Lowest possible score on PARQ = 24 (very positive of parent); highest possible score on PARQ = 96 (very negative perception of parent); Error bars: 95% CI.

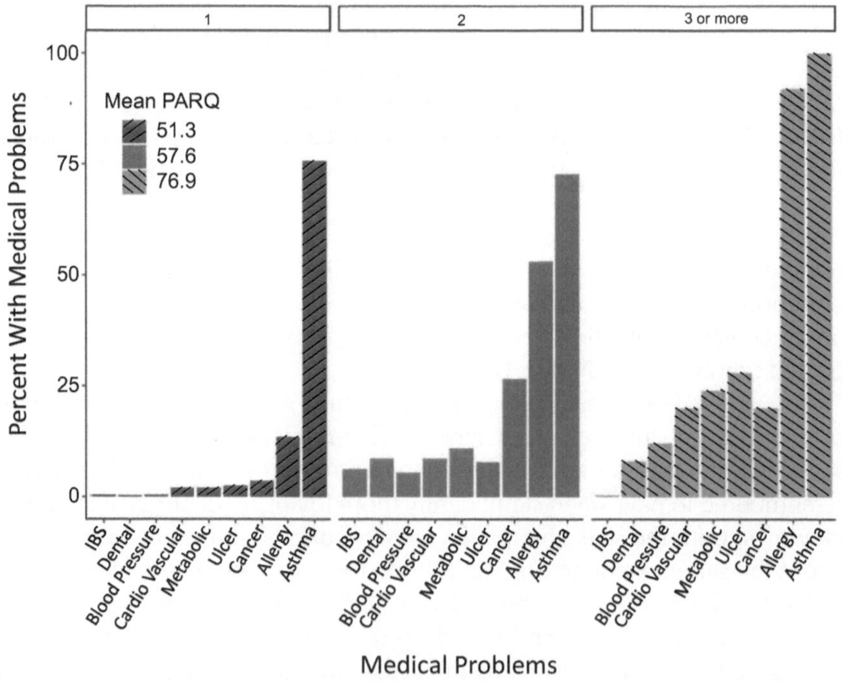

FIGURE 10.2 Relation Between Remembered Parental Acceptance-Rejection and Percentage of Individuals With Specific Medical Problems.

Note: 1 = one medical problem; 2 = two medical problems; 3 or more = 3 or more medical problems.

conclusion pertains to asthma, which tends to be equally prevalent among adults who experienced minor rejection in childhood versus adults who experienced substantial rejection. But, the prevalence of asthma is much higher among participants who experienced very serious rejection.

Further, we computed a regression analysis model using maternal and paternal rejection as predictor variables and continuous raw data on medical problems as the outcome variable. Multiple linear regression analysis, after controlling for participants' age, gender, education level, ethnicity, religion, employment, socio-economic background, and marital status, indicated that 80% of the variance in offspring's medical problems [$F(1,265) = 1133.8$, $p < 0.001$] was associated with the experience of parental rejection during childhood. Results also showed that both paternal rejection ($\beta = .49$, $p < .001$) but especially maternal rejection ($\beta = .56$, $p < .001$) predicted the number of medical problems experienced by young adults.

Discussion

This study adds to the limited literature available on relations among young adults' memories of parental (maternal and paternal) acceptance-rejection during childhood and adults' current medical problems. Importantly, young adults in this study who recall having been loved (accepted) in childhood tend to have few if any serious medical problems. However, young adults who remember having been essentially loved by both parents, but who also experienced minor elements of maternal and paternal rejection in childhood, tend to report having at least one serious medical problem. Those young adults who reported serious rejection by both their mothers and fathers in childhood tend to self-report at least two medical problems. Finally, young adults who experienced very serious parental rejection in terms of emotional coldness, hostility and aggression, indifference and neglect, or undifferentiated rejection in childhood tend to have three or more medical problems.

These group differences may be at least partially explained by the fact that when stress responses are activated frequently, intensely, and persistently during childhood—as they tend to be in the context of serious parental rejection—the biological systems involved may become permanently calibrated to activate more easily (Rohner, 2021). These systems may not turn off as readily as they should (Peña et al., 2017). Thus, over time, these repeated activations might lead to a greater risk for stress-related diseases well into adulthood (Miller et al., 2011a, 2011b; Springer et al. 2007).

It is also important to note that, on average, young adults in this study see their fathers as having been slightly less accepting than their mothers at all levels of self-reported medical problems except for those adults who reported having three or more medical problems. For the latter group, remembered maternal rejection in childhood is not significantly different from remembered paternal rejection. It is unclear at this time what medical effect these differences in parenting might have had on the physical development of young adults. If such medical effects exist, it is wholly unclear what biopsychological mechanisms might have produced them. Answers to questions such as these await future research.

Overall, results of this research show that the stressful experiences in childhood that are linked with parental rejection are associated with an increased risk of developing an array of troublesome medical conditions, including allergies, asthma, high blood pressure, cancers, cardiovascular problems, periodontal disease, irritable bowel syndrome, metabolic abnormality, and ulcers.

These results, however, must be considered in relation to the study's limitations. First, all participants were college students who had been raised in two-parent households, that is, raised by both their mothers and fathers, thus limiting generalizability to other populations. Additionally, we have no information about the effects of other potentially confounding adverse childhood experiences (e.g., parents' mental illness or substance abuse; poverty; neighborhood risk). Further, the study cannot demonstrate a causal chain from remembered parental rejection in childhood to subsequent medical problems in adulthood. Ultimately, longitudinal research that considers all these factors is needed to clearly establish causal relations between parental rejection and subsequent medical problems. Future research with broader populations should also try to determine the relative severity of medical problems that are often associated with interpersonal rejection.

Despite these limitations, this research does show that the form of childhood adversity known as parental rejection tends to reliably predict medical problems in adulthood. Interventions directed at enabling warm, loving, and accepting parenting in childhood should be a protective factor for improving individuals' physical health in adulthood.

Data availability statement

The data that support the findings of this article are available on request from Sumbleen Ali (sumbleen.ali@uconn.edu)

Funding Information

This work was funded by the Brain Imaging Research Center (BIRC) and by the Department of Human Development and Family Sciences (HDFS) at the University of Connecticut to Preston A. Britner, PhD.

References

Anda, R. F., Butchart, A., Felitti, V. J., & Brown, D. W. (2010). Building a framework for global surveillance of the public health implications of adverse childhood experiences. *American Journal of Preventive Medicine, 39*, 93–98.

Anda, R. F., Dong, M., Brown, D. W., Felitti, V. J., Giles, W. H., Perry, G. S., ... & Dube, S. R. (2009). The relationship of adverse childhood experiences to a history of premature death of family members. *BMC Public Health, 9*(1), 1–10.

Bayer, J. K., Sanson, A. V., & Hemphill, S. A. (2006). Parent influences on early childhood internalizing difficulties. *Journal of Applied Developmental Psychology, 27*(6), 542–559.

Carroll, J. E., Gruenewald, T. L., Taylor, S. E., Janicki-Deverts, D., Matthews, K. A., & Seeman, T. E. (2013). Childhood abuse, parental warmth, and adult multisystem biological risk in the coronary artery risk development in young adults' study. *Proceedings of the National Academy of Sciences, 110*(42), 17149–17153.

Centers for Disease Control and Prevention. (2013). *Adverse Childhood Experiences Study: Prevalence of individual adverse childhood experiences*. Retrieved from http://cdc.gov/ace/prevalence.htm

Chen, Y., Kubzansky, L. D., & VanderWeele, T. J. (2019). Parental warmth and flourishing in mid-life. *Social Science & Medicine, 220*, 65–72.

Davidson, G., Devaney, J., & Spratt, T. (2010). The impact of adversity in childhood on outcomes in adulthood: Research lessons and limitations. *Journal of Social Work, 10*(4), 369–390.

Dong, M., Anda, R. F., Felitti, V. J., Dube, S. R., Williamson, D. F., Thompson, T. J., ... Giles, W. H. (2004). The interrelatedness of multiple forms of childhood abuse, neglect, and household dysfunction. *Child Abuse & Neglect, 28*, 771–784.

Drossman, D. A., Leserman, J., Nachman, G., Li, Z., Gluck, H., Toomey, T. C., & Mitchell, C. M. (1990). Sexual and physical abuse in women with functional or organic gastrointestinal disorders. *Annals of Internal Medicine, 113*, 828–833.

Drury, S. S., Theall, K., Gleason, M. M., Smyke, A. T., De Vivo, I., Wong, J. Y. Y., ... Nelson, C. A. (2012). Telomere length and early severe social deprivation: linking early adversity and cellular aging. *Molecular Psychiatry, 17*(7), 719–727.

Fagundes, C. P., Glaser, R., Malarkey, W. B., & Kiecolt-Glaser, J. K. (2013). Childhood adversity and herpesvirus latency in breast cancer survivors. *Health Psychology, 32*(3), 337–344.

Felitti, V. J., Anda, R. F., Nordenberg, D., Williamson, D. F., Spitz, A. M., Edwards, V., & Marks, J. S. (1998). Relationship of childhood abuse and household dysfunction to many of the leading causes of death in adults: The Adverse Childhood Experiences (ACE) Study. *American Journal of Preventive Medicine, 14*(4), 245–258.

Felitti, V. J., Anda, R. F., Nordenberg, D., Williamson, D. F., Spitz, A. M., Edwards, V., ...Marks, J. S. (2019). Relationship of childhood abuse and household dysfunction to many of the leading causes of death in adults: The adverse childhood experiences (ACE) study. *American Journal of Preventive Medicine, 56*(6), 774–786.

Fisher, H. L., Craig, T. K., Fearon, P., Morgan, K., Dazzan, P., Lappin, J., ... Murray, R. M. (2011). Reliability and comparability of psychosis patients' retrospective reports of childhood abuse. *Schizophrenia Bulletin, 37*(3), 546–553.

Garner, A. S., Shonkoff, J. P., Siegel, B. S., Dobbins, M. I., Earls, M. F., McGuinn, L., ... Committee on Early Childhood, Adoption, and Dependent Care. (2012). Early childhood adversity, toxic stress, and the role of the pediatrician: Translating developmental science into lifelong health. *Pediatrics, 129*(1), e224–e231.

Israel, S., Moffitt, T. E., Belsky, D. W., Hancox, R. J., Poulton, R., Roberts, B., ... Caspi, A. (2014). Translating personality psychology to help personalize preventive medicine for young adult patients. *Journal of Personality and Social Psychology, 106*(3), 484.

Khaleque, A. (2013). Perceived parental warmth and children's psychological adjustment, and personality dispositions: A meta-analysis. *Journal of Child and Family Studies, 22*, 297–306. https://doi.org/10.1007/s10826-012-9579-z

Khaleque, A., & Ali, S. (2017). A systematic review of meta-analyses of research on interpersonal acceptance–rejection theory: Constructs and measures. *Journal of Family Theory & Review, 9*(4), 441–458.

Kiecolt-Glaser, J. K., Gouin, J. P., Weng, N. P., Malarkey, W. B., Beversdorf, D. Q., & Glaser, R. (2011). Childhood adversity heightens the impact of later-life caregiving stress on telomere length and inflammation. *Psychosomatic Medicine, 73*(1), 16–22.

Kiecolt-Glaser, J. K., Renna, M. E., Shrout, M. R., Madison, A. A. (2020). Stress reactivity: What pushes us higher, faster, and longer—and why it matters. *Current Directions in Psychological Science*, https://doi.org/10.1177/0963721420949521

Lansford, J. E., Rothenberg, W. A., Jensen, T. M., Lippold, M. A., Bacchini, D., Bornstein, M. H., ... Al-Hassan, S. M. (2018). Bidirectional relations between parenting and behavior problems from age 8 to 13 in nine countries. *Journal of Research on Adolescence, 28*(3), 571–590.

Lehman, B. J., Taylor, S. E., Kiefe, C. I., & Seeman, T. E. (2009). Relationship of early life stress and psychological functioning to blood pressure in the CARDIA study. *Health Psychology, 28*(3), 338.

Matthews, K. A., Chang, Y. F., Thurston, R. C., & Bromberger, J. T. (2014). Child abuse is related to inflammation in mid-life women: Role of obesity. *Brain, Behavior, and Immunity, 36*, 29–34.

Matthews, K. A., & Gallo, L. C. (2011). Psychological perspectives on pathways linking socioeconomic status and physical health. *Annual Review of Psychology, 62*, 501–530.

McEwen, B. S., & Seeman, T. (1999). Protective and damaging effects of mediators of stress: Elaborating and testing the concepts of allostasis and allostatic load. *Annals of the New York Academy of Sciences, 896*(1), 30–47.

Miller, G. E., Chen, E., & Parker, K. J. (2011a). Psychological stress in childhood and susceptibility to the chronic diseases of aging: Moving toward a model of behavioral and biological mechanisms. *Psychological Bulletin, 137*(6), 959.

Miller, G. E., Lachman, M. E., Chen, E., Gruenewald, T. L., Karlamangla, A. S., & Seeman, T. E. (2011b). Pathways to resilience: Maternal nurturance as a buffer against the effects of childhood poverty on metabolic syndrome at midlife. *Psychological Science, 22*(12), 1591–1599.

Norman, R. E., Byambaa, M., De, R., Butchart, A., Scott, J., & Vos, T. (2012). The long-term health consequences of child physical abuse, emotional abuse, and neglect: A systematic review and meta-analysis. *PLoS Med, 9*(11), e1001349.

Peña, C. J., Kronman, H. G., Walker, D. M., Cates, H. M., Bagot, R. C., Purushothaman, I., ... Goodman, E. (2017). Early life stress confers lifelong stress susceptibility in mice via ventral tegmental area OTX2. *Science, 356*(6343), 1185–1188.

Pesonen, A-K. & Räikkönen, K. (2012) The lifespan consequences of early life stress. *Physiological Behavior, 106*(5),722–727.

Pinquart, M. (2017). Associations of parenting dimensions and styles with externalizing problems of children and adolescents: An updated meta-analysis. *Developmental Psychology, 53*(5), 873.

Putnick, D. L., Bornstein, M. H., Lansford, J. E., Malone, P. S., Pastorelli, C., Skinner, A. T., Sorbring, E., Tapanya, S., Uribe Tirado, L. M., Zelli, A., Alampay, L. P., Al-Hassan, S. M., Bacchini, D., Bombi, A. S., Chang, L., Deater-Deckard, K., Di Giunta, L., Dodge, K. A., & Oburu, P. (2015). Perceived mother and father acceptance-rejection predict four unique aspects of child adjustment across nine countries. *Journal of Child Psychology and Psychiatry, 56*, 923–932.

Repetti, R. L., Robles, T. F., & Reynolds, B. (2011). Allostatic processes in the family. *Development and Psychopathology, 23*(3), 921–938.

Reuben, A., Moffitt, T.E., Caskpi, A., Belsky, D.W., Harrington, H., Schroeder, F. ...Danese, A. (2016). Lest we forget: Comparing retrospective and prospective assessments of adverse childhood experiences in the prediction of adult health. *Journal of Child Psychology and Psychiatry, 57*, 1103–1112

Rich-Edwards, J. W., Spiegelman, D., Hibert, E. N. L., Jun, H. J., Todd, T. J., Kawachi, I., & Wright, R. J. (2010). Abuse in childhood and adolescence as a predictor of type 2 diabetes in adult women. *American Journal of Preventive Medicine, 39*(6), 529–536.

Rohner, R. P. (1986). *The warmth dimension: Foundations of parental acceptance-rejection theory*. Sage Publications, Inc.

Rohner, R. P. (2004a). The parental "acceptance–rejection syndrome": Universal correlates of perceived rejection. *American Psychologist, 59*, 830–840.

Rohner, R. P. (2004b). *Parental Acceptance-Rejection Questionnaire (PARQ)* Father version. Rohner Research Publications.

Rohner, R. P. (2004c). *Parental Acceptance-Rejection Questionnaire (PARQ)* Mother version. Rohner Research Publications.

Rohner, R. P. (2005). *Parental Acceptance-Rejection Questionnaire (PARQ)*. Rohner Research Publications.

Rohner, R. P. (2021). Introduction to Interpersonal Acceptance-Rejection Theory (IPARTheory) and evidence. *Online Readings in Psychology and Culture, 6*(1), 1–65. https://doi.org/10.9707/2307-0919.1055

Rohner, R. P., & Britner, P. A. (2002). Worldwide mental health correlates of parental acceptance-rejection: Review of cross-cultural and intracultural evidence. *Cross-Cultural Research, 36*(1), 16–47.

Rohner, R. P. & Khaleque, A. (Eds.). (2005). *Handbook for the study of parental acceptance and rejection* (4th ed). Rohner Research Publications.

Rohner, R. P., & Lansford, J. E. (2017). Deep structure of the human affectional system: Introduction to interpersonal acceptance–rejection theory. *Journal of Family Theory & Review, 9*(4), 426–440.

Rothenberg, W. A. (2019). A review of intergenerational continuity in parenting: Identifying developmental pathways and moderating factors. *Marriage & Family Review, 55*(8), 701–736.

Rothenberg, W. A., Lansford, J. E., Bornstein, M. H., Chang, L., Deater-Deckard, K., Di Giunta, L., ... & Bacchini, D. (2020). Effects of parental warmth and behavioral control on adolescent externalizing and internalizing trajectories across cultures. *Journal of Research on Adolescence, 30*(4), 835–855.

Seeman, T., Epel, E., Gruenewald, T., Karlamangla, A., & McEwen, B. S. (2010). Socio-economic differentials in peripheral biology: Cumulative allostatic load. *Annals of the New York Academy of Sciences, 1186*(1), 223–239.

Solís, C. B., Kelly-Irving, M., Fantin, R., Darnaudéry, M., Torrisani, J., Lang, T., & Delpierre, C. (2015). Adverse childhood experiences and physiological wear-and-tear in midlife: Findings from the 1958 British birth cohort. *Proceedings of the National Academy of Sciences, 112*(7), E738–E746.

Spertus, I. L., Yehuda, R., Wong, C. M., Halligan, S., & Seremetis, S. V. (2003). Childhood emotional abuse and neglect as predictors of psychological and physical symptoms in women presenting to a primary care practice. *Child Abuse & Neglect, 27*(11), 1247–1258.

Suglia, S.F., Campo, R.A., Brown, A.G.M., Stoney, C., Boyce, C.A.,... Watamura, S.E. (2020). Social determinants of cardiovascular health: Early life adversity as a contributor to disparities in cardiovascular diseases. *The Journal of Pediatrics, 219*, 267–273.

Springer, K. W. (2009). Childhood physical abuse and midlife physical health: Testing a multi-pathway life course model. *Social Science & Medicine, 69*(1), 138–146.

Springer, K. W., Sheridan, J., Kuo, D., & Carnes, M. (2007). Long-term physical and mental health consequences of childhood physical abuse: Results from a large population-based sample of men and women. *Child Abuse & Neglect, 31*(5), 517–530.

van IJzendoorn, M. H. & Juffer, F. (2006). The Emanuel Miller memorial lecture 2006: Adoption as intervention. Meta-analytic evidence for massive catch-up and plasticity in physical, socio-emotional, and cognitive development. *Journal of Child Psychology and Psychiatry, 47*, 1228–1245

Varese, F., Smeets, F., Drukker, M., Lieverse, R., Lataster, T., Viechtbauer, W., ... Bentall, R. P. (2012). Childhood adversities increase the risk of psychosis: A meta-analysis of patient-control, prospective-and cross-sectional cohort studies. *Schizophrenia Bulletin, 38*(4), 661–671.

Wegman, H. L., & Stetler, C. (2009). A meta-analytic review of the effects of childhood abuse on medical outcomes in adulthood. *Psychosomatic Medicine, 71*(8), 805–812.

Witek-Janusek, L., Tell, D., Albuquerque, K., & Mathews, H. L. (2013). Childhood adversity increases vulnerability for behavioral symptoms and immune dysregulation in women with breast cancer. *Brain, Behavior, and Immunity, 30*, S149–S162.

PART III

Clinical Implications and Practical Applications of IPARTheory

11

CLINICAL APPLICATIONS OF INTERPERSONAL ACCEPTANCE-REJECTION THEORY (IPARTHEORY)

M. Selenga Gürmen

Interpersonal acceptance-rejection theory (IPARTheory) is an evidence-based theory that examines one's need for love, care, and acceptance from significant others. According to the theory, feeling rejected is hurtful and linked worldwide to significant mental, social, emotional, and even physical health problems. Although IPARTheory first started in the 1960s by examining the causes, consequences, and other correlates of *parental* rejection in childhood, the theory expanded its scope to include all significant relationships throughout the lifespan (Rohner, 2014).

The theory has been tested for more than six decades on every continent except Antarctica. Thousands of children, adolescents, and adults have repeatedly confirmed IPARTheory's main tenets in research (see Ali et al., 2019, 2023; Khaleque & Ali, 2017; Rohner & Ali, 2025; Chapter 1, this book). Despite its extensive research and clear links with psychological maladjustment and mental health problems, the clinical implications and adaptations of IPARTheory have only recently begun in the last 15 years. Therefore, this chapter aims to examine the clinical correlates as well as clinical applications of the main tenets of the theory. It is also important to note that although IPARTheory formulates acceptance-rejection as a continuum, this chapter features mostly interpersonal rejection and its impact on individuals' emotions and behaviors.

The chapter focuses heavily on clinical symptoms and problematic relational patterns such as rejection sensitivity and fear of intimacy as well as IPARTheory's relational diagnosis, the *Acceptance-Rejection Syndrome*. The chapter also describes two existing clinical adaptations of the theory.

DOI: 10.4324/9781003441243-14

One is a clinical Manual created by Rising and Rohner (2021) and the other is a clinical protocol for relational therapy by Rigazio-DiGilio and Rohner (2006, 2015) and first implemented by Donoghue (2010). Further, the chapter discusses therapy models and techniques that sometimes incorporate IPARTheory's evidence-based orientation and tenets.

Fundamentals of IPARTheory

Rohner (2004, 2023) defined rejection as the absence or significant withdrawal of warmth, affection, care, comfort, concern, nurturance, support, or simply love from another person. Both children's and adults' reactions to interpersonal rejection show resemblances across cultures (Khaleque & Rohner, 2004; Rohner & Khaleque, 2010). These reactions, discussed later, form personality dispositions that describe different sets of beliefs, affective responses, and behavioral patterns of self and other significant relationships. If not treated, the personality dispositions are expected to be maintained throughout the lifespan (Rohner & Ali, 2025; Chapter 1 this book).

Although IPARTheory's concepts and themes are studied cross-culturally and show similarities across cultures, it is important to note that sociocultural values and meanings play an important role. The theory's sociocultural subtheory takes into account the crucial role of society and the cultural context. One should consider the role of social institutions, cultural values, traditions, and rituals when evaluating interpersonal acceptance-rejection and their psychological consequences for well-being and relational patterns. This is especially important for therapists who work with rejection in clinical practice.

IPARTheory's Conceptualization of Clinical Symptoms and Diagnoses

According to IPARTheory's personality subtheory, the perception of rejection by significant others such as parents in childhood and peers and intimate partners in adulthood may lead to extreme levels of psychological distress. These, in turn, are likely to lead to psychological maladjustment problems (Rohner & Ali, 2025; Chapter 1, this book). The theory postulates that rejecting parents or partners—either in the form of being emotionally cold, indifferent, or hostile—may elicit destructive insecurities and negative personality dispositions (Khaleque & Rohner, 2012; Rohner & Khaleque 2010). Those dispositions include the following: anxiety; insecurity; *hostility; aggression, passive aggression, or problems with the management of anger; negative self-esteem; negative self-adequacy; emotional instability; emotional unresponsiveness; dependence or defensive independence depending on the form, frequency, and severity of the rejection; and negative worldview; and cognitive distortions.*

Additionally, cross-cultural studies consistently show that parental rejection experienced in childhood predicts *rejection sensitivity* (Rohner, 2021) in adult relationships (Rohner & Ali, 2025; Chapter 8, this book. See also Ibrahim et al., 2015; Khaleque et al., 2019; Whittington & Mullinax, 2024). Rejection sensitivity is often associated with aggressiveness or victimization later in intimate partner relationships. Those responses, in turn, may result in higher levels of partner rejection (Gao et al., 2021). Studies show that higher levels of rejection sensitivity also tend to be associated with higher levels of jealousy and aggressive behaviors in romantic relationships (Murphy & Russell, 2018; Choi & Lim, 2023).

Another important relational concept in IPARTheory is *fear of intimacy*. Individuals with a fear of intimacy have typically been hurt and rejected in past relationships and they are fearful of further rejection in the current relationship. Whereas individuals with rejection sensitivity may act clingy, jealous, and aggressive, individuals with a fear of intimacy may distance themselves from their intimate partners and withdraw from commitment (Aracı-İyiaydın et al., 2022; İyiaydın & Sümer 2021). Several IPARTheory studies have found that offspring's memories of maternal and paternal rejection during childhood predicted fear of intimacy in adult relationships across cultures (Aracı-İyiaydın et al., 2022; Rohner, 2016. See also Khaleque, 2025; Chapter 5, this book).

In addition to these personality dispositions, interpersonal rejection tends to be associated with other physical and mental-health issues such as internalizing problems including depression and anxiety. Depression and anxiety are significantly associated with interpersonal rejection both in children and adults across cultures (Gao et al., 2017; Rohner 2021). In addition to internalizing problems, externalizing behaviors (e.g., angry outbursts, and destructive behaviors) often results from parental rejection in childhood and can extend into adulthood. Putnick et al. (2014) showed in their longitudinal study that externalizing behaviors and decreased-prosocial behavior and social competence are common among children who experienced rejection from their parents (see also Lansford, 2025; Chapter 7, this book).

Additionally, studies show that drug and alcohol abuse and physical health problems tend to be universally associated with experiences of interpersonal rejection (Rohner & Britner, 2002). Moreover, parental rejection and early childhood trauma are often associated with significant physical health problems in adulthood such as cardiovascular diseases, cancer, asthma, and gastrointestinal problems (see Ali, Rohner, & Britner, 2025; Chapter 10, this book). Based on robust findings regarding the psychological effects of interpersonal acceptance-rejection, Rohner (2004) conceptualized a new term to diagnose the relational impact of interpersonal rejection: "*the acceptance-rejection syndrome*." The syndrome encapsulates all the negative personality dispositions discussed so far in this chapter.

To date, there are 39 measures available in more than 77 languages and dialects internationally that were created to study the effects, causes, and other correlates of IPARTheory's main variables. The measures not only look at parental and partner acceptance but also explore acceptance-rejection from best friends, siblings, teachers, in-laws, grandparents, coaches, supervisors, and others. There is also a questionnaire to measure acceptance-rejection within organizational contexts. Almost all of these questionnaires have practical applications, and many are useful in clinical settings. Initially the questionnaires were often utilized in family courts, specifically in parental alienation cases. Bernet et al. (2020), for example, used the child version of the Parental Acceptance-Rejection Questionnaire to help differentiate unjustified parental alienation from justified parental "estrangement". The measure was unusually successful. As Bernet et al. (2020) wrote, the "PARQ-Gap criterion used in this study distinguished severely alienated children from neglected and other children with 99% accuracy" (p.1232; see also Bernet & Alvarez, 2025; Chapter 14 this book).

Adapting IPARTheory into Treatment Models and Techniques

To date, there are two important applications of IPARTheory in clinical practice. One is a clinical Manual created by Rising and Rohner (2023) on *Recovery from Rejection: A Manual of Client Handouts for Clinical Practice*. The other is a treatment protocol for relational therapy created by Rigazio-DiGilio and Rohner (2006 & 2015) and first implemented in relational therapy by Donoghue (2010). Each of these applications is described below.

Recovery from Rejection: A Manual of Client Handouts Clinical Practice

The first edition of the Manual was created by Rising and Rohner in 2021, but it is currently in its third edition (Rising and Rohner, 2021). The goal of the Manual is to elucidate the *Acceptance-Rejection Syndrome* but most especially to offer treatment objectives and guidelines to professionals who work with clients experiencing rejection in their significant relationships. The Manual, which is available gratis online, was designed in such a way that professionals can use individual sections as targeted client Handouts. *Recovery from Rejection* is now available in English, German, Persian, Turkish, and Urdu. It is pending in Bengali, Bulgarian, Czech, and Dutch. Other languages are also under consideration by potential translators.

The Manual starts with a detailed description of the *Acceptance-Rejection Syndrome* with its etiology (types of interpersonal rejection) and behavioral consequences symptoms (personality dispositions). It offers guidelines to assess rejection and its impact on clients. Then treatment goals and methods are listed. Some of the therapeutic goals include building trust and strong alliances, encouraging emotional expression and processing of emotion; providing a new set of skills to both identify healthy relationships and to change maladaptive behavioral and thought processes. Building a strong support system with healthy relationships and utilizing spiritual beliefs and practices is emphasized as a tool to create acceptance for oneself and interpersonal relationships. The Manual also provides valuable resources for clients to read. Nine personality dispositions are described and explained in the Manual, and a case example is provided for each disposition. Each Handout also lists a set of treatment recommendations for clients.

IPARTheory in Relational Therapy

A major clinical application of IPARTheory was conducted by Donoghue (2010) with 12 couples who sought relational counseling. Based on the therapy model proposed by Rigazio-DiGilio and Rohner (2006), the main idea was that self and relational awareness of past and current rejection will enhance the couple's intimate relationship and increase their empathy and love for each other. Two sets of IPARTheory questionnaires were used as interactive assessment tools at different time points during the treatment. These measures were the (1) Adult version of the Parental Acceptance-Rejection Questionnaire (PARQ), Mother & Father forms, and (2) the Intimate Adult Relationship Questionnaire (IARQ). The primary research objectives were to (1) use the questionnaires as a way to generate therapeutic dialogue, (2) create graphs of questionnaire-related findings to reflect clients' own and their partners' experiences of rejection, (3) use the interactive assessments as a way to guide the therapy process and treatment planning, and (4) examine changes over time in clients' perceptions of rejection and use of language about themselves and their partner.

The treatment protocol was designed in seven steps. The first step provided couples with the Mother and Father versions of the Adult PARQ. These were completed by each client separately at home after the first session. After the couple completed the questionnaires, the next two sessions included therapeutic discussions of the results of their responses while using Ivey and Ivey's (2007) Microcounseling Skills (explained further below). Additionally, two joint sessions also employed graphic displays of each client's perceptions of maternal and paternal acceptance-rejection in childhood, as well as from each other using the IARQ. In those sessions, the therapist co-created a treatment plan with important points from the assessment sessions. After the treatment sessions, steps 1–3 were repeated to assess clients' new perceptions of parental and partner acceptance-rejection. In the last session, the couple and the therapist evaluated the therapy process and progress achieved in therapy.

The findings showed that self-reports of experienced rejection along with the in-depth discussions of these in sessions helped couples increase their empathy toward one another. Clients' understanding of their own and their partner's past hurts from childhood changed clients' feelings and behaviors in their current romantic relationships. Through the systematic protocol, the repeated measures and discussions allowed couples to track progress and positive changes throughout the therapy process. Employing different methods—questionnaires, graphs, and in-depth discussions—enhanced and enriched the couples' ability to understand each other's individual perceptions and experiences. According to Rigazio-DiGilio and Rohner (2015) the findings "confirm the efficacy and practicality of using IPARTheory assessments and measures in relational therapy, and they form the foundation from which a more exhaustive evidence-based model can be constructed" (p. 512).

In addition to the clinical Manual and the Rigazio-DiGilio and Rohner protocol for relational therapy, IPARTheory concepts, and themes can be used in other ways in clinical treatment. Almost all therapeutic approaches can incorporate the main tenets of the theory because its main focus deals with individuals' own personal perceptions and experiences of rejection, and the way those perceptions and experiences translate into relational patterns. Some of those modalities and techniques as well as the concept of therapeutic alliance are discussed in the following section.

Therapy Models That Can Incorporate IPARTheory Concepts

Psychodynamic Therapy

Psychodynamic therapy is considered one of the first forces of psychotherapy. Based on Freud's psychoanalytic theories, psychodynamic therapy focuses on unconscious processes and unresolved inner conflicts (Mitchell & Black, 2016). Psychodynamic approaches presume that difficult early childhood experiences are responsible for psychological maladjustment and mental disorders. The therapy's goal is to help clients process their past experiences and increase their self-awareness around inner conflicts (Messer & Warren, 1995). IPARTheory's premises regarding childhood rejection and its impact on adult relationships are parallel to how psychodynamic therapy formulates mental and emotional difficulties.

Undifferentiated rejection, especially, appears to fit well with psychodynamic emphases on unconscious processes. According to Rohner (2021), undifferentiated rejection "refers to individuals' beliefs that the significant others do not really care about them or love them, even though there might not be clear behavioral indicators that the parent or significant other is neglecting, unaffectionate, or aggressive toward them". (p. 5). Clinicians who employ a psychodynamic perspective might say that the person who experienced rejection could have repressed their memories of rejection in order to cope with difficult maladaptive experiences from early childhood.

Cognitive-Behavioral Therapy

As discussed above, IPARTheory posits that individuals develop mental representations of themselves, others, and the world in line with their experiences of acceptance-rejection. The cognitive-behavioral therapy (CBT) model focuses on maladaptive thoughts (i.e., mental representations) and behavioral patterns to understand mental health problems. It is one of the most studied therapy models that is effective for treating anger, anxiety, and avoidance (Scaini et al., 2016).

Because CBT asserts that mental health problems stem from maladaptive thoughts and false beliefs, interventions usually focus on changing those negative thoughts and false beliefs in therapy (Beck, 2011). For instance, negative self-esteem—one of the negative personality dispositions associated with interpersonal rejection—includes individuals' negative views of themselves as "not being good enough". Utilizing CBT, negative self-esteem can be treated via recognizing and challenging those negative mental representations and false beliefs about themselves. In CBT, becoming aware of one's thoughts and beliefs is pivotal. IPARTheory's assessment tools can be very helpful for clients to identify their negative mental representations and behavioral patterns.

Acceptance and Commitment Therapy (ACT)

ACT is a derivative from CBT. It focuses on thoughts and values, and helps clients let go of the suffering that stems from false beliefs and negative values they hold about themselves (Hayes et al., 2012). According to ACT, individuals are encouraged to discover and clarify their values that are most important to them in life. Individuals can use IPARTheory principles to investigate how their experiences of acceptance and rejection affect their values and what they value in their relationships. This can lead to a more in-depth awareness of the roles of acceptance and rejection in their lives, as well as their value-based aspirations.

Rising and Rohner's (2023) *Recovery from Rejection* Manual recommends CBT and ACT techniques. Client Handouts in the Manual specifically recommend that clients identify and challenge current false beliefs and thoughts. Forgiveness is also recommended in some of the Handouts. It is important to note that forgiveness was not used to refer to reconciliation with the rejecting individual. Rather, it aimed to remind clients that they carry strong negative emotions and form false beliefs about people and themselves. Forgiveness offers individuals an opportunity to let go of past hurt and open themselves to new healthy relationships.

Emotion-Focused Therapy

Emotion-Focused Therapy (EFT) is a psychotherapy model based on attachment theory (Ainsworth, 1989; Bowlby, 1982). Its main goal is to help clients explore and experience negative and vulnerable emotions, especially feelings of rejection. In EFT, feelings of rejection can be considered an attachment injury. That is, it is a "relational trauma that occurs when one partner feels betrayed or abandoned by the other, particularly during a moment of need, such as when experiencing a loss or a major life change" (Lafontaine et al., 2022, p.1). Behavioral and emotional descriptions of rejection sensitivity seem similar to anxious attachment; fear of intimacy can be considered as an avoidant attachment style (Bowlby, 1982).

Emotion-focused therapy is a therapy modality that focuses on emotional experiences and expressions, especially in couples therapy. The aim is to help partners process raw emotions and transform them into acceptance and empathy (S. M. Johnso, 2007; D. R. Johnson, 2012) The EFT therapist aims to "create the attuned synchrony of emotional responsiveness that builds and maintains secure emotional bonds" (Johnson & Wittenborn, 2012, p. 2). Therapists evaluate the attachment styles and needs of the partners and help them heal their past and present attachment injuries. EFT is one of the best empirically supported therapy models. Research consistently shows that marital satisfaction increases and emotional hurts due to rejection decreases, and that those changes tend to be maintained over time (Beasley & Ager, 2019; Marren et al., 2022; Spengler et al., 2022).

The most important step in EFT treatment is softening the partner who has anxious attachment—called the *pursuer*. Because of prior attachment injury or rejection, pursuers usually react with anxiety or hostility and constantly worry that their partner will reject or abandon them at any time (rejection sensitivity). On the other hand, the partner with avoidant-attachment usually avoids intimacy bids and withdraws from emotional connection. This person is called the *withdrawer*. The behavioral expressions of the withdrawer resemble IPARTheory's description of the fear of intimacy. The therapist aims to soften the pursuer while simultaneously trying to re-engage the withdrawer.

Family Therapy

In addition to how past relationships might indirectly impact existing relationships through rejection sensitivity and fear of intimacy, existing relationships with significant others appear to have an impact on other relationships. For instance, perceptions of spousal acceptance correlate with adolescents' perceptions of their parents' acceptance-rejection (Gürmen & Rohner, 2014). So, acceptance-rejection in one dyad (husband & wife) often has an effect on another dyad (parent–child). This concept strongly supports systemic therapy's central idea of interdependence of relationships.

The systemic approach, which is the core idea of marriage and family therapy (MFT), looks at relationships as entities that are interdependent and interrelated (Minuchin, 1974). For example, one relational entity in a family such as the spousal/parental dyad affects and is affected by another relational entity such as parent–child or sibling dyad. This approach is applicable to the central tenets of IPARTheory. Sabah et al. (2022), for example showed that parental rejection is linked with sibling rejection and bullying behaviors in sibling dyads.

Systemic therapy is also interested in the intergenerational transmissions of relational, emotional, and behavioral patterns. In fact, some systemic therapy models such as Bowen's model (Bowen, 1978) utilized *genograms* to map relational patterns across generations. Genograms are symbolic maps of intergenerational relationships (McGoldrick et al., 2020). Given that parental acceptance-rejection has an impact on both psychological adjustment as well as on rejection sensitivity and fear of intimacy representations of individuals, and that parental acceptance-rejection has an impact on intimate partner acceptance-rejection in adult relationships, we can speculate that the intergenerational transmission of acceptance-rejection is likely to be observed in genograms. One study showed an indirect transmission of perceived parental rejection across three generations of grandmothers, mothers, and adult-granddaughters (Turkdogan, 2021).

Children are limited by their still developing capacity for insight and self-reflection. Thus, a rejecting caregiver can serve as the primary vehicle for modification of the child's negative mental representations. Family therapy can facilitate safe and healthy modeling for interpersonal acceptance for both parent–child relationships and spousal/partner relationships.

Family therapists can help parents learn healthy communication skills that foster acceptance. Further, wounds from past rejection can be discussed and repaired in conjoint family sessions. Such, present-focused interventions designed to foster healthy caregiver-parent relationships is likely to help with children's problematic behaviors and psychological maladjustment. The interventions may involve helping to instill appropriate emotion regulation skills in the child. This approach includes having caregivers examine their own mental representations of self as a parent and a partner as well as examining memories of any of their own adverse childhood experiences. In fact, one study showed that interventions such as parenting programs that focus on parental rejection may serve as a protective factor for helping to eliminate adverse effects for future generations (Rothenberg et al., 2023).

In family therapy, the caregiver may learn alternative ways of responding to the child with love, warmth, nonthreatening, and noncoercive behavior. While designing interventions and therapeutic conjoint sessions, clinicians should consider the child's age and current level of cognitive ability. Having spousal/partner sessions to discuss issues related to spousal rejection is required in order to protect healthy boundaries between parents and children.

Parent–Child Interaction Therapy

Parent–child interaction therapy (PCIT) is a specific treatment model for young children and their parents (Eyberg & Calzada, 1998). It aims to foster secure, warm, and healthy relationships between young children and their parents. PCIT is shown to be effective for children between the ages of 2 and 6 with behavioral problems such as tantrums and negative attention-seeking behaviors (Herschell et al., 2002). PCIT includes live coaching sessions for parents to foster discipline, warmth, and acceptance while they interact and play with their children. IPARTheory principles may be used to assist parents in understanding how their communication style is likely to affect their child's perception of acceptance or rejection.

Postmodern Approaches: Gestalt and Narrative Therapy

In both individual and relational therapy, awareness and meaning-making play pivotal roles in identifying the problem and facilitating change. In the *Gestalt* approach, it is suggested that awareness helps people to organize themselves, their relationships, and their lives in a meaningful manner so that individuals can understand themselves and the world better (Yontef, 1982, 1983, 1993). IPARTheory helps people understand their own subjective experiences of rejection and provides opportunities for meaning-making around their past and current experiences.

Past experiences are prone to affect and be affected by an individual's current meaning–making processes (White & Epston, 1990). That notion is one of the most important features of how therapy can change one's perceptions of past and present self and relationships. In the interpersonal acceptance-rejection realm, as individuals mentally process past hurt and rejection through their present relationships, it helps them to (1) change their perceptions of what they experienced in the past, (2) free themselves from the experience of rejection sensitivity and fear of intimacy.

Narrative therapy focuses mainly on meaning-making processes and the way in which individuals live their experiences as a unique story (White & Epston, 1990). For people who experienced parental rejection in childhood, the story usually involves strong emotions and beliefs about not being loved and cared for, not deserving love, and believing that people cannot be trusted. Experiences of parental rejection are traumatic stories that continue from previous relationships to present and future relationships.

In narrative therapy, the therapist respectfully listens to the clients' stories and encourages them to look for alternative stories through unique loving experiences that they may have experienced (White, 1995). Emotions are processed throughout story descriptions and explorations of alternative stories. The process of re-authoring their story helps clients feel empowered and changes their belief systems around traumatic rejection.

Treatment Techniques and Tools That Can Incorporate IPARTheory Concepts

Mapping Out: Use of Genograms

Another possible way of becoming aware and challenging existing rejection beliefs and behaviors can be achieved through the use of genograms. A genogram is a specific technique used to map out intergenerational transmissions of behaviors, beliefs, symptoms, diseases, etc. (McGoldrick et al., 2020). It is a symbolic family tree that focuses on emotions, behavioral patterns, and relationships. Experiences of acceptance-rejection as well as parenting behaviors (rejection styles) can be easily tracked and described by genograms.

Genograms can be used both in individual and relational therapy. Similar to the use of IPARTheory questionnaires, genograms are also considered as interactive assessment and treatment tools. When individuals or their partners become aware of their behavior patterns and rejection experiences, they have the opportunity to restructure the meanings and schemas associated with these, as well as their interactional patterns with their significant others (Bowen, 1978; McGoldrick & Carter, 2001).

In relational therapy, just as with the use of IPARTheory questionnaires, individuals witness an extensive and deep level of discussion of their partner's family of origin themes, traumas, rejections, and emotional wounds. Exposure to these issues help clients increase empathy and understanding as well as acceptance of each other's wounds rather than trying to fight against or change them. At this point, the couple starts to appreciate each other's efforts to change their past behavioral patterns of rejection sensitivity or fear of intimacy.

Action: Psychodrama, Empty Chair Technique, and Enactments

Therapeutic change may be achieved through experiential practices in that clients may create different fictional or real experiences. For instance, *psychodrama* is a psychotherapy approach and technique that allows clients to explore and experience emotions in a more dramatic way (Moreno, 1993). Clients—usually with an audience of other clients or experts—perform their emotions and relationships on a stage. This is a form of individual therapy conducted in a group setting. The dramatic performance of emotions and relationships help the individual to have a different perspective on their experiences, thoughts, beliefs, and emotions (Cruz et al., 2018).

IPARTheory's concepts of interpersonal rejection (past or current) can be explored and processed by psychodrama techniques. For instance, role-playing is common in psychodrama, and role reversal can be a powerful way for participants to learn empathy and understanding of how rejection and acceptance affect others. Participants can play the role of both the person experiencing rejection and the person providing it. In this way, the individual gains insight into the emotions and views associated with being rejected and rejecting others. Further, creating scenes or scenarios that represent actual life events is common in psychodrama. These scenes can be especially created to address concerns of rejection and acceptance, allowing participants to explore these relationships in a safe and controlled therapeutic setting.

The *empty chair technique* is another effective psychotherapy technique that fosters clients' processing and experiencing their interpersonal or inner conflicts (Perls et al., 1951). It is derived from Gestalt therapy and resembles role-playing. But in this case, the other person is an empty chair. By talking to an imaginary person, situation, or a problem, clients may have a chance to converse and process more deeply their own thoughts and feelings (Mann, 2010). In the case of interpersonal rejection, clients can express their feelings, thoughts, and concerns related to the rejection they have experienced in the relationship by engaging in a conversation with the imaginary other. Switching roles can help the client gain insights into the other person's perspective and feelings, thereby fostering greater empathy and understanding.

Another experiential technique is called *enactments*. This technique is usually used in couple and family therapy sessions. The main goal is to help clients experience new and healthy behavioral patterns, and play out them in the session with the guidance of a therapist (Gardner & Butler, 2009). The EFT approach in couples therapy utilizes enactments in order for clients to "bridge the inner world of experience and the outer world of interaction and help give expression to newly processed inner emotional experience" (Tilley & Palmer, 2012). Clients' partners or family members can process the feelings of rejection as well play out newly gained healthy communication skills through enactments. This process may help the couple or the family to foster greater interpersonal acceptance and warmth.

Role-modeling an Accepting Relationship: Therapeutic Alliance

Another important use of IPARTheory's concepts in clinical practice becomes possible through the *therapeutic relationship*. In his conceptualization of treatment and recovery from rejection in IPARTheory, Rohner (1986, 2021) was concerned about the therapist serving as a trusted individual who enables a healthy relationship between client and therapist. This can enable clients to understand and analyze unpleasant aspects of past and/or present experiences. Moreover, clients become aware of their mental representations (cognitive frameworks for interpreting and organizing experiences). After achieving this insight, clients are likely to begin thinking and feeling in new, more adaptive ways.

Therapists for a relatively short period of time may become a significant other who can show warmth, care, and support toward the client. According to Carl Rogers (1957) therapist's warmth, acceptance, and unconditional positive regard has healing effects on the client. A meta-analysis of several studies showed that therapist's support, empathy, and care, "sets the stage for other mutual interventions and, at least in some cases, may prove sufficient to effect positive change." (Farber et al., 2018- p. 419). IPARTheory's emphasis on love and acceptance can be applied to therapeutic relationships and become a vehicle for therapeutic change in and of itself.

A strong and trusted relationship with a therapist can provide a baseline potential for clients to challenge their negative worldview and negative self-esteem. Further, their reactive behaviors such as anger and hostility, emotional unresponsiveness, and dependence or defensive independence can find a loving re-bound and that creates a new overwriting experience. The therapist as the active agent and a solid support can help clients reestablish a safe and healthy relationship to experience interpersonal acceptance.

Conclusion

IPARTheory is a well-established and extensively studied theory of interpersonal acceptance-rejection. Findings consistently show that there are detrimental effects of interpersonal rejection on children's and adults' well-being and psychological adjustment. Hurtful past relationships may also impact current relationships through rejection sensitivity and fear of intimacy. The clinical correlates of IPARTheory call both individual and relational therapists for action. To date, there are two important clinical adaptations of IPARTheory: The clinical Manual and the protocol in relational therapy. Those applications are extensive and have detailed guidelines and protocols. More applications and research studies to examine their effectiveness are needed for further growth. Also, other treatment suggestions that incorporate IPARTheory's main tenets and concepts are included in this chapter to spark new approaches for clinical practice and research.

References

Ainsworth, M. D. S. (1989). Attachment beyond infancy. *American Psychologist, 44,* 709–716. http://doi.org/10.1037/0003-066X.44.4.709

Ali, S., Khatun, N., Khaleque, A., & Rohner, R. P. (2019). They love me not: A meta-analysis of relations between parental undifferentiated rejection and offspring's psychological maladjustment. *Journal of Cross-Cultural Psychology, 50*(2), 185–199. https://doi.org/10.1177/0022022118815599

Ali, S., Khatun, M. N., Khaleque, A., & Rohner, R. P. (2023). Perceived parental undifferentiated rejection and children's personality dispositions: A meta-analysis of multicultural studies. *The Journal of Genetic Psychology, 184*(1), 9–22.

Ali, S., Rohner, R. P., Britner, P. A. & Hoeft, F. (2025). Memories of parental rejection in childhood predict medical problems in adulthood. *Global perspectives on parental acceptance and rejection: Lessons learned from IPARTheory* (pp. 191–206). Routledge.

Aracı-İyiaydın, A., Toplu-Demirtaş, E., Akçabozan-Kayabol, N. B., & Fincham, F. D. (2022). I ruminate therefore I violate: The tainted love of anxiously attached and jealous partners. *Journal of Interpersonal Violence, 37*(9–10), NP7129–NP7155.

Beasley, C. C., & Ager, R. (2019). Emotionally focused couples therapy: A systematic review of its effectiveness over the past 19 years. *Journal of Evidence-Based Social Work, 16*(2), 144–159. https://doi.org/10.1080/23761407.2018.1563013

Beck, J.S. (2011). *Cognitive behavior therapy: Basics and beyond* (2nd ed.), New York: The Guilford Press.

Bernet, W., & Alvarez, M. (2025). From normal to lethal: the continuum of parental denigration and parental alienation. *Global perspectives on parental acceptance and rejection: Lessons learned from IPARTheory* (pp. 267–278). Routledge.

Bernet, W., Gregory, N., Rohner, R. P., & Reay, K. M. (2020). Measuring the difference between parental alienation and parental estrangement: The PARQ-gap. *Journal of Forensic Sciences, 65*(4), 1225–1234.

Bowen, M. (1978). *Family Therapy in Clinical Practice,* New York: Jason Aronson.

Bowlby, J. (1982). Attachment and loss: Retrospect and Prospect. *American Journal of Orthopsychiatry, 52*(4), 664–678. https://doi.org/10.1111/j.1939-0025.1982.tb01456.x
Choi, J., & Lim, J. (2023). Does your childhood attachment make you bully your lover? The role of rejection sensitivity and romantic relationship satisfaction. *Emerging Adulthood, 11*(6), 1423–1432. https://doi.org/10.1177/21676968231193185
Cruz, A., Sales, C., Alves, P., & Moita, G. (2018). The core techniques of Morenian psychodrama: A systematic review of literature. *Frontiers in Psychology*, 1-11 .
Donoghue, J. M. (2010). Clinical application of parental acceptance- rejection theory (PARTheory) measures in relational therapy, assessment, and treatment. Unpublished doctoral dissertation, University of Connecticut, Storrs, CT
Eyberg, S. M., & Calzada, E.J. (1998). *Parent-Child Interaction Therapy: Treatment manual* Unpublished manuscript, University of Florida.
Farber, B. A., Suzuki, J. Y., & Lynch, D. A. (2018). Positive regard and psychotherapy outcome: A meta-analytic review. *Psychotherapy, 55*(4), 419.
Gao, S., Assink, M., Liu, T., Chan, K. L., & Ip, P. (2021). Associations between rejection sensitivity, aggression, and victimization: A meta-analytic review. *Trauma, Violence, & Abuse, 22*(1), 125–135. http://doi.org/10.1177/1524838019833005
Gao, S., Assink, M., Cipriani, A., & Lin, K. (2017). Associations between rejection sensitivity and mental health outcomes: A meta-analytic review. *Clinical Psychology Review, 57*, 59–74. http://doi.org/10.1016/j.cpr.2017.08.007
Gardner, B. C., & Butler, M. H. (2009). Enacting relationships in MFT: The empirical, theoretical, and clinical case for incorporating enactments as common factors in the best practice model. *Journal of Couple & Relationship Therapy, 8*(4), 306–324.
Gürmen, M. S., & Rohner, R. P. (2014). Effects of marital distress on Turkish adolescents' psychological adjustment. *Journal of Child and Family Studies, 23*(7), 1155–1162. https://doi.org/10.1007/s10826-013-9773-7
Hayes, S. C., Strosahl, K. D., & Wilson, K. G. (2012). *Acceptance and Commitment Therapy, second edition: The process and practice of Mindful Change*. Guilford Publications.
Herschell, A. D., Calzada, E. J., Eyberg, S. M., & McNeil, C. B. (2002). Parent-child interaction therapy: New directions in research. *Cognitive and Behavioral Practice, 9*(1), 9–16.
Ibrahim, D. M., Rohner, R. P., Smith, R. L., & Flannery, K. M. (2015). Adults' remembrances of parental acceptance–rejection in childhood predict current rejection sensitivity in adulthood. *Family and Consumer Sciences Research Journal, 44*(1), 51–62. http://doi.org/10.1111/fcsr.12119
Ivey, A. E., & Ivey, M. B. (2007). *Intentional interviewing and counseling: Facilitating client development in a multicultural society* (6th ed.). Belmont, CA: Thomson Learning.
İyiaydın, A. A., & Sümer, Z. H. (2021). The mediational role of intimate partner acceptance and psychological adjustment in the relationship between intimate partner control and marital adjustment. *Current Psychology, 42*(2), 1598–1608. https://doi.org/10.1007/s12144-021-01468-2
Johnson, S. M. (2007). The contribution of emotionally focused couples therapy. *Journal of Contemporary Psychotherapy, 37*(1), 51. https://doi.org/10.1007/s10879-006-9034-9
Johnson, D. R. (2012). Transportation into a story increases empathy, prosocial behavior, and perceptual bias toward fearful expressions. *Personality and Individual Differences, 52*(2), 150–155.

Johnson, S. M., & Wittenborn, A. K. (2012). New research findings on emotionally focused therapy: Introduction to special section. *Journal of Marital and Family Therapy, 38*(1), 18–22. https://doi.org/10.1111/j.1752-0606.2012.00292.x

Khaleque, A. (2025). Influence of parental acceptance-rejection on adult intimate relationships. In R. P. Rohner & S. Ali, (Eds.), *Global perspectives on parental acceptance and rejection: Lessons learned from IPARTheory* (pp. 107–119). Routledge.

Khaleque, A., & Ali, S. (2017). A systematic review of meta-analyses of research on interpersonal acceptance- rejection theory: Constructs and measures. *Journal of Family Theory & Review, 9*(4), 441–458. https://doi.org/10.1111/jftr.12228

Khaleque, A., & Rohner, R. P. (2004). Perceived parental acceptance–rejection and psychological adjustment: A meta-analysis of cross cultural and intracultural studies. *Journal of Marriage and Family, 64*(1), 54–64.

Khaleque, A., & Rohner, R. P. (2012). Pancultural associations between perceived parental acceptance and psychological adjustment of children and adults: A meta-analytic review of worldwide research. *Journal of Cross-Cultural Psychology, 43*, 784–800. http://dx.doi.org/10.1177/0022022111406120

Khaleque, A., Uddin, M. K., Hossain, K. N., Siddique, M. N. E. A., & Shirin, A. (2019). Perceived parental acceptance–rejection in childhood predict psychological adjustment and rejection sensitivity in adulthood. *Psychological Studies, 64*(4), 447–454. http://doi.org/10.1007/s12646-019-00508-z

Lafontaine, M.-F., Bolduc, R., Lonergan, M., Clement, L. M., Brassard, A., Bureau, J.-F., Godbout, N., & Péloquin, K. (2022). Attachment injury severity, injury-related stress, forgiveness, and sexual satisfaction in injured adult partners. *The Journal of Sex Research, 60*(8), 1138–1147. https://doi.org/10.1080/00224499.2022.2086677

Lansford, J. E. (2025). Developmental correlates of parental acceptance-rejection from childhood to adulthood in nine countries. In R. P. Rohner & S. Ali, (Eds.), *Global perspectives on parental acceptance and rejection: Lessons learned from IPARTheory* (pp. 136–152). Routledge.

Marren, C., Mikoška, P., O'Brien, S., & Timulak, L. (2022). A qualitative meta-analysis of the clients' experiences of emotion-focused therapy. *Clinical Psychology & Psychotherapy, 29*(5), 1611–1625. https://doi.org/10.1002/cpp.2745

Mann, D. (2010). *Gestalt therapy: 100 key points and techniques*. New York: Routledge.

McGoldrick, M. & Carter, B. (2001). Advances in coaching: Family therapy with one person. *Journal of Marital and Family Therapy, 27*(3), 281–300. https://doi.org/10.1111/j.1752-0606.2001.tb00325.x

McGoldrick, M., Gerson, R., & Petry, S. (2020). *Genograms: Assessment and Treatment*, Fourth edition. Norton and Company.

Messer, S. B., & Warren, C. S. (1995). *Models of brief psychodynamic therapy*. New York: Guilford.

Minuchin, S. (1974). *Families & Family Therapy*. Harvard U. Press.

Mitchell, S. A., & Black, M. J. (2016). *Freud and beyond: A history of modern psychoanalytic thought*. Basic Books, A Member of the Perseus Books Group.

Moreno, J. L. (1993). *Psicodrama*, São Paulo; New York, NY: Cultrix; Beacon House, Inc.

Murphy, A. M., & Russell, G. (2018). Rejection sensitivity, jealousy, and the relationship to interpersonal aggression. *Journal of Interpersonal Violence, 33*(13), 2118–2129. http://doi.org/10.1177/0886260515622572

Perls, F., Hefferline, R. F., & Goodman, P. (1951). *Gestalt therapy: Excitement and growth in the human personality*. New York: Gestalt Journal Press.

Putnick, D. L., Bornstein, M. H., Lansford, J. E., Malone, P. S., Pastorelli, C., Skinner, A. T., Sorbring, E., Tapanya, S., Tirado, L. M. U., Zelli, A., Alampay, L. P., Al-Hassan, S. M., Bacchini, D., Bombi, A.S., Chang, L., Deater-Deckard, K., Di Giunta, L., Dodge, K. A., & Oburu, P. (2014). Perceived mother and father acceptance-rejection predict four unique aspects of child adjustment across nine countries. *Journal of Child Psychology and Psychiatry, 56*(8), 923–932. https://doi.org/10.1111/jcpp.12366

Rigazio-DiGilio, S. A., & Rohner, R. P. (2006). Clinical adaptation of parental acceptance-rejection theory questionnaires as interactive assessment and treatment tools in relational therapy. In F. Erkman (Ed.), *Acceptance: The Essence of Peace*. Selected papers from the 1st International Congress on Interpersonal Acceptance-Rejection (pp. 3–23). Instanbul: Turkish Psychological Association.

Rigazio-DiGilio, S. A. & Rohner, R. P. (2015). Interpersonal acceptance-rejection theory and clinical applications. In E. Kourkoutas & A. Hart (Eds.), *Innovative practices and interventions for children and adolescents with psychosocial difficulties and disorders* (pp. 476–515). Newcastle upon Tyne, UK: Cambridge Scholars Publications.

Rising, D. G., & Rohner, R. P. (2021). *Recovery from Rejection: A Manual of Client Handouts for Clinical Practice*. (2nd ed. 3.0). Rohner Research Publications. www.rohnerresearchpublications.com

Rogers, C. R. (1957). The necessary and sufficient conditions of therapeutic personality change. *Journal of Consulting Psychology, 21*(2), 95.

Rohner, R. P. (1986). *The warmth dimension: Foundations of parental acceptance-rejection theory*. Beverly Hills, CA: Sage Publications, Inc. (Available as e-book from Rohner Research Publications, Storrs, CT).

Rohner, R. P. (2004). The parental" acceptance-rejection syndrome": Universal correlates of perceived rejection. *American Psychologist, 59*(8), 830–840. https://doi.org/10.1037/0003-066X.59.8.830

Rohner, R. P. (2014). Parental acceptance-rejection theory gets a new name: Interpersonal acceptance-rejection theory (IPARTheory). *Interpersonal Acceptance, 8*(3), 6.

Rohner, R. P. (2016). Introduction to interpersonal acceptance-rejection Theory (IPARTheory) and evidence. *Online Readings in Psychology and Culture, 6*(1), 1–40. https://doi.org/10.9707/2307-0919.1055

Rohner, R. P. (2021). Introduction to Interpersonal Acceptance-Rejection Theory (IPARTheory) and Evidence. *Online Readings in Psychology and Culture, 6*(1). https://doi.org/10.9707/2307-0919.1055

Rohner, R. P. (2023, May). *Glossary of significant concepts in IPARTheory: Center for the study of Interpersonal Acceptance & Rejection*. Center for the Study of Interpersonal Acceptance Rejection. https://csiar.uconn.edu/glossary/

Rohner, R. P. & Ali, S. (2025). IPARTheory, evidence, and methods from conception through maturity. In Rohner, R. P., & Ali, S. (Eds.). *Global perspectives on parental acceptance and rejection: Lessons learned from IPARTheory* (pp. 3–38). Routledge.

Rohner, R. P., & Britner, P. A. (2002). Worldwide mental health correlates of parental acceptance-rejection: Review of cross-cultural and intracultural evidence. *Cross-Cultural Research, 36*(1), 16–47. https://doi.org/10.1177/106939710203600102

Rohner, R. P., & Khaleque, A. (2010). Testing central postulates of Parental Acceptance-Rejection Theory (PARTheory): A meta-analysis of cross-cultural studies. *Journal of Family Theory & Review, 2*(1), 73–87. https://doi.org/10.1111/j.1756-2589.2010.00040.x

Rothenberg, W. A., Lansford, J. E., Tirado, L. M. U., Yotanyamaneewong, S., Alampay, L. P., Al-Hassan, S. M., ... Bornstein, M. H. (2023). The intergenerational transmission of maladaptive parenting and its impact on child mental health: Examining cross-cultural mediating pathways and moderating protective factors. *Child Psychiatry & Human Development, 54*(3), 870–890.

Sabah, A., Aljaberi, M. A., Lin, C.-Y., & Chen, H.-P. (2022). The associations between sibling victimization, sibling bullying, parental acceptance–rejection, and school bullying. *International Journal of Environmental Research and Public Health, 19*(23), 16346. https://doi.org/10.3390/ijerph192316346

Scaini, S., Belotti, R., Ogliari, A., & Battaglia, M. (2016). A comprehensive meta-analysis of cognitive-behavioral interventions for social anxiety disorder in children and adolescents. *Journal of Anxiety Disorders, 42,* 105 112. https://doi.org/10.1016/j.janxdis.2016.05.008

Spengler, P. M., Lee, N. A., Wiebe, S. A., & Wittenborn, A. K. (2022). A comprehensive meta-analysis on the efficacy of emotionally focused couple therapy. *Couple and Family Psychology: Research and Practice*. https://doi.org/10.1037/cfp0000233

Tilley, D., & Palmer, G. (2012). Enactments in emotionally focused couple therapy: Shaping moments of contact and change. *Journal of Marital and Family Therapy, 39*(3), 299–313. https://doi.org/10.1111/j.1752-0606.2012.00305.x

Turkdogan, T. (2021). Intergenerational transmission of perceived parental acceptance–rejection and psychological adjustment: Grandmothers, mothers, and adult granddaughters. *Journal of Child and Family Studies, 30*(5), 1327–1341. https://doi.org/10.1007/s10826-021-01942-2

White, M. & Epston, D. (1990). *Narrative Means to Therapeutic Ends,* New York: W.W. Norton.

White, M. (1995). *Re-authoring lives: Interviews and essays*. Adelaide, Australia: Dulwich Centre Publications.

Whittington, D. D., & Mullinax, H. (2024). An examination of college students' unwanted pursuit of ex-romantic partners: relations to parental warmth and difficulties in emotion regulation. *European Journal of Developmental Psychology, 21*(1), 1–19.

Yontef, G. (1982). Gestalt Therapy: Its inheritance from Gestalt psychology. *Gestalt Theory, 4*(1/2), 23–39.

Yontef, G. (1983). The self in Gestalt Therapy: Reply to Tobin. *The Gestalt Journal, 6*(1), 55–70.

Yontef, G. M. (1993). *Awareness, dialogue, and process*. Highland, NY: Gestalt Journal Press.

12

INTERPERSONAL ACCEPTANCE-REJECTION AND NEUROBIOLOGICAL DEVELOPMENT

Jonas G. Miller and Sumbleen Ali

Parents serve as the primary source of early social input. The nature of this input is reflected, in part, in the quality and types of parental caregiving behaviors, which help to regulate children's neurobiological development in ways that have short- and long-term implications for personal and interpersonal well-being. Six decades of research on interpersonal acceptance-rejection (IPARTheory) suggest that the parent–child relationship serves as a model for children's relationships with others and has implications for adjustment across the lifespan (see Rohner & Ali, 2025; Chapter 1, this book). Broadly, parents who adopt a nurturing orientation toward their children develop strong, high-quality bonds with them, and this serves as the foundation for children's adjustment and prosocial orientation toward others (Miller & Hastings, 2019). Many children, however, are exposed to adverse, stressful experiences in the family context. These experiences are powerful predictors of health and well-being. As children develop and spend more time outside the family, peer relationships become increasingly important. Adolescence, in particular, is characterized by heightened sensitivity to peer influence, social evaluation, and the quality of close friendships (Blakemore & Mills, 2014). Childhood and adolescence are thus periods of great opportunity and risk.

The acceptance-rejection continuum is a core dimension that underlies variation in the quality of early social input in family and peer environments. This continuum is the central focus of IPARTheory which posits that humans have an enduring and universal emotional need for acceptance and feeling cared about by individuals important to them, including

DOI: 10.4324/9781003441243-15

parents, peers, and intimate partners. Rejection from significant others undermines individuals' fundamental need to belong, thus increasing the risk of experiencing maladjustment across the lifespan (Rohner, 2004).

This chapter focuses on the way in which neurobiological states change when individuals' fundamental need for interpersonal acceptance is met versus not met. What are the immediate consequences of interpersonal acceptance versus rejection on the nervous system? In addition, the chapter considers how relationships characterized by acceptance versus rejection are associated with neurobiological development in children and adolescents. What are the developmental implications of parents' behaviors? The chapter covers neurobiological research related to social acceptance-rejection through four lenses. First, it begins by reviewing the patterns of neurobiological activity in the brain and body that are observed in response to tasks that simulate social acceptance and rejection. This research considers the neural, hormonal, and autonomic changes in response to experiences of social acceptance versus rejection. Second, it reviews current understanding of the links between parental acceptance and rejection and neurodevelopment and psychobiology. This includes presenting findings from studies focused on relationship quality, parenting behaviors, or family-level adversity (e.g., maltreatment) in relation to brain structure and function, and other systems implicated in socioemotional development such as the hypothalamic pituitary adrenal (HPA) axis and parasympathetic nervous system (PNS). Third, the chapter considers the developmental neuroscience and developmental psychobiology literature focused on social acceptance and rejection in the context of peer relationships, particularly in adolescents. Fourth, the chapter discusses how neurobiology informs an understanding of individual differences in sensitivity to the effects of acceptance-rejection on development. The chapter concludes with a discussion of potential future directions for research at the intersection of developmental neuroscience, psychobiology, and IPARTheory.

How Does the Nervous System Respond to Interpersonal Acceptance-Rejection?

The immediate neurobiological consequences and correlates of interpersonal acceptance and rejection can be studied using experimental paradigms. Perhaps the most widely used paradigm in neuroimaging research and the gold standard for studying social rejection is the *Cyberball* task (Williams et al., 2000). In *Cyberball*, participants play an online ball-tossing game with partners whom they believe to be other participants but, in fact, are computerized players. *Cyberball* includes an inclusion (acceptance) condition, during which participants toss the ball to the other players, and an exclusion (rejection) condition, during which the computerized players toss the ball to each other and exclude the participant. The exclusion condition has been shown to effectively elicit negative emotions in children, adolescents, and young adults (Ali et al., 2024; Wölfer & Scheithauer, 2013).

At the neural level, studies have found that the exclusion condition elicits increased activation in brain regions that underpin social pain (Rotge et al., 2015) defined as "the unpleasant experience that is associated with actual or potential damage to one's sense of social connection or social value owing to social rejection, exclusion, negative social evaluation or loss" (Eisenberger, 2012, p. 421). This includes increased activation in various subdivisions within the anterior cingulate cortex (ACC) that are involved in error and conflict monitoring (dorsal ACC; Shen et al., 2015), emotion regulation (ventral ACC; Etkin et al., 2011), and subjective feelings of distress (subgenual and pregenual ACC; Rotge et al., 2015). Exclusion in *Cyberball* also elicits increased activation in insula regions that are implicated in pain and salience processing (Mwilambwe-Tshilobo & Spreng, 2021) and medial and ventrolateral prefrontal cortex regions important for emotion regulation (Vijayakumar et al., 2017; see Figure 12.1).

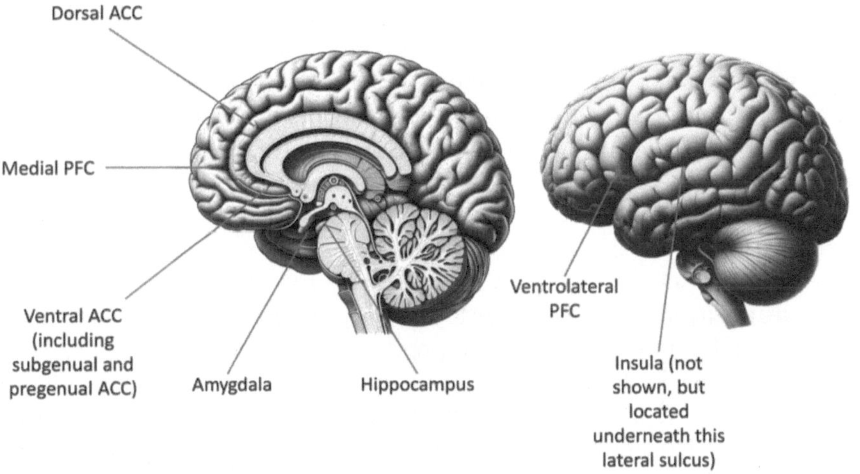

FIGURE 12.1 Brain Regions Most Frequently Implicated in Rejection and Acceptance.

Note: The ACC, PFC, and insula regions are reliably activated by social exclusion. Weaker functional connectivity between ventral ACC regions and the amygdala is related to parental warmth and acceptance. Hippocampus and amygdala regions show structural alterations in relation to social experiences involving rejection (e.g., maltreatment, deprivation). ACC = anterior cingulate cortex; PFC = prefrontal cortex. Part of this image was created using the DALL-E artificial intelligence art generator.

A recent meta-analysis suggests that many of the regions that are reliably activated by *Cyberball* exclusion have significant spatial overlap with the default mode network (Mwilambwe-Tshilobo & Spreng, 2021). This network includes regions that are thought to contribute to the theory of mind (i.e., mentalizing) and autobiographical recollection (Spreng et al., 2009). Social exclusion appears to elicit widespread activity in brain networks that support affective and salience processing and emotion regulation that is important for managing distress related to exclusion. Further, experiencing rejection recruits regions important for social cognition and self-reflection that could contribute to thoughts about why they are excluded (Mwilambwe-Tshilobo & Spreng, 2021). Thus, the experience of social rejection is characterized by representing the mental states of others, self-referential processes, and social-emotional pain.

Adolescence is widely considered to be a period of heightened rejection sensitivity compared to other age groups; adolescents demonstrate stronger increases in negative affect and self-evaluation following rejection, and they experience a heightened risk for anxiety and depression (Blakemore & Mills, 2014). Thus, most developmental neuroscience research examining neural responses to social rejection has focused on adolescents. Other research areas, however, have used different methodologies to study adolescent neurobiological responses to exclusion/rejection and related experiences like social evaluation. Without the constraints imposed by use of magnetic resonance imaging scanners (e.g., keeping one's head still, exposure to loud noises from the scanner, and lying flat in the scanner), researchers can utilize interpersonal laboratory tasks that may have even greater ecological validity than *Cyberball*. For example, the Yale Interpersonal Stressor (YIS) task involves participants interacting with two confederates trained to gradually exclude them using verbal and non-verbal cues (Stroud et al., 2000). Adolescents show increased neuroendocrine and cardiovascular reactivity to this task relative to children, as demonstrated by increased cortisol, alpha-amylase, and blood pressure (Stroud et al., 2009).

The Trier Social Stress Test (TSST) is another widely used and reliable laboratory protocol for inducing physiological stress related to social evaluation (Dickerson & Kemeny, 2004). This task typically requires participants to prepare and deliver a speech and to perform a serial subtraction task in the presence of a judge or panel of evaluators trained to maintain a neutral expression. In adolescents, the TSST effectively elicits autonomic reactivity characterized by increased heart rate, increased blood pressure, decreased PNS activity, increased sympathetic nervous system (SNS) activity, and increased HPA-axis activity as measured by salivary cortisol (Miller et al., 2019a; Stroud et al., 2009). Consistent with findings suggesting that adolescence is a period of heightened rejection sensitivity, adolescents demonstrate greater physiological reactivity to social-evaluative stressors than do children (Stroud et al., 2009), and this reactivity increases with age and pubertal development (Sumter et al., 2010). These findings suggest that interpersonal rejection and closely related experiences such as social evaluation activate coordinated stress responses that mobilize metabolic resources. Some activation of stress response systems can support coping, but extreme and persistent responses can be metabolically costly and support fight-or-flight responses. Adolescents demonstrate increased biological reactivity to rejection and social evaluation relative to other age groups. These findings are consistent with the perspective that adolescents' avoidance of social rejection and the desire for social acceptance from peers is particularly strong (Blakemore & Mills, 2014).

It is important to highlight the fact that most of the research on the immediate effects of social rejection on neurobiology has focused on rejection from peers or, in TSST research, social evaluation from adults. In infant studies, however, researchers have used the still-face paradigm (SFP) to assess infants' neurobiological response to insensitive caregiving from parents. Specifically, the SFP includes episodes in which caregivers either play with their infants or present a neutral face without response to infant cues. This play episode of the SFP elicits increased parasympathetic activity in infants, whereas the neutral face episode leads to increased cardiac arousal represented by increased heart rate and decreased parasympathetic activity (Conradt & Ablow, 2010). Thus, not responding to infant cues in the SFP—which may simulate early neglect or insensitive caregiving—appears to activate stress responses similar to responses observed with social rejection in older children, adolescents, and adults.

Social rejection is a powerful experience, eliciting widespread changes in neurobiology that contribute to negative emotions, social cognitive processes, and coping efforts. However, many of these immediate effects can be dampened or buffered in the presence of social acceptance or support, especially from significant others and attachment figures (Hostinar & Gunnar, 2015). For example, the presence of an attachment figure or presentation of stimuli associated with the attachment figure has been found to reduce neural activity in regions implicated in pain, threat, and negative emotion. Coan et al. (2006) found that holding the hand of a supportive spouse reduced threat-related activation in the insula and superior frontal gyrus. Viewing pictures of long-term romantic partners increases activation in regions involved in emotion regulation, such as the ventromedial prefrontal cortex (Eisenberger et al., 2011). The neural effects of social acceptance may partially rely on oxytocin, a neuropeptide implicated in caregiving and social bonding (Hostinar & Gunnar, 2015). Some brain regions important for affective processing—such as the amygdala—show high oxytocin receptor density (Insel & Shapiro, 1992). Oxytocin also upregulates social engagement and safety-signaling systems, such as the PNS (Carter et al., 2008), and downregulates activity in stress response systems, such as the HPA-axis (Uvnäs-Moberg, 1998). Thus, social acceptance may induce neurobiological states that support evaluating the environment as safe.

In childhood, parental acceptance and support are potent sources of coregulation and safety, but these effects may diminish in adolescence. For instance, children showed reduced cortisol reactivity to TSST when parents expressed acceptance and support before the task, whereas parental support had no buffering effect among adolescents (Hostinar et al., 2015). Similarly, children—not adolescents—show more mature forms of amygdala reactivity and connectivity and improved emotion regulation in the presence of maternal stimuli (Gee et al., 2014). It is possible that adolescents increasingly rely on people other than parents, such as peers, for social support and acceptance, and that this switch is partially mediated by neurobiological changes related to puberty (Doom et al., 2015). Thus, the effects of social acceptance on neurobiology may vary depending on the source of acceptance and stage of development.

Neurobiological Correlates of Parental Acceptance and Rejection

Parenting behaviors indicative of acceptance, including sensitivity, responsiveness, and warmth toward the child, are consistently linked to children's prosocial orientation, including greater empathy (see also Lansford, 2025; Chapter 7, this book). Parental sensitivity and support also aid in developing emotion regulation and self-regulatory capacities (Miller & Hastings, 2019). These skills are crucial for emotional adjustment (Memmott-Elison et al., 2020), and serve as protective factors in contexts of risk (Armstrong-Carter et al., 2021a). They are also foundational for future life success (Moffitt et al., 2011).

Positive caregiving behaviors may lead to positive child outcomes by shaping the development of neurobiological systems implicated in children's own caregiving behaviors, health, and emotion regulation (Miller & Hastings, 2019). Early expressions of affection and care in infancy, toddlerhood, and childhood are linked to the development of regulatory systems, including the HPA-axis and parasympathetic nervous system (PNS). The HPA axis stimulates the release of the hormone cortisol in response to stressful events and increases alertness and arousal (Sapolsky et al., 2000). The PNS downregulates cardiovascular activity through the vagus nerve and can facilitate social engagement (Porges, 2022). These systems may serve as critical mediators of the effects of parenting. For example, a recent meta-analysis of 103 studies with more than 13,000 participants found that warm, sensitive, and supportive parenting behaviors are associated with higher resting PNS activity in children (Alen et al., 2022). This is generally thought to be associated with increased capacity for effective regulation of emotion and attention (Porges, 2022; Thayer et al., 2012). Other studies have focused on how parents' harsh, controlling, and neglectfulbehaviors—which are indicative of rejection—are associated with atypical or less healthy development of regulatory systems. Harsh and controlling maternal behaviors may negatively impact the development of children's PNS response to emotional and social challenges (Hastings et al., 2008). Taken together, caregiving behaviors that suggest parental acceptance tend to shape neurobiological systems important for coping and perceiving the environment as safe.

The last decade has seen tremendous growth in developmental neuroscience research focused on the links between parenting practices and brain outcomes and development (Tan et al., 2020). On the positive side, parental warmth and sensitivity have been shown to be prospectively associated with adolescent development of weaker resting-state functional connectivity between the amygdala and subgenual ACC (sgACC) (Miller et al., 2021). The amygdala is involved in rapid detection and responding to salient events (LeDoux, 2007), whereas the sgACC is involved in depressive rumination (Hamilton et al., 2015). Miller et al. (2021) found that weaker amygdala–sgACC connectivity was related to reduced depressive symptoms. Thus, the neurophenotype that was more common in the context of parental warmth and acceptance was related to fewer mental health problems.

Similarly, other research has found that parental warmth is associated with adolescents' reduced amygdala and sgACC response to parental criticism (Butterfield et al., 2021). Further, parental warmth was linked to lower levels of adolescents' anxiety and depression through its relation with reduced sgACC activation (Butterfield et al., 2021). Other studies focused on broader networks involved in social and affective processes have found that parental expressions of positive affect are associated with neurodevelopmental patterns thought to reflect healthy brain maturation (Pozzi et al., 2021). Similarly, youth who perceive their parents as warm and accepting showed heightened connectivity within the default mode network, a pattern associated with reduced psychopathology (Davis et al., 2022).

More recently, researchers have considered whether parental acceptance-rejection plays a role in how individuals react to acceptance-rejection in other contexts. Parental rejection in the form of emotional maltreatment has been linked to activity in adolescent brain regions important for salience processing during the social exclusion versus inclusion portions of the Cyberball task (Schulz et al., 2022). Children with positive parent representations at preschool age (i.e., portrayed their parents as helpful and supportive) showed cardiac slowing in later response to social exclusion at school age. This pattern, in turn, predicted fewer peer problems (White et al., 2021). These findings raise the possibility that early parental acceptance-rejection experiences may be foundational for how children respond to rejection in the future and whether they are likely to navigate peer relationships effectively. However, more research is needed on the implications of the history of parental acceptance-rejection for neurobiological response to acceptance-rejection.

Another developmental neuroscience approach to examining the sequelae of chronic or early exposure to rejection has been neuroimaging individuals with a history of childhood maltreatment or severe social-emotional and physical deprivation, frequently due to institutional rearing. These experiences often reflect extreme rejection and caregiving experiences that are outside the normative range of parenting (Farber et al., 2022). This literatures points to the possibility that exposure to rejection in the form of trauma, abuse, and neglect leads to widespread alterations in brain structure, activation, and connectivity (Miller et al., 2022). Some of these alterations may underpin the adverse psychological consequences of rejection.

At the level of brain structure, developmental neuroscience consistently implicates exposure to maltreatment and deprivation in alterations in the prefrontal cortex (PFC) and subcortical regions that are important for emotional processing and mental health. Compared to other parts of the brain, the prefrontal cortex undergoes protracted development over time, which may make this region particularly sensitive to caregiving input. Subcortical regions rich in glucocorticoid receptors may also be sensitive to stress related to the quality of caregiving. Indeed, individuals who experience childhood maltreatment or early deprivation due to institutionalization show reduced volume and accelerated thinning in prefrontal regions implicated in emotion, motivation, and psychopathology (Sheridan et al., 2022). These individuals also show volumetric alterations in stress-sensitive subcortical regions like the hippocampus (Hanson et al., 2015) and the amygdala (Tottenham et al., 2010). Children who experience severe neglect have also been found to have overall reductions in the volume and integrity of white matter and corpus callosum (Bick et al., 2015), frontal-striatal tracts (Bick et al., 2015), and frontal-parietal tracts (Govindan et al., 2010). This suggests less robust structural connectivity. In turn, these structural alterations in the prefrontal cortex, subcortical regions, and white matter have been associated with indicators of maladjustment, such as behavioral problems (e.g., Hanson et al., 2015).

In addition to structural alterations, children exposed to extreme forms of parental rejection show altered functioning of brain regions implicated in emotion and the production of stress responses. For example, research on maltreatment, family violence, and institutionalization consistently finds that these experiences are related to amygdala hyperactivity to emotional faces (Gee et al., 2013; Suzuki et al., 2014). Similar findings have been observed for adverse experiences in community samples (Miller et al., 2020). Some of these effects appear to be specific to the centromedial subdivision of the amygdala (Miller et al., 2020; Suzuki et al., 2014), which mediates autonomic, endocrine, and behavioral responses to salient stimuli (LeDoux, 2007). Thus, early experiences of rejection appear to be associated with patterns of amygdala activation that may support hypervigilance to cues signaling threat, such as angry and fearful faces. This rapid detection of potential dangers may promote safety in hostile family conditions that are characterized by frequent parental rejection. But this brain alteration also increases long-term risk for psychosocial maladjustment.

Children and adolescents exposed to early and severe rejection also show blunted activation in prefrontal regions important for cognitive control (Weissman et al., 2020) and in striatum regions involved in reward processing (Goff et al., 2013). Reduced activation in prefrontal regions may contribute to the deficits in executive functioning that have been documented in children exposed to parental rejection (Ma et al., 2022). Blunted striatum reactivity to reward-related stimuli may underpin specific mental health difficulties, such as anhedonia, which emerge in the context of poor family-relationship quality (Kouros & Garber, 2014). Further, the functional connectivity between these various regions is altered in youth exposed to severe forms of parental rejection such as physical abuse and neglect (VanTieghem & Tottenham, 2018). For instance, these experiences have been linked to weaker negative functional connectivity between prefrontal regions and the amygdala, a pattern implicated in less effective emotion regulation and vulnerability to psychopathology (Marusak et al., 2015).

Overall, the literature suggests that parental rejection in the forms of psychosocial deprivation and maltreatment is associated with a wide range of neurobiological outcomes that contribute to social, emotional, cognitive, and behavioral development and functioning. The range of developmental sequelae related to parental rejection may be mediated by widespread alterations in the brain and body. Sensitive parenting provides young children with sensory, motor, linguistic, and social stimulation, which foster learning. Thus, the absence of sensitive caregiving deprives young children of interactions crucial for shaping neurobiological systems underlying well-being and positive development. In addition, overt parental rejection in the form of harsh or abusive caregiving may alter neurobiological systems in ways that promote personal safety in dangerous environments but also increase the long-term risk for psychopathology and other adverse outcomes.

Neural Correlates of Peer Rejection in Adolescence

As discussed earlier in this chapter, parents or caregivers are primary sources of social input in childhood, but social importance gradually shifts toward peers through late childhood and adolescence. This shift is associated with maturation in neural systems involved in social processing (Blakemore & Mills, 2014). Peer rejection in the forms of social exclusion or bullying is associated with enhanced sensitivity to social rejection that may be supported by increased activity and connectivity within circuits important for implementing behavioral, cognitive, and emotional adaptations (Lee et al., 2017).

The enhanced sensitivity to social rejection in adolescents who have experienced peer victimization is likely to affect the implementation of self-regulation and decision-making in social situations such as engaging in risky behavior. For example, Telzer et al. (2018) found that experiences of peer victimization can lead adolescents to make risky decisions such as crossing a busy intersection when they see a yellow traffic light rather than waiting for the light to turn red. The authors found that during risky decisions there was increased recruitment of affective sensitivity regions (amygdala, ventral striatum, and orbitofrontal cortex) and social cognition regions (superior temporal sulcus, STS, and temporoparietal junction) of the brain. Other researchers have found that exposure to adverse experiences was associated with reduced activation in critical regions of the inhibitory function network, including the dACC and the mPFC (Cará et al., 2019). These brain regions are known to be involved in self-regulation.

Preliminary evidence suggests that the right supramarginal gyrus response to rejection is enhanced in adolescents who experience social rejection (Asscheman et al., 2019). This region appears to be involved in internalizing problems. Research has also found that there is an increased risk for internalizing and externalizing behavior problems because of experiences of peer victimization (Reijntjes et al., 2010; see also Rohner & Ali, 2025; Chapter 1, this book). According to IPARTheory, positive experience with significant others such as parents is likely to serve as a protective function, mitigating the detrimental impact of peer rejection (Rohner, 2004, 2021).

Neurobiological Correlates of Coping and Resilience to Interpersonal Rejection

Despite the well-documented psychosocial and neurobiological effects of social rejection, not all humans exposed to interpersonal rejection, especially parental rejection, demonstrate unhealthy development. IPARTheory recognizes that some individuals are better able than others to emotionally cope with experiences of interpersonal rejection (Rohner, 2021; Rohner & Ali, 2025; Chapter 1, this book). In IPARTheory, such individuals are referred to as *"affective copers"* (Rohner, 2021). IPARTheory defines affective copers as "individuals whose emotional and overall mental health is fairly good despite having been raised in seriously rejecting families or despite being seriously rejected by other attachment figures throughout life" (Rohner, 2023). Thus, IPARTheory's research argues that there are significant individual-level variations in the psychosocial and neurobiological factors involved in vulnerability and resilience to experiences of interpersonal rejection.

IPARTheory explains this individual-level variation in vulnerability and resilience by employing a multivariate model of behavior (Rohner 2023; see also Rohner & Ali, 2025; Chapter 1, this book). IPARTheory states that the behavior of an affective coper is a function of the interaction between self, other, and context. *"Self"* characteristics include an individual's mental representations and other internal (affective, cognitive, perceptual, and motivational dispositions) and external (observable behaviors) characteristics. *"Other"* includes the personal and interpersonal characteristics of the rejecting other, including variation in the severity, type, duration, and timing of specific events related to experiences of interpersonal rejection. *"Context"* characteristics include other significant people in the individual's life, along with social-situational characteristics of the person's environment. Further, IPARTheory emphasizes specific social-cognitive capabilities that allow some children and adults to cope with perceived rejection more effectively than others. These capabilities include a differentiated sense of self, a sense of self-determination, and the capacity to depersonalize (Rohner, 1986, 2021).

Research suggests that some of these tendencies and processes may be represented in the brain as specific patterns, functioning, profiles, or signatures of neural structure, activity, and connectivity (i.e., neurophenotypes) that confer risk versus resilience. For example, the right temporoparietal junction (TPJ) is a region that distinguishes between self and others (Lamm et al., 2019). To our knowledge, however, researchers have yet to consider the role of the right TPJ in coping and resilience to interpersonal rejection experiences. Decreased neural reactivity to rejection experiences in a social pain network may support protection against the effects of peer victimization on adolescent psychopathology (Rudolph et al., 2016). This decreased neural reactivity may support decreased psychological sensitivity and vigilance to rejection cues (Rudolph et al., 2016). However, most of the research on the neurobiology of resilience to rejection and related factors has not identified neurophenotypes that map to specific psychological resilience and coping processes.

Instead, one of the more common approaches to studying resilience processes is considering the interactive effects of rejection-related factors and neurobiology on well-being (i.e., a moderation-based approach) (Miller et al., 2022). This approach focuses on whether the strength of association between interpersonal rejection and adjustment is weakened in the context of a particular pattern of brain structure or function. This area of research is still in the early stages. However, there is evidence that some neurobiological consequences of interpersonal rejection may be adaptations that confer some degree of resilience (Miller et al., 2022). For example, accelerated cortical thinning and smaller hippocampal volume related to interpersonal rejection may also moderate the adverse effects of rejection in a manner that reflects reduced sensitivity to environmental influence. This relative insensitivity may represent a developmental adaptation that helps to reduce vulnerability to subsequent rejection experiences. Conversely, other neural processes may support vulnerability and play a role in magnifying sensitivity to rejection experiences.

Future Directions

Little is known about potential gender differences in the effects of interpersonal acceptance and rejection on neural function and development. Many IPARTheory behavioral studies, however, have noted gender differences. For example, a meta-analysis of 66 studies (N=19,511) found differences in adult sons' versus adult daughters' perceptions of maternal versus paternal acceptance (Ali et al., 2015). Specifically, adults' memories of *maternal* acceptance in childhood have significantly stronger relations with adult sons' current psychological adjustment than adult daughters' adjustment. Conversely, adults' recollections of *paternal* acceptance in childhood have a significantly stronger relation with adult daughters' psychological adjustment than adult sons' adjustment. Investigating gender differences in how interpersonal acceptance and rejection are related to brain functioning may help researchers understand gender differences in psychological effects.

Most affective neuroscience research focuses on within-individual analyses that consider the associations of socioemotional processes with individual differences in neurobiology. One question of great interest to investigators is how the accepting and rejecting behavior of one member of a dyad affects the behavior and neurobiology of the other member. Exploration of this issue requires within-dyad analyses that consider transactional processes between dyad members. In research focused on parasympathetic regulation, there is a great deal of interest in the synchrony of fluctuations in neurobiological states in parent–child dyads (Miller et al., 2023). Some studies examine the directional effects of parent-to-child and child-to-parent (Armstrong-Carter et al., 2021b). Parent–child synchrony of parasympathetic nervous system activity has been considered in conflict discussions (Suveg et al., 2019) but has not been extended to other rejection-acceptance paradigms. One promising technology for considering IPARTheory in relation to within-dyad synchrony analyses in brain activity is functional near-infrared spectroscopy (fNIRS). It has been used to study dyadic processes, including parent–child interaction and relationship quality (Miller et al., 2019b) as well as expressing and receiving appreciation in adult dyads (Balters et al., 2023). In addition, compared to fMRI, fNIRS is more robust to motion artifacts and allows for the measurement of changes in cortical oxygenation in more social and ecologically valid contexts. Given these strengths, fNIRS may be promising for future research on neural correlates of IPARTheory in childhood and infancy.

Most neuroscience studies offer a snapshot of interpersonal acceptance and rejection and its effects cross-sectionally or in two-time points. How neurobiological function and structure change over time in relation to early or changing experiences of acceptance-rejection remains largely unknown. Thus, more prospective studies are needed to examine the critical influence of early parent–child relationships in governing neural responses to interpersonal rejection. In addition, repeated assessments of neurobiology and acceptance-rejection will allow researchers to model developmental trajectories. Recent work has linked insecure attachment assessed in early adolescence to trajectories of accelerated cortical thinning in early adulthood (Puhlmann et al., 2023). Threat-related adversity has been associated with stable and high brain network connectivity throughout adolescence (Chahal et al., 2022). Future research should build on these studies using different measures of parental acceptance-rejection and consider the possibility of non-linear trajectories. Study designs with repeated measures also allow researchers to model transactional processes between parent and child that link the development of parent–child relationships to child neurobiology.

The field of neuropsychology primarily uses variable-focused analyses to examine relations between measures of acceptance-rejection and developmental outcomes. A promising alternative for future research is to adopt more person-centered analyses. One example is brain-based biotyping applied to defining subgroups of participants characterized by different patterns of within- and between-network functional connectivity (Miller et al., 2022). This work often utilizes data-driven, exploratory methods to search for connectivity-based subgroups that can be compared to other variables. For instance, biotyping could reveal brain-based differences that may be related to different histories of acceptance-rejection, and sensitivity to the psychosocial effects of these experiences.

Last, studying the neurobiology of interpersonal relationships represents an opportunity for interdisciplinary collaboration among neuroscientists, psychologists, biologists, physicians, and others. This area of research demands a multilevel perspective. Therefore, professionals from diverse scientific traditions stand to make essential and complementary contributions to this research. This chapter serves as a call for more interdisciplinary collaboration.

Conclusion

This chapter synthesizes studies of how experiences of interpersonal acceptance and rejection influence human neurobiology, with a particular emphasis on development. To integrate IPARTheory into neurobiological research, the chapter includes discussions of the neurobiological correlates of interpersonal acceptance and rejection. Across diverse fields and measures of neurobiology, studies provide converging evidence that interpersonal acceptance, especially parental acceptance, helps children evaluate the environment as safe, engage in prosocial processes, and cope with challenges. Conversely, rejection can set off multisystem changes in neurobiology that support stress responding, negative affect, and self-referential and social cognitive processes. Chronic early rejection from caregivers may shape the development of neurophenotypes in ways that increase vulnerability and maladjustment. Nevertheless, not all individuals are equally sensitive to acceptance-rejection's short-term and long-term effects. Incorporating new methodologies and interdisciplinary approaches in future research will help advance an understanding of the neurobiological correlates and pathways of acceptance-rejection on development and individual differences in coping and resilience to rejection. Further, this area of research may shed light on efforts to foster resilience to rejection. This research also has the potential of using social acceptance experiences to improve developmental outcomes and well-being.

References

Alen, N. V., Shields, G. S., Nemer, A., D'Souza, I. A., Ohlgart, M. J., & Hostinar, C. E. (2022). A systematic review and meta-analysis of the association between parenting and child autonomic nervous system activity. *Neuroscience & Biobehavioral Reviews, 139*, 104734. https://doi.org/10.1016/j.neubiorev.2022.104734

Ali, S., Rohner, R. P., Britner, P. A., & Jahn, A. (2024). Longing for belonging: Feeling loved (or not) and why it matters. *Family Relations: An Interdisciplinary Journal of Applied Family Studies, 73*(4), 2639–2654. https://doi.org/10.1111/fare.13029

Ali, S., Khaleque, A., & Rohner, R. P. (2015). Pancultural gender differences in the relation between perceived parental acceptance and psychological adjustment of children and adult offspring: A meta-analytic review of worldwide research.

Journal of Cross-Cultural Psychology, *46*(8), 1059–1080. https://doi.org/10.1177/0022022115597754

Armstrong-Carter, E., Miller, J. G., Hill, L. J. B., & Domingue, B. W. (2021a). Young children's prosocial behavior protects against academic risk in neighborhoods with low socioeconomic status. *Child Development*, *92*(4), 1509–1522. https://doi.org/10.1111/cdev.13549

Armstrong-Carter, E., Miller, J. G., & Obradović, J. (2021b). Parent–child physiological synchrony: Concurrent and lagged effects during dyadic laboratory interaction. *Developmental Psychobiology*, *63*(7), e22196. https://doi.org/10.1002/dev.22196

Asscheman, J. S., Koot, S., Ma, I., Buil, J. M., Krabbendam, L., Cillessen, A. H. N., & van Lier, P. A. C. (2019). Heightened neural sensitivity to social exclusion in boys with a history of low peer preference during primary school. *Developmental Cognitive Neuroscience*, *38*, 100673. https://doi.org/10.1016/j.dcn.2019.100673

Balters, S., Miller, J. G., & Reiss, A. L. (2023). Expressing appreciation is linked to interpersonal closeness and inter-brain coherence, both in person and over Zoom. *Cerebral Cortex*, *33*(11), 7211–7220. https://doi.org/10.1093/cercor/bhad032

Bick, J., Zhu, T., Stamoulis, C., Fox, N. A., Zeanah, C., & Nelson, C. A. (2015). Effect of early institutionalization and foster care on long-term white matter development: A randomized clinical trial. *JAMA Pediatrics*, *169*(3), 211–219. https://doi.org/10.1001/jamapediatrics.2014.3212

Blakemore, S.-J., & Mills, K. L. (2014). Is adolescence a sensitive period for sociocultural processing? *Annual Review of Psychology*, *65*, 187–207. https://doi.org/10.1146/annurev-psych-010213-115202

Butterfield, R. D., Silk, J. S., Lee, K. H., Siegle, G. S., Dahl, R. E., Forbes, E. E., Ryan, N. D., Hooley, J. M., & Ladouceur, C. D. (2021). Parents still matter! Parental warmth predicts adolescent brain function and anxiety and depressive symptoms 2 years later. *Development and Psychopathology*, *33*(1), 226–239. https://doi.org/10.1017/S0954579419001718

Cará, V. M., Esper, N. B., de Azeredo, L. A., Iochpe, V., Dalfovo, N. P., Santos, R. C., Sanvicente-Vieira, B., Grassi-Oliveira, R., Franco, A. R., & Buchweitz, A. (2019). An fMRI study of inhibitory control and the effects of exposure to violence in Latin-American early adolescents: Alterations in frontoparietal activation and performance. *Social Cognitive and Affective Neuroscience*, *14*(10), 1097–1107. https://doi.org/10.1093/scan/nsz092

Carter, C. S., Grippo, A. J., Pournajafi-Nazarloo, H., Ruscio, M. G., & Porges, S. W. (2008). Oxytocin, vasopressin and sociality. In I. D. Neumann & R. Landgraf (Eds.), *Progress in Brain Research* (Vol. 170, pp. 331–336). Elsevier. https://doi.org/10.1016/S0079-6123(08)00427-5

Chahal, R., Miller, J. G., Yuan, J. P., Buthmann, J. L., & Gotlib, I. H. (2022). An exploration of dimensions of early adversity and the development of functional brain network connectivity during adolescence: Implications for trajectories of internalizing symptoms. *Development and Psychopathology*, *34*(2), 557–571. https://doi.org/10.1017/S0954579421001814

Coan, J. A., Schaefer, H. S., & Davidson, R. J. (2006). Lending a hand: Social regulation of the neural response to threat. *Psychological Science*, *17*(12), 1032–1039. https://doi.org/10.1111/j.1467-9280.2006.01832.x

Conradt, E., & Ablow, J. (2010). Infant physiological response to the still-face paradigm: Contributions of maternal sensitivity and infants' early regulatory behavior. *Infant Behavior and Development*, *33*(3), 251–265. https://doi.org/10.1016/j.infbeh.2010.01.001

Davis, K., Hirsch, E., Gee, D., Andover, M., & Roy, A. K. (2022). Mediating role of the default mode network on parental acceptance/warmth and psychopathology in youth. *Brain Imaging and Behavior, 16*(5), 2229–2238. https://doi.org/10.1007/s11682-022-00692-z

Dickerson, S. S., & Kemeny, M. E. (2004). Acute stressors and cortisol responses: A theoretical integration and synthesis of laboratory research. *Psychological Bulletin, 130*(3), 355–391. https://doi.org/10.1037/0033-2909.130.3.355

Doom, J. R., Hostinar, C. E., VanZomeren-Dohm, A. A., & Gunnar, M. R. (2015). The roles of puberty and age in explaining the diminished effectiveness of parental buffering of HPA reactivity and recovery in adolescence. *Psychoneuroendocrinology, 59*, 102–111. https://doi.org/10.1016/j.psyneuen.2015.04.024

Eisenberger, N. I. (2012). The pain of social disconnection: Examining the shared neural underpinnings of physical and social pain. *Nature Reviews. Neuroscience, 13*(6), 421–434. https://doi.org/10.1038/nrn3231

Eisenberger, N. I., Master, S. L., Inagaki, T. K., Taylor, S. E., Shirinyan, D., Lieberman, M. D., & Naliboff, B. D. (2011). Attachment figures activate a safety signal-related neural region and reduce pain experience. *Proceedings of the National Academy of Sciences of the United States of America, 108*(28), 11721–11726. https://doi.org/10.1073/pnas.1108239108

Etkin, A., Egner, T., & Kalisch, R. (2011). Emotional processing in anterior cingulate and medial prefrontal cortex. *Trends in Cognitive Sciences, 15*(2), 85–93. https://doi.org/10.1016/j.tics.2010.11.004

Farber, M. J., Gee, D. G., & Hariri, A. R. (2022). Normative range parenting and the developing brain: A scoping review and recommendations for future research. *European Journal of Neuroscience, 55*(9–10), 2341–2358. https://doi.org/10.1111/ejn.15003

Gee, D. G., Gabard-Durnam, L. J., Flannery, J., Goff, B., Humphreys, K. L., Telzer, E. H., Hare, T. A., Bookheimer, S. Y., & Tottenham, N. (2013). Early developmental emergence of human amygdala-prefrontal connectivity after maternal deprivation. *Proceedings of the National Academy of Sciences of the United States of America, 110*(39), 15638–15643. https://doi.org/10.1073/pnas.1307893110

Gee, D. G., Gabard-Durnam, L., Telzer, E. H., Humphreys, K. L., Goff, B., Shapiro, M., Flannery, J., Lumian, D. S., Fareri, D. S., Caldera, C., & Tottenham, N. (2014). Maternal buffering of human amygdala-prefrontal circuitry during childhood but not during adolescence. *Psychological Science, 25*(11), 2067–2078. https://doi.org/10.1177/0956797614550878

Goff, B., Gee, D. G., Telzer, E. H., Humphreys, K. L., Gabard-Durnam, L., Flannery, J., & Tottenham, N. (2013). Reduced nucleus accumbens reactivity and adolescent depression following early-life stress. *Neuroscience, 249*, 129–138. https://doi.org/10.1016/j.neuroscience.2012.12.010

Govindan, R. M., Behen, M. E., Helder, E., Makki, M. I., & Chugani, H. T. (2010). Altered water diffusivity in cortical association tracts in children with early deprivation identified with Tract-Based Spatial Statistics (TBSS). *Cerebral Cortex (New York, N.Y.: 1991), 20*(3), 561–569. https://doi.org/10.1093/cercor/bhp122

Hamilton, J. P., Farmer, M., Fogelman, P., & Gotlib, I. H. (2015). Depressive rumination, the default-mode network, and the dark matter of clinical neuroscience. *Biological Psychiatry, 78*(4), 224–230. https://doi.org/10.1016/j.biopsych.2015.02.020

Hanson, J. L., Nacewicz, B. M., Sutterer, M. J., Cayo, A. A., Schaefer, S. M., Rudolph, K. D., Shirtcliff, E. A., Pollak, S. D., & Davidson, R. J. (2015). Behavioral problems after early life stress: Contributions of the hippocampus and amygdala. *Biological Psychiatry, 77*(4), 314–323. https://doi.org/10.1016/j.biopsych.2014.04.020

Hastings, P. D., Nuselovici, J. N., Utendale, W. T., Coutya, J., McShane, K. E., & Sullivan, C. (2008). Applying the polyvagal theory to children's emotion regulation: Social context, socialization, and adjustment. *Biological Psychology, 79*(3), 299–306. https://doi.org/10.1016/j.biopsycho.2008.07.005

Hostinar, C. E., & Gunnar, M. R. (2015). Social support can buffer against stress and shape brain activity. *AJOB Neuroscience, 6*(3), 34–42. https://doi.org/10.1080/21507740.2015.1047054

Hostinar, C. E., Johnson, A. E., & Gunnar, M. R. (2015). Parent support is less effective in buffering cortisol stress reactivity for adolescents compared to children. *Developmental Science, 18*(2), 281–297. https://doi.org/10.1111/desc.12195

Insel, T. R., & Shapiro, L. E. (1992). Oxytocin receptor distribution reflects social organization in monogamous and polygamous voles. *Proceedings of the National Academy of Sciences of the United States of America, 89*(13), 5981–5985. https://doi.org/10.1073/pnas.89.13.5981

Kouros, C. D., & Garber, J. (2014). Trajectories of individual depressive symptoms in adolescents: Gender and family relationships as predictors. *Developmental Psychology, 50*(12), 2633–2643. https://doi.org/10.1037/a0038190

Lamm, C., Rütgen, M., & Wagner, I. C. (2019). Imaging empathy and prosocial emotions. *Neuroscience Letters, 693*, 49–53. https://doi.org/10.1016/j.neulet.2017.06.054

Lansford, J. E. (2025). Developmental correlates of parental acceptance-rejection from childhood to adulthood in nine countries. In Rohner, R. P., & Ali, S. (Eds.). *Global perspectives on parental acceptance and rejection: Lessons learned from IPARTheory* (pp. 136–152). Routledge.

LeDoux, J. (2007). The amygdala. *Current Biology: CB, 17*(20), R868–874. https://doi.org/10.1016/j.cub.2007.08.005

Lee, S. W., Choi, J., Lee, J.-S., Yoo, J. H., Kim, K. W., Kim, D., Park, H., & Jeong, B. (2017). Altered function of ventrolateral prefrontal cortex in adolescents with peer verbal abuse history. *Psychiatry Investigation, 14*(4), 441–451. https://doi.org/10.4306/pi.2017.14.4.441

Ma, Y., Xing, X., & Zhang, M. (2022). Parental rejection and school-aged children's externalizing behavior problems in China: The roles of executive function and callous-unemotional traits. *Child Psychiatry & Human Development*. https://doi.org/10.1007/s10578-022-01397-6

Marusak, H. A., Martin, K. R., Etkin, A., & Thomason, M. E. (2015). Childhood trauma exposure disrupts the automatic regulation of emotional processing. *Neuropsychopharmacology, 40*(5), 1250–1258. https://doi.org/10.1038/npp.2014.311

Memmott-Elison, M. K., Holmgren, H. G., Padilla-Walker, L. M., & Hawkins, A. J. (2020). Associations between prosocial behavior, externalizing behaviors, and internalizing symptoms during adolescence: A meta-analysis. *Journal of Adolescence, 80*, 98–114. https://doi.org/10.1016/j.adolescence.2020.01.012

Miller, J. G., Armstrong-Carter, E., Balter, L., & Lorah, J. (2023). A meta-analysis of mother–child synchrony in respiratory sinus arrhythmia and contextual risk. *Developmental Psychobiology, 65*(1), e22355.

Miller, J. G., Chahal, R., & Gotlib, I. H. (2022). Early life stress and neurodevelopment in adolescence: Implications for risk and adaptation. In K. A. Miczek & R. Sinha (Eds.), *Neuroscience of Social Stress* (pp. 313–339). Springer International Publishing. https://doi.org/10.1007/7854_2022_302

Miller, J. G., Gillette, J. S., Manczak, E. M., Kircanski, K., & Gotlib, I. H. (2019a). Fine particle air pollution and physiological reactivity to social stress in adolescence: The moderating role of anxiety and depression. *Psychosomatic Medicine, 81*(7), 641–648. https://doi.org/10.1097/PSY.0000000000000714

Miller, J. G., & Hastings, P. D. (2019). Parenting, neurobiology, and prosocial development. In D. J. Laible, G. Carlo, & L. M. P. Walker, (Eds.), *The Oxford handbook of parenting and moral development* (pp. 129–144). Oxford Library of Psychology.

Miller, J. G., Ho, T. C., Humphreys, K. L., King, L. S., Foland-Ross, L. C., Colich, N. L., Ordaz, S. J., Lin, J., & Gotlib, I. H. (2020). Early life stress, frontoamygdala connectivity, and biological aging in adolescence: A longitudinal investigation. *Cerebral Cortex (New York, NY), 30*(7), 4269–4280. https://doi.org/10.1093/cercor/bhaa057

Miller, J. G., Ho, T. C., Kirshenbaum, J. S., Chahal, R., Gifuni, A. J., & Gotlib, I. H. (2021). Testing a developmental model of positive parenting, amygdala–subgenual anterior cingulate cortex connectivity, and depressive symptoms in adolescents before and during the covid-19 pandemic. *Biological Psychiatry Global Open Science, 1*(4), 291–299. https://doi.org/10.1016/j.bpsgos.2021.07.005

Miller, J. G., Vrtička, P., Cui, X., Shrestha, S., Hosseini, S. M. H., Baker, J. M., & Reiss, A. L. (2019b). Inter-brain synchrony in mother-child dyads during cooperation: An fNIRS hyperscanning study. *Neuropsychologia, 124*, 117–124. https://doi.org/10.1016/j.neuropsychologia.2018.12.021

Moffitt, T. E., Arseneault, L., Belsky, D., Dickson, N., Hancox, R. J., Harrington, H., Houts, R., Poulton, R., Roberts, B. W., Ross, S., Sears, M. R., Thomson, W. M., & Caspi, A. (2011). A gradient of childhood self-control predicts health, wealth, and public safety. *Proceedings of the National Academy of Sciences, 108*(7), 2693–2698. https://doi.org/10.1073/pnas.1010076108

Mwilambwe-Tshilobo, L., & Spreng, R. N. (2021). Social exclusion reliably engages the default network: A meta-analysis of Cyberball. *NeuroImage, 227*, 117666. https://doi.org/10.1016/j.neuroimage.2020.117666

Porges, S. W. (2022). Polyvagal theory: A science of safety. *Frontiers in Integrative Neuroscience, 16*. https://doi.org/10.3389/fnint.2022.871227

Pozzi, E., Vijayakumar, N., Byrne, M. L., Bray, K. O., Seal, M., Richmond, S., Zalesky, A., & Whittle, S. L. (2021). Maternal parenting behavior and functional connectivity development in children: A longitudinal fMRI study. *Developmental Cognitive Neuroscience, 48*, 100946. https://doi.org/10.1016/j.dcn.2021.100946

Puhlmann, L. M., Derome, M., Morosan, L., Kilicel, D., Vrtička, P., & Debbané, M. (2023). Longitudinal associations between self-reported attachment dimensions and neurostructural development from adolescence to early adulthood. *Attachment & Human Development, 25*(1), 162–180. https://doi.org/10.1080/14616734.2021.1993628

Reijntjes, A., Kamphuis, J. H., Prinzie, P., & Telch, M. J. (2010). Peer victimization and internalizing problems in children: A meta-analysis of longitudinal studies. *Child Abuse & Neglect, 34*(4), 244–252. https://doi.org/10.1016/j.chiabu.2009.07.009

Rohner, R. P. (1986). *The warmth dimension: Foundations of parental acceptance-rejection theory* (p. 248). Sage Publications, Inc.

Rohner, R. P. (2004). The parental "acceptance-rejection syndrome": Universal correlates of perceived rejection. *American Psychologist, 59*(8), 830–840. https://doi.org/10.1037/0003-066X.59.8.830

Rohner, R. P. (2021). Introduction to interpersonal acceptance-rejection theory (IPARTheory) and evidence. *Online Readings in Psychology and Culture, 6*(1), 1–65. Doi:10.9707/2307-0919.1055

Rohner, R. P. (2023, September 3). *Glossary of Significant Concepts in IPARTheory | Center for the Study of Interpersonal Acceptance & Rejection*. https://csiar.uconn.edu/glossary/

Rohner, R. P. & Ali, S. (2025). Interpersonal acceptance-rejection theory (IPAR-Theory): From conception through maturity. In Rohner, R. P., & Ali. S. (Eds.). *Global perspectives on parental acceptance and rejection: Lessons learned from IPARTheory* (pp. 3–38). Routledge.

Rotge, J.-Y., Lemogne, C., Hinfray, S., Huguet, P., Grynszpan, O., Tartour, E., George, N., & Fossati, P. (2015). A meta-analysis of the anterior cingulate contribution to social pain. *Social Cognitive and Affective Neuroscience, 10*(1), 19–27. https://doi.org/10.1093/scan/nsu110

Rudolph, K. D., Miernicki, M. E., Troop-Gordon, W., Davis, M. M., & Telzer, E. H. (2016). Adding insult to injury: Neural sensitivity to social exclusion is associated with internalizing symptoms in chronically peer-victimized girls. *Social Cognitive and Affective Neuroscience, 11*(5), 829–842. https://doi.org/10.1093/scan/nsw021

Sapolsky, R. M., Romero, L. M., & Munck, A. U. (2000). How do glucocorticoids influence stress responses? Integrating permissive, suppressive, stimulatory, and preparative actions. *Endocrine Reviews, 21*(1), 55–89. https://doi.org/10.1210/edrv.21.1.0389

Schulz, C. C., Klitzing, K. von, Deserno, L., Sheridan, M. A., Crowley, M. J., Schoett, M. J. S., Hoffmann, F., Villringer, A., Vrtička, P., & White, L. O. (2022). Emotional maltreatment and neglect impact neural activation upon exclusion in early and mid-adolescence: An event-related fMRI study. *Development and Psychopathology, 34*(2), 573–585. https://doi.org/10.1017/S0954579421001681

Shen, C., Ardid, S., Kaping, D., Westendorff, S., Everling, S., & Womelsdorf, T. (2015). Anterior cingulate cortex cells identify process-specific errors of attentional control prior to transient prefrontal-cingulate inhibition. *Cerebral Cortex (New York, N.Y.: 1991), 25*(8), 2213–2228. https://doi.org/10.1093/cercor/bhu028

Sheridan, M. A., Mukerji, C. E., Wade, M., Humphreys, K. L., Garrisi, K., Goel, S., Patel, K., Fox, N. A., Zeanah, C. H., Nelson, C. A., & McLaughlin, K. A. (2022). Early deprivation alters structural brain development from middle childhood to adolescence. *Science Advances, 8*(40), eabn4316. https://doi.org/10.1126/sciadv.abn4316

Spreng, R. N., Mar, R. A., & Kim, A. S. N. (2009). The common neural basis of autobiographical memory, prospection, navigation, theory of mind, and the default mode: A quantitative meta-analysis. *Journal of Cognitive Neuroscience, 21*(3), 489–510. https://doi.org/10.1162/jocn.2008.21029

Stroud, L. R., Foster, E., Papandonatos, G. D., Handwerger, K., Granger, D. A., Kivlighan, K. T., & Niaura, R. (2009). Stress response and the adolescent transition: performance versus peer rejection stressors. *Development and Psychopathology, 21*(1), 47–68. https://doi.org/10.1017/S0954579409000042

Stroud, L. R., Tanofsky-Kraff, M., Wilfley, D. E., & Salovey, P. (2000). The Yale Interpersonal Stressor (YIPS): Affective, physiological, and behavioral responses to a novel interpersonal rejection paradigm. *Annals of Behavioral Medicine: A Publication of the Society of Behavioral Medicine, 22*(3), 204–213. https://doi.org/10.1007/BF02895115

Sumter, S. R., Bokhorst, C. L., Miers, A. C., Van Pelt, J., & Westenberg, P. M. (2010). Age and puberty differences in stress responses during a public speaking task: Do adolescents grow more sensitive to social evaluation? *Psychoneuroendocrinology, 35*(10), 1510–1516. https://doi.org/10.1016/j.psyneuen.2010.05.004

Suveg, C., Braunstein West, K., Davis, M., Caughy, M., Smith, E. P., & Oshri, A. (2019). Symptoms and synchrony: Mother and child internalizing problems moderate respiratory sinus arrhythmia concordance in mother-preadolescent dyads. *Developmental Psychology, 55*(2), 366–376. https://doi.org/10.1037/dev0000648

Suzuki, H., Luby, J. L., Botteron, K. N., Dietrich, R., McAvoy, M. P., & Barch, D. M. (2014). Early life stress and trauma and enhanced limbic activation to emotionally valenced faces in depressed and healthy children. *Journal of the American Academy of Child and Adolescent Psychiatry, 53*(7), 800–813.e10. https://doi.org/10.1016/j.jaac.2014.04.013

Tan, P. Z., Oppenheimer, C. W., Ladouceur, C. D., Butterfield, R. D., & Silk, J. S. (2020). A review of associations between parental emotion socialization behaviors and the neural substrates of emotional reactivity and regulation in youth. *Developmental Psychology, 56*(3), 516–527. https://doi.org/10.1037/dev0000893

Telzer, E. H., Miernicki, M. E., & Rudolph, K. D. (2018). Chronic peer victimization heightens neural sensitivity to risk taking. *Development and Psychopathology, 30*(1), 13–26. https://doi.org/10.1017/S0954579417000438

Thayer, J. F., Ahs, F., Fredrikson, M., Sollers, J. J., & Wager, T. D. (2012). A meta-analysis of heart rate variability and neuroimaging studies: Implications for heart rate variability as a marker of stress and health. *Neuroscience and Biobehavioral Reviews, 36*(2), 747–756. https://doi.org/10.1016/j.neubiorev.2011.11.009

Tottenham, N., Hare, T. A., Quinn, B. T., McCarry, T. W., Nurse, M., Gilhooly, T., Millner, A., Galvan, A., Davidson, M. C., Eigsti, I.-M., Thomas, K. M., Freed, P. J., Booma, E. S., Gunnar, M. R., Altemus, M., Aronson, J., & Casey, B. J. (2010). Prolonged institutional rearing is associated with atypically large amygdala volume and difficulties in emotion regulation. *Developmental Science, 13*(1), 46–61. https://doi.org/10.1111/j.1467-7687.2009.00852.x

Uvnäs-Moberg, K. (1998). Oxytocin may mediate the benefits of positive social interaction and emotions. *Psychoneuroendocrinology, 23*(8), 819–835. https://doi.org/10.1016/s0306-4530(98)00056-0

VanTieghem, M. R., & Tottenham, N. (2018). Neurobiological programming of early life stress: Functional development of amygdala-prefrontal circuitry and vulnerability for stress-related psychopathology. *Current Topics in Behavioral Neurosciences, 38*, 117–136. https://doi.org/10.1007/7854_2016_42

Vijayakumar, N., Cheng, T. W., & Pfeifer, J. H. (2017). Neural correlates of social exclusion across ages: A coordinate-based meta-analysis of functional MRI studies. *NeuroImage, 153*, 359–368. https://doi.org/10.1016/j.neuroimage.2017.02.050

Weissman, D. G., Jenness, J. L., Colich, N. L., Miller, A. B., Sambrook, K. A., Sheridan, M. A., & McLaughlin, K. A. (2020). Altered neural processing of threat-related information in children and adolescents exposed to violence: A transdiagnostic mechanism contributing to the emergence of psychopathology. *Journal of the American Academy of Child and Adolescent Psychiatry, 59*(11), 1274–1284. https://doi.org/10.1016/j.jaac.2019.08.471

White, L. O., Bornemann, B., Crowley, M. J., Sticca, F., Vrtička, P., Stadelmann, S., Otto, Y., Klein, A. M., & von Klitzing, K. (2021). Exclusion expected? Cardiac slowing upon peer exclusion links preschool parent representations to school-age peer relationships. *Child Development, 92*(4), 1274–1290. https://doi.org/10.1111/cdev.13494

Williams, K. D., Cheung, C. K., & Choi, W. (2000). Cyberostracism: Effects of being ignored over the Internet. *Journal of Personality and Social Psychology, 79*(5), 748–762. https://doi.org/10.1037//0022-3514.79.5.748

Wölfer, R., & Scheithauer, H. (2013). Ostracism in childhood and adolescence: Emotional, cognitive, and behavioral effects of social exclusion. *Social Influence, 8*(4), 217–236. https://doi.org/10.1080/15534510.2012.706233

13

UNDERSTANDING THE CURRENT STATUS OF PARENTAL ACCEPTANCE-REJECTION FOR LGBTQ+ YOUTH ACROSS THE GLOBE

Kimberly Fuller

Lesbian, gay, bisexual, transgender, queer, and other sexual and gender minority (LGBTQ+) individuals experience the process of "coming out." Coming out is lifelong—LGBTQ+ people continuously disclose their identities to new people, including friends, siblings, and parents (Toomey et al., 2013). For many people, parents are among the most important and most difficult people to come out to. The importance of parents cannot be minimized—the role that families of origin, particularly parents, have cannot be replaced, even by chosen family (i.e., friends who become family) systems (Ryan, 2009; Shilo & Savaya, 2011). Studies consistently highlight the importance of family's acceptance in proximity to coming out and throughout the LGBTQ+ person's life as the family becomes more familiar with the identity and begins to understand the implications of choosing to be an affirming parent (Ryan, 2009). Many studies indicate both the benefit of parental acceptance on identity formation and mental health and the challenges of experiencing rejection from families. For those who face rejection, there are increased mental health concerns, including depression, anxiety, substance use, and increased suicidal ideation and suicide attempts (Haas et al., 2010; Human Rights Campaign, 2013; Ryan et al., 2009). Parental acceptance helps protect against these physical and mental health disparities.

There has been little empirical and practical application of interpersonal acceptance-rejection theory (IPARTheory) on the experiences of parental acceptance and rejection for the LGBTQ+ population. The two studies that have attempted to advance this literature (Davis & Anderson, 2021; Fuller & Rutter, 2018) only do so for LGB individuals and not transgender and

DOI: 10.4324/9781003441243-16

gender-diverse individuals. The latter two groups may experience parental acceptance-rejection in distinctly different ways. Despite the lack of implementation of IPARTheory in LGBTQ+ literature, the theory does align with LGBTQ+ people's experiences coming out to and living with families who might accept or reject their sexual identity. These familial experiences follow similar patterns as shown in the vast body of global research on IPARTheory conducted with a majority cisgender and heterosexual populations (Rohner, 2021). This chapter describes the current status of parental acceptance-rejection toward LGBTQ+ children across the globe and the impact of parental acceptance-rejection on the mental health and well-being of LGBTQ+ youth and adults.

Coming Out

Coming out is a critical stage in an LGBTQ+ individual's life. It marks the beginning of conversations and decisions to disclose one's identity with significant others (i.e., family, friends, peers). The decision to come out can be a challenging one because not all people within a LGBTQ+ person's life may be accepting and affirming. Notably, many individuals worry about the response of family members and friends (Ryan, 2009). Coming out is an important milestone for building self-acceptance (Cass, 1984; Ragins, 2004) by allowing LGBTQ+ people to live more authentically (Bosson et al., 2012). Choosing not to share this identity can significantly interfere with building self-acceptance and reducing internalized homo/bi/transphobia (Critcher & Ferguson, 2014). It can even inhibit relationship development and maintenance (Pachankis, 2007) and satisfaction (Fuller & Rutter, 2018). Choosing not to disclose or delay disclosure can also increase psychological distress for transgender and gender diverse (TGD) people who may anticipate rejection in the future when they feel ready to disclose to their families (Rood et al., 2016). This is even more true for those who have multiple intersecting minority identities (Chen & Tryon, 2012).

Rates of acceptance of LGBTQ+ people vary across the globe (Pew Research Center, 2020). Many western countries such as Spain, France, UK, Netherlands, Sweden, Germany, Canada, Australia, and the United States have fairly high acceptance rates—often over 70%. Those numbers are in stark contrast to countries across the globe, including countries in Africa (e.g., Nigeria, Tunisia) and Asia (e.g., Indonesia), which have less than 10% acceptance rates (Pew Research Center, 2020). Although many countries still have low acceptance levels, there has been a steady increase over the past two decades in most countries' acceptance rates of LGBTQ+ people (Pew Research Center, 2020). Even in countries like the United Kingdom, coming out to family as an LGBTQ+ person can influence the type and depth of relationships that individuals have with their parents. Less than a third of LGBTQ+ young adults have a very close relationship with their family compared to 50% of cisgender and heterosexual people. Slightly more than half of LGBTQ+ young people describe their family relationships as close, less than 20% describe them as not very close, and 4% describe their relationships with their family as not being close at all (Grossman et al., 2021). Only 9% of LGBTQ+ people feel like their families understand what is important to them in their life.

The Trevor Project (2022) reported that the age of coming out has decreased over the last decade. Individuals between 13 through 17 years old were most likely to come out around age 13, whereas those who were 18 through 24 were most likely to come out around age 16. Coming out at younger ages means that parents are likely to have an earlier awareness of their children's sexual and gender identities (Ryan, 2009). Younger LGBTQ+ adolescents tend to experience instances of rejection and internalized identity-based negativity and may be more sensitive than older youth to interpersonal acceptance-rejection. They are also more likely to have problems with depression, anxiety, or suicidal ideation (Baams et al., 2020; Russell & Fish, 2019). Research demonstrates that across the board, parents' responses to their children's sexual and gender identities can have a long-lasting impact on their long-term health and well-being. These outcomes are essentially the same as those reported in studies on parental acceptance-rejection conducted using IPARTheory as a theoretical basis.

Applying IPARTheory to LGBTQ+ Populations

IPARTheory's descriptions of the consequences and other correlates of interpersonal acceptance and rejection (Rohner, 2021) are consistent with much of the research on parental acceptance-rejection faced by LGBTQ+ individuals and their families. Elements other than *parental* acceptance-rejection in the theory could be applied to the experiences of interpersonal acceptance and rejection among LGBTQ+ populations (such as acceptance-rejection by peers, siblings, and teachers). I focus here on parents, however, because of their critical influence in children's lives (Rohner, 2021).

IPARTheory utilizes a multidimensional approach to study acceptance and rejection. Its personality subtheory focuses on the warmth dimension of parenting and the long-term effects of acceptance-rejection. Its coping subtheory focuses on affective coping versus instrumental coping, and why some individuals are better able to deal emotionally with the negative effects of perceived rejection than most individuals. Its sociocultural systems subtheory and model attempts to explain and predict major worldwide causes of parental acceptance-rejection, as well as to explain and predict major correlates of institutionalized expressive systems and of individual expressive behaviors. The remainder of this chapter discusses specific applications of these topics to LGBTQ+ populations.

Personality Subtheory

The basic premise of personality subtheory is that all people need to feel cared about by significant others in their lives (Rohner, 2021). Many LGBTQ+ people have a strong desire for significant others to support and nurture them in crucial moments such as coming out. Rohner (2021) theorizes that individuals' perceptions of their parents' actions can influence the internal psychological state of a person. These are often earmarked in LGBTQ+ literature as internalized homophobia/biphobia/transphobia. Often a parent's demonstration of acceptance through physical, verbal, and symbolic actions is appropriately interpreted by the child. However, occasionally what the parent intends as accepting behavior is not interpreted that way by the child. For example, some parents may believe that saying "I love you even though you are gay" is affirming, but the LGBTQ+ child may not perceive the statement as acceptance.

The Warmth Dimension

The warmth dimension of parenting describes psychological states ranging from acceptance to rejection that individuals may encounter with their parental figure(s) over time (Rohner, 2021). Although research has demonstrated that certain types of families, traits, and characteristics may be more or less likely to be accepting or rejecting of their children (D'Amico & Julien, 2012; Rohner, 1986; Ryan et al., 2009), little research from an IPARTheory perspective describes precisely how parents may support their children's sexual and gender identities. Below are two tables that depict potential demonstrations of acceptance-rejection. Table 13.1 describes how this may appear for lesbian, gay, and bisexual (LGB) individuals, and Table 13.2 describes how this may appear for transgender and gender diverse (TGD) individuals. Even though there is significant overlap between the examples in the two tables, there are specific differences between what LGB individuals experience compared to what transgender and gender-diverse people may experience.

Parents can demonstrate their acceptance of their child's identity in the ways that many parents of cisgender and heterosexual people do, such as hugging or kissing their child or attending events or activities that are important to the child (Rohner, 2021). LGB and TGD individuals may experience additional warmth when parents demonstrate thoughtful and

TABLE 13.1 Application of IPARTheory to LGB Persons: Warmth Dimension Depiction of LGB Parental Acceptance–Rejection

Parenting Behavior	*Observable behavior*	*Types*	*Example behaviors*
Warmth	Affection	Verbal	Say "I love you" (Rohner, 1986); proudly tell other people about child's identity (SAMHSA, 2014)
		Symbolic	Invite partner over (SAMHSA, 2014); go to PFLAG meetings (SAMHSA, 2014); defend child from school bullying (Ryan, 2009)
Hostility	Aggression	Physical	Kiss, hug, cuddle (Rohner, 1986)
		Verbal	Telling the child they are disgusting, gross, or sick (Ryan, 2009); using gay slurs (Ryan, 2009); calling their child's identity a lifestyle or choice (SAMHSA, 2014)
		Symbolic	So-called praying the gay away (Ryan, 2009)
Indifference	Neglect	Physical	Hitting child (Rohner, 2021)
			Refusing to talk about sexual identity (Ryan, 2009); keeping a distance from child (Rohner, 1986); not welcoming partners or friends when they come to the home (Ryan, 2009) Not acting on discrimination or harassment (Ryan, 2009); paying no attention to needs of the child (Rohner, 1986)
Undifferentiated rejection			Individual feels unloved, unappreciated, or uncared for despite lack of evidence (Rohner, 1986)

considerate actions that express affirmation of their children's identities. Whereas LGB people may want their family's aid in proudly sharing their sexual identity (e.g., sharing their child is gay), TGD individuals may feel more warmth if their parents do not share their sex assigned at birth except under necessary circumstances, such as with medical professionals (Andrzejewski et al., 2021). LGBTQ+ individuals may also feel accepted when parents help them reach out to affirming medical providers. However, transgender people may need more significant levels of connectivity to endocrinologists and surgeons who are trans-competent. Hence, having parents do the additional work of facilitating these appointments and financially supporting them is significant (Andrzejewski et al.,

TABLE 13.2 Application of IPARTheory to Transgender & Gender Diverse Persons: Warmth Dimension Depiction of Transgender Parental Acceptance–Rejection

Parenting Behavior	*Observable behavior*	*Types*	*Example behaviors*
Warmth	Affection	Verbal	Say "I love you" (Rohner, 1986); using the child's chosen name/pronouns; not outing their child unless necessary and beneficial (Andrzejewski et al., 2021)
		Symbolic	go to PFLAG meetings (SAMHSA, 2014); defend child from school bullying (Ryan, 2009); help child secure new clothing that aligns with gender presentation; establish and attend medical appointments relevant to transitioning (Andrzejewski et al., 2021)
Hostility	Aggression	Physical	Kiss, hug, cuddle (Rohner, 1986)
		Verbal	Telling the child they are disgusting, gross, or sick (Ryan, 2009); using transphobic slurs; calling their child's identity a lifestyle or choice (SAMHSA, 2014)
		Symbolic	Putting the child in conversion therapy or treatments to try to change the child
Indifference	Neglect	Physical	Hitting child (Rohner, 1986)
			Refusing to talk about gender identity; keeping a distance from child (Rohner, 1986); not welcoming partners or friends when they come to the home (Ryan, 2009) Not acting on discrimination or harassment (Ryan, 2009); paying no attention to needs of the child (Rohner, 1986)
Undifferentiated rejection			Individual feels unloved, unappreciated, or uncared for despite lack of evidence (Rohner, 1986)

2021). Even though these may be outstanding opportunities for parents to demonstrate acceptance, these are not the only ways that LGBTQ+ children may feel accepted and affirmed by their families. Even if parents put forward these efforts, LGBTQ+ youth may still perceive a lack of support or parental rejection.

There are four primary ways that LGBTQ+ individuals can experience a sense of rejection from their families. They may be defined as coldness/lack of warmth, hostility/aggression, indifference/neglect, and undifferentiated rejection. One of the most notable demonstrations of rejection is characterized as hostility/aggression, which can be shown through physical abuse such as hitting, kicking, and throwing objects or as verbal abuse such as the use of homophobic or transphobic slurs (American Academy of Pediatrics, 2021). LGB and TGD individuals may experience parental hostility or aggression in similar ways. For example, their parents may say they do not accept them and refuse to accept any potential partners. Parents may even become physically aggressive (Human Rights Campaign, 2013). TGD individuals may experience additional hostility/aggression when family members refuse to use their chosen names and pronouns or intentionally misuse the ones used by their child.

Parents can also neglect their children's sexual and gender identity. They may not ask about romantic relationships (Ryan, 2009) or be curious about the stages and processes the youth would like to undergo for transitioning (Andrzejewski et al., 2021). They may also not talk with the child when they are together or they may not discuss anything about the individual's relationships, gender, or gender presentation (Koken et al., 2009). Undifferentiated rejection is another form of rejection that LGBTQ+ people may experience. It is characterized by an ongoing pattern of emotional disconnect with the parent without any significant instances of abuse and neglect, but also no explicit instances of warmth and affection. For LGBTQ+ people, parents may comment that *choosing* their identity is choosing not to have a relationship with the family, which ultimately can lead to great social and emotional distancing within the family (Koken et al., 2009). Many LGBTQ+ people with rejecting parents experience a combination of these types of rejection.

Parental Responses of Rejection

LGB individuals often encounter heightened levels of rejection stemming explicitly from their sexual identity (Human Rights Campaign, 2013). Research consistently shows the profound impact of acceptance and rejection on LGBTQ+ youths' development (Haas et al., 2010; Ryan et al., 2009). That research tends to employ a variety of theoretical models to explain this phenomenon. Often the research focuses unilaterally on the perspective of one subset of the parent/child dynamic. Studies that focus exclusively on the perspective of LGBTQ+ youth themselves provide limited insight into familial experiences—for example, how families can foster acceptance and self-acceptance, and how acceptance-rejection may change over time (Saltzburg, 2004). Several studies have examined how family responses change over time (Grossman et al., 2021; Huebner et al., 2019). One of the studies found that parents of LGB youth continued to struggle more than two years after initially coming out, though at a lower frequency and intensity than when the youth initially disclosed (Huebner et al., 2019). A study on TGD youth and their parents looked at the difference between parents' reactions. This study found that even though both parents tended to become more accepting of their transgender youth over time, 53% of the mothers but only 45% of the fathers were accepting (Grossman et al., 2021).

A small number of studies have examined parents' cognitive and affective responses to learning about their child's sexual identity (Chrisler, 2017; Goodrich, 2009; Grafsky, 2014) and gender identity (Riley et al., 2011). Goodrich (2009) explored both parents' immediate adjustments in their parenting roles following the disclosure of sexual identity and the long-term consistency of parental responses. The author noted the many ways in which parents initially responded and continued to respond over time to their LGB child's identity. Chrisler (2017) analyzed key themes in the literature about parental responses to their child's LGB identity. The authors found that parents varied from skepticism, uncertainty of a child's identity, appraising the situation, responding, coping, and reappraisal. Riley et al. (2011) described the mourning and adjustment process that parents of transgender youth went through as they grieved the loss of one identity and—ideally—moved toward acceptance of the child's new identity.

These studies do not describe parents' *internal* feelings about their LGBTQ+ children. Instead, they more often focus on observable behaviors. Additionally, these studies very often reflect only parents who do not presently accept their child's sexual and gender identity. Despite studies on the child's perceptions of parents' responses and parents' reports of their child's identities, the concurrent perspectives and responses of both parents and children during and after coming out remain unexamined.

Mental Health and Parental Acceptance-Rejection

The increased discrimination, marginalization, and stigmatization of LGBTQ+ individuals contribute to increased mental health challenges. There is a negative correlation between the age of coming out and mental health (The Trevor Project, 2022). Fifty-six percent of LGBTQ+ youth who came out before 13-years-old have considered suicide compared to 42% who came out later in life. Almost half of all youth who came out before age 13 mentioned threats or actual harm related to their sexual and gender identity (The Trevor Project, 2022). There are also differences in discrimination as well with 83% of LGBTQ+ youth who came out before age 13 experiencing discrimination compared to 72% of people who came out later in life (The Trevor Project, 2022). Coming out early increases the duration and often the intensity of exposure to discrimination by peers and-family members.

Parental acceptance appears to mitigate this risk for younger people (The Trevor Project, 2022). The likelihood of suicidal ideation was reduced by over one-half among LGBTQ+ youth who came out before age 13 but had high family support. Building on this foundational work, a subsequent study by Ryan et al. (2009) examined three distinct strata of familial acceptance (low, moderate, high) and their interconnectedness with various health outcomes. Findings from the research underscored the fact that LGBTQ+ youth who reported higher levels of familial acceptance were predisposed to exhibit elevated self-esteem, augmented social support networks, and overall improved well-being. Additionally, negative correlations were established between high levels of familial acceptance and depression, substance use, suicidal ideation, and suicide attempts.

Ryan et al's study (2009) unveiled a troubling escalation in detrimental health behaviors such as suicidal ideation, substance abuse, and risky sexual conduct as rejection intensified.

For those whose parents were rejecting, these experiences were often nuanced and could range from subtle rejection to more explicit methods (Ryan et al., 2009) Individuals encountering moderate levels of familial rejection faced heightened vulnerabilities, notably in the form of depression and suicide attempts (Ryan et al., 2009).

LGB Health Disparities

Many investigations have shown the destructive impact of familial rejection on the mental health of LGB individuals and a negative correlation between parental acceptance and decreased mental health issues (Haas et al., 2010). Importantly, LGB individuals frequently internalize the deleterious physical, verbal, and symbolic manifestations of rejection, often conflating these experiences with their sense of intrinsic worth and value (Frost & Meyer, 2009). This phenomenon resembles the development of rejection sensitivity stemming from internalized rejection (Rohner, 2021).

The concept of rejection sensitivity provides a salient framework for explaining the genesis and experiential facets of internalized homophobia (IH) among LGB individuals (Baams et al., 2020). IH may be construed as the internalization of societal discrimination based on sexual orientation and manifested as hatred, dislike, or shame toward oneself (Frost & Meyer, 2009). Negative societal and media attitudes toward LGB people can often be perpetuated by family members, friends, and other significant figures within one's world (Frost & Meyer, 2009). IH can be reinforced even more by ongoing negative feedback throughout adolescence after coming out (Frost & Meyer, 2009). Because of society's emphasis on heterosexism, IH can be self-perpetuating (Meyer & Dean, 1998). When parents reject their children's sexual identity, it is not uncommon for LGB individuals to internalize this negative evaluation as an evaluation of their own negative self-worth and value (Frost & Meyer, 2009). This internalization may persist even when overt rejection is no longer evident, leading individuals to harbor feelings of inadequacy and self-doubt about their LGB identity.

Driven by a pervasive anticipation of rejection—even when no tangible evidence of rejection exists—individuals afflicted by internalized homophobia may grapple with reluctance in coming out and with disclosing their sexual orientation to others. The process of internalization can culminate in the adoption of heterosexist attitudes and ultimately, self-rejection of one's sexual identity (Frost & Meyer, 2009). In turn, this may result in strain and dissatisfaction within intimate relationships (Fuller & Rutter, 2018; Mohr & Fassinger, 2006; Otis et al., 2006).

Paralleling research on rejection sensitivity, research on internalized homophobia has demonstrated a pronounced association with difficulties in forming and sustaining intimate relationships (Coyne et al., 1987; Mohr & Fassinger, 2006; Otis et al., 2006). Individuals burdened by robust internalized homophobia often contend with ambivalence, interpersonal conflict, incongruous relationship objectives, and misunderstandings within their intimate partnerships (Mohr & Fassinger, 2006). The depression precipitated by IH can introduce feelings of anxiety, tension, and othernegative emotions into these relationships, perpetuating a cycle of miscommunication and perceived rejection that erodes the quality and satisfaction of these relationships (Fuller & Rutter, 2018; Mohr & Fassinger, 2006).

Transgender-Gender Diverse Health Outcomes

Research on TGD individuals has consistently shown that TGD youth experience worse health outcomes and more significant health disparities compared to their cisgender peers (American Psychological Association, 2015). Studies demonstrate that TGD high school students report three times greater risks of chronic mental health issues and are two times more likely to have poor general health concerns than cisgender peers (Rider et al., 2018; Veale et al., 2017). They are also less likely to have social support, even compared to lesbian, gay, and bisexual peers (Connolly et al., 2016; McConnell et al., 2016). These disparities likely stem from chronic stress due to stigmatization and oppression faced by TGD individuals (Bockting et al., 2013; Hendricks & Testa, 2012).

Parental acceptance and family support are protective factors for TGD youth (Shelton & Bond, 2017). However, TGD young people are less likely than cisgender youth to have strong family relationships. This may be due to parental rejection of the youth's gender identity, to the youth's anticipation of rejection, or to the same reasons that some cisgender youth do not have strong family ties (e.g., because of family discord, poor parental mental health, and youth behavior issues; Shelton & Bond, 2017). Parental rejection can be as varied as referring to the youth by their legal name despite knowing that they have chosen a new name, using incorrect pronouns, not supporting efforts toward the youth's transition (such as hormone replacement therapy or gender affirmation surgeries), or physically abusing the youth. Parental rejection can ultimately lead to enhanced social and economic marginalization (Klein & Golub, 2016), including food insecurity (Russomanno & Jabson Tree, 2020), housing insecurity and homelessness (Glick et al., 2019, 2020), incarceration, and physical violence and abuse (Bouris & Hill, 2017; Katz-Wise et al., 2018; Simons et al., 2013). This marginalization can also lead to higher risks of drug abuse and contracting HIV and other STIs. Furthermore, familial rejection can inhibit access to transition-related healthcare (Koch et al., 2020; White Hughto et al., 2017), which is especially likely for youth and young adults. Prohibiting transition-related care can significantly affect physical and mental health outcomes (Dickey & Budge, 2020).

Rejection experienced by TGD individuals may also add to an increased feeling of not belonging in their family, feeling as though they are burdening their family, and feeling a sense of hopelessness about their situation and future (Grossman et al., 2016). Some of these youth may even feel they are better off dead and consider suicide as their only way out of the situation (Grossman et al., 2016; Van Orden et al., 2010). Conversely, the benefits of supportive and accepting parents are essential for TGD health and well-being (Budge et al., 2018; Lefevor et al., 2019; Schimmel-Bristow et al., 2018; Shelton & Bond, 2017). Demonstrating support for a TGD individual's identity can be a crucial component of that support. This might include using a chosen name and the appropriate pronouns or pushing for more affirmative policies at their child's school. Acceptance of the youth's gender identity can even reduce the impact of trans-negativity encounters external to the family.

Positive family relationships have been linked to improved mental health outcomes (Ryan et al., 2009), reduced complications of chronic conditions (Leeman et al., 2016), and reduced health-risk behaviors (McCormick et al., 2016; Sieving et al., 2017). Transgender individuals with family support report increased quality of life, reduced perceived burden of a transgender identity, and fewer symptoms of depression (Simons et al., 2013).

A study conducted with Hawaiian natives found connections between family support and increased self-esteem, sexual self-efficacy, and delay of first sexual experiences (Stotzer, 2011). Family's appreciation and affection, particularly from mothers, are strongly linked to improved health and well-being outcomes (Bouris & Hill, 2017; Katz-Wise et al., 2018; Taliaferro et al., 2018; Taliaferro et al., 2019). The greater the maternal warmth experienced, the lower the frequency of suicidal ideation (Bouris & Hill, 2017). Additionally, when TGD youth were satisfied with their families they had less depression and fewer anxiety symptoms, less non-suicidal self-injury, and an increase in self-esteem (Katz-Wise et al., 2018).

The ways in which parents communicate with their TGD children is also important. Various authors (e.g., Bouris & Hill, 2017; Katz-Wise et al., 2018; Taliaferro et al., 2018; Taliaferro et al., 2019) have found that positive communication within the family is associated with positive outcomes such as feeling safe and supported at school, lower levels of depressive and anxiety symptoms, higher self-esteem, and greater resiliency (Katz-Wise et al., 2018).

Sociocultural Systems Subtheory

IPARTheory's Sociocultural Systems subtheory describes how variability in culture, religion, family values, socio-environmental, and diversity of life experiences are associated with the extent to which parents tend to be accepting or rejecting toward their children. Ethnic minorities, including immigrants who are highly religious and come from a lower socioeconomic background are less likely to be as accepting of their LGBTQ+ children than are other parents (Richter et al., 2017). This often results from the multigenerational transmission of family values (Rohner, 2021). The family's religion is a good example of this transmission. A study of the relation between religion and acceptance demonstrated greater acceptance of LGBTQ+ youth by people with no religion or religions like non-Orthodox Judaism than people whose families were Muslim or Orthodox Christian (Miller et al., 2020).

Cultural differences too make a difference in the likelihood of parents accepting or not accepting their children's LGBTQ+ identities. For example, a 2021 study of Greek LGB individuals (Drydakis, 2021) found that parental acceptance had increased from 2013 to 2018, but overall acceptance was still relatively low. A 2020 study of LGBT Chinese individuals examined disclosure rates and family's response to disclosure. Lesbians were significantly more likely to disclose to family members at a rate of 70% compared to gay, bisexual, and transgender individuals who reported less than 50% disclosure rates (Wang et al., 2020). All participants reported anticipating discrimination and disappointment from their families because of their perception of incongruence between being LGBT and societal norms and expectations. China's emphasis on men's responsibility to create a nuclear family and produce offspring may be a significant contributing factor for Chinese gay, bisexual, and transgender (GBT) men expecting familial disappointment and discrimination. A report from Thailand demonstrated the same type of family responsibility that delayed or prevented Thai LGBTQ+ persons from living authentically (UDNP, USAID, 2014). Hlalele & Matsumunyane (2022) conducted a study in Lesotho southern Africa. They found that most people in their sample rejected their LGBTQ+ children whereas some were marginally accepting. Biswas (2018) found in India that a major reason for LGBTQ people choosing to come out was an attempt to reduce family pressure to marry (Biswas, 2018). However, many LGBTQ+ people chose to keep their gender identity hidden. These studies indicate the role of culture in influencing both familial response, and LGBTQ+ individuals decisions to come out to their family.

Coping Subtheory

IPARTheory's coping subtheory describes how people cope with theongoing negative outcomes of rejection (Rohner, 2021). One element ofcoping—hardiness—tends to be associated with the potential of resiliency for LGB people (Figueroa & Zoccola, 2016) and may influence whether someone is an instrumental or affective coper. The levels of external social support may also influence how well TGD people manage familial rejection (Yadegarfard et al., 2014). The literature surrounding LGBTQ+ individuals who cope with family distress often describes the need to prioritize oneself (Bjorkman & Malterud, 2012; Hequembourg & Brallier, 2009), and to build more stable and solid relationships with other members of the LGBTQ+ community (Hequembourg & Brallier, 2009; Meyer, 2007).

Affective copers are typically people who have a reasonably healthy mental status despite their experiences of parental rejection. They have a greater ability than non-copers to connect to their resources and networks, and to create a better sense of community (Rohner, 2021). One of the skillsets that healthy LGBTQ+ people learn is the necessity to take care of their mental health needs by prioritizing themselves and their identities over negative responses of significant others (Bjorkman & Malterud, 2012; Hequembourg & Brallier, 2009). LGBTQ+ individuals can benefit from acknowledging their parents' decision to reject them and separating it from their view of self (Hequembourg & Brallier, 2009). Very often this is difficult to achieve without help from a mental health professional (Bjorkman & Malterud, 2012). Affective copers are also more likely than non-copers to reach out to their support systems and utilize them as supportive agents—and to seek out supportive people from new contexts such as LGBT centers (Cohen et al., 2006).

Instrumental copers may have difficulty finding healthy ways to manage their feelings of rejection (Rohner, 2021). They may focus on more task-oriented activities, such as being overly invested in a job or school. Despite the instrumental success they experience, they may not have worked to improve their emotional and mental health. They may be very successful individuals, but they have a greater likelihood than affective copers to experience mental illness, including depression, anxiety, and substance abuse disorders. And they may have increased suicidal ideation and attempts (Cochran & Mays, 2017; Fredricksen-Goldsen et al., 2013). Instrumental copers are more likely than affective copers to need tailored prevention, advocacy, and treatment to mitigate the development of psychological symptoms (Cochran et al., 2016).

Limitations of Current Measurement and Application of IPARTheory

The Parental Acceptance-Rejection Questionnaire (PARQ; Rohner, 2004) measures an individual's perceptions of parental acceptance and rejection. The measure assesses mothers' and fathers' behaviors individually, which is especially important for LGBTQ+ individuals as one parent—often the mother—may be warmer and more accepting than the other (Davis & Anderson, 2021). Three versions of the PARQ measure perceived parental acceptance-rejection: the Child PARQ, the Adult PARQ, and the parent PARQ. The Child PARQ measures youth's current feelings of parental acceptance-rejection, whereas the Adult PARQ measures an older individual's memories of parental acceptance-rejection in childhood. The Child PARQ may be particularly helpful for LGBTQ+ youth, with the current age of coming out being around 13 years old. The Parent PARQ measures parents' (mothers' and fathers') perceptions of their own accepting or rejecting behaviors toward their child.

One challenge of this measure is its limited adaptability for LGBTQ+ people who come out in adulthood. Many LGBTQ+ people wait until they have left the homes of their family of origin to fully live in their identity, arising out of safety concerns with disclosure (Morton et al., 2018; Watson et al., 2019). Older LGBTQ+ adults may also not disclose until later adulthood after their children have departed from the home out of a reluctance to disrupt the current family system. Currently, no measure exists to capture those experiences directly or to articulate the reasons why an LGBTQ+ person may choose not to disclose until later in life.

Another limitation of IPARTheory measures is their lack of items to assess the unique acceptance-rejection experiences of LGBTQ+ persons. For example, many LGBTQ+ individuals find their families to be supportive and accepting of them across school, friends, and life stressors, but their parents may not support or accept their sexual or gender identities. The measure may currently reflect one or both parents to be generally accepting, but this may be very different from the way the LGBTQ+ person experiences their parents' response to their identity.

Although Davis and Anderson (2021) proposed a Sexual Orientation Acceptance Questionnaire (SAQ) and tested it for internal consistency, the measure has not been integrated into IPARTheory. If an IPARTheory measure is developed for LGBTQ+ populations, careful thought must be utilized when selecting specific items to give to LGB versus TGD individuals because their experiences of parental acceptance and rejection tend to be divergent. Items specifically related to homophobic and transphobic behaviors and verbal responses affirming their identity and indicating love would be necessary to capture these experiences. TGD people should receive items related to gender-affirming care and the purchase of clothing and other items that align with their gender presentation. Additionally, the adult IPARTheory metric should include specific partner behaviors, such as their partner's treatment of them, potentially over-sexualizing their friendships, or instances of transphobic behaviors. This would ensure that both groups can be well studied on how their families may demonstrate acceptance and rejection.

Conclusions

LGBTQ+ people undergo a continuous process of coming out to significant others. Their parents are the most significant people whose reactions often have a life-long impact. Although minimally utilized in studying the process of coming out, IPARTheory is an applicable theoretical perspective to understand the sequelae of rejection and the protective factors of acceptance on LGBTQ+ individuals. Parental support can significantly lessen psychological distress and health disparities experienced by LGBTQ+ people, even when the discrimination and stigma are coming from external sources such as schools or peers. IPARTheory should be developed more thoroughly to capture the unique experiences of LGBTQ+ people with accepting or rejecting parents.

References

American Academy of Pediatrics. (2021). Lesbian, gay, bisexual, and transgender (LGBT) teens: Information for parents. Retrieved from https://publications.aap.org/patiented/article-abstract/doi/10.1542/ppe_document240/554/Lesbian-Gay-Bisexual-and-Transgender-LGBT-Teens

American Psychological Association. (2015). Key terms and concepts in understanding gender diversity and sexual orientation among students. Retrieved from www.apa.org/pi/lgbt/programs/safe-supportive/lgbt/key-terms.pdf

Andrzejewski, J., Palpate, S., Steiner, R. J., Boyce, L., & Johns, M. M. (2021). Perspectives of transgender youth on parental support: Qualitative findings from the resilience and transgender youth study. *Health Education & Behavior: The Official Publication of the Society for Public Health Education, 48*(1), 74–81. https://doi.org/10.1177/1090198120965504

Baams, L., Kiekens, W. J., & Fish, J. N. (2020). The rejection sensitivity model: Sexual minority adolescents in context. *Archives of Sexual Behavior, 49,* 2259–2263.

Biswas, M. (2018). Socio-economically convenient 'coming-out' decision of India's lesbian, gay, bisexual community. *International Journal of Research Culture Society, 2*(2), 324–337.

Bjorkman, M. & Malterud, K. (2012). Lesbian women coping with challenges of minority stress: A qualitative study. *Scandinavian Journal of Public Health, 40,* 239–244. https://doi.org/10.1177/1403494812443608

Bockting, W. O., Miner, M. H., Swinburne Romine, R. E., Hamilton, A., & Coleman, E. (2013). Stigma, mental health, and resilience in an online sample of the US transgender population. *American Journal of Public Health, 103*(5), 943–951.

Bosson, J., Weaver, J., & Prewitt-Freilino, J. (2012). Concealing to belong, revealing to be known: Classification expectations and self-threats among persons with concealable stigmas. *Self & Identity, 11*(1), 114–135. https://doi.org/10.1080/15298868.2010.513508

Bouris, A., & Hill, B. J. (2017). Exploring the mother–adolescent relationship as a promotive resource for sexual and gender minority youth. *Journal of Social Issues, 73*(3), 618–636.

Budge, S. L., Belcourt, S., Conniff, J., Parks, R., Pantalone, D., & Katz-Wise, S. L. (2018). A grounded theory study of the development of trans youths' awareness of coping with gender identity. *Journal of Child and Family Studies, 27,* 3048–3061.

Cass, V. (1984). Homosexual identity formation: Testing a theoretical model. *Journal of Sex Research, 20*(2), 143–167. https://doi.org/10.1080/00224498409551214

Chen, Y. & Tryon, G.S. (2012). Dual minority stress and Asian American gay men's psychological distress. *Journal of Community Psychology, 40,* 539–554.

Chrisler, A. J. (2017). Understanding parent reactions to coming out as lesbian, gay, or bisexual: A theoretical framework. *Journal of Family Theory & Review, 9*(2), 165–181. https://doi.org/10.1111/JFTR.12194

Cochran, S. C., & Mays, V. M. (2017). Advancing the LGBT health research agenda: Differential health trends within the lesbian, gay, and bisexual populations. *American Journal of Public Health, 107*(4), 497–498. https://doi.org/10.2105/AJPH.2017.303677

Cochran, S.C., Mays, V. M., Max, W., Stark, B., Hai-Yen, S., & Offen, N. (2016). A strategic approach to eliminating sexual orientation-related health disparities. *American Journal of Public Health, 106*(9), e4–e5. https://doi.org/10.2105/AJPH.2016.303271

Cohen, H. L., Padilla, Y. C., & Aravena, V. C. (2006). Psychosocial support for families of gay, lesbian, bisexual, and transgender people. In: Morrow D, Messinger L, editors. *Sexual orientation & gender expression in social work practice: Working with gay, lesbian, bisexual, & transgender people*. (pp. 153–176). New York, NY: Columbia University Press.

Connolly, M. D., Zervos, M. J., Barone II, C. J., Johnson, C. C., & Joseph, C. L. (2016). The mental health of transgender youth: Advances in understanding. *Journal of Adolescent Health, 59*(5), 489–495.

Coyne, J., Kessler, R., Tal, M., Turnbull, J., & Wortman, C. B. (1987). Family burden depression. *Journal of Consulting & Clinical Psychology, 55*(3), 347–352. https://doi.org/10.1037//0022-006x.55.3.347

Critcher, C., & Ferguson, M. (2014). The cost of keeping it hidden: Decomposing concealment reveals what makes it depleting. *Journal of Experimental Psychology: General, 143*(2), 721–735. https://dx.doi.org/10.1037/a0033468

D'Amico, E., & Julien, D. (2012). Disclosure of sexual orientation and gay, lesbian, and bisexual youths' adjustment: Associations with past and current parental acceptance and rejection. *Journal of GLBT Family Studies, 8*(3), 215–242. doi:10.1080/1550428X.2012.677232

Davis, K. C., & Anderson, J. L. (2021). The role of perceived parental acceptance-rejection on personality psychopathology in sexual orientation minority young adults. *Journal of Child and Family Studies, 30*, 276–291.

Dickey, L. M., & Budge, S. L. (2020). Suicide and the transgender experience: A public health crisis. *American Psychologist, 75*(3), 380–390. https://doi.org/10.1037/amp0000619

Drydakis, N. (2021). Social rejection, family acceptance, economic recession, and physical and mental health of sexual minorities. *Sexuality Research and Social Policy*, 1–23.

Figueroa, W. S., & Zoccola, P. M. (2016). Sources of discrimination and their associations with health in sexual minority adults. *Journal of Homosexuality, 63*(6), 743–763. doi:10.1080/00918369.2015.1112193

Fredricksen-Goldsen, K. F., Hyun-Jun, K., Barkan, S. E., Muraco, A., & Hoy-Ellis, C. P. (2013). Health disparities among lesbian, gay, and bisexual older adults: Results from a population-based study. *American Journal of Public Health, 103*(10), 1802–1809. https://dx.doi.org10.2105/AJPH.2012.301110

Frost, D., & Meyer, I. (2009). Internalized homophobia and relationship quality among lesbians, gay men, and bisexuals. *Journal of Counseling Psychology, 56*(1), 97–109. https://doi.org/10.1037/a0012844

Fuller, K. A., & Rutter, P. A. (2018). Perceptions of parental acceptance or rejection: How does it impact LGB adult relationship quality and satisfaction? *Journal of GLBT Family Studies, 14*(4), 317–336.

Glick, J. L., Lopez, A., Pollock, M., & Theall, K. P. (2019). "Housing insecurity seems to almost go hand in hand with being trans": Housing stress among transgender and gender non-conforming individuals in New Orleans. *Journal of Urban Health, 96*(5), 751–759. https://doi.org/10.1007/s11524-019-00384-y

Glick, J. L., Lopez, A., Pollock, M., & Theall, K. P. (2020). Housing insecurity and intersecting social determinants of health among transgender people in the USA: A targeted ethnography. *International Journal of Transgender Health, 21*(3), 337–349. https://doi.org/10.1080/26895269.2020.1780661

Goodrich, K. M. (2009). Mom and dad come out: The process of identifying as a heterosexual parent with a lesbian, gay, or bisexual child. *Journal of LGBT Issues in Counseling, 3*, 37–61. https://doi.org/10.1080/15538600902754478

Grafsky, E. L. (2014). Becoming the parent of a GLB son or daughter. *Journal of GLBT Family Studies, 10*, 36–57. https://doi.org/10.1080/1550428X.2014.857240

Grossman, A. H., Park, J. Y., Frank, J. A., & Russell, S. T. (2021). Parental responses to transgender and gender nonconforming youth: Associations with parent support, parental abuse, and youths' psychological adjustment. *Journal of Homosexuality, 68*(8), 1260–1277. https://doi.org/10.1080/00918369.2019.1696103

Grossman, A. H., Park, J. Y., & Russell, S. T. (2016). Transgender youth and suicidal behaviors: Applying the interpersonal psychological theory of suicide. *Journal of Gay & Lesbian Mental Health, 20*(4), 329–349. https://doi.org/10.1521/suli.2007.37.5.527

Haas, A., Eliason, M., Mays, V., Mathy, R., Cochran, S., & D'Augelli, A., & Clayton, P. J. (2010). Suicide and suicide risk in lesbian, gay, bisexual, and transgender populations: Review and recommendations. *Journal of Homosexuality, 58*(1), 10–51. https://doi.org/10.1080/00918369.2011.534038

Hendricks, M. L., & Testa, R. J. (2012). A conceptual framework for clinical work with transgender and gender nonconforming clients: An adaptation of the Minority Stress Model. *Professional Psychology: Research and Practice, 43*(5), 460.

Hequembourg, A., & Brallier, S. (2009). An exploration of sexual minority stress across the lines of gender and sexual identity. *Journal of Homosexuality, 56*(3), 273–298. https://dx.doi.org/10.1080/00918360902728517

Hlalele, D., & Matsumunyane, K. (2022). Sexual Diversity: Peer and family rejection or acceptance in Lesotho?. *Journal of Asian and African Studies, 57*(4), 635–649.

Huebner, D. M., Roche, K. M., & Rith, K. A. (2019). Effects of family demographics and the passage of time on parents' difficulty with their lesbian, gay, or bisexual youth's sexual orientation. *Archives of Sexual Behavior, 48*(5), 1581–1588. https://doi.org/10.1007/s10508-019-1430-9

Human Rights Campaign. (2013). *GrowingupLGBT in America: HRC youth survey*. Washington, DC: Author. Retrieved from https://assets.hrc .org//files/assets/resources/NCOD-Youth-Report.pdf?_ga=2.190843690.168437395.1500052736-1480285383.1500052736

Katz-Wise, S. L., Ehrensaft, D., Vetters, R., Forcier, M., & Austin, S. B. (2018). Family functioning and mental health of transgender and gender-nonconforming youth in the trans teen and family narratives project. *The Journal of Sex Research, 55*(4-5), 582–590.

Klein, A., & Golub, S. A. (2016). Family rejection as a predictor of suicide attempts and substance misuse among transgender and gender nonconforming adults. *LGBT Health, 3*(3), 193–199. https://doi.org/10.1089/lgbt.2015.0111

Koch, J. M., McLachlan, C. T., Victor, C. J., Westcott, J., & Yager, C. (2020). The cost of being transgender: Where socio-economic status, global health care systems, and gender identity intersect. *Psychology & Sexuality, 11*(1–2), 103–119. https://doi.org/10.1080/19419899.2019.1660705

Koken, J. A., Bimbi, D. S., & Parsons, J. T. (2009). Experiences of familial acceptance-rejection among transwomen of color. *Journal of Family Psychology, 23*(6), 853–860. https://doi.org/10.1037/a0017198

Leeman, J., Crandell, J. L., Lee, A., Bai, J., Sandelowski, M., & Knafl, K. (2016). Family functioning and the well-being of children with chronic conditions: A meta-analysis. *Research in Nursing & Health, 39*(4), 229–243.

Lefevor, G. T., Sprague, B. M., Boyd-Rogers, C. C., & Smack, A. C. (2019). How well do various types of support buffer psychological distress among transgender and gender nonconforming students? *International Journal of Transgenderism, 20*(1), 39–48.

McConnell, E. A., Birkett, M., & Mustanski, B. (2016). Families matter: Social support and mental health trajectories among lesbian, gay, bisexual, and transgender youth. *Journal of Adolescent Health, 59*(6), 674–680.

McCormick, E. M., Qu, Y., & Telzer, E. H. (2016). Adolescent neurodevelopment of cognitive control and risk-taking in negative family contexts. *NeuroImage, 124*, 989–996.

Meyer, I. (2007). Prejudice and discrimination as social stressors. In I. Meyer & M. Northridge, *The health of sexual minorities* (pp. 242–267). New York, NY: Springer.

Meyer, I., & Dean, L. (1998). Internalized homophobia, intimacy, and sexual behavior among gay and bisexual men. In G. Herek (Ed.), *Stigma and sexualorientation: Understanding prejudice against lesbians, gay men* (pp. 160–186). Thousand Oaks, CA: Sage.

Miller, K. K., Watson, R. J., & Eisenberg, M. E. (2020). The intersection of family acceptance and religion on the mental health of LGBTQ youth. *Annals of LGBTQ Public and Population Health, 1*(1), 27–42.

Mohr, J., & Fassinger, R. (2006). Sexual orientation identity and romantic relationship quality in same-sex couples. *Personality & Social Psychology Bulletin, 32*(8), 1085–1099. https://doi.org/10.1177/0146167206288281

Morton, M. H., Dworsky, A., Matjasko, J. L., Curry, S. R., Schlueter, D., Chávez, R., & Farrell, A. F. (2018). Prevalence and correlates of youth homelessness in the United States. *Journal of Adolescent Health, 62*(1), 14–21.

Pachankis, J. (2007). The psychological implications of concealing a stigma: A cognitive-affective-behavioral model. *Psychological Bulletin, 133*(2), 328–345. https://doi.org/10.1037/0033-2909.133.2.328

Pew Research Center. (2020). *The Global Divide on Homosexuality Persists*. Retrievedfromfile:///Users/kimfuller/Downloads/PG_2020.06.25_Global-Views-Homosexuality_FINAL%20(2).pdf

Ragins, B. (2004). Sexual orientation in the workplace: The unique work and career experiences of gay, lesbian and bisexual workers. *Research in Personal & Human Resources Management, 23*, 35–120. https://doi.org/10.1016/S0742-7301%2804%2923002-X

Richter, B., Lindahl, K., & Malik, N. (2017). Examining ethnic differences in parental rejection of LGB youth sexual identity. *Journal of Family Psychology, 31*(2), 244–249. https://doi.org/10.1037/fam0000235

Rider, G. N., McMorris, B. J., Gower, A. L., Coleman, E., & Eisenberg, M. E. (2018). Health and care utilization of transgender and gender nonconforming youth: A population-based study. *Pediatrics, 141*(3), e20171683. https://doi.org/10.1542/peds.2017-1683

Riley, E. A., Sitharthan, G., Clemson, L., & Diamond, M. (2011). The needs of gender-variant children and their parents: A parent survey. *International Journal of Sexual Health, 23*(3), 181–195.

Rohner, R. P. (1986). *The warmth dimension: Foundations of parental acceptance-rejection theory*. Beverly Hills, CA: Sage Publications, Inc. (Available as e-book from Rohner Research Publications, Storrs, CT).

Rohner, R. P. (2004). The parental "acceptance-rejection syndrome:" Universal correlates of perceived rejection. *American Psychologist, 59*, 830–840.

Rohner, R. P. (2021). Introduction to Interpersonal Acceptance-Rejection Theory (IPARTheory) and Evidence. *Online Readings in Psychology and Culture*, 6(1), 1–65. https://doi.org/10.9707/2307-0919.1055

Rood, B. A., Reisner, S. L., Surace, F. I., Puckett, J. A., Maroney, M. R., & Pantalone, D. W. (2016). Expecting rejection: Understanding the minority stress experiences of transgender and gender-nonconforming individuals. *Transgender Health, 1*(1), 151–164.

Russell, S. T., & Fish, J. N. (2019). Sexual minority youth, social change, and health: A developmental collision. *Research in Human Development, 16*(1), 5–20.

Russomanno, J., & Jabson Tree, J. M. (2020). Food insecurity and food pantry use among transgender and gender non-conforming people in the Southeast United

States. *BMC Public Health, 20*(1), 1–11. https://doi.org/10.1186/s12889-020-08684-8

Ryan, C. (2009). *Supportive families, healthy children: Helping families support their lesbian, gay, bisexual, and transgender (LGBT) children*. Washington, DC: National Center for Cultural Competence. Retrieved from https://familyproject.sfsu.edu/sites/default/files/FAP_English%20Booklet_pst.pdf

Ryan, C., Huebner, D., Diaz, R., & Sanchez, J. (2009). Family rejection as a predictor of negative health outcomes in White and Latino lesbian, gay, and bisexual young adults. *Pediatrics, 123*(1), 346–352. https://doi.org/10.1542/peds.2007-3524

Saltzburg, S. (2004). Learning that an adolescent child is gay or lesbian: The parent experience. *Social Work, 49*(1), 109–118.

Schimmel-Bristow, A., Haley, S. G., Crouch, J. M., Evans, Y. N., Ahrens, K. R., McCarty, C. A., & Inwards-Breland, D. J. (2018). Youth and caregiver experiences of gender identity transition: A qualitative study. *Psychology of Sexual Orientation and Gender Diversity, 5*(2), 273.

SAMHSA (2014). *SAMHSA's Concept of Trauma and Guidance for a Trauma-Informed Approach*. US Department of Health and Human Services.

Shelton, J., & Bond, L. (2017). "It just never worked out": How transgender and gender expansive youth understand their pathways into homelessness. *Families in Society, 98*(4), 284–291.

Shilo, G., & Savaya, R. (2011). Effects of family and friend support on LGB youths' mental health and sexual orientation milestones. *Family Relations, 60*(3), 318–330. doi:10.1111/j.1741-3729.2011.00648.x

Sieving, R. E., McRee, A. L., McMorris, B. J., Shlafer, R. J., Gower, A. L., Kapa, H. M., … Resnick, M. D. (2017). Youth–adult connectedness: A key protective factor for adolescent health. *American Journal of Preventive Medicine, 52*(3), S275–S278.

Simons, L., Schrager, S. M., Clark, L. F., Belzer, M., & Olson, J. (2013). Parental support and mental health among transgender adolescents. *Journal of Adolescent Health, 53*(6), 791–793.

Stotzer, R. L. (2011). Family cohesion among Hawai 'i's māhūwahine. *Journal of GLBT Family Studies, 7*(5), 424–435.

Otis, M. D., Rostosky, S. S., Riggle, E. D. B., & Hamrin, R. (2006). Stress and relationship quality in same-sex couples. *Journal of Social and Personal Relationships, 23*(1), 81–99. doi:10.1177/0265407506060179

Taliaferro, L. A., McMorris, B. J., & Eisenberg, M. E. (2018). Connections that moderate risk of non-suicidal self-injury among transgender and gender nonconforming youth. *Psychiatry Research, 268*, 65–67.

Taliaferro, L. A., McMorris, B. J., Rider, G. N., & Eisenberg, M. E. (2019). Risk and protective factors for self-harm in a population-based sample of transgender youth. *Archives of Suicide Research, 23*(2), 203–221.

The Trevor Project. 2022. Research Brief: Age of Sexual Orientation Outness and Suicide Risk. Retrieved from https://www.thetrevorproject.org/wpcontent/uploads/2022/10/October-2022-Research-Brief-Final.pdf

Toomey, R., Ryan, C., Diaz, R., Card, N., & Russell, S. (2013). Gender-nonconforming lesbian, gay, bisexual, and transgender youth: School victimization and young adult psychosocial adjustment. *Psychology of Sexual Orientation & Gender Diversity, 1*, 71–80. https://doi.org/10.1037/2329-0382.1.s.71

UNDP, USAID (2014). Being LGBT in Asia: Thailand Country Report. Bangkok.

Van Orden, K. A., Witte, T. K., Cukrowicz, K. C., Braithwaite, S. R., Selby, E. A., & Joiner, T. E. Jr, (2010). The interpersonal theory of suicide. *Psychological Review, 117*(2), 575–600. https://doi.org/10.1037/a0018697

Veale, J. F., Watson, R. J., Peter, T., & Saewyc, E. M. (2017). Mental health disparities among Canadian transgender youth. *Journal of Adolescent Health*, *60*(1), 44–49.
Wang, Y., Hu, Z., Peng, K., Rechdan, J., Yang, Y., Wu, L., ... Chen, R. (2020). Mapping out a spectrum of the Chinese public's discrimination toward the LGBT community: results from a national survey. *BMC Public Health*, *20*(1), 1–10.
Watson, R. J., Grossman, A. H., & Russell, S. T. (2019). Sources of social support and mental health among LGB youth. *Youth & Society*, *51*(1), 30–48.
White Hughto, J. M., Rose, A. J., Pachankis, J. E., & Reisner, S. L. (2017). Barriers to gender transition-related healthcare: Identifying underserved transgender adults in Massachusetts. *Transgender Health*, *2*(1), 107–118. https://doi.org/10.1089/trgh.2017.0014
Yadegarfard, M., Meinhold-Bergmann, M. E., & Ho, R. (2014). Family rejection, social isolation, and loneliness as predictors of negative health outcomes (depression, suicidal ideation, and sexual risk behavior) among Thai male-to-female transgender adolescents. *Journal of LGBT youth*, *11*(4), 347–363.

14

FROM NORMAL TO LETHAL

The Continuum from Parental Denigration to Parental Alienation

William Bernet and Mary Alvarez

Parental alienation theory (PA theory) addresses a phenomenon that sometimes occurs in children of separated and divorced parents. Parental alienation (PA) is a mental state in which a child—usually one whose parents are engaged in a high-conflict separation or divorce—allies strongly with one parent (the favored parent) and rejects a relationship with the other parent (the alienated or targeted parent) without a good reason (Bernet & Greenhill, 2022, p. 591). PA occurs when one parent (the alienating parent) influences or indoctrinates the child to fear and resist a relationship with the other parent (the alienated parent). Baker (2007, 2010) argued that parents who manifest alienating behaviors create a feeling of rejection in their children by making parental love conditional on the child's rejection of the other parent. Also, using alienating behaviors results in children internalizing the false belief that the alienated parent does not love or care for them, resulting in a perception of rejection.

Baker and Bernet proposed a five-factor model for the diagnosis of parental alienation. The model consists of the following five factors: (1) the child manifests contact resistance or refusal, that is, avoids a relationship with one of the parents; (2) the presence of a prior positive relationship between the child and the rejected parent; (3) the absence of abuse, neglect, or seriously deficient parenting on the part of the rejected parent; (4) the use of multiple alienating behaviors on the part of the favored parent; and (5) the child exhibits many of the eight behavioral manifestations of alienation (Baker, 2020; Bernet and Greenhill, 2022).

DOI: 10.4324/9781003441243-17

Not all children exposed to alienating behaviors reject the targeted parent. The children who do develop the mental condition of PA share certain behavioral characteristics, that is, Factor 5 of the Baker Model for the identification of PA. These behaviors include (1) a campaign of denigration against the alienated parent; (2) frivolous rationalizations for the child's criticism of the alienated parent; (3) lack of ambivalence toward both parents with one parent becoming all good and the other parent becoming all bad, that is, "splitting"; (4) the "independent thinker" phenomenon in which the child strongly denies being influenced by one parent to reject the other; (5) reflexive support of the favored parent against the alienated parent; (6) absence of guilt over exploitation and mistreatment of the alienated parent; (7) the use of "borrowed scenarios"; and (8) spread of the child's animosity toward the alienated parent's extended family (Gardner, 1992, pp. 63–92). It is important to note that not all children who manifest contact refusal were influenced to do so by the favored parent, and not all children exposed to alienating behaviors reject the targeted parent.

IPARTheory and Parental Alienation Theory

IPARTheory and PA theory have overlapping domains of interest. Both theories pertain to how children relate to parents and other significant caregivers. They both posit that parents and other adults influence—for good or bad—the behavior, attitudes, interpersonal relationships, and psychological development and functioning of children. To some extent, both theories have ways of quantifying parental behavior and its effects on children.

Unlike PA theory, however, IPARTheory focuses specifically on individuals' experiences of interpersonal acceptance and rejection, especially from parent(s). IPARTheory argues that parents may express their love (acceptance) physically, verbally, or symbolically by acts of emotional support, caring, nurturance, warmth, and affection. Parental rejection, in contrast, is manifested in physical, verbal, and symbolically hurtful behaviors such as (1) emotional coldness and lack of affection; (2) anger, hostility, and aggression (e.g., insulting, yelling, hitting, rude behaviors); (3) indifference and neglect (i.e., being physically or psychologically unavailable or not interested in supporting the emotional needs of the child); and (4) undifferentiated rejection (i.e., children believe their parents do not really care about them, want them, or love them without any behavioral manifestations from the prior three forms of rejection) (Rohner, 2021).

IPARTheory argues that children and adults tend the world over to react in ten specific ways when they experience rejection from people important to them such as parents. They tend to become (1) anxious, (2) insecure, (3) angry, hostile, aggressive, or have problems with the management of hostility and aggression, (4) emotionally unresponsive, (5) develop impaired self-esteem, (6) develop impaired self-adequacy, (7) become emotionally unstable, (8) develop a negative worldview, and (9) develop other cognitive distortions and become dependent or defensively independent depending on the form, intensity, and duration of rejection. They also tend to develop other psychological, behavioral, and physical health problems such as depression and suicidal ideation (Rohner, 2021). The effects of childhood acceptance and rejection tend to extend into adulthood (Rohner, 2021; see also Rohner & Ali, 2025, Chapter 1, this book). PA theory, on the other hand, has a much narrower scope of interest. It pertains chiefly to one type of parental behavior, that is, the methods by which the favored parent indoctrinates and influences the child to fear and reject the alienated parent. It also pertains to one type of outcome, that is, the child's intense rejection of the alienated parent.

IPARTheory and PA theory interact in a significant way. For example, IPARTheory has 35 self-report questionnaires in up to 78 languages and dialects that can be used in PA research. Especially popular are the Parental Acceptance-Rejection Questionnaire (PARQ) and the Personality Assessment Questionnaire (PAQ). The PARQ is used to quantitively measure aspects of PA such as the "lack of ambivalence" (Jaffe, Thakkar, & Piron, 2017, p. 1; Lee & Olesen, 2001, p. 284). Typical or nonalienated children usually experience minor ambivalence about parents and other significant individuals. That is, they realize that the mother has some strong points and some weak points, and the same goes for the father. Severely alienated children, in contrast, usually perceive one parent (the favored or alienating parent) in an overwhelmingly positive manner and the second parent (the rejected or alienated parent) in an extremely negative manner. This mental phenomenon is known as "splitting" (Vaillant, 1992). As noted earlier, splitting is one of the eight behavioral signs of PA in alienated children (Bernet & Greenhill, 2022; Gardner, 1992).

Administration and Scoring of the PARQ

The child PARQ is a self-report questionnaire administered to children and adolescents. Youth respond to it with paper and pencil or by computer. The standard (long) form of the PARQ: Mother version contains 60 questions about the child's mother; the long form of the PARQ: Father version contains the same 60 questions about the child's father. Youth respond to each item with one of four options: 4 = Almost Always True, 3 = Sometimes True, 2 = Rarely True, and 1 = Almost Never True. Some of the questions are phrased in a way that requires reverse scoring. Possible scores for the questionnaires range from 60 to 240. Low scores indicate the child's positive perception of that parent (i.e., perceived parental acceptance). High scores indicate a negative perception of that parent (i.e., perceived parental rejection).

The short 24-item version of the PARQ may also be used with children. Possible scores for the short form range from 24 to 96. It is sometimes more convenient to administer the short version because it takes less time to complete than the long version. This may be an important consideration if the participants are expected to complete several questionnaires for a research project. However, because of its greater length, the long version can provide subtler and more nuanced information than the short version (Table 14.1 provides information about interpreting PARQ scores).

The parent version of the PARQ is used with parents to assess their perception of their relationship with their child. And the adult version is used by adult offspring to reflect on their childhood experiences of parental acceptance-rejection. The PARQ has been administered to tens of thousands of children in more than 1000 studies worldwide. Most commonly children in those studies report experiencing significant parental acceptance, though a minority of youth in most studies report varying degrees of parental rejection. It is important to note here that the PARQ was not developed specifically for use in child custody evaluations or for aiding in PA identification. Its current use in these contexts illustrates how an important tool in IPARTheory has influenced a specific dimension of PA theory.

The degree of splitting among alienated children can be measured by the PARQ and is characterized by the PARQ-Gap (Bernet et al., 2018; Bernet et al., 2020). The PARQ-Gap is the absolute numerical difference between children's responses on the "PARQ: Mother" version versus the "PARQ: Father" version. If the PARQ: Mother and PARQ: Father scores are

TABLE 14.1 Interpretation of Parental Acceptance-Rejection Questionnaire (PARQ) Scores Based on Previous Research

PARQ (long form) (60 items)	*PARQ (short form) (24 items)*	*Interpretation of scores*
60–80 (Bernet et al., 2018)	24–30 (Alvarez and Turner, 2023)	Unusual. Extremely positive perception of the parent.
90–110 (Bernet et al., 2018; Campo & Rohner, 1992; Rohner, 2005; Veneziano, 2000).	35–45 (Artemis and Touloumakos, 2014; Aktar et al., 2023)	Child's perception of loving acceptance by the parent, a normal response.
120–140 (Rohner, 2005)	50–60 (Alvarez and Turner, 2023)	Child's perception of mild to moderate rejection by the parent.
150–190 (Rohner, 2005)	65–75 (Alvarez and Turner, 2023)	Child's perception of serious rejection by the parent.
200–240 (Bernet et al., 2018)	80–90 (Rohner, 2019)	Unusual. Child's extremely negative perception of the parent.

similar (as occurs in most loving, intact families), the PARQ-Gap is very low. However, if the PARQ: Mother and PARQ: Father scores are very different from each other, the PARQ-Gap is likely to be very high. For example, there could be a 90- to 180-point difference between them on the long version of the PARQ, or a 35- to 72-point difference on the short version.

The Continuum from Parental Denigration to Parental Alienation

The most important features of PA include the pattern of one parent's badmouthing and denigrating the other parent, and the painful dilemma for children caught between battling parents. Although both of these characteristics are very prominent in cases of PA, they also occur in other family scenarios. It is possible to construct a continuum of family dynamics that includes: normal family relations, parental denigration, loyalty conflict, mild PA, moderate PA, severe PA, and extreme PA. Extreme PA involves the death of a family member. This chapter explains the seven steps on the continuum from typical families through denigration to extreme alienation. The steps reflect increasing "doses" of parental denigration and other alienating behaviors. The early steps of denigration and loyalty conflict do not constitute PA, per se, but in some cases are precursors to its onset. Increasing levels of denigration lead to increasingly severe behavioral indicators of PA in children. This process may also be characterized as increasing levels of coercive control by the alienating parent. Favored parents use their children as weapons when they use coercive control to negatively affect the child's relationship with the target parent (Harman, Kruk, & Hines, 2018). This chapter discusses how the PARQ and PARQ-Gap can help characterize each step. PA theory researchers have data regarding typical PARQ scores of children for some of these steps. In other steps, we suggest how future research can fill in the missing data.

Normal Families

Typical children in loving, intact families perceive both of their parents in a generally positive manner. These children generally have PARQ scores on the long form ranging from 90 to 110 (Bernet et al., 2018, p. 780; Campo & Rohner, 1992, pp. 433–434; Rohner, 2005, p. 49; Veneziano, 2000, pp. 126–127). Alternatively, these children typically have PARQ scores on the short form ranging from 35 to 45 (Aktar et al., 2023, Appendix S1; Artemis & Touloumakos, 2014, p. 1237). Scores such as these reveal that children perceive both parents to be more-or-less equally loving, so their mother and father PARQ scores are close in value, and their PARQ-Gap scores are very low (Bernet et al., 2020, p. 1231).

Parental Denigration

Parental denigration refers to problematic interactions between married, separated, and divorced parents. In this context, Parent A engages in occasional badmouthing of Parent B. Typical examples of badmouthing are: "This parent said bad things about my other parent in front of me," and "This parent made me feel guilty if I enjoyed time with my other parent." Badmouthing tends to occur sporadically in the context of a low level of parental conflict. Rowen and Emery (2014, 2018, 2019) published several research studies regarding parental denigration based on questionnaires administered to college students. The authors drew an unexpected conclusion in their research when they reported that the young adults who experienced parental denigration tended to have a closer relationship with the denigrated parent than with the denigrating parent. These results are the opposite of what occurs in cases in PA, where children ally with the denigrating or alienating parent and reject a relationship with the denigrated or alienated parent.

Rowen and Emery wrongly concluded, however, that their data challenged PA theory, saying, "Perhaps most important, no support was found for the alienation hypothesis among mothers or fathers, married or divorced families ..." (Rowen & Emery, 2019, p. 13). Their three articles regarding this topic were seriously flawed because they conflated mild, infrequent levels of denigration found in their surveys of college students with the incessant, intense, and pervasive denigration that occurs in severe PA. Rowen and Emery's (2019) research would have been enhanced if they had administered the adult version of the PARQ to participants who reported mild levels of parental denigration. PA theory researchers would have expected to find a normal level of perceived acceptance by the denigrated parent (e.g., scores between 90 and 110 on the long form) and perhaps a slightly elevated level of rejection by the denigrating parent (e.g., scores between 120 and 130 on the long form). There would also likely have been slight differences between PARQ: Mother and PARQ: Father scores such that the PARQ-Gap would be slightly elevated. These predictions involve speculation, but they are hypotheses that can be tested in future research.

Loyalty Conflicts

Loyalty conflicts occur when parents attempt to enlist children's support and affection in opposition to the other parent. Generally, when children are caught in the battleground between the two parents, they initially attempt to maintain a good relationship with both parents. This is likely to create an uncomfortable state of cognitive dissonance (Festinger, 1957; Mills & Harmon-Jones, 1999). Children with severe loyalty conflict often say to themselves: "I'm unhappy when I'm with Dad because I miss Mom, and I'm unhappy when I'm with Mom because I miss Dad."

We are not aware of any research where the PARQ has been systematically administered to children with loyalty conflicts. However, if that were to occur, PA theorists would predict that the children would have slightly negative perceptions of both parents, perhaps with PARQ scores in the range of 120–130. These scores reveal that children perceive both parents more or less equally, so their Mother and Father PARQ scores would be predicted to be close in value but slightly elevated. Thus, their PARQ-Gap scores would also be minimal, perhaps ranging from 0 to 10 points (Bernet et al., 2020).

Mild Parental Alienation

Mild PA refers to cases where children say they do not want to visit the rejected parent, but when they do have parenting time with that parent they do just fine. The children appear to have a satisfactory relationship with both parents as long as they deal with only one parent at a time. The behavior of children experiencing loyalty conflicts and mild parental alienation may be similar in that both may be uncomfortable transitioning from the home of one parent to the home of the other. However, children with a loyalty conflict try to have good feelings about both parents whereas children with mild PA have already started to ally with Parent A and reject Parent B.

Alvarez and Turner (2023) administered the short form of the PARQ to court-referred children who manifested mild and moderate parental alienation. The mildly alienated children had low PARQ scores for the favored parent (short form PARQ, $M = 29.49$) and normal scores for the targeted parent (short form PARQ, $M = 37.71$). These scores indicated that the child was starting to ally with the favored or alienating parent. However, the PARQ short form scores for the favored parent and the targeted parent are close to each other, so their PARQ-Gap score was small ($M = 9.03$).

Moderate Parental Alienation

Moderate PA refers to cases where children say they do not want to visit the rejected parent, but are required to have parenting time with that parent anyway. During that parenting time, moderately alienated children tend to be oppositional and negative. However, there may be brief episodes when they are pleasant and enjoy time with the targeted parent. The transition from loyalty conflict to mild PA and then to moderate PA was described by

Klosinski (1993) who said that when children are caught in loyalty conflicts and can no longer bear the feelings of guilt, "A frequently observed defensive reaction of the child is a sudden and exaggerated taking of sides with one parent and turning against the other: resorting to unrealistic black and white, good and bad dichotomous thinking" (p. 561). These children resolve the extreme cognitive dissonance created by the loyalty conflict and give up trying to please both parents. They solve the dilemma by gravitating to the favored parent and rejecting the alienated parent.

Alvarez and Turner (2023) administered the short form of the PARQ to moderately alienated children. They found that PARQ scores for the favored parent (short form PARQ, $M = 29.14$) were slightly lower than typical; but the PARQ scores for the rejected parent (short form PARQ, $M = 66.16$) were much higher than typical, revealing the perception of significantly more rejection than acceptance. Their PARQ-Gap scores (short form PARQ, $M = 36.49$) were significant. As expected, the scores of children experiencing moderate PA were midway between those of mildly alienated and severely alienated children.

Severe Parental Alienation

Severe PA refers to cases in which children adamantly assert that they do not want to visit or have a relationship with the rejected parent. They may refuse to visit or have any relationship with that parent for months or years. Some severely alienated children do have parenting time with the rejected parent—for example, in response to a court order—but during that time, they tend to be persistently oppositional and negativistic. For example, they may stay in their bedroom during the entire parenting time, and continue to communicate with the favored parent through text messages and phone conversations.

Severely alienated children have been found to have significant changes from the normal range on the PARQ. Bernet et al. (2018, p. 780), for example, found that in cases of severe PA, the mean PARQ (long form) scores for the favored or alienating parents were extremely low (long form PARQ, $M = 64.87$, alienating mother; $M = 67.86$, alienating father), expressing an unrealistically positive perception of the alienating mother or father. The mean PARQ (long form) scores for the rejected parents were extremely high (long form PARQ, $M = 212.52$, rejected father; $M = 231.87$, rejected mother), expressing a seriously negative perception of those parents. Likewise, Bernet et al. (2020, p. 1231) found that the mean PARQ-Gap scores of severely alienated children were extremely high (long form PARQ, $M = 144.67$, alienated mother; $M = 167.21$, alienated father), indicating a high degree of splitting. They also found that a PARQ-Gap of 90 points separated severely alienated from nonalienated children with 99% accuracy.

Extreme Parental Alienation

Extreme PA refers to the rare circumstance in which one or more members of the extreme alienation triad are killed. According to Korosi et al. (2023), the possibilities are: "an alienated child killing their alienated parent; an alienating parent killing the child and then themselves; an alienated child or alienated parent becoming so hopeless and frustrated that they kill themself" (p. 117). Of course, when severely alienated children commit suicide, PA theorists have no way of knowing precisely what they were thinking. However, those theorists hypothesize that the children had become so depressed, angry, confused, and frustrated that they were no longer able to engage in extreme splitting as a way to deal with the conflict between their parents. Instead of allying with Parent A and rejecting Parent B, they gave up on both parents and felt they had no meaningful support from anyone. Of course, researchers have no way to measure PARQ scores among these suicidal youth. However, PA theorists predict that they had very negative perceptions of both parents at the time they ended their lives.

Discussion

The denigration-to-alienation continuum discussed here differs from the "continuum of child-parent relationships after separation and divorce" described by Kelly and Johnston (2001, p. 251). The Kelly and Johnston continuum consists of the relationships children might experience with their parents after separation and divorce: positive relationship with both parents; affinity with one parent; alliance with one parent; estranged from one parent; and alienation from one parent. Those authors emphasized several psychosocial processes that cause this diversity of parent–child relationships. The continuum of denigration to alienation described in this chapter, on the other hand, is a way to describe the psychological processes that children might go through as they experience increasing levels of indoctrination and coercive control from one or both parents.

The parental denigration to parental alienation continuum described here resolves the counter-intuitive observation of Rowen and Emery (2019), who argued that low levels of denigration cause the child to turn away from the denigrating parent. In contrast, they argued, high levels of alienating behaviors cause children to ally with the alienating or favored parent. However, this phenomenon is not counter-intuitive when one understands the difference between the low levels of denigration (studied by Rowen and Emery) and the pervasive, intense alienating behaviors (described in PA theory). It makes sense that children exposed to low levels of denigration are likely to ally with the denigrated parent. In contrast, children exposed to pervasive alienating behaviors are likely to ally with the alienating parent.

There is a dose–response relationship (or exposure–response relationship) as cases proceed from loyalty conflict to mild PA, to moderate PA, and finally to severe levels of PA. A dose–response relationship means that the magnitude of an individual's response is a function of the level of their exposure to a stimulus or stressor. Children on the continuum are exposed to increasing levels of parental coercion and indoctrination. The resulting dose–response effect is reflected in children's behaviors, clinical signs and symptoms, and PARQ scores (see Table 14.2). This dose–response effect helps demonstrate that the expression of PA in children is the outcome of continuing and increasingly pathological interactions between the alienating parent and the children. This observation is consistent with early research by Burrill-O'Donnell (2001), who compared the level of alienating behaviors on the part of the favored parent with the level of negativity expressed by the children. She found that "The more negative symptoms the parent had, the more negative the behaviors of the child" (p. 59).

Research reported in this chapter supports the value of using the PARQ as one component of a comprehensive child custody evaluation. The PARQ, by itself, does not create a diagnosis of PA. However, it can be used effectively as part of a comprehensive evaluation to examine children's perceptions of the parent–child relationship. For example, if the PARQ-Gap on the long version of the measure is very high (e.g., greater than 90) and the PARQ score of the favored parent is very low (e.g., less than 80), the profile is consistent with an extreme level of splitting and suggests severe

TABLE 14.2 Estimated Parental Acceptance-Rejection Questionnaire (PARQ) and PARQ-Gap Scores at Various Steps Along the Continuum from Parental Denigration to Parental Alienation

Step on Continuum	*PARQ Scores*	*PARQ-GAP Score*
Typical children	Normal for both parents.	Very small
Parental denigration	Slightly high for denigrating parent; normal for denigrated parent.	Small
Loyalty conflicts	Slightly high for both parents.	Very small
Mild PA	Slightly low for favored parent; normal for rejected parent.	Small
Moderate PA	Slightly low for favored parent; moderately high for rejected parent.	Moderate
Severe PA	Very low for favored parent; very high for rejected parent.	Very large
Extreme PA	Moderately or severely high for both parents.	Small to moderate

Note: PA = parental alienation. Some estimates are based on research; some on hypotheses or educated speculation.

PA. However, suppose the PARQ-Gap is high (e.g., 90 points), but the PARQ scores of both parents on the long form of the measure are elevated (e.g., 140 or more). In that case, the profile is consistent with the child feeling strongly rejected by both parents, which suggests a history of abuse and neglect (Bernet et al., 2020, p. 1231).

Empirical data are lacking for some of the steps in the continuum from parental denigration to PA. For example, researchers should measure PARQ scores for children who experience parental denigration as well as children with severe loyalty conflicts. It is also important to collect PARQ scores from children who experience mild, moderate, and severe levels of PA, as well as from children who experience mild, moderate, and severe levels of abuse and neglect. Continuing collaboration among IPARTheory researchers and PA theory researchers will strengthen the underlying evidence base of both developmental theories.

Acknowledgments

The authors appreciate the contributions of Christine Turner, MSW, J.D., and Ronald P. Rohner, Ph.D., to the development of this chapter.

References

Aktar, R., Sugiura, Y., & Hiraishi, K. (2023). "They love me, they love me not": An IRT-based investigation of the Child Parental Acceptance-Rejection Questionnaire (PARQ) with a Japanese sample. *Japanese Psychological Research, 65*(1), 21–36.

Alvarez, M., & Turner, C. (2023). Unpublished data.

Artemis, G., & Touloumakos, A. K. (2014). "They accept me, they accept me not": Psychometric properties of the Greek version of the child Parental Acceptance-Rejection Questionnaire –Short Form. *Journal of Family Issues, 37*(9), 1226–1243.

Baker, A. J. L. (2007). *Adult children of parental alienation syndrome: Breaking the ties that bind*. New York, NY: W. W. Norton.

Baker, A. J. L. (2010). Adult recall of parental alienation in a community sample: Prevalence and associations with psychological maltreatment. *Journal of Divorce & Remarriage, 51*(1), 16–35.

Baker, A. J. L. (2020). Parental alienation and empirical research. In D. Lorandos & W. Bernet (Eds.), *Parental alienation – Science and law* (pp. 207–253). Springfield, IL: Charles C Thomas.

Bernet, W., & Greenhill, L. L. (2022). The five-factor Model for the diagnosis of parental alienation. *Journal of the American Academy of Child & Adolescent Psychiatry, 61*(5), 591–594.

Bernet, W., Gregory, N., Reay, K. M., & Rohner, R. P. (2018). An objective measure of splitting in parental alienation: The Parental Acceptance-Rejection Questionnaire (PARQ). *Journal of Forensic Sciences, 63*(3), 776–783.

Bernet, W., Gregory, N., Rohner, R. P., & Reay, K. M. (2020). Measuring the difference between parental alienation and parental estrangement: The PARQ-Gap. *Journal of Forensic Sciences*, 65(4), 1225–1234.

Burrill-O'Donnell, J. (2001). *Parental alienation syndrome in court referred custody cases* (Doctoral dissertation). Northcentral University, Prescott Valley, Arizona.

Campo, A. T., & Rohner, R. P. (1992). Relationships between perceived parental acceptance-rejection, psychological adjustment, and substance abuse among young adults. *Child Abuse & Neglect, 16*, 429–440.

Festinger, L. (1957). *A theory of cognitive dissonance*. Stanford, CA: Stanford University Press.

Gardner, R. A. (1992). *The parental alienation syndrome: A guide for mental health and legal professionals*. Cresskill, NJ: Creative Therapeutics.

Harman, J. J., Kruk, E., & Hines, D. A. (2018). Parental alienating behaviors: An unacknowledged form of family violence. *Psychological Bulletin, 144*(12), 1275–1299.

Jaffe, A. M., Thakkar, M. J., & Piron, P. (2017). Denial of ambivalence as a hallmark of parental alienation. *Cogent Psychology, 4*, 1327144.

Kelly, J. B., & Johnston, J. R. (2001). The alienated child: A reformulation of parental alienation syndrome. *Family Court Review, 39*(3), 249–266.

Klosinski, G. (1993). Psychological maltreatment in the context of separation and divorce. *Child Abuse & Neglect, 17*(4), 557–563.

Korosi, S. A., Bernet, W., Graham, S. P., & Ross, D. (2023). Parental alienation: A violent and potentially lethal social and psychological phenomenon. *European Journal of Parental Alienation Practice*, 1, 114–138.

Lee, S. M., & Olesen, N. W. (2001). Assessing for alienation in child custody and access evaluations. *Family Court Review, 39*(3), 282–298.

Mills, J., & Harmon-Jones, E. (1999). *Cognitive dissonance: Progress on a pivotal theory in social psychology*. Washington, DC: American Psychological Association.

Rohner, R. P. (2005). Parental Acceptance-Rejection Questionnaire (PARQ): Test manual. In R. P. Rohner & A. Khaleque (Eds.), *Handbook for the study of parental acceptance and rejection*, 4th ed. (pp. 43–106). Rohner Research Publications.

Rohner, R. P. (2019). Interpreting the Short Form (24-items) of the Child and Adult PARQ. [unpublished manuscript]. Storrs, CT: Center for the Study of Interpersonal Acceptance and Rejection, University of Connecticut.

Rohner, R. P. (2021). Introduction to Interpersonal Acceptance-Rejection Theory (IPARTheory) and Evidence. *Online Readings in Psychology and Culture, 6*(1), 1–65.

Rohner, R. P. & Ali, S. (2025). Interpersonal acceptance-rejection theory (IPARTheory): From conception through maturity. In Rohner, R. P., & Ali. S. (Eds.). *Global perspectives on parental acceptance and rejection: Lessons learned from IPARTheory* (pp. 3–38). Routledge.

Rowen, J., & Emery, R. (2014). Examining parental denigration behaviors of co-parents as reported by young adults and their association with parent–child closeness. *Couple and Family Psychology Research and Practice, 3*(3), 165–177.

Rowen, J., & Emery, R. (2018). Parental denigration: A form of conflict that typically backfires. *Family Court Review, 56*(2), 258–268

Rowen, J., & Emery, R. E. (2019). Parental denigration boomerangs versus alienates: Parent–child closeness, reciprocity, and well-being using multiple informants. *Family Relations: An Interdisciplinary Journal of Applied Family Studies, 68*(1), 119–134.

Vaillant, G. E. (1992). *Ego mechanisms of defense: A guide for clinicians and researchers*. Washington, DC: American Psychiatric Publishing.

Veneziano, R. A. (2000). Perceived paternal and maternal acceptance and rural African American and European American youths' psychological adjustment. *Journal of Marriage and the Family, 62*(1), 123–132.

APPENDIX A

Glossary of Significant Concepts in Interpersonal Acceptance-Rejection Theory (IPARTheory)

Ronald P. Rohner

Note: All entries in this glossary are implicitly prefaced by the phrase, "In IPARTheory, the defined concept refers to…" Some of the concepts may be defined differently in other theoretical paradigms. See the References at the end of the Glossary to discover how the concepts fit into IPARTheory. Concepts written in italics within a definition are centrally important to that concept and are defined elsewhere in the Glossary. © 2004, 2021, 2024, 2025 by Rohner Research Publications.

Acceptance The warmth, affection, care, comfort, concern, nurturance, emotional support, or simply love that parents and others can feel and express toward their children, *attachment figures*, and others. Acceptance has two principle behavioral expressions: physical and verbal. Physical expressions of acceptance include hugging, cuddling, caressing, approving glances, kissing, smiling, and other such indications of endearment, approval, or support. Expressions of verbal acceptance include praising, complimenting, saying nice things to or about the child or other person, perhaps singing songs or telling stories to a young child, and the like. Acceptance may also be expressed by culturally approved symbolic gestures. Finally, acceptance is characterized by the absence or minimal presence of *rejection*.(See the *warmth dimension of parenting*)

Acceptance-rejection syndrome A relational diagnosis composed of two complementary sets of factors. First, four classes of behaviors appear universally to convey the symbolic message that "my parent…" (or other attachment figure) "...loves me" (or does not love me—i.e., rejects me). These classes of behavior include perceived *warmth/affection* (or its opposite, *coldness/lack of affection*), *hostility/aggression*, *indifference/neglect*, and *undifferentiated rejection*. Second, the psychological adjustment of children and adults (defined by the constellation of ten specific personality dispositions described in *personality subtheory*) tends universally to vary directly with the extent to which individuals perceive themselves to be accepted or rejected in their relationship with individuals most important to them. (See *syndrome*; see also Rohner & Ali, 2025, Chapter 1, this book).

Affection Observable behaviors that result when individuals act on their feelings of *warmth* or love. Affection can be shown either physically (hugging, kissing, caressing, comforting, and the like), verbally (praising, complimenting, saying nice things to or about the child or others, and so forth), or in other symbolic forms. These and many other caring, nurturing, supportive, and loving behaviors help define the behavioral expressions of *acceptance*.

Aggression Any behavior where there is the intention of hurting someone, something, or oneself. It is differentiated into physical, verbal, and symbolic forms. Physical aggression includes hitting, biting, pushing, shaking, pinching, scratching, burning, tying up, and the like. Verbal aggression, on the other hand, includes sarcasm, belittling, cursing, scapegoating, denigrating, and saying other thoughtless, unkind, cruel things to or about the person. Symbolic aggression includes the use of angry or rude hand gestures or facial expressions. Aggression is to be distinguished from *assertiveness*.

Anthroponomy The science of human behavior that searches for worldwide principles (i.e., *universals*) of human behavior—that is, principles of behavior and of human development that can be shown empirically to hold true for people everywhere regardless of differences in culture, race, language, ethnicity, gender, and other such defining conditions. *IPARTheory* and research illustrate the anthroponomical endeavor. (See *universalist approach; phylogenetic perspective; phylogenetic model*)

Anxiety Diffuse, often unfocused fear frequently evoked by the disruption or threatened disruption of an individual's relationship with an *attachment figure* (e.g., with a *parent* for the child or an intimate partner for an adult). (See *personality subtheory; psychological adjustment*).

Assertiveness Individuals' attempts to place themselves in physical, verbal, or social equality with, or superiority over another person. When one does this with the intent of hurting someone else, then the act becomes one of *aggression*. But generally, assertiveness is to be distinguished from aggression.

Attachment figure Any person with whom a child or adult has a relatively long-lasting emotional bond, who is uniquely important to an individual, and who is interchangeable with no one else. That is, an attachment figure is a *significant other*. But an attachment figure has at least one additional criterion not included in the definition of significant other. Specifically to be an attachment figure, as defined in IPARTheory, one's sense of emotional security, happiness, and well-being must be dependent to some degree on the quality of the relationship with the other person. As with all affectional bonds—such as those felt for significant others and attachment figures—individuals are likely to feel the need to establish at least periodic physical closeness or proximity to their partner, experience "distress upon inexplicable separation, pleasure or joy upon reunion, and grief at loss..." (Ainsworth, 1989, p. 711). Assessment of the extent to which an individual is a significant other or an attachment figure may be made by responding to the Intimate Partner Attachment Questionnaire (*IPAQ*), and the Intimate Adult Relationship Questionnaire (*IARQ*). An attachment figure in these measures is defined by an affirmative response to the question "Is your overall sense of emotional security, comfort, and well-being affected by your feelings about your relationship with your partner?" A measure of the intensity of attachment one person has for another is available in the Intensity of Attachment Scale (*IAS*).

Behavior observations (BOs) One of the *procedures* along with the interview (e.g., *PARIS*), and self-report questionnaires (e.g., *PARQ*), available to assess parents' accepting and rejecting behaviors—or individuals' perceptions of these behaviors.

Biological state Refers in the *phylogenetic perspective* and the *phylogenetic model*, to the complete range of genetic dispositions (See *genotype*) found in populations throughout the human species. It also includes biological structure and processes of the living body, for example the nervous system, the endocrine system, and our senses of sight, hearing, taste, smell, and touch. From a developmental point of view, biological state is more or less synonymous with maturation or organismic growth. Overall, "biological state" is humankind's complete biological—including genetic—endowment.

Cognition Mental activity including the capacity to know, comprehend, understand, reason, and remember. (See *mental representation; phylogenetic model*).

Cognitive Distortions Cognitive distortions refer to chronic thought patterns where individuals tend to inaccurately interpret events, the behavior of others, or their own personal dispositions in a negative way. This is sometimes referred to as "automatic negative thinking". Examples of cognitive distortions include *personalizing, rejection sensitivity, imposter syndrome*, and *negative worldview*. Cognitive distortions are often caused in childhood by the perception of parental rejection and the resulting *acceptance-rejection syndrome*. Cognitive distortions can also emerge—though probably in a less intense form—in the context of other troubled *attachment* relationships throughout the lifespan (e.g., by perceived rejection from an intimate partner). The more prolonged and severe the rejection is, the more likely it is that cognitive distortions will develop, and the more severe they are likely to be.

Coldness On the warmth/affection scale of the *warmth dimension of parenting*, coldness refers to the lack or absence (or perceived absence) of emotional *warmth*. (See *rejection*).

Community study approach Refers in the anthroponomical research design of *IPARTheory* to long-term ethnographic research within a given community in order to place styles of parenting and other relevant behaviors within their full sociocultural context. (See *convergence of methodologies and procedures; anthroponomy; multimethod research strategy; universalist approach*).

Control dimension of parenting A continuum of parenting defined at one pole by *permissiveness* and at the other by *restrictive control*. Intermediate between these poles are *moderate control* and *firm control*, which are sometimes combined to form *flexible control*. Conceptually, behavioral control has two components: (1) the extent to which parents place limits or restrictions on their children's behavior (i.e., the extent to which parents use directives requiring compliance, make demands, and establish family or household rules). Behavioral control also pertains to (2) the extent to which parents insist on compliance with these proscriptions and prescriptions. The concept of behavioral control does not refer to the methods or techniques parents use to enforce compliance with their proscriptions and prescriptions. This latter issue deals with styles of parental discipline (e.g., *physical punishment*). In *IPARTheory* research, behavioral control is measured most often by the Parental Control Scale (*PCS*) or by scores on the control scale of the *PARQ/Control*.

Convergence of methodologies and procedures The areas of overlap or convergence of results across two or more discrete *methodologies* or *procedures*, as displayed in Figures A.1 and A.2 below. (See *anthroponomy; multimethod research strategy; universalist approach*)

Differentiated sense of self (self-differentiation) The capability of individuals to (a) understand another person's feelings, thoughts, and motivations, and—crucially—(b) clearly distinguish or differentiate those dispositions from their own feelings, thoughts, and motivations,

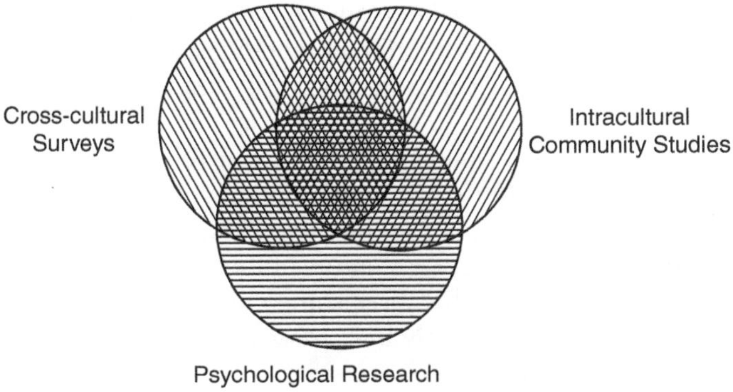

FIGURE A.1 Convergence of Methodologies.

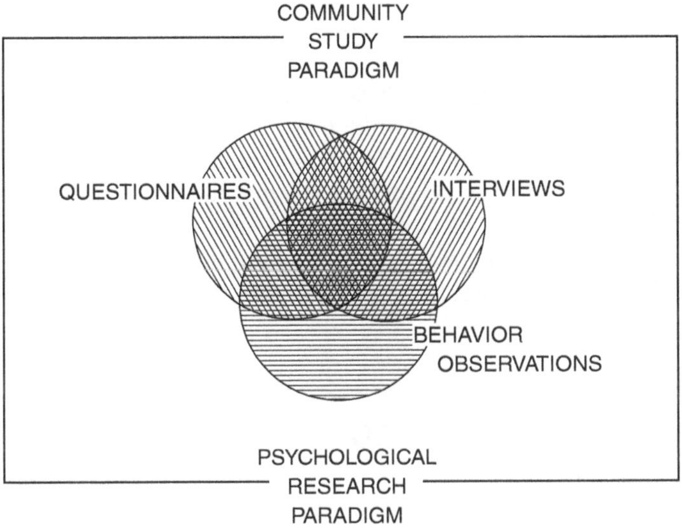

FIGURE A.2 Convergence of Procedures. © 2004, 2021, 2024 , 2025 by Rohner Research Publications.

especially in emotionally close relationships. In effect, self-differentiation involves the ability to maintain psychological individuality in the context of emotionally intense relationships. (See *sense of self*).

Copers, affective Those people whose emotional and overall *psychological adjustment* is reasonably good despite having been rejected as children. Affective copers are able to escape many but not all of the pernicious psychological effects of rejection as specified in *IPARTheory's personality subtheory* and in the *acceptance-rejection syndrome*. (See *copers, instrumental*)

Copers, instrumental Rejected persons who do well in their professions, occupations, and other task-oriented activities, but whose emotional and overall *psychological adjustment* is impaired as defined in *IPARTheory's personality subtheory* and in the *acceptance-rejection syndrome*. These individuals maintain high levels of task competence and occupational performance despite living with the expectable psychological consequences of parental rejection. (See *copers, affective*).

Coping subtheory One of the three subtheories of *IPARTheory*. It addresses the question: what gives some children and adults the resilience to cope more effectively than most with the experiences of perceived rejection? (See Figure A.3)

Counter rejection The situation where rejected individuals (e.g., adolescents) reject the other person in turn (e.g., the rejecting parent). Counter rejection appears to occur most often in the context of *defensive independence*. (See *personality subtheory*).

Culture Learned symbolic meanings approximately shared by most members of a society or by identifiable segments of the society (e.g., status groups), and generally transmitted from one generation to the next. (Note: this definition and concepts within it are amplified in Rohner, 1984.) The important point here is that the concept "culture" in *IPARTheory* refers exclusively to some degree of *consensus* about symbolic *meanings* among members of a population. The concept does not include behavior except insofar as behavior is motivated by or expresses

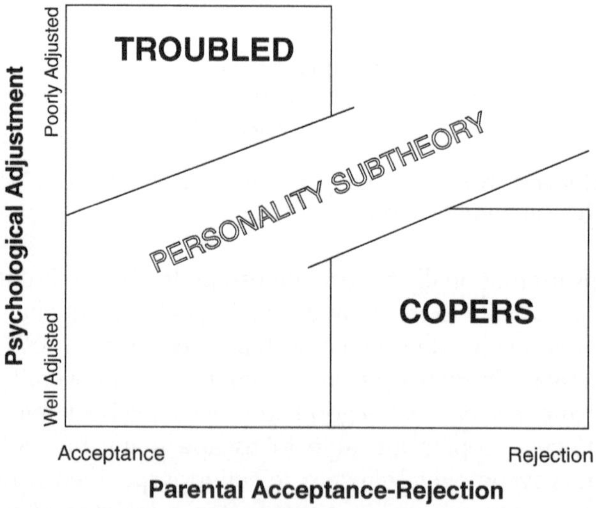

FIGURE A.3 Coping Subtheory within Personality Subtheory. © 2004, 2021, 2024, 2025 by Rohner Research Publications.

symbolic meanings. (See *culture learning; enculturation; equivalence of meaning; mental representation*).

Culture learning The process through which one becomes a responsible adult member of a given society, as defined by the norms of that society. (See *anthroponomy; culture; enculturation*; the *universalist approach*).

Defensive independence The commonplace tendency for seriously rejected persons to make fewer and fewer bids over time for *positive response* (See *dependence*) because of their growing anger and increasing emotional unresponsiveness. Many defensively independent persons say, in effect, "To hell with you! I don't need you. I don't need anybody!" Defensive independence is one way many rejected persons attempt to defend themselves against further hurt of rejection in situations over which they feel they have little control. Defensive independence is like healthy *independence* in that individuals make relatively few behavioral bids for positive response. But it is unlike healthy independence in that defensively independent people continue to emotionally crave positive response, though they sometimes do not recognize it. Indeed, because of the overlay of anger, distrust, and other negative emotions generated by chronic rejection, defensively independent individuals often actively deny their need for love, support, encouragement, sympathy, and other forms of positive response. (See *acceptance-rejection syndrome; personality subtheory*).

Dependence The internal, psychologically felt wish or yearning for emotional (vs. instrumental or task oriented) support, care, comfort, attention, nurturance, and similar responses from *significant others* and *attachment figures*. Dependence in IPARTheory also refers to the actual behavioral bids individuals make for such responsiveness. For young children, these bids may include clinging to parents, whining or crying when parents unexpectedly depart, and seeking physical proximity with them when they return. Older children and adults may express their need for positive response more symbolically—especially in times of distress—by seeking reassurance, approval, or support, as well as comfort, affection, or solace from people who are important to them—particularly from parents for youths, and from nonparental significant others for adults. Dependence in *IPARTheory* is construed as a continuum, with *independence* defining one end of the continuum and dependence the other. (See *acceptance-rejection syndrome; personality subtheory*) (See Figure A.4).

Emotional dysregulation Inability to effectively manage emotional states, resulting in inappropriately intense and often prolonged emotional reactions such as uncontrolled angry outbursts; inability to exert reasonable control over emotions and to express emotions appropriately in most situations. See also *emotional stability*.

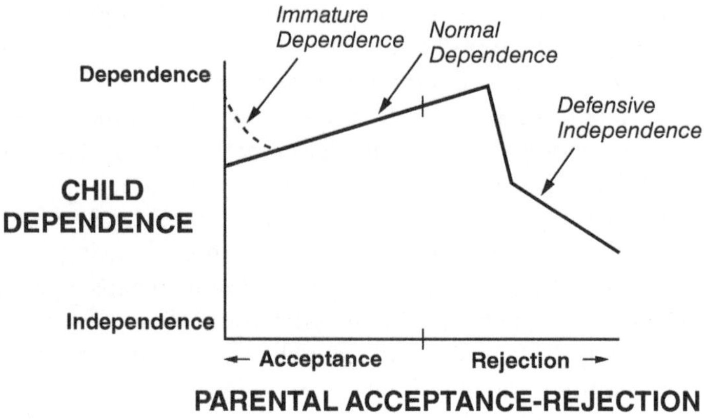

FIGURE A.4 The Dependency Curve in IPARTheory. © 2004, 2021, 2024, 2025 by Rohner Research Publications.

Emotional insecurity An individual's feelings of anxious distress, unease, uncertainty, or nervousness about being vulnerable in a desired relationship with a significant other (e.g., with an attachment figure), or in one's abilities, or goals.

Emotional responsiveness Persons' ability to express their emotions freely and openly. Emotional responsiveness is revealed by the spontaneity and ease with which a person is able to respond emotionally to another person, the extent to which the individual—adult or child—feels comfortable forming warm, intimate, involved, lasting, and non-defensive attachments with other people, attachments that are untroubled by emotional wariness, constriction, or lack of trust. The interpersonal relationships of emotionally responsive people tend to be close and personal, and such people have little trouble responding to the friendship advances of others. In contrast, emotionally unresponsive people are emotionally insulated from others. They have restricted and often only defensive emotional involvement with others. They may, however, be sociable and friendly, but friendliness is not to be confused with the ability to enter into intimate relationships. Some people who are friendly are impaired in their capacity to have intimate, involved, non-defensive relationships; their relationships tend to be non-personal and somewhat distant emotionally. (See *acceptance-rejection syndrome; personality subtheory*).

Emotional stability Individuals' steadiness of mood, their ability to withstand minor setbacks, failures, difficulties, and other stresses without becoming upset emotionally. Emotionally stable persons tolerate minor stresses and strains of day to day living without becoming emotionally upset, anxious, nervous, tense, or angry. They are able to maintain composure under minor emotional stress. They are fairly constant in their basic mood, and they generally revert quickly to that state following those occasions when they have experienced considerable stress or have been exceptionally provoked. The unstable person, on the other hand, is subject to fairly wide, frequent, and often unpredictable mood shifts that may swing from pole to pole. IPARTheory's conception of *emotional instability* includes:

1 Frequent shifts in emotion.
2 High emotional intensity.
3 Rapid rise time in the onset of emotion.
4 Slow rate of return to emotional baseline.
5 Excessive reactivity to negative psychosocial cues.
6 Random, chaotic, or rapidly cycling fluctuation in affect (See *acceptance-rejection syndrome; personality subtheory*).

Enculturation The process of learning to become a responsible adult member of a society as defined by the norms of that society. (See *culture, culture learning*).

Equivalence of meaning Refers to qualitatively different symbolic behaviors that share essentially the same underlying meaning. For example (1) receiving a peeled and segmented orange from a parent in West Bengal has much the same symbolic meaning as verbally praising a child in North America; (2) hissing at a woman in St. Kitts, West Indies is roughly equivalent to giving a wolf-whistle in the in the US—both behaviors express a man's sexual admiration for a woman. In cross-cultural and multi-ethnic studies of parental acceptance-rejection one must strive to be sensitive to issues regarding the equivalence of meaning. (See *culture*).

Experience Refers in IPARTheory's *phylogenetic perspective* and the *phylogenetic model* to anything that individuals perceive or anything to which they react as living organisms. It includes experiences with the physical world, the social or interpersonal world, and very importantly, with oneself, including one's inner world. Also included in the concept of experience is a person's total history of experiences, probably from the moment of conception but certainly from birth onward. It also includes the kinds of experiences called "learning," including *culture learning* (See *culture*).

Expressive behaviors Refer in the *sociocultural systems model* to beliefs and behaviors of individuals that express or reflect their internal psychological states. For example, why do some people prefer simplicity in art whereas others prefer more complex art? Or, why do some believe God is harsh and punitive whereas others believe God is warm and loving—and others do not believe in God at all? These and many other expressive beliefs, preferences, and behaviors tend worldwide to be reliably associated with childhood experiences of parental acceptance-rejection. (See *sociocultural systems subtheory; universals in human behavior*).

Fear of intimacy Refers in IPARTheory to the condition where individuals are afraid to form—or are anxious about forming—a personal or intimate relationship with another person, especially a person who is important to them. More specifically, the concept refers in IPARTheory to an individual's reluctance or anxiousness about exchanging thoughts and feelings of a deeply personal nature with someone, especially with a *significant other*. Self-disclosure of deeply personal information leaves the individual vulnerable or at risk for being hurt emotionally or in some other way by the other person.

Firm control Conditions where parents exercise firm but not rigid or moment-by-moment control over children's behavior. Children's (often selfish) demands are effectively resisted. Parents exert firm control at times of parent-child disagreement, but do not hem in the child with many restrictions. Children's behavior is guided by regimen and parental intervention. (See the *control dimension of parenting*).

Flexible control The portion of the *control dimension of parenting* that includes *moderate control* and *firm control* (but excludes *permissiveness* and *restrictive control*).

Forgiveness Forgiveness in IPARTheory refers to dispositional forgiveness, that is, to an individual's general, long-term tendency to forgive interpersonal offenses. More specifically, IPARTheory adopts the American Psychological Association's (VandenBos, 2007) definition of forgiveness which states that forgiveness refers to,

> Willfully putting aside feelings of resentment toward an individual who has committed a wrong, been unfair or hurtful, or otherwise harmed one in some way. Forgiveness is not equated with reconciliation or excusing another, and it's not merely accepting what happened or ceasing to be angry. Rather, it involves a voluntary transformation of one's feelings, attitudes, and behavior toward the individual, so that one is no longer dominated by resentment and can express compassion, generosity, or the like toward the individual.
>
> *(p. 385)*

As such, forgiveness tends to be associated with a reduction of negative emotions such as anger, hostility, resentment, and bitterness following a perceived offense it is also likely to be associated with a greater sense of personal and relational well-being than is characteristic of individuals who are unable or unwilling to be forgiving. Individuals who are dispositionally forgiving tend not to be vengeful. *(See Vengeance).*

Genotype The complete genetic endowment of the individual. (See *phylogenetic model; phylogenetic perspective*).

Holocultural method A paradigm of research for testing hypotheses "by means of correlations found in a worldwide, comparative study whose units of study are entire societies or cultures, and whose sampling universe is either (a) all known cultures… or (b) all known primitive tribes" (Naroll, Michik, & Naroll, 1976).

Hostility An internal or emotional feeling of enmity, anger, or resentment. Hostility is a principal motivator of *aggression*. (See *aggression; personality subtheory*; the *warmth dimension of parenting*).

Idiographic A focus on the unique, individual case (versus attempting to generalize to the larger class of which the case is an element). Idiographic contrasts with *nomothetic*. IPARTheory's anthroponomical emphasis is nomothetic. (See *anthroponomy; universalist approach*).

Immature dependence High levels of parental warmth and affection combined with *intrusive parental control*—that is, moment-by-moment control over and manipulation of a child's behavior—are likely to produce an especially noticeable spiking in the dependency curve (see Figure A.4). That is, parents who continually say, in effect, "Oh, Honey, don't do that! You might hurt yourself. Let mommy do it for you," are likely to reinforce the child's dependency needs at the same time they interfere with the child's normal exploration and self-testing. Thus these children often do not develop a full sense of age-appropriate competence, mastery, and a realistic sense of their own limitations. The parent reinforces an infantalizing form of dependency. In *IPARTheory* the form of parenting producing this immature dependency is sometimes called *smother love* or "smother mothering." (See *dependence; personality subtheory*)

Imposter syndrome Feelings of personal inadequacy and incompetence despite objective evidence to the contrary. Persons experiencing the syndrome typically see themselves as being fake. They are often unable to emotionally recognize or acknowledge their own accomplishments even though others do. And they are frequently fearful that others will see through their "façade" and recognize them to be the fraud they believe themselves to be. In fact, they often say to themselves something like "I'm a total fraud, and sooner or later people are going to find out".

Independence An individual's relative freedom from the felt-need for *positive response*. That is, the independent person is one who does not often feel the need to rely on others for emotional support, encouragement, reassurance, comfort, and so forth. Emotionally healthy individuals are able to make these bids from time to time as needed. The important issue is how often and how intensely they feel the need for such positive response. Independence is distinguished in IPARTheory from *self-reliance*. (See *dependence; defensive independence; personality subtheory*).

Indeterminance in human behavior The view held in *IPARTheory* that, by their very nature, human behavior and development are to some degree indeterminate and therefore probabilistic; they do not follow strict laws or forces such as those postulated in Newtonian physics. Rather, IPARTheory postulates that mental activity (See *mental representation*) coordinates all human experience. That is, *experience* is given meaning through mental activity. Experience is thus susceptible to many interpretations. Individual variability in the interpretation of experience may be a major source of partial indeterminance of behavior and development. This variability in the interpretation of experience contributes to IPARTheory's emphasis on a *phenomenological perspective*. (See *culture*; the *probability model; universals in human behavior*).

Indifference An emotional state characterized by a lack of concern for or interest in an individual, or not really caring about that person. (See *neglect*; the *warmth dimension of parenting*).

Insecurity Apprehensiveness and anxiousness often evoked by the disruption or threatened disruption of an individual's relationship with a *significant other* or *attachment figure* (e.g., with a parent for the child or with an intimate partner for an adult). (See *personality subtheory; psychological adjustment*).

Institutionalized expressive systems Refer in the *sociocultural systems model* (see Figure A.6) to ubiquitous but essentially nonsurvival oriented features of a society such as a people's religious beliefs, artistic and musical traditions, their games, folklore, and the like. (See *culture; expressive behaviors; sociocultural systems subtheory*).

Intracultural variability The natural variation that occurs with respect to almost any given behavior, belief, or other human characteristic in a given sociocultural system. In IPARTheory research—as in all anthroponomical investigations—one must examine intracultural variability as well as cross-cultural variability. (See *anthroponomy; culture; universalist approach*)

Interpersonal Acceptance-Rejection Theory See *IPARTheory*.

Interpersonal Rejection Sensitivity (IRS) A heightened readiness or disposition to perceive negative or hurtful intent in the behavior of others, even when no such intent is present. IRS also includes a readiness to interpret the ambiguous behavior of others as being intentionally hurtful in some way. As such, it involves hypervigilance or watchfulness for the possibility of being criticized, ridiculed, slighted, disrespected, minimized, ignored, excluded, or rejected in some other way. As construed in IPARTheory, IRS is associated with the experience of hurt feelings or emotional pain, including but not limited to sadness, dejection, depression, anger, and irritation resulting from the real or imagined rejection by others. (See *Rejection Expectancy*).

Intrusive control A form of behavioral control (usually firm or restrictive) where parents intrude into the child's activities without regard to the child's feelings or needs. Intrusive control tends to be motivated more by the parent's own personal needs or wishes than by a realistic need to monitor or control the child's actions. Intrusive or interfering parents impose their will on the child with little regard for the child's own emotional state or current activity. (See *control dimension of parenting; immature dependence; restrictive control*).

IPARTheory Interpersonal acceptance-rejection theory (IPARTheory) is an evidence-based theory of socialization and lifespan development that attempts to predict and explain major consequences, causes, and other correlates of interpersonal acceptance and rejection within the U.S. and worldwide. It attempts to answer five classes of questions divided into three subtheories. Two classes of questions define IPARTheory's *personality subtheory*. A third class of questions defines IPARTheory's *coping subtheory*. The last two classes of questions define IPARTheory's *sociocultural systems subtheory* and *sociocultural systems model*. The theory includes intimate adult relationships, peer relationships, and all other close interpersonal relationships throughout the lifespan.

Loneliness A feeling of unhappiness resulting from the absence of and longing for desired companionship, or as a result of separation from a wanted relationship.

Maintenance systems Refers in the *sociocultural systems model* (see Figure A.6) to those features of a society that ensure the survival of the family and members of the community, and help maintain the integrity of the population in its physical and cultural sense. Illustrations of maintenance systems include: the way people make a living, ensure social control, and ensure the procreation and socialization of children. (See *culture; sociocultural systems subtheory*).

Maladjustment An emotional disturbance, usually of a relatively mild nature. In IPARTheory, maladjustment is operationalized primarily in terms of the 10 universal effects of perceived interpersonal rejection described in the *acceptance-rejection syndrome* (e.g., anxiety; emotional insecurity; anger; impaired self-esteem; impaired self-adequacy; emotional unresponsiveness; emotional instability; negative worldview; cognitive distortions; dependence, or defensive independence). (See also *psychological adjustment*).

Mechanical model The belief (rejected in *IPARTheory*) that human behavior is strictly ruleful, and that if the rules, mechanisms, or processes are fully understood, human behavior and development can be predicted with perfect fidelity. Mechanical model theories are typically stated in the form of invariants, constants, or absolutes. For example, G. Stanley Hall's notions about the universality of adolescent stress, illustrates this when he wrote about adolescence being universally and inevitably a period of storm and stress. Freud's notion about the universality and inevitability of the Oedipus complex (for the normal development of males) is a second illustration.

Mediation model The fact (as displayed in Figure A.5 below) that perceived parental acceptance-rejection has both a direct and indirect

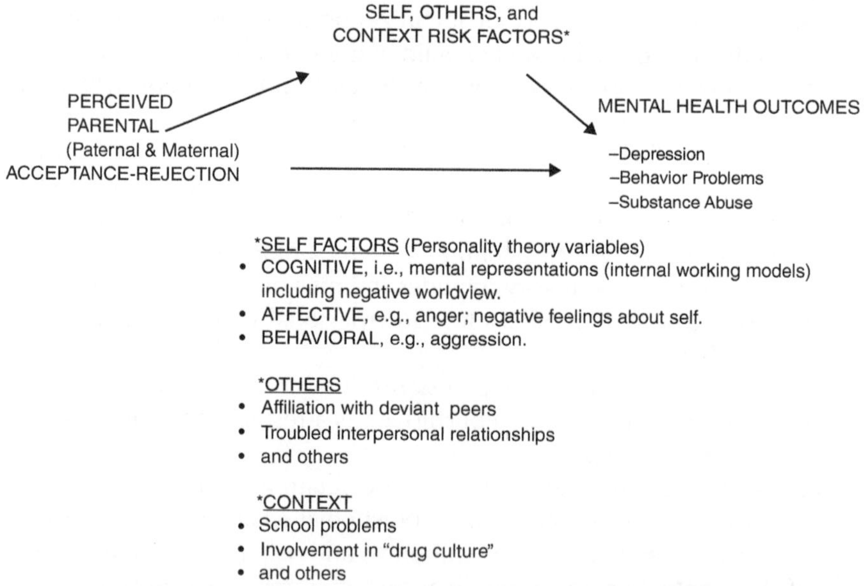

FIGURE A.5 Mediation Model of the Relation Between Parental (Paternal and Maternal) Acceptance-Rejection and Mental Health Outcomes. © 2004, 2021, 2024, 2025 by Rohner Research Publications.

effect on the development of *psychological adjustment* (and other) behavioral and developmental outcomes.

Mental representation An individual's more-or-less coherent but usually implicit conception of reality. The conception consists largely of cognitive generalizations about self, others, and the experiential world constructed from emotionally significant past and current *experience*. Mental representations about a specific domain (e.g., beliefs and expectations about oneself, *significant others, attachment figures*, or interpersonal relationships) fall along at least three continua: (1) from being consciously recognized to being wholly unconscious, (2) from being internally consistent and organized to being inconsistent and perhaps chaotic, and (3) from being loosely or flexibly scripted to being tightly or rigidly ruleful. Along with one's emotional state—which both influences and is influenced by one's conception of reality—mental representations tend to shape the way in which individuals perceive, construe, and react to new experiences, including interpersonal relationships. Mental representations also influence what and how individuals store and remember experiences. Once created, individuals' mental representations of self, of significant others, attachment figures, and of the world around them tend to induce them to seek or to avoid certain situations and kinds of people. (See *cognition; culture; personality subtheory*).

Methodology A class or tradition of research; a research paradigm; a body of methods, postulates, and rules for doing a specific type of research. Illustrations of methodologies include the *holocultural method*, the experimental method, and survey research. Methodology is to be distinguished from *procedure*. (See *anthroponomy; universalist approach; convergence of methodologies*).

Moderate control Conditions where parents make relatively few demands on children (e.g., for household responsibility or orderly behavior). Parents allow their children to regulate their own activities as much as possible, but within a few clearly defined and enforced limits. Parents avoid strict, unyielding control. (See *control dimension of parenting*).

Multimethod research strategy The need to employ a variety of discrete, unrelated research *procedures* and *methodologies* in anthroponomical research in order to reduce or even eliminate the likelihood that the results achieved might be an artifact of the potential bias (i.e., systematic error) inherent in every measurement process. If the same results emerge across multiple but independent procedures and methodologies—each containing the potential for its own unique form of bias—then one can be reasonably confident the results are not an artifact of the measurements used. (See *anthroponomy; convergence of methodologies and procedures; universalist approach*).

Multivariate model of behavior States that the behavior of the individual (e.g., a child's coping with perceived rejection) is a function of the interaction between self, other, and context. "Self" characteristics include the child's *mental representations* and other internal and external (*personality*) characteristics. "Other" characteristics include the personal characteristics of the loving or rejecting parent(s), along with the form, frequency, duration, and severity of such behaviors. "Context" characteristics include other significant persons in the child's life, along with social-situational characteristics of the child's environment. The multivariate model is often written in quasi-mathematical form: $B_I = f[SOC]$. Where B_I refers to the behavior of the individual, *f* refers to "a function of," *S* refers to "self," *O* refers to "other," and *C* refers to "context." The parentheses indicate an interaction among elements within their bounds.

Neglect A condition where parents fail to attend appropriately to the physical, medical, educational, social, emotional, and other needs of the child. Often, neglecting parents pay little attention to children's needs for comfort, solace, help, or attention. And they may remain physically as well as *psychologically unavailable*, unresponsive, or inaccessible to the child. (See *indifference*; the *warmth dimension of parenting*).

Nomothetic An interest in or attempt to generalize about some phenomenon, for example the worldwide effects of perceived rejection. Nomothetic contrasts with *idiographic*. (See *anthroponomy; universalist approach*).

Parent Any person who has more or less long-term, primary caregiving responsibility for a child. This person may be a mother, father, grandparent, other relative, or even a non-kinsperson such as a foster parent or parent surrogate in an institutional setting. Parents are generally *attachment figures*.

Parental Acceptance-Rejection Theory (See *PARTheory*)

Parental alienation The condition where children—usually ones whose parents are engaged in high-conflict separation or divorce—align themselves strongly with one parent (the preferred or alienating parent) and reject a relationship with the other parent (the alienated or target parent) without legitimate justification. The children are led by the alienating parent to believe that the targeted parent is evil, dangerous, or not worthy of love. As a result, the children try to reject any further relationship with the targeted parent. Many professionals regard parental alienation to be a form of child abuse. Parental alienation is to be distinguished from *Parental Estrangement*.

Parental estrangement Refers to the condition where children reject or refuse to have contact with a parent (the target parent) for justifiable reasons such as a history of parental rejection, abuse, or neglect. Parental estrangement is to be distinguished from *Parental Alienation*.

PARTheory (Parental Acceptance-Rejection Theory) was the original name for what is now known as *IPARTheory* (interpersonal acceptance-rejection theory). The name was changed to IPARTheory in June, 2014.

Passive aggression Non-active forms of aggression such as pouting, passive obstructionism, sulking, stubbornness, and intentional procrastination when these behaviors are motivated by the intent of irritating or getting back at another person. (See *hostility; aggression; personality subtheory*).

Permissiveness Conditions where parents attempt to exercise only minimum control over the child's behavior. The rules, proscriptions, and prescriptions that parents impose on children include only the barest controls needed for safety and physical health. Sometimes little attempt is made to enforce the few rules or restrictions that do exist. Parents are non-directive about much of what the child does. These parents are willing to allow children to do things their own way. Decisions about the child are usually dependent on the child's own will, whim, or desires about the matter. (See the *control dimension of parenting; PCS*).

Personality An individual's more-or-less stable set of internally motivated predispositions to respond (i.e., affective, cognitive, perceptual, and motivational dispositions) and actual modes of responding (i.e., observable behaviors) in various life situations or contexts. These dispositions and behaviors usually have regularity and orderliness across time and space. (See *psychological adjustment*).

Personality subtheory One of the three subtheories of *IPARTheory*. Personality subtheory focuses on a constellation of ten personality dispositions that are postulated to characterize rejected children and adults the world over. These dispositions include *interpersonal anxiety; emotional insecurity; dependence*; or *defensive independence*; depending on the form, frequency, timing, and severity of rejection; *emotional unresponsiveness; anger; hostility, aggression, passive aggression*, or *problems with the management of hostility and aggression*; negative *self-esteem*; negative *self-adequacy*; negative *worldview; emotional instability*; and *cognitive distortions*. Each of these personality dispositions falls on a continuum of "more" or "less." The ten personality dispositions in their "negative" expressions (e.g., emotional unresponsiveness) represent a constellation of interrelated and measurable characteristics that are predicted in personality subtheory and in the *acceptance-rejection syndrome* to result from the experience of interpersonal rejection in all sociocultural systems, races, and languages of the world.

Personalizing The act of reflexively or automatically and egocentrically relating life events to oneself; the act of inappropriately interpreting events primarily in terms of oneself, usually in a negative sense. People who are unable to depersonalize tend to interpret interpersonal encounters, and even accidental events, as having special and direct reference to themselves. That is, they tend to "take everything personally." According to IPARTheory's *coping subtheory*, the capacity to depersonalize provides a social-cognitive (See *mental representation*) resource that allows rejected children and adults to psychologically process hurtful interpersonal interaction in a more benign way.

Phenomenological perspective IPARTheory's emphasis on individuals' own perceptions or subjective appraisals of their parents' (or other *attachment figures'*) accepting or rejecting behaviors versus an outsiders' (e.g., the researcher's) appraisals of individuals' experiences. (See also *indeterminance in human behavior; probability model*).

Phylogenetic model Asserts that the behavior and development of an individual is a function in some unspecified way of the interaction between an individual's *biological state* and *experience* as modified by *cognition* or mental activity. The phylogenetic model is sometimes symbolized by a quasi-mathematical formula $B_I = f[(B \times E)C]$, where B_I is the behavior of the individual; *f* is "a function of;" *B* is the individual's biological state; *E* is experience, and; *C* is cognition or mental activity. The brackets and parentheses within brackets convey the idea of complex interactions among enclosed elements. (See *mental representation; phylogenetic perspective*).

Phylogenetic perspective Asserts that the contemporary behavior and behavior-potential of the species Homo sapiens is a function in an as yet unspecified way of interactions over the millennia between humankind's *biological state* and *experience*. The phylogenetic perspective is sometimes symbolized by a quasi-mathematical formula $B_h = f(B \times E)$, where B_h is the behavior potential of humans, *f* is "a function of," *B* is biological state, and *E* is experience. The product symbol (x) conveys the idea of an interaction between elements within the parentheses. In effect, this perspective recognizes an almost inextricable interaction between nature and nurture.

Physical punishment The direct or indirect infliction of physical discomfort or pain on a child by a person in a position of authority over the child (e.g., *parent*), usually for the purpose of (1) stopping a child's unwanted behavior, (2) preventing the recurrence of unwanted behavior, or (3) because the child failed to do something (s)he was supposed to do. In IPARTheory research, physical punishment is measured most often on the Physical Punishment Questionnaire (PPQ).

Positive response, need for IPARTheory's *personality subtheory* begins with the probably untestable assumption that humans have developed over the course of evolution (See *phylogenetic perspective*) the enduring, biologically based emotional need for positive response from people most important to them (*attachment figures*). The need for positive response includes an emotional wish, desire, or yearning (whether consciously recognized or not) for comfort, support, care, concern, nurturance, and the like. In adulthood the need becomes more complex and differentiated to include the wish (recognized or unrecognized) for positive regard from *significant others* and attachment figures. When individuals act on the emotionally felt need for positive response (e.g., for comfort, nurturance, support, or love) the resulting behavior is generally called *dependence*.

Probability model The view that little in human behavior is absolutely fixed, constant, or invariant. Rather, any given behavior or other outcome has varying degrees of likelihood (probability) of occurring under specific conditions. Part of the reason for this variability in behavioral (and developmental) outcomes—according to IPARTheory—revolves around almost inevitable imperfections in theory and measurement. But it also revolves around the presumption that human behavior is to some degree inherently indeterminant (See *indeterminance in human behavior*). Unlike *mechanical model* theories, probability model theories (such as IPARTheory) tend to be written in probabilistic language stating that "perceived parental rejection *tends* to be associated everywhere with [specific outcomes or antecedents]." (See *universals; phylogenetic model*)

Problems with the management of hostility and aggression Conditions where individuals have psychological difficulty recognizing or dealing emotionally with their own feelings of anger, irritation, resentment, *hostility*, or propensity toward *aggression*. Problems with the management of hostility and aggression may be revealed in disguised or symbolic forms such as: worried preoccupation about one's own or others' imagined hostility; aggressive fantasies, daydreams, or night dreams, and; unusual interest in violent events or activities. (See *acceptance-rejection syndrome; personality subtheory*).

Procedure A specific measurement process. That is, a procedure is a single assessment device, measure, or technique of data collection such as interviewing or the use of questionnaires. Each of these is a single, coherent, and integrated procedure for collecting information, and is to be distinguished from a *methodology*. (See *universalist approach; convergence of methodologies*).

Psychological adjustment Refers to a state of positive affect or a state of positive mental health. Adjustment is a continuum, not a simple dichotomy of being adjusted versus maladjusted. (See also *maladjustment*).

Psychological unavailability A form of *neglect* where parents or intimate partners may be physically present, but do not give the individual psychological access to them. The parent or partner does not respond to the individual or interact psychologically with him or her. The parent or partner is inattentive or insensitive to the individual's requests for help, emotional support, or nurturance when the individual is in need. Such behaviors are sometimes motivated by *indifference*. (See the *warmth dimension of parenting*).

Rejection The absence or significant withdrawal of warmth, affection, care, comfort, concern, nurturance, support, or simply love by *parents* and other *attachment figures* toward children and adults, and the presence of a variety of physically and psychologically hurtful behaviors and emotions. Worldwide, rejection tends to take four principal forms: (1) emotional *coldness* and the absence or withdrawal of behaviorally expressed *affection*; (2) *hostility* and *aggression* (3) *indifference* and *neglect* and, (4) *undifferentiated rejection*. The terms parental acceptance and rejection tend to connote positive and negative behaviors, respectively. In everyday American English the phrase "parental rejection" implies bad parenting and sometimes even bad people. In cross-cultural and ethnic research, however, one must try hard not to make such value judgments. Rather, one should attempt to view the phrase as being *descriptive* of parents' and others' behavior, not judgmental or evaluative. This is because parents in about 25% of the world's societies (Rohner, 1975, 1984) tend to reject their children (as defined in IPARTheory), though they generally behave in ways they regard as culturally appropriate. (See *acceptance; culture*; the *warmth dimension of parenting*).

Rejection expectancy Interpersonal rejection expectancy refers in IPARTheory to the anxious expectation of being criticized, ridiculed, slighted, disrespected, minimized, ignored, excluded, or rejected in some other way by others. Rejection expectancy may be an indicator of serious interpersonal rejection sensitivity. (See *Interpersonal Rejection Sensitivity*; IRS).

Rejection Sensitivity (See *Interpersonal Rejection Sensitivity*; IRS).

Restrictive control Condition where parents impose many—sometimes moment-by-moment—restrictions or rules (proscriptions and prescriptions) on the child in a wide variety of situations, and firmly enforce these rules, often by physical means if necessary. These parents often limit children's autonomy to try out their own skills or to behave on their own without parental interference or guidance. (See the *control dimension of parenting*).

Self-adequacy Judgment individuals make about their own competence or ability to meet the instrumental/task-oriented demands of day-to-day living. Feelings of positive self-adequacy imply that one views oneself as capable of dealing satisfactorily with problems; as a success or capable of success in the things one sets out to do; as self-assured, self-confident, and socially adequate. Feelings of negative self-adequacy, on the other hand, are feelings of incompetence, the perceived inability to meet day-to-day demands successfully. (See *self-evaluation; self-esteem; personality subtheory; imposter syndrome*).

Self-determination Refers to the extent to which individuals feel they have personal control or influence over important life events and their outcomes. A positive sense of self-determination is one of the social-cognitive dispositions (*mental representations*) postulated in *coping subtheory* to help many rejected persons cope more effectively than most with the experience of perceived rejection—though one's sense of self-determination is itself likely to be affected by the experience of rejection (See *copers, affective*).

Self-differentiation The capability of individuals to (a) understand another person's feelings, thoughts, and motivations, and—crucially—(b) to clearly distinguish or differentiate those dispositions from their own feelings, thoughts, and motivations, especially in emotionally close relationships. In effect, self-differentiation involves the ability to maintain psychological individuality in the context of emotionally intense relationships. (See *differentiated sense of self*).

Self-esteem Refers to the global emotional judgment individuals make about themselves in terms of worth or value. Feelings of positive self-esteem imply that one likes oneself; that one approves of, accepts, and is comfortable with oneself; that one is rarely disappointed in oneself; and that one perceives oneself to be a person of worth and worthy of respect. Negative self-esteem, on the other hand, implies that one dislikes or disapproves of oneself; that one devalues oneself and sometimes feels inferior to others; that one perceives oneself to be a worthless person or worthy of condemnation. (See *self-evaluation; self-adequacy; personality theory*).

Self-evaluation Refers to the global judgment individuals tend to make about themselves. It has two principal expressions, as postulated in *personality subtheory*. These are *self-esteem* and *self-adequacy*.

Self-reliance An individual's relative freedom from feeling the need to rely on others for help with instrumental or task-oriented activities (vs. emotional reliance on significant others/attachment figures). In IPARTheory self-reliance is distinguished from *dependence* and *independence*.

Sense of self Individuals' (e.g., young children's) relative awareness of their own individual personhood, internally (that is, distinguishing self from nonself, psychologically, as well as differentiating specific aspects of self from other aspects of self) as well as externally (that is, distinguishing self from nonself as a physical organism). In the course of normal development children gain over time an increasing awareness of self, the world, and interpersonal relationships. At any given age some children have a more differentiated sense of self than do others. *Coping subtheory* postulates that the more aware children are of themselves (physically and psychologically) as distinct from others (e.g., parents) and all that is not self, the greater the potential they have for being able to distinguish negative/rejecting messages given by parents from messages that children give themselves. This social-cognitive (*mental representation*) capacity is thought in *IPARTheory* to provide a resource for helping children cope more effectively than most with the destructive effects of perceived rejection. (See *coping, affective*).

Significant other Any person with whom a child or adult has a relatively long-lasting emotional tie, who is uniquely important to the individual, and who is interchangeable with no one else. (See also *attachment figure*).

Smother love The form of parenting where caregivers intrude (often inappropriately) into the child's activities in an apparently loving but excessively controlling, manipulative way. The child is often smothered with infantilizing, affectionate control, producing a tendency toward *immature dependence*. (See the dependency curve illustrated under *dependence*).

Sociocultural systems model A graphic framework (shown in Figure A.6) to guide conceptual thinking about the antecedents, consequences, and other correlates of parental acceptance-rejection within individuals and within total sociocultural systems. Elements and relations within the model are detailed in Rohner (1986). (See *culture; sociocultural systems subtheory; maintenance systems; institutionalized expressive systems*).

Sociocultural systems subtheory One of three subtheories in *IPARTheory*. This subtheory attempts to explain and predict major worldwide causes of interpersonal (especially parental) acceptance-rejection. The subtheory also attempts to explain and predict major *institutionalized expressive systems* correlates and individual *expressive behavior* correlates of interpersonal acceptance-rejection. (See *sociocultural systems model*).

Species specific A phenomenon that is unique to a given species of animal, and to only that species. Species specific is distinguished in *IPARTheory* from *species wide*. The effects of perceived parental rejection are postulated in IPARTheory to be species wide, but not necessarily species specific.

Species wide A phenomenon that is characteristic of an entire species. For example the song of a specific species of bird, or in *IPARTheory* the postulated effects of perceived *rejection*. To be species wide is not necessarily to be *species specific*. (See *anthroponomy; IPARTheory*).

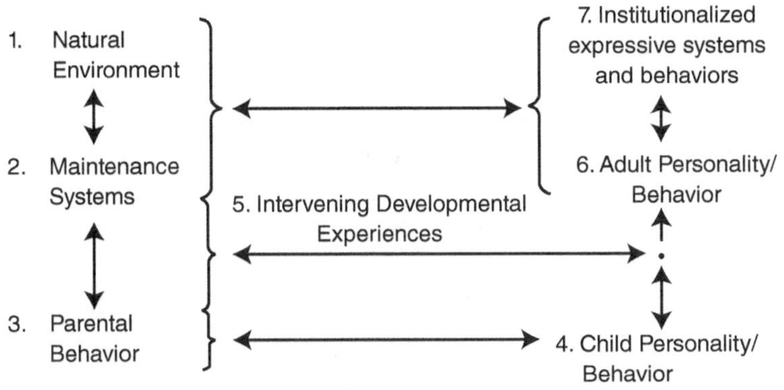

FIGURE A.6 Interpersonal Acceptance-Rejection Theory's Sociocultural Systems Model. © 2004, 2021, 2024, 2025 by Rohner Research Publications.

Syndrome a pattern of behaviors, traits, or dispositions that occur together and that characterize a particular disorder or condition (See *acceptance-rejection syndrome*). Any single disposition may be found in other conditions. It is the full configuration of dispositions that compose the syndrome.

Troubled individuals Those persons who are psychologically distressed or maladjusted in ways characteristic of rejected individuals, despite being raised in warm and loving (accepting) families. (See Figure A.3; see also *personality subtheory; acceptance-rejection syndrome*).

Undifferentiated rejection Individuals' affectively charged belief that their parents or other attachment figures do not really care about them, want them, or love them, but clear behavioral indicators are absent that the parents or other attachment figures are neglecting, unaffectionate, or aggressive toward them. (See the *warmth dimension of parenting*).

Universalist approach Addresses the methodological question: If one is serious about establishing *universals* in human behavior, how does one go about doing it? In serving the interests of *anthroponomy*, the universalist approach generally requires (1) a *multimethod research strategy* (looking for the convergence of results across disparate *methodologies* and *procedures*), and; (2) an adequate worldwide, cross-cultural sampling of races, languages, ethnic groups, genders, and other significant variations relevant to the issue investigated. (See *convergence of methodologies and procedures*).

Universals Scientifically derived principles of human behavior and human development that can be shown empirically to generalize across our species (See *species wide*) under specified conditions wherever they occur. Universals have a high probability of occurring but are not necessarily invariant or constant throughout our species. (See *anthroponomy; probability model; species wide; universalist approach*).

Vengeance Vengeance in IPARTheory refers to the (cognitive) wish or (behavioral) attempt to get even with, or to take revenge on—that is, to hurt physically, emotionally, socially, or in some other way—persons who are perceived to have wronged the individual. Individuals who are vengeful tend not to be forgiving. (See *Forgiveness*).

Warmth The emotional (vs. behavioral) experience of caring, nurturance, concern, or simply love of one person (e.g., a parent) for another (e.g., a child). (See *affection*; the *warmth dimension of parenting*).

Warmth dimension of interpersonal relationships A continuum of parenting or other interpersonal relationships defined at one end by perceived *acceptance* and at the other end by perceived *rejection*. All humans can be placed (or place themselves) somewhere along this continuum. The warmth dimension has to do with the quality of the affectional bond between individuals (e.g., between parents and their children) and with the physical and verbal behaviors used to express these feelings. The warmth dimension of interpersonal relationships must be distinguished from *warmth* per se on the warmth/affection scale in Figure A.7.

Worldview A person's often unverbalized overall evaluation of life, the universe, or the very essence of existence as being more or less positive or negative. A person with a positive worldview sees life as basically

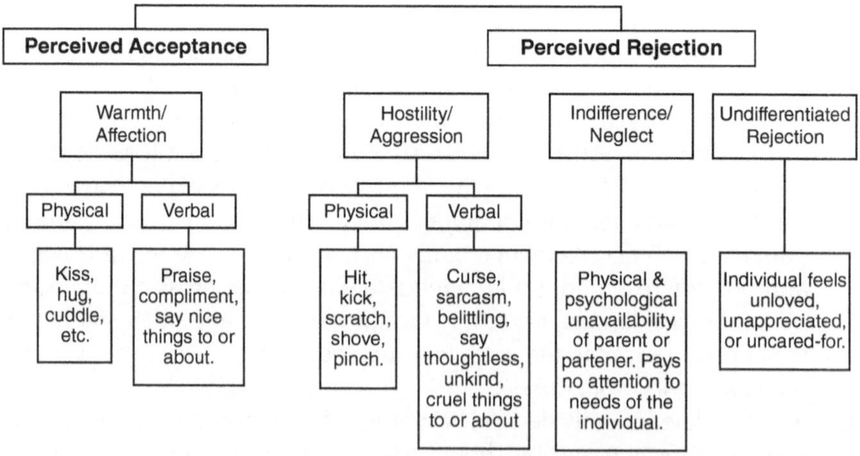

FIGURE A.7 Warmth Dimension of Interpersonal Relationships. © 2004, 2021, 2024, 2025 by Rohner Research Publications.

good, secure, friendly, happy, or unthreatening, or having some other positive valence. For a person with a negative worldview, on the other hand, life is seen as essentially bad, insecure, threatening, unpleasant, hostile, uncertain, and/or full of many dangers. Worldview, then, is a judgment that individuals make about the quality of existence. It is not to be confused with one's empirical knowledge of social, economic, political, or other events. (See *mental representation; personality subtheory; cognitive distortions*).

References

Ainsworth, M. (1989). Attachments beyond infancy. *American Psychologist, 44*, 709–716.

Naroll, R., Michik, G. L., Naroll, F. (1976). *Worldwide theory testing*. New Haven, CT: Human Relations Area Files.

Rohner, R. P. (1975). *They love me, they love me not: A worldwide study of the effects of parental acceptance and rejection*. New Haven: HRAF Press, 1975. (now published by Rohner Research Publications, Storrs, CT.)

Rohner, R. P. (1984). Toward a conception of culture for cross-cultural psychology. *Journal of Cross-Cultural Psychology, 15*, 111–138.

Rohner, R. P. (1986). *The warmth dimension: Foundations of parental acceptance-rejection theory*. Newbury Park, CA: Sage Publications, Inc. (now published by Rohner Research Publications, Storrs, CT.)

VandenBos, G. R. (Ed.). (2007). APA Dictionary of Psychology. American Psychological Association

APPENDIX B

Measures of Interpersonal Acceptance-Rejection and Its Effects

Ronald P. Rohner

By 2024, Rohner had created 35 measures to be used in IPARTheory research, as shown in Table B.1. Many of these measures are available in up to 78 languages or dialects worldwide. All were developed to help researchers, practitioners, and others study issues of interpersonal acceptance-rejection. The measures are available through Rohner Research Publications (rohnerresearchpublications.com).

Extensive information about the reliability and validity of many of these measures for use internationally and among American ethnic groups is available in the *Handbook for the Study of Parental Acceptance and Rejection* (Rohner & Khaleque, 2005) and elsewhere (Khaleque & Rohner, 2002; Rohner & Ali, 2020a, 2020b, Rohner & Khaleque, 2003; Rohner et al., 2024). Further, references to approximately 6,000 quantitative psychological studies using these and related measures may be found in Rohner Center's bibliography (csiar.uconn.edu). There, interested students, researchers, and practitioners may do keyword searches to locate authors, articles, and books dealing with specific acceptance-rejection topics of special interest to them.

TABLE B.1 Self-Report Measures Used in IPARTheory Research

1. Best Friend Acceptance-Rejection Control/Questionnaire (BFARQ/CQ)
2. Best Friend Acceptance-Rejection Questionnaire (BFARQ)
3. Coach Acceptance-Rejection Questionnaire (CARQ)
4. Early Childhood Best Friend Acceptance-Rejection Questionnaire (ECBFARQ)
5. Early Childhood Parental Acceptance-Rejection Questionnaire (ECPARQ: mother, father)
6. Early Childhood Teacher Acceptance-Rejection Questionnaire (ECTARQ)
7. Elder Sibling Acceptance-Rejection Questionnaire (ESARQ)
8. Elder Sibling Acceptance-Rejection/Control Questionnaire (ESAR/CQ)
9. Gender Inequality Scale (GIS)
10. Grandparent Acceptance-Rejection Questionnaire (GARQ)
11. In-Law Acceptance-Rejection Questionnaire (ILARQ: mother in-law and father in-law)
12. In-Law Acceptance-Rejection/Control Questionnaire (ILAR/CQ)
13. Intensity of Attachment Scale (IAS)
14. Interpersonal Acceptance-Rejection Loneliness Scale (IPARLS)
15. Interpersonal Rejection Sensitivity Scale (IRSS)
16. Interpersonal Relationship Anxiety Questionnaire (IRAQ)
17. Intimate Adult Relationship Questionnaire (IARQ)
18. Intimate Adult Relationship/Control Questionnaire (IARQ/CQ)
19. Intimate Partner Attachment Questionnaire (IPAQ)
20. Intimate Partner Attachment/Control Questionnaire (IPAQ/CQ)
21. Organizational Acceptance-Rejection Questionnaire (OARQ)
22. Organizational Acceptance-Rejection/Control Questionnaire (OARQ/CQ)
23. Parent's Evaluation of Child's Conduct (PECC)
24. Parental Acceptance-Rejection Interview Schedule (PARIS)
25. Parental Acceptance-Rejection Questionnaire (PARQ)
26. Parental Acceptance-Rejection/Control Questionnaire (PARQ/C)
27. Parental Control Scale (PCS)
28. Parental Power-Prestige Questionnaire (3PQ)
29. Personal Information Forms (PIF)
30. Personality Assessment Questionnaire (PAQ)
31. Physical Punishment Questionnaire (PPQ)
32. Substance Use Questionnaire (SUQ)
33. Supervisor Acceptance-Rejection Questionnaire (SARQ)
34. Teacher Acceptance-Rejection Questionnaire (TARQ)
35. Teacher's Evaluation of Student's Conduct (TESC)

References

Khaleque, A., & Rohner, R. P. (2002). Reliability of measures assessing the pancultural association between perceived parental acceptance-rejection and psychological adjustment: A meta-analysis of cross-cultural and intracultural studies. *Journal of Cross-Cultural Psychology, 33*, 87–99. https://doi.org/10.1177/0022022102033001006

Rohner, R. P., & Ali, S. (2020a). The parental acceptance-rejection questionnaire (PARQ). In V. Zeigler-Hill, & T. Shackelford (Eds.), *Encyclopedia of personality and individual differences*. New York: Springer.

Rohner, R. P., & Ali, S. (2020b). The personality assessment questionnaire (PAQ). In V. Zeigler-Hill, & T. Shackelford (Eds.), *Encyclopedia of personality and individual differences*. New York: Springer.

Rohner, R. P., Ali. S., Filus, A., ... Britner, P. (2024). Reliability and validity of the interpersonal rejection sensitivity scale: A multicultural study. *Current Psychology, 43*, 7986–7996.

Rohner, R. P., & Khaleque, A. (2003). Reliability and validity of the Parental Control Scale: A meta-analysis of cross-cultural and intracultural studies. *Journal of Cross-Cultural Psychology, 34*, 643–649. https://doi.org/10.11770022022103255650

Rohner, R. P., & Khaleque, A. (Eds.) (2005). *Handbook for the study of parental acceptance and rejection* (4th ed.). Storrs, CT: Rohner Research Publications.

SUBJECT INDEX

Pages in *italics* refer to figures, pages in **bold** refer to tables, and pages followed by n refer to notes.

AUTHOR INDEX

Pages in **bold** refer to tables and pages followed by n refer to notes.